Catalog of
Published Concert Music
by
American Composers

by
Angelo Eagon

Second Edition

The Scarecrow Press, Inc.
Metuchen, N. J.   1969

Copyright 1969, by Angelo Eagon

Library of Congress Card No. 68-9327

SBN 8108-0175-2

FOREWORD

Designed as a current reference for the extensive repertory of concert music by American composers, this catalog includes works in various categories which are generally available in some printed form for purchase. Suitable for performance, these compositions have been selected for the professional and non-professional musician, for music groups and organizations, schools of music, colleges and universities, libraries and research institutions.

In some instances, only a study or miniature score of a work has been published or, in some cases, issued in offset or in a blueprint edition. For those works of which a study score is available in print but of which the instrumental parts may be acquired only on a rental basis, the symbol "(R)" is used. For example: for William Schuman's Symphony No. 8, only a study or miniature score is available for purchase from the publisher, Theodore Presser Company (TP), but the orchestral parts may be obtained on a rental basis. Such a work is listed under the composer's name in the appropriate section entitled "Full Symphony Orchestra" as follows: "Symphony No. 8 TP(R)."

The different sections as listed in the table of contents include music for solo voice and for solo instruments, for choral music (mixed chorus--SATB; women's chorus--SSA; men's chorus--TTBB), for choral music with instrumental accompaniment, for music for various ensemble combinations, for music for orchestra (string orchestra, chamber orchestra, and full symphony), for band (including works for wind symphony), and for percussion (percussion ensembles as well as for those works for symphonic and other ensembles in which the percussion section is given a prominent part by the composer). Compositions for soloist or for soloists are included under the listings for string, chamber, and full symphony orchestras and for band. Other listings include operas and also selected jazz scores composed, primarily, for concert performance: jazz combos and music for big band jazz. Electronic music or that music for which a performance relies on mechanical devices has, with the exception of its use in connection with certain works for percussion, been omitted but will be included in subsequent supplements, which are planned to be issued on an average of every two years.

iii

With few exceptions, so-called "arrangements" of works by composers other than by the original composers themselves have been excluded.

Numerous cross references have been included. Many works of larger dimensions, such as concerti, are listed only under "String or Chamber Orchestra with Solo Instrument or Voice" or under "Full Symphony Orchestra with Solo Instrument or Voice" or under "Band." Thus, Aaron Copland's symphony with organ solo is listed under "Full Symphony Orchestra with Solo Instrument or Voice" and not under "Organ." The same is true for Paul Creston's concerti for marimba, saxophone, violin, and for accordion; for Samuel Barber's concerti for violin, cello, and for piano; and for Walter Piston's concerti for viola and for violin. None of those works is listed under the individual solo instrument.

Two types of indexes are included: one listing the composers; the other listing the authors or sources of texts of the vocal and choral music and also for those works of larger ensembles in which texts are narrated.

In compiling a catalog of such a wide coverage, an arbitrary decision had to be made on what constitutes an "American" composer. The following criteria were established: in addition to native-born composers, compositions are included of those foreign-born composers who became naturalized American citizens before the age of 26 and who have made significant contributions to the American musical scene.

Every effort has been exerted to make the entries current as of June 1, 1968. It is inevitable that in a work of this scope and variety, there may be some inadvertent omissions.

Without the magnificent assistance and patient cooperation that the many music publishers and individual composers have given, such a compilation as this catalog would not have been possible.

Angelo Eagon
Denver, Colorado
July 3, 1968

TABLE OF CONTENTS

---

* With piano unless otherwise indicated.
**All durations or timings are approximate.

KEY TO ABBREVIATIONS

A	alto voice	E-hn	English horn
acc	accompaniment	fl	flute
acdn	accordion	full	full symphony orchestra
a-cl	alto clarinet	glock	glockenspiel
a-fl	alto flute	gtr	guitar
a-rec or rec(A)	alto recorder	high hn	high voice French horn
a-sax	alto saxophone	har	harmonica
anon	anonymous	hp	harp
B	bass voice	hpcd	harpsichord
b-rec or rec(B)	bass recorder	low man	low voice mandolin
Bar	baritone voice	mar	marimba
bar	baritone horn	med	medium voice
bar-sax	baritone saxophone	min	minutes (approximate duration)
B-Bar	bass baritone voice	mov	movement
b-cl	bass clarinet	m-S	mezzo soprano voice
b-dr	bass drum	ms	manuscript
bsn	bassoon	Mu	mute
b-trb	bass trombone	Narr	narrator
clav	clavichord	ob	oboe
c-b	contra bass or double bass	obb	obbligato
c-bsn	contra bassoon	opt	optional
cel	celesta	orch	full orchestra
cent	century	org	organ
Ch	chorus	perc	percussion
cham	chamber orchestra	picc	piccolo
cl	clarinet	pno	piano
cmb	cymbals	pt	parts
Col	coloratura voice	(R)	parts on rental
cor	cornet	rec	recorder
dr	drum or drums	rev	revised or revision

S	soprano voice
SATB	mixed chorus (Soprano, Alto, Tenor, Bass)
sax	saxophone
sc	scenes
sn-dr	snare drum
Sp	speaker
s-rec or rec(S)	soprano recorder
SSA	women's chorus (Sopranos I & II, Alto)
str	strings
str qrt	string quartet
susp	suspended
sym	symphony
tam	tambourine
T	tenor voice
t-dr	tenor drum
tba	tuba
timp	timpani
trad	traditional
trans	translator or translation
trb	trombone
tri	triangle
trp	trumpet
t-rec or rec(T)	tenor recorder
t-sax	tenor saxophone
t-trb	tenor trombone
TTBB	men's chorus (Tenors I & II, Basses I & II)
unacc	unaccompanied
vib	vibraphone
vla	viola
vlc	violoncello
vln	violin
xy	xylophone

1. VOICE

SOLO VOCAL MUSIC (Piano Accompaniment Unless Otherwise Indicated)

Composer, Title and Publisher	Range	Author of Text
ADLER, Samuel		
Four poems OX	high	James Stephens
And it was stormy weather.		
Chill of the eve. The piper. The wind.		
ALETTE, Carl		
God's world TP	med	Edna St. Vincent Millay
Three secular songs TP	med	
Ashes of life		Edna St. Vincent Millay
The moon has gone		C. Brandt
What lips my lips have kissed		Edna St. Vincent Millay
AMES, William		
Dream pang AMP	med	Robert Frost
Fire and ice AMP	med	Robert Frost
Judgment MER	med	William Rose Benét
A minor bird AMP	med	Robert Frost
Nothing gold can say AMP	med	Robert Frost
A patch of old snow AMP	med	Robert Frost
Spring pools AMP	med	Robert Frost
ANTHEIL, George		
Five songs B&H	high	Adelaide Crapsey
November night. Triad.		
Fate defied. Suzanna and the elders.		
Morning.		
ARGENTO, Dominick		
Ode to the west wind B&H	high	Percy B. Shelley
(See also "Mixed Chorus")		
AVSHALOMOV, Jacob		
The glass town GAL	high	Alastair Reid
BABBITT, Milton		
Du (song cycle) AMP	high	August Stramm
Wiedersehen. Wankelmut.		
Begegnung. Verzweifelt.		
Allmacht. Traum. Schwermut.		
Sounds and words (in: New vistas in song)EBM	high	Milton Babbitt
The widow's lament in springtime AMP	high	William Carlos Williams
BACON, Ernst		
Adam and Eve CF	low, med	trad, USA
Brady B&H	low	Ernst Bacon
Buffalo gals CF	low, med	trad, USA

Composer, Title and Publisher	Range	Author of Text
The commonplace AMP	med	Walt Whitman
Five poems by Emily Dickinson GS	med, high	Emily Dickinson
It's all I have to bring. So bashful.		
Poor little heart. To make a prairie.		
In this of all my hopes.		
The grass AMP	med	Emily Dickinson
Is there such a thing as day?	med	Emily Dickinson
The lonesome grove CF	med, high	trad, USA
O friend AMP	med	Emily Dickinson
Quiet airs MER	med	
The divine ship		Walt Whitman
Eden		Emily Dickinson
Fond affection		anon
Gentle greeting		Emily Brontë
The heart		Emily Dickinson
The lamb		William Blake
The little stone		Emily Dickinson
Of love		Robert Herrick
Song of snow-white heads		Cho Wen-Chun
Stars		A. E. Housman
To musique, to becalm his fever		Robert Herrick
Twilight		Sara Teasdale
The red rose B&H	med	Robert Burns
Six songs NME	low	
Ancient Christmas carol		trad
The banks of the Yellow Sea		Emily Dickinson
A clear midnight		Walt Whitman
No dew upon the grass		Emily Dickinson
Omaha		Carl Sandburg
World take notice		Walt Whitman
Velvet people CF	med	Emily Dickinson
BAKSA, Robert F.		
Think no more, lad B&H	med	A. E. Housman
When I was one-and-twenty B&H	med	A. E. Housman
BALES, Richard		
Mary's gift PIC	med	Dorothy Callaway
Ozymandias PIC	med	Percy B. Shelley
BARAB, Seymour		
An explanation B&H	med	Walter Learned
Four songs B&H	med, high	
Go lovely rose		Edmund Waller
I can't be talkin' of love		Esther Matthews
Minstrel's song		Thomas Chatterton
She's somewhere in the sunlight strong		Richard LeGallienne
A maid me loved B&H	med	Patrick Hannay
Songs of perfect propriety B&H	med	Dorothy Parker
Song of perfect propriety. Now at liberty.		
Ultimatum. Renunciation. Inventory.		
Social note. A very short song.		
One perfect rose. Wisdom. Men.		
Lullaby. Comment.		

Composer, Title and Publisher	Range	Author of Text
BARBER, Samuel		
Andromache's farewell, Op. 39 (orch(R)) GS	S	John Patrick Creagh after the Greek of Euripides' The Trojan Women
Collected songs GS	low, high	
Bessie Bobtail		James Stephens
The daisies		James Stephens
Hermit songs		anon, Irish, VIII-XIII cent

At St. Patrick's purgatory. Church
bell at night. Saint Ita's vision. The
heavenly banquet. The crucifixion.
Sea-snatch. Promiscuity. The monk
and his cat. The praises of God. The
desire for hermitage.

I hear an army (with cham orch or pno acc)		James Joyce
Mélodies passagères		Rainer Maria Rilke

Puisque tout passe. Un cygne. Tombeau
dans un parc. Le clocher chante. Depart.

Monks and raisins (with cham orch or pno acc)		Jose Garcia Villa
Nocturne (with cham orch or pno acc)		Frederick Prokosch
A nun takes the veil		Gerard M. Hopkins
(See also "Mixed-", "Women's" & "Men's Chorus")		
Nuvoletta		James Joyce
The queen's face on the summery coin		Robert Horan
Rain has fallen		James Joyce
The secrets of the old		Wm. Butler Yeats
Sleep now		James Joyce
Sure on this shining night (with cham orch or pno acc)		James Agee
(See also "Mixed Chorus")		
With rue my heart is laden		A.E. Housman
Dover beach (with str qrt acc) GS	med	Matthew Arnold
Must the winter come so soon (from Vanessa) GS	med, high	Gian Carlo Menotti
Two scenes from Antony and Cleopatra (orch(R)) GS	S	Shakespeare; adapted by Franco Zeffirelli

1. Give me some music
2. Death of Cleopatra

Under the willow tree (from Vanessa) GS	high	Gian Carlo Menotti
(See also "Mixed Chorus")		
BASSETT, Leslie		
To music GAL	high	
Great art thou, O music		William Billings
Slow, slow, fresh fount		Ben Jonson
To music		Robert Herrick
BAUER, Marion		
Night in the woods GS	med	Edward R. Still
Through the upland meadows GS	high	John Gould Fletcher

Composer, Title and Publisher	Range	Author of Text

BEACH, Bennie
Peace (in: <u>Contemporary American songs</u>)S-B   low, high   Sara Teasdale

BEESON, Jack
Calvanistic evensong MIL   Bar   John Betjeman
Five songs PIC   med   Francis Quarles
  On a spiritual fever. A good night.
  On the world. Epigram. On death.

BERGER, Arthur
Three poems of Yeats (fl, cl, vlc acc) NME   med   Wm. Butler Yeats
  Crazy Jane on the day of judgment.
  His confidence. Girl's song.

BERGSMA, William
Bethsabe bathing GAL   med   George Peele
Lullee, Lullay CF   high   Janet Lewis
Six songs to poems by e.e. cummings CF   high   e.e. cummings
  When God lets my body be. Doll's boy's
  asleep. Hist whist little ghost things.
  Thy fingers make early flowers. It may
  not always be so. Jimmie's got a goil.

BERNSTEIN, Leonard
Afterthought (from <u>Facsimile</u>) GS   high   Leonard Bernstein
La bonne cuisine (four recipes) GS   high   Emile Dumont
  Plum pudding. Ox-tails. Tavouk
  Gueunksis. Rabbit at top speed.
Glitter and be gay (from <u>Candide</u>) GS   high   Richard Wilbur
I hate music (a cycle of kid songs) W-7   high   Leonard Bernstein
  A big Indian and a little Indian. I hate
  music. I just found out today. Jupiter
  has seven moons. My mother says that
  babies come in bottles.
Lamentation (from <u>Jeremiah Symphony</u>) W-7   med, high   Biblical
Silhouette, "Galilee" GS   med   Leonard Bernstein
Two love songs GS   high   Rainer Maria Rilke
  Extinguish my eyes.
  When my soul touches yours.

BIALOSKY, Marshall
An old picture (in: <u>Contemporary American</u>   low, high   Howard Nemerov
  <u>songs</u>) S-B

BLACKWOOD, Easley
Un voyage à Cythère, Op. 20 GS   S   Charles Baudelaire
  picc (also 2nd fl), fl, ob (also E-hn),
  2 cl, bsn, trp, hn, trb, c-b(R)

BLITZSTEIN, Marc
From· Marion's book CHAP   med   e.e. cummings
  o by the by. when life is quite through
  with. what if a much of a which of a
  wind. silent unday by silently not night.
  until and i heard. yes is a pleasant
  country. open your heart.

Composer, Title and Publisher	Range	Author of Text
Jimmie's got a goil (in: Cos Cob song album) B&H	med	e.e. cummings
Six Elizabethan songs CHAP		
Court song	med	anon
Lullaby	med	Shakespeare
Shepherd's song	med	Shakespeare
Song of the glove	med	Ben Jonson
Sweet is the rose	med	Amoretti
Vendor's song	med	Shakespeare
BOATWRIGHT, Howard		
Black is the color (with vln) OX	m-S	trad
Cock Robin (with rec) OX	m-S	trad
Gypsy laddie (with 2 melody instruments) OX	m-S	trad
One morning in May (with vln) OX	S	trad
O Waly Waly OX	m-S or Bar	trad
BONDS, Margaret		
Three dream portraits COL	med, high	Langston Hughes
Dream variation. I, too.		
Minstrel man.		
BOWLES, Paul		
Ainsi parfois nos seuils (in: Cos Cob song album) B&H	med	St. Jean Perse
Blue mountain ballads GS	med	Tennessee Williams
Cabin. Heavenly grass. Lonesome man.		
Sugar in the cane.		
David AMP	med	Frances Frost
Four Spanish songs AME	med	Garcia Lorca
In the woods AMP	med	Paul Bowles
Letter to Freddy GS	med	Gertrude Stein
On a quiet conscience MER	med	Charles I
Three HAR	med	Tennessee Williams
Two skies HAR	med	Jane Bowles
BRANSCOMBE, Gena		
Old woman rain (in: Contemporary American songs) S-B	low, high	Louise Driscoll
BRICCETI, T.		
Three songs, Op. 2 MM	med	Elizabeth Royce
Epitaph. Verse. Portrait.		
BUCCI, Mark		
Concerto for a singing instrument (with hp, pno (cel), str orch acc - (R)) FM	high	vocalise
Promenade. Vocalise.		
Tug of war.		
CADMAN, Charles Wakefield		
The brooklet GS	low	Henry W. Longfellow
Joy GS	med, high	Elsie Long
The moon behind the cottonwood GS	low, high	Nelle R. Eberhart

Composer, Title and Publisher	Range	Author of Text
CAGE, John		
Aria (1958) CFP	high	vocalise (vowels, consonants and words from English and various foreign languages)
Experiences II (1945-48) CFP	med	e. e. cummings
Five songs (1938) CFP	low	e. e. cummings
little four paws. little Christmas tree. in Just-. hist whist. another comes.		
A flower (1950) (with closed pno acc) CFP	med	vocalise
Forever and sunsmell (1942) (with perc duo) CFP	med	e. e. cummings
(See also "Percussion")		
She is asleep (1943) (prepared pno acc) CFP	med	vocalise
(See also "Percussion")		
Solo for voice 1 (1958) (unacc) CFP	any	John Cage
Solo for voice 2 (1960) (unacc) CFP	any	John Cage
The wonderful widow of eighteen springs (1942) (with closed pno acc)	any	James Joyce
CALDWELL, Mary E.		
A lute carol (fl or vln obb opt) HWG	med	Robert Herrick
CARPENTER, John Alden		
The cock shall crow GS	med	Robert L. Stevenson
A cradle song GS	med	William Blake
Four Negro songs GS	low	Langston Hughes
The cryin' blues. Jazz-boys. Shake your brown feet, honey. That soothin' song.		
Gitanjali, song offerings GS	med	Rabindranath Tagore
When I bring you colored toys. On the day when death will knock at the door. The sleep that flits on baby's eyes. I am like a remnant of a cloud of autumn. On the seashore of endless worlds. Light my light.		
Water-colors (Four Chinese tone poems) GS	med	
Highwaymen		Li-She
On a screen		Li-Po
The odalisque		Yu-Hsi
To a young gentleman		Confucius
CARR, Benjamin		
No. 17 of Carr's miscellany, the history of England from the close of the Saxon Heptarchy to the Declaration of American Independence in familiar verse MA	med	Benjamin Carr
CARTER, Elliott		
Dust of snow (1942) AMP	med	Robert Frost
The rose family AMP	med	Robert Frost
Voyage VAL	high	Harte Crane
Warble for lilac-time PIC	high	Walt Whitman
CARTER, John		
Cantata SMPC	high	trad

Composer, Title and Publisher	Range	Author of Text
Prelude. Rondo. Recitative. Air. Toccata.		
CHADWICK, George		
Bobolink GS	med	David Stevens
In my beloved's eyes GS	med	W. M. Chauvenet
The voice of Philomel GS	low, high	David Stevens
CHANLER, Theodore		
The children GS	med	Leonard Feeney
The children. Once upon a time. Wind. Sleep. The rose. Grandma. Spick and span. Moo is a cow. One of us.		
The doves HAR	med	Leonard Feeney
Eight epitaphs B&H	low, med	Walter de la Mare
Alice Rodd. Susannah Fry. Three sisters. Thomas Logge. A midget. No voice to scold. Ann Poverty. Be very quiet now.		
The flight AMP	med	Leonard Feeney
Four rhymes from peacock pie AMP	med	Walter de la Mare
The ship of Rio. Old Shellover. Cake and sack. Tillie.		
The lamb AMP	med	William Blake
Memory AMP	med	William Blake
O mistress mine B&H	med	Shakespeare
These my Ophelia (in: Cos Cob song album) B&H	high	Archibald MacLeish
Three husbands (Epitaph No. 9) B&H	S	Walter de la Mare
CHILDS, Barney		
Seven epigrams TP	S	Robert Herrick
CHOU, Wen-Chung		
Seven poems of T'ang Dynasty (winds, pno, perc acc) NME	T	Chinese poets of 8th and 9th cent; trans: Louise Varèse
CITKOWITZ, Israel		
Gentle lady (in: Cos Cob song album) B&H	med	James Joyce
CONE, Edward T.		
Silent noon (in: New vistas in song) EBM	high	Dante Gabriel Rossetti
COPLAND, Aaron		
As it fell upon a day (1923) (with fl & cl acc) B&H	high	Richard Barnefield
Dirge in the woods (1957) B&H	high	George Meredith
Laurie's song (from Tender land) B&H	med	Horace Everett
Old American songs (with pno or cham or full orch (R))	med	trad, USA
Set I (1950): The boatman's dance. The dodger. Long time ago. Simple gifts. I bought me a cat.		

Composer, Title and Publisher	Range	Author of Text

Set II (1952):   The little horses. Zion's
walls. The golden willow
tree. At the river. Ching-
a-ring chaw.

Poet's song B&H	high	e.e. cummings
(also included in Cos Cob Song		
Album (B&H) under title "Song (1927)")		
Song (1927) (in: Cos Cob song album) B&H	high	e.e. cummings
Twelve songs of Emily Dickinson (1950) B&H	med	Emily Dickinson

Nature, the gentlest mother. There came
a wind like a bugle. Why do they shut me
out of heaven? The world feels dusty.
Heart, we will forget him. Dear March,
come in! Sleep is supposed to be. When
they come back. I felt a funeral in my
brain. I've heard an organ talk some-
times. Going to Heaven! The chariot.

Vocalise (1928) B&H	high	

CORIGLIANO, John

The Cloisters (also with orch (R)) GS	med	William Hoffman

Christmas at The Cloisters.
Fort Tryon Park: September.
Song to the witch of The Cloisters.
The unicorn.

CORTÉS, Ramiro

The falcon CFP	high	anon
The Spanish songs PIC	med	Federico García
Adivinanza de la guitarre (The riddle of		Lorca
the guitar). La guitarre (The guitar).		
Las seis cuerdas (The six strings).		

CORY, Richard

Most men GEN	med	Douglass Cross

COWELL, Henry

Daybreak PIC	high	William Blake
Firelight and lamp CFP	med	Gene Baro
The donkey MER	med	G.K. Chesterton
The little black boy CFP	med	William Blake
The pasture (in: New vistas in song) EBM	high	Robert Frost
Spring comes singing (1954) AMP	high	Dora Hagemeyer
St. Agnes morning MER	high	Maxwell Anderson
Toccanta (vlc, fl, pno or orch acc) B&H	S	vocalise
Vocalise (fl and pno acc) CFP	S	

CRESTON, Paul

Ave Maria COL	med, high	liturgical
The bird of wilderness GS	high	Rabindranath Tagore
Fountain song, Op. 46, No. 3 MCA	high	John G. Neidardt
Lullaby, Op. 46, No. 2 MCA	med	John G. Neidardt
Psalm XXIII GS	med, high	Biblical
Serenade, op. 46, No. 1 MCA	high	Edward C. Pinkney
A song of joys COL	med, high	Walt Whitman

Composer, Title and Publisher	Range	Author of Text
CRIST, Bainbridge		
Chinese Mother Goose rhymes CF	med	from the Chinese;
Baby is sleeping. Lady bug. The		trans: I. T. Headland
mouse. Of what use is a girl. Pat		
a cake. What the old cow said.		
Coloured stars CF	high	from the Chinese;
		trans: E. Powys
		Mathers
Garden of bamboos (Street song of Annam)CF	med	trad
Into a ship, dreaming CF	med	Walter de la Mare
Leila (Song of Nepal) CF	high	trans: E.
		Powys Mathers
CRUMB, George		
Night music I (with pno (cel) and perc acc) MIL	high	García Lorca
(See also "Percussion")		
Three madrigals (with vib and c-b) MIL	S	trad
CUMMING, Richard		
Go lovely rose B&H	med	Edmund Waller
Little black boy B&H	med	William Blake
Memory, hither come B&H	med	William Blake
deGASTYNE, Serge		
May my heart EV	med	e. e. cummings
Three young maidens EV	med	from the Cancion-
		eros (15th cent)
		anon
Two elegies EV	med	
The last words		Maurice Maeterlinck
The sleeper of the valley		Arthur Rimbaud
DELLO JOIO, Norman		
The assassination CF	low	Robert Hillyer
The creed of Pierre Cauchon		
(from "The trial at Rouen") COL	Bar	Norman Dello Joio
Lament CF	med	Chidlock Tichborne
Lamentation of Saul (with orch or fl, ob,	Bar	text adapted from
cl, vla, vlc, pno (R)) CF		the play "David" by
		D. H. Lawrence
The listeners CF	low	Walter de la Mare
Mill doors CF	med	Carl Sandburg
New born CF	med	Lenore G. Marshall
Six love songs CF		
All things leave me	high	Arthur Symonds
The dying nightingale	high	Stark Young
Eyebright	med	J. Addington
		Symonds
How do I love thee	high	Eliz. B. Browning
Meeting at night	high	Robert Browning
Why so pale and wan?	med	Sir John Suckling
There is a lady sweet and kind CF	med	anon, Elizabethan
Three songs of adieu EBM	high	
After love		Arthur Symonds
Fade, vision bright		anon

Composer, Title and Publisher	Range	Author of Text
Farewell		John Addington Symonds
Un sonetto de Petrarca (in: New vistas in song) EBM	high	Petrarch
DIAMOND, David		
Anniversary in a country cemetery B&H	med	Katherine A. Porter
As life, what is so sweet B&H	med	anon, c. 1624
Be music, night CF	high	Kenneth Patchen
Brigid's song MER	med	James Joyce
Chatterton SMPC	high	John Keats
Children of the poor MCA	med	Victor Hugo
David weeps for Absolom MER	med	Biblical
Epitaph (1945) AMP	med	Herman Melville
Even though the world keeps changing (from Sonnets to Orpheus) CF	high	Rainer Maria Rilke
Five songs EV	med	
The epitaph		Logan Pearsall Smith
Monody		Herman Melville
A portrait		Herman Melville
Somewhere		Logan Pearsall Smith
This world is not my home		anon
Five songs (from The tempest) CHAP	med	Shakespeare
Come unto these yellow sands. Full fathom five. No more dams I'll make for fish. Where the bee sucks. While you here do snoring lie.		
A flower given to my daughter B&H	med	James Joyce
For an old man SMPC	med	T.S. Eliot
Four ladies SMPC	high	Ezra Pound
How it was with them MCA	med	Walt Whitman
I have longed to move away SMPC	med	Dylan Thomas
If you can't MCA	med	e.e. cummings
Let nothing disturb thee (1945) AMP	med	H.W. Longfellow
Lift not the painted veil SMPC	high	Percy B. Shelley
Love is more SMPC	med	e.e. cummings
The mad maid's song (fl & hpcd, or pno, acc) SMPC	med	Robert Herrick
The midnight meditation SMPC	med	Elder Olson
Music when soft voices die (1943) AMP	med	Percy B. Shelley
My spirit will not haunt the mound SMPC	med	Thomas Hardy
On death (1943) AMP	med	John Clare
Seven songs EV		
Billy in the Darbies	high	Herman Melville
Four uncles	high	e.e. cummings
The lover as mirror	med	Edward Stringham
My little mother	med	Katherine Mansfield
Sister Jane	med	Jean de la Fontaine
Souvent j'ai dit à mon mari	med	Katherine Mansfield
The twisted trinity	med	Carson McCullers
The shepherd boy sings in the valley SMPC	med	John Bunyan
To Lucasta on going to the wars AMP	med	Richard Lovelace
We two (song cycle) SMPC	med	Shakespeare
I. Shall I compare thee to a summer's day?		
II. Let me confess that we two must		

Composer, Title and Publisher	Range	Author of Text
be twain		
III. Those pretty wrongs that liberty commits		
IV. For shame deny that thou bear'st love to any		
V. O from what power hast thou this powerful might		
VI. My love is a fever longing still		
VII. No longer mourn for me when I am dead		
VIII. When in disgrace with fortune and men's eyes		
IX. When to the sessions of sweet silent thought		
Vocalises (with vla) SMPC	high	
DIERCKS, John		
About a lamb TP	med	William Blake
DONATO, Anthony		
To my neighbor at the concert (in: Contemporary American songs) S-B	low, high	Jeanne De Lamarter
DONOVAN, Richard		
Four songs VAL	high	
Away, delights		John Gould Fletcher
Here comes a lusty wooer		anon
O love, how thou art tired out with rhyme		Duchess of Newcastle
Song for a dance		Francis Beaumont
DOUGHERTY, Celius		
Listen! the wind B&H	high	Humbert Wolfe
little fourpaws GS	med	e.e. cummings
Loveliest of trees B&H	med	A.E. Housman
Madonna of the evening flowers B&H	med	Amy Lowell
New England pastoral B&H	med	Emily Dickinson
o by the way GS	med	e.e. cummings
Song of jasmine B&H	high	from "The Arabian Nights"
Song for autumn GS	med	Mary Webb
sweet spring is your time (vocal duet) GS		e.e. cummings
The taxi CF	med	Amy Lowell
thy fingers make early flowers GS	med	e.e. cummings
until and I heard GS	med	e.e. cummings
Upstream GS	med	Carl Sandburg
DRUCKMAN, Joseph		
Dark upon the harp (Psalms) (with 2 trp, hn, trb, tba, perc (R)) TP	m-S	Biblical
DUKE, John		
Acquainted with the night SMPC	med	Robert Frost
April elegy GS	med	Alfred Young Fisher
Bells in the rain CF	high	Elinor Wylie
Central Park at dusk B&H	med	Sara Teasdale
The door B&H	med	Orrick Johns

Composer, Title and Publisher	Range	Author of Text
The end of the world VAL	med	Archibald MacLeish
Evening CF	med	Frederick Prokosch
For a dead kitten SMPC	med	Sara Henderson Ray
Four poems by Edwin Arlington Robinson CF		Edwin A. Robinson
Luke Havergal	med	
Richard Cory	low	
Miniver Cheevy	low	
Calvary	low	
Here in this spot with you GS	med	Robert Nathan
Hist...whist SMPC	med	e.e. cummings
I can't be talkin' of love	high	Esther Mathews
I carry your heart GS	med	e.e. cummings
I ride the great black horses GS	med	Robert Nathan
I watched the Lady Caroline GS	low, med	Walter de la Mare
In the fields CF	low	Charlotte Mew
Just spring CF	high	e.e. cummings
Last word of a bluebird GS	med	Robert Frost
Loveliest of trees GS	med	A.E. Housman
Love's secret B&H	med	William Blake
Morning in Paris CF	high	Robert Hillyer
The mountains are dancing CF	high	e.e. cummings
My soul is an enchanted boat VAL	med	Percy B. Shelley
Only for me B&H	med	Mark van Doren
Peggy Mitchell GS	med	James Stephens
A piper GS	high	Seumas O'Sullivan
Remembrance SMPC	med	Emily Brontë
Shelling peas GS	med, high	Jessica Jackson
Silver GS	low, med	Carl Sandburg
There will be stars B&H	med	Sara Teasdale
Three Gothic ballads SMPC	med	
The coward's lament		Edna St. Vincent Millay
The mad knight's song		John Heath-Stubs
The old king		John Heath-Stubs
To Karen, singing EV	med	John Duke
To the thawing wind SMPC	med	Robert Frost
Two songs GS	med	Elinor Wylie
The bird. Little elegy.		
Two songs VAL	med	
XXth century		Robert Hillyer
White in the moon		A.E. Housman
When slim Sophia mounts her horse MER	med	Walter de la Mare
The white dress GS	med	Humbert Wolfe
Wild swans MER	med	Edna St. Vincent Millay

DUKELSKY, Vladimir (DUKE, Vernon)

Four songs BB	med	William Blake
Nurse's song. The fly.		
The blossom. How sweet I roam'd.		
Six songs (from A Shropshire lad) BB	med	A.E. Housman
Into my heart. With rue my heart is		
laden. When I watch the living.		
Loveliest of trees. Oh, when I was		
in love. Now hollow fires.		
Three Chinese songs CF	med	Michael Kuzmin; trans: Andre Skalski

Composer, Title and Publisher	Range	Author of Text

Cradle song.   After the tryst.
Adolescence.

EATON, John
Holy sonnets of John Donne (song cycle)   high   John Donne
(with pno or orch acc) SHAW
Batter my heart, three person'd
God (#XIV).   Spit in my face, you
Jewes (#XI).   O my black soule! (#IV).
What if the present were the world's
last night (#XIII).   At the round earth's
imagined corner (#VII).

EDMUNDS, John
Folk songs BOS   low, high   trad, USA
Billy boy.   Come all you fair and
tender ladies.   Every night when the
sun goes in.   Fare you well.   Jesus,
Jesus, rest your head.   On top of Old
Smokey.   The crawfish song.
Have these for yours SMPC   med   A.E. Housman
The isle of Portland B&H   med   A.E. Housman
The lonely CF   med   George Wm. Russell
O death, rock me asleep SMPC   med   Anne Boleyn
The drummer MIL   med   Thomas Hardy

EFFINGER, Cecil
Mary's soliloquy (from cantata "The St.   low   Lucy Vessey
Luke Christmas story") GS

ELWELL, Herbert
Agamede's song VAL   high   Arthur Upson
Renouncement GS   med   Alice Meynell
The road not taken GS   med   Robert Frost
Suffolk owl VAL   high   Thomas Vautor

EPSTEIN, David
Four songs (a cycle) (solo hn & string acc) MER S
Cuckoo   Gerard M. Hopkins
Spring and fall   Gerard M. Hopkins
Strike, churl...   Gerard M. Hopkins
To sleep   John Keats

EVETT, Robert
First mass of Christmas (with org) WLP   S and Bar   Biblical
Gradual.   Alleluia.

FARBERMAN, Harold
"N.Y. Times--Aug. 30, 1964" (with   S   text from N.Y.
pno and perc) GEN   Times, ed. of Aug.
The blue whale.   Politics.   Science.   30, 1964
Civil rights.   (See also "Percussion")

FELCIANO, Richard
Glossolalia (Psalm 150) (speaking with   Bar or dra- Biblical
tongues) (with org, perc, electronic   matic T

Composer, Title and Publisher	Range	Author of Text
tape (R))		
(See also "Percussion")		
FELDMAN, Morton		
For Franz Kline (with vln, vlc, hn,	S	vocalise
chimes, pno) CFP		
Four songs to e.e. cummings (with	S	e.e. cummings
vlc and pno acc) CFP		
Intervals (with vlc, trp, vib, perc (R)) CFP	b-Bar	vocalise
Journey to the end of night (with fl, cl,	S	
b-cl, bsn) CFP		
The O'Hara songs (with vln, vla, vlc,	b-Bar	John O'Hara
chimes, pno) CFP		
FERGUSON, Edwin Earle		
Two Spanish songs (with pno, 4-hands) AMP	med	Cancioneros; trans:
Lune que reluces (Moon with thy loveli-		Edwin E. Robinson
ness beaming). Quiero dormir y no		
puedo ('Tis love that keeps me from		
sleeping).		
FINE, Irving		
Childhood fables for grownups B&H	med	Gertrude Normon
Vol. 1: Polaroli. Tigeroo. Lenny the		
leopard. The frog and the snake.		
Vol. 2: Two worms. The duck and the yak.		
Mutability MIL	med, high	Irene Orgel
I have heard the hoofbeats of happiness.		
My father. The weed. Peregrine.		
Jubilation. Now God be thanked for		
mutability.		
FINE, Vivian		
Four songs NME	m-S	
Comfort to a youth (vln, vla acc)		Robert Herrick
The lover in winter plaineth for the		
spring (vla acc)		anon, XVI cent
She weeps over Rahoon (2 vln, vla, vlc acc)		James Joyce
Tilly (2 vln, vlc acc)		James Joyce
The great wall of China (with fl, vlc, pno) NME	med	Franz Kafka
FINK, Michael		
Rain comes down ECS	S	Edna St. Vincent
		Millay
What lips my lips have kissed ECS	S	Edna St. Vincent
		Millay
FINNEY, Ross Lee		
Poems by Archibald MacLeish AME	med	Archibald MacLeish
They seemed to be waiting. Go secretly.		
The flowers of the sea. Salute. These,		
my Ophelia.		
Poor Richard (song cycle) GS	high	Benjamin Franklin
Epitaph. Here Skuff lies. Wedlock, as		
old men note. Drinking song. When		
Mars and Venus. Epitaph on a talkative		
old maid. In praise of wives.		

Composer, Title and Publisher	Range	Author of Text
Three 17th century lyrics VAL	med	
Look how the floor of heaven		Shakespeare
On May morning		John Milton
On the life of man		Henry Vaughan
Three love songs VAL		John Donne
Of weeping	med	
Forbidding mourning	med	
Love's growth	high	

FLAGELLO, Nicolas

Contemplatzioni di Michelangelo (pno or	high	Michelangelo; trans:
orch acc) GEN		Joseph Tusiani
Come può esser (How can it be)		
Ben doverrieno (For all this anguish)		
Ben fu (Preparing for your eyes)		
Di più cose (My eyes are grieved)		
An island in the moon (pno or orch acc) GEN	high	William Blake
As I walked forth. This frog he would		
a-wooing ride. O father, O father.		
Good English hospitality. Leave, O		
leave me to my sorrows. Doctor Clash		
and Signor Falalasole.		
La bella Aurora GEN	T	Tasso
Good English hospitality GEN	med	William Blake
The land (pno or cham acc) GEN	b-Bar	Alfred Lord
The eagle. The owl. The throstle.		Tennyson
The oak. The snowdrop. Flower in		
the cranny.		
Leave, O leave me to my sorrows GEN	med	William Blake
L'infinito (pno or cham acc) GEN	med	Giacomo Leopardi

FLANAGAN, William

The dugout PIC	high	Siegfried Sassoon
Go and catch a falling star PIC	high	John Donne
Good-bye my fancy (fl & gtr or pno acc) PIC	S	Walt Whitman
Heaven haven PIC	med	Gerard M. Hopkins
Horror movie CFP	med	Howard Moss
If you can CFP	high	Howard Moss
Plants cannot travel CFP	high	Howard Moss
See how they love me CFP	med	Howard Moss
Send home my long strayed eyes PIC	high	John Donne
Song for a winter child PIC	med	Edward Albee
The upside-down man PIC	med	Howard Moss
Valentine to Sherwood Anderson PIC	med	Gertrude Stein

FLOYD, Carlisle

Ain't it a pretty night (from Susannah) B&H	high	Carlisle Floyd
Blitch's prayer of repentance (from	Bar	Carlisle Floyd
Susannah) B&H		
The mystery (5 songs of motherhood) (with	S	Gabriela Mistral;
pno or orch (R)) B&H		trans: Anita K.
1. He kissed me. 2. Gentleness.		Fleet
3. To my husband. 4. At dawn.		
5. Rocking.		
Pilgrimage (pno or orch acc) B&H	Bar	Biblical
Man that is born of a woman (Job 14).		

Composer, Title and Publisher	Range	Author of Text

Save me, O Lord, for the waters are
come into my soul (Psalm 69). O Lord,
thou hast searched me and known me
(Psalm 139). Praise the Lord, O my
soul (Psalms 148 & 149). For I am
persuaded (Romans 8).

The trees on the mountains (from Susannah) B&H	high	Carlisle Floyd

FONTRIER, Gabriel

Sleep now, dream now GEN	med	Gabriel Fontrier

FOSS, Lukas

Song of anguish (with pno or full or cham orch (R)) CF	Bar	Biblical
The song of songs (from Song of Solomon) CF	med, high	Biblical

Awake, O north wind. Come, my beloved.
By night on my bed. Set me as a seal.

Time cycle (with full or cham orch(R)) CF	S	
We're late		W. H. Auden
When the bells justle		A. E. Housman
Sechzehnter Januar		Franz Kafka
O Mensch, gib Acht		Frederich Nietzsche
Wanderers Gemuetsruhe SMPC	med	Goethe
Where the bee sucks (from The tempest) GS	high	Shakespeare

FOSTER, Stephen

Foster album of songs GS	any	Stephen Foster

Beautiful dreamer. Camptown races.
Come where my love lies dreaming.
Jeannie with the light brown hair.
Laura Lee. Massa's in de cold, cold
ground. My old Kentucky home. Nell
and I. Nelly Bly. Oh! Susanna. Old
black Joe. Old dog Tray. Old folks at
home. Open thy lattice, love. Ring,
ring de banjo. Under the willow she's
weeping.

The unknown Foster: Seven songs TP	med, high	trad & Stephen Foster

Summer longings. Some folks. I cannot
sing tonight. Katy Bell. Thou art the
queen of my song. Why, no one to love?
There are plenty of fish in the sea.

FREED, Arnold

Acquainted with the night B&H	med	Robert Frost

FREED, Isadore

Chartless CF	med	Emily Dickinson
Crossing the plains CF	med	Joaquin Miller
November SMPC	med	Thomas Hood
Psalm Viii SMPC	med	Biblical
When I was one-and-twenty SMPC	med	A. E. Housman

FULEIHAN, Anis

My Ahmed has gone to give battle SMPC	med	Anis Fuleihan

Voice: Solo Vocal Music   25

Composer, Title and Publisher	Range	Author of Text
GABOR, Harley		
Voice II (with a-fl and perc) AP	med, high	from 7 Japanese
(See also "Percussion")		Haiku poems
GABURO, Kenneth		
The night is still CF	high	Rabindranath Tagore
GERSHWIN, George		
Porgy and Bess CHAP		Du Bose Heyward--
		Ira Gershwin
Bess, you is my woman now	S & Bar	
I got plenty o' nuttin'	low	
It ain't necessarily so	med	
Summertime	S	
GIANNINI, Vittorio		
Be still, my heart EV	med, high	Karl Flaster
Far above the purple hills COL	high	Karl Flaster
Heart cry COL	med	Karl Flaster
I did not know EV	high	Karl Flaster
I only know EV	med, high	Karl Flaster
I shall think of you COL	med	Karl Flaster
Longing EV	med	Karl Flaster
Sing to my heart a song EV	med, high	Karl Flaster
Tell me, oh blue, blue sky COL	med	Karl Flaster
There were two swans EV	high	Karl Flaster
GOLD, Ernest		
Songs of love and parting GS	high	
Gifts		James Thomson
Music, when soft voices die		Percy B. Shelley
Parting		Emily Dickinson
Peace		Emily Dickinson
A red, red rose		Robert Burns
Shall I compare thee		Shakespeare
Time does not bring relief		Edna St. Vincent Millay
GOLDMAN, Richard Franko		
My kingdom MER	S	Robert L. Stevenson
Two poems of William Blake MER	med	William Blake
To a lovely myrtle bound.		
The shepherd.		
The weary yeare MER	high	Edmund Spenser
GRAVES, William		
Song for St. Cecelia's day (cantata) (pno	high	W.H. Auden
or cl and str qrt (R)) CF		
GREEN, Ray		
Concluded lives AME	med	Emily Dickinson
Conversation with a cloud AME	med	Evelyn Barlow
Four short songs AME	med	Carl Sandburg
Fog. Nocturn cabbage.		
Summer grass. Broken sky.		
Songs to children's poems AME		Herbert & Pierre Salinger

Composer, Title and Publisher	Range	Author of Text
Books	med	
Fog	med	
Machines	med	
The motorcycle	high	
Rain	med	
GRIFFES, Charles		
By a lonely forest pathway GS	high	Lenau;
		trans: Chapman
The dreamy lake GS	high	Mosen; trans: Dole
Evening song GS	high	Sidney Lanier
Five poems from the ancient Far East	med	
(with orch or pno acc) GS		
A feast of lanterns		Yaun Mei
Landscape		Sada-ihe
The old temple among the mountains		Chang Wen-Chang
So-fei gathering flowers		Wang Chang-Ling
Tears		Wang Seng-Ju
La fuite de la lune GS	med	Oscar Wilde
The half-ring moon GS	med	John Tabb
If I could go with you GS	high	Mosen;
		trans: Untermeyer
In a myrtle shade GS	high	William Blake
Lament of Ian the Proud (with orch or	med, high	Fiona MacLeod
pno acc) GS		
An old song resung GS	any	John Masefield
O'er the tarn's unruffled mirror GS	med, high	Lenau;
		trans: Chapman
Phantoms GS	med	Arturo Giovannetti
Rose of the night (with orch or pno acc) GS	high	Fiona MacLeod
Sorrow of Mydath GS	med	John Masefield
Symphony in yellow GS	med	Oscar Wilde
Thy dark eyes to mine (with orch or pno	high	Fiona MacLeod
acc) GS		
Time was, when I in anguish lay GS	high	Geibel;
		trans: Chapman
Upon their grave GS	med, high	Heine;
		trans: Untermeyer
Waikiki GS	med, high	Rupert Brooke
We'll to the woods and gather may GS	med	Wm. Ernest Henley
GRIFFIS, Elliot		
Songs from Poe HE	med	Edgar Allen Poe
Eldorado. To Helen. To the river.		
GRIMM, Johann D.		
O Jesus show Thy great compassion B&H	S & A duet	source of text un-
		known
GRUENBERG, Louis		
Lieder, Op. 24 TP	med	
HAIEFF, Alexei		
In the early hours (song cycle) CHAP	med	Alexei Haieff
At dusk. Any time. Before dawn.		
In the afternoon.		

Composer, Title and Publisher	Range	Author of Text
HAMM, Charles anyone lived in a pretty how town VAL	med	e.e. cummings
HARRIS, Roy Abraham Lincoln walks at midnight (a cantata of lamentation) (with vln, vlc, pno) AMP	m-S	Vachel Lindsay
Fog CF	med	Carl Sandburg
Give me the splendid silent sun (with orch acc) AMP	Bar	Walt Whitman
HARRISON, Lou Air from Rapunzel (with fl, vln, vla, vlc, hp, pno) PIC	high	William Morris
Alma redemptoris mater (1951) (vln, trb, tack-pno acc) PIC	Bar	liturgical
Fragment from Calamus (1946) AMP	Bar	Walt Whitman
HAUBIEL, Charles Sea songs HE Sea Gulls. Fog. Sea wind.	low, high	Grace H. White
HAUFRECHT, Herbert The clock shop (1955) BB Alarm clock. Banjo clock. The clock in the steeple. Cuckoo clock. Electric clock. Grandfather's clock. The ship's clock. The station clock.	med	Elfrida Norden
HELLER, Alfred Two Heine songs MER Der Tod, das ist die kuehle Nacht (Death- it is a still, cold night). Ein Fichtenbaum steht einsam (A pine tree towers lonely).	med	Heinrich Heine; trans: Aaron Kramer
HELM, Everett Lament HAR	med	Thomas Chatterton
Prairie waters by night CF	med	Carl Sandburg
Two love songs MER It is so long. For my lady.	med	e.e. cummings
HOAG, Charles Three songs VAL Love's snare. What menys thys. Words.	med	Thomas Wyatt
HOIBY, Lee Go, and catch a falling star B&H	high	John Donne
An immortality GS	med	Ezra Pound
The tides of sleep B&H (See also "Symphony with Solo Instru- ment or Voice")	low	Thomas Wolfe
HOLDEN, David A land dirge VAL	high	John Webster

Composer, Title and Publisher	Range	Author of Text
HOPKINSON, Francis		
Beneath a weeping willow's shade CF	med	Francis Hopkinson
My days have been so wondrous free CF	med	Thomas Parnell
My love is gone to sea CF	med	Francis Hopkinson
O'er the hills and far away CF	med	Francis Hopkinson
HOVHANESS, Alan		
Avak, the healer, Op. 65 (with C-trp, str) CFP	med	Alan Hovhaness
Black pool of cat CFP	med	Jean Harper
Dawn at Laona, Op. 153 CFP	med	Alan Hovhaness
1. Prelude. 2. Vision of dark places.		
3. The hosts flew white. 4. Motionless		
breath.		
Hercules (with vln) CFP	S	Alan Hovhaness
How I adore thee, Op. 7 CFP	med	Alan Hovhaness
I heard thee singing CFP	high	Consuelo Cloos
Innisfallen CFP	med	Jean Harper
Layla, Op. 29 CFP	med	from Persian poet
		Jami (1400); trans:
		Edward Fitzgerald
Live in the sun, Op. 169 (with cel) CFP	med	Alan Hovhaness
Love songs of Hafiz CFP	med	adapted by Alan
1. Hafiz, like Lord Krishna, darting.		Hovhaness
2. Hafiz is a merry old thief. 2. O		
flowing of my tears. 4. Hafiz wanders,		
weeping. 5. Day of Hafiz vision. 6. O		
love, hear my cry. 7. Where is my		
beloved? 8. Love for the soul.		
Lullaby of the lake CFP	med	Consuelo Cloos
The moon has a face, Op. 158 CFP	med	R. L. Stevenson
O goddess of the sea, Op. 151 CFP	low	Alan Hovhaness
O lady moon (in: New vistas in song)	high	Lafcadio Hearn
(pno and cl acc) EBM		
Out of the depths (Psalm 130) (with pno or	high	Biblical
org) CFP		
Advent, Confession, Faith, Humilation,		
Prayer, concert, general.		
Pagan saint CFP	high	Consuelo Cloos
Persephone, Op. 154 CFP	med	Alan Hovhaness
Raven river CFP	low	Consuelo Cloos
Starlight of noon, Op. 32 CFP	med	Alan Hovhaness
Three odes of Solomon (with pno or org) CFP	med	from ancient Syriac
As the wings of doves. As the work of		
the husbandman. No way is hard.		
Three songs CFP	med	Jean Harper
Describe me. Green stones.		
Fans of blue.		
Yar Nazani, Op. 24 CFP	med	Hamasdegh
HOWE, Mary		
Berceuse GS	med	anon
Let us walk in the white snow CF	high	Elinor Wylie
Songs (in 7 volumes) GAL	med, high	English, French,
		German

Composer, Title and Publisher	Range	Author of Text
HUGGLER, John		
Sculptures (orch (R)) CFP	S	Robinson Jeffers
HUNDLEY, Richard		
Ballad on Queen Anne's death (1619) GEN	med	trad
For your delight GEN	med	Robert L. Stevenson
Maiden snow GEN	med	Kenneth Patchen
Postcard from Spain GEN	high	Richard Hundley
Softly the summer GEN	high	Richard Hundley
Spring (When daisies pied) GEN	med	Shakespeare
Wild plum GEN	med	Orrick Johns
HYMAN, Dick		
"The popular Shakespeare": Songs from the plays of Shakespeare GEN	med	Shakespeare
When that I was and a little tuny boy. Under the Greenwood tree. When daffodils begin to peer. It was a lover and his lass. Come away, come away, death. Winter (when icicles hang on the wall). Spring (when daisies pied and violets blue). Sigh no more, ladies. Will you buy any tape. O mistress mine. Take O take those lips away. Blow thou winter wind. Lawn as white as driven snow. Who is Sylvia?		
IVES, Charles		
Chanson de Florian MER	med	Charles Ives
Flag song PIC	med	Charles Ives
Four songs MER	med	
Duty		Ralph W. Emerson
Luck and work		Charles Ives
1, 2, 3		Charles Ives
Vita		Manilius
Fourteen songs PIC	med	
The cage		Charles Ives
De la drama: Rosamunde		Belanger
In Flanders field		John McCrae
Marie		R.V. Gottschall
Nature's way		Charles Ives
Naught that country needeth	(Bar only)	Henry Alford (from Bernard)
On the counter		Charles Ives
Romanzo di Central Park		Leigh Hunt
A song--for anything		Charles Ives
Songs my mother taught me		Heyduk
The things our fathers loved		Charles Ives
Those evening bells		Thomas Moore
Watchman!		John Bowring
Weil' auf mir (Eyes so dark)		Charles Ives
From "Lincoln, the great commoner" NME	med	Edwin Markham
Ilmenau (Over the tree tops) PIC	med	Goethe
It strikes me that... MER	med	Charles Ives
The light that is felt MER	med	John Greenleaf Whittier

Composer, Title and Publisher	Range	Author of Text
A night song PIC	med	Thomas Moore
Nine songs PIC	med	
Autumn		Harmony T. Ives
Dreams		Porteous
Elegy		Gallet
Evidence		Charles Ives
Grantchester		Rupert Brooke
His exaltation		Robert Robinson
A son of a gambolier		anon
There is a lane		Harmony T. Ives
They are there		Charles Ives
(See also "Mixed Chorus")		
Nineteen songs NME	med	
Aeschylus and Sophocles		Walter Savage Landor
Canon		Thomas Moore
A Christmas carol		trad
Cradle song		A. L. Ives
An election		Charles Ives
A farewell to land		Lord Byron
From "Night of frost in May"		George Meredith
From "Paracelsus"		Robert Browning
General William Booth enters into heaven		Vachel Lindsay
In summer fields		Almers;
		trans: Chapman
The innate		Charles Ives
La fede		Lodovico Ariosto
Majority		Charles Ives
On the antipodes		Charles Ives
Requiem		Robert L. Stevenson
Resolution		Charles Ives
Slugging a vampire		Charles Ives
Tom sails away		Charles Ives
Two little flowers		Charles Ives
Sacred songs PIC		
Abide with me	med	Rev. Henry F. Lyte
The camp meeting	med	Charlotte Elliott
The collection	med	Stanzas from old
		hymns
Disclosure	med	Charles E. Ives
Down East	med	Charles E. Ives
Forward into light	T or S	Charles E. Ives
His exaltation	low	Robert Robinson
Naught that country needeth	Bar	Henry Alford
		(from Bernard)
Religion	med	James T. Bixby
The waiting soul	low	William Cowper
Watchman!	low	John Bowring
Where the eagle	med	M. P. Turnbull
Seven songs AMP	med	
Charlie Rutlage		cowboy song
Evening		John Milton
The Indians		Charles Sprague
Maple leaves		Thomas B. Aldrich
The see'r		Charles Ives
Serenity		J. Greenleaf Whittier
Walking		Charles Ives

Composer, Title and Publisher	Range	Author of Text
Ten songs PIC		
from "Amphion"	med	Alfred Lord Tennyson
The circus band	med	Charles E. Ives
Forward into light	T or S	Henry Alford (from Bernard)
I travelled among unknown men	med	William Wordsworth
Memories (a. very pleasant; b. rather sad)	med	Charles E. Ives
Mirage	med	Christina Rossetti
Omens and oracles	med	anon
Slow march	med	Charles E. Ives
To Edith	med	Harmony T. Ives
The world's wanderers	med	Percy B. Shelley
Thirteen songs PIC	med	
Abide with me		Rev. Henry F. Lyte
Allegro		Harmony T. Ives
Berceuse		Charles Ives
The camp meeting		Charlotte Elliott
The collection		from old hymns
Down East		Charles Ives
In the alley		Charles Ives
Old home day		Charles Ives
An old flame		Charles Ives
The old mother		Vinje; trans: Corder
Tarrant Moss		Rudyard Kipling
Where the eagle		M. P. Turnbull
The world's highway		Harmony T. Ives
Thirty-four songs NME	med	
Afterglow		J. Fenimore Cooper
Ann Street		Maurice Morris
At parting		Frederick Peterson
At the river		Charles Ives
At sea		Robert Underwood Johnson
The childrens' hour		Henry W. Longfellow
December		Folgore da San Geminiano
Duty (a) and Vita (b)		Ralph W. Emerson & Manilius
From the "Incantation"		Lord Byron
From "The swimmers"		Louis Untermeyer
The greatest man		Anne Collins
Harpalus		Thomas Percy
Hymn		anon
Ich grolle nicht		Heinrich Heine
Immortality		Charles Ives
The last reader		Oliver W. Holmes
Like a sick eagle		John Keats
Luck and work		Robert Underwood Johnson
Mists		Harmony T. Ives
The new river		Charles Ives
A night thought		Thomas Moore
Premonitions		Robert Underwood Johnson
The rainbow		William Wordsworth

Composer, Title and Publisher	Range	Author of Text
Rough wind		Percy B. Shelley
September		Folgore da San Geminiano
Soliloquy (or a study in 7ths and other things)		Charles Ives
Song for harvest season		old hymn
The south wind		Charles Ives
Thoreau		Charles Ives
Tolerance		Arthur T. Hadley
Walt Whitman		Walt Whitman
West London		Matthew Arnold
When stars are in the quiet skies		Edward Bulwer-Lytton
The white gulls		Maurice Morris
Twelve songs PIC	med	
August		Folgore da San Geminiano
Disclosure		Charles Ives
The Housatonic at Stockbridge		Robert Underwood Johnson
Karen		anon
My native land		anon
Qu'il m'irait bien		anon
Religion		James T. Bixby
Remembrance		Charles Ives
The side show		Charles Ives
Spring song		Harmony T. Ives
Waltz		Charles Ives
The waiting soul		William Cowper
Vote for names PIC	med	Charles Ives
Where the eagle (in: Cos Cob song album) B&H	med	M. P. Turnbull
JACOBI, Frederick		
Three songs VAL	high	Philip Freneau
On the sleep of plants. Elegy.		
Ode to freedom.		
JAMES, Philip		
Uncertainty CF	high	Mavor Moore
KAGEN, Sergius		
All day I hear WEIN	med	James Joyce
Because I could not stop for death MCA	med	Emily Dickinson
Drum MER	med	Langston Hughes
I think I could turn MER	low	Walt Whitman
I'm nobody WEIN	med	Emily Dickinson
A June day WEIN	high	Sara Teasdale
Let it be forgotton WEIN	med	Sara Teasdale
London MER	med	William Blake
Mag WEIN	med	Carl Sandburg
Maybe WEIN	med	Carl Sandburg
Prayer MCA	med	Langston Hughes
Sleep now MCA	med	James Joyce
Three satires MER	Bar	
How pleasant it is to have money		Arthur Hugh Clough
Persons of intelligence and culture		Louis MacNeice

Composer, Title and Publisher	Range	Author of Text
Yonder see the morning blink		A. E. Housman
Upstream WEIN	med	Carl Sandburg
KALMANOFF, Martin		
George Washington comes to dinner CF	med	Geo. Washington's Rules of Civility & Decent Behavior in Company & Conversation
Twentieth century (in: Contemporary American songs) S-B	low, high	Robert Hillyer
KENNEDY, John Brodbin		
All things that heal B&H	med	Samuel Menashe
Broken dialogue B&H	med	Jean Garrigue
KERR, Harrison		
Six songs EBM	med, high	Adelaide Crapsey
Triolet. Old love. Fate Dirge. The old, old winds. A white moth flew.		
KETTERING, Eunice Lee		
Compensation (in: Contemporary American songs) S-B	low, high	Sara Teasdale
KIM, Earl		
Letters found near a suicide (in: New vistas in song) EBM	high	Frank Horne
KLEIN, John		
Illusion AMP	med	Jeanne Hislop
Night mist AMP	med	Jeanne Hislop
Song is so old AMP	med	Herman Hagedorn
Sonnet to the sea AMP	med	Jeanne Hislop
There was a little girl AMP	med	Pearl Stevens
To evening AMP	med	Jeanne Hislop
KOCH, Frederick		
River night TP	med	Frances Frost
KOCH, John		
Calico pie GEN	med	Edward Lear
Ditty GEN	med	Robert L. Stevenson
An epitaph GEN	med	Walter de la Mare
An immortality GEN	med	Ezra Pound
Silver GEN	med	Walter de la Mare
Tame cat GEN	med	Ezra Pound
The tea shop GEN	med	Ezra Pound
KREUTZ, Arthur		
Chloe AMP	med	Robert Burns
A red, red rose AMP	med	Robert Burns
KREUTZ, Robert		
December lark (in: Contemporary American songs) S-B	low, high	Oliver Herford

Composer, Title and Publisher	Range	Author of Text

KUBIK, Gail
Songs about women SMPC — med
  Like a clear, deep pool — Somerset Maugham
  She was all piety — Audrey Wurdemann
  A woman's armor — Mary Bickel
Songs for Karen CHAP — med
  Bedtime song — Gertrude Norman
  A Christmas sing-song poem — Arthur Kramer
  I don't like dragons — Gertrude Norman

KUPFERMAN, Meyer
Island in a room (1963) GEN — med — Robert Winner

LADERMAN, Ezra
Songs for Eve OX — high — Archibald MacLeish
  1. What Eve sang. 2. Eve's exile.
  3. Eve's now-I-lay-me. 4. Eve in
  the dawn. 5. The riddles (also published separately). 6. Eve's rebuke
  to her child. 7. Eve quiets her
  children. 8. Eve explained to the
  thrush who repeats everything.

LA MONTAINE, John
Fragments from "The Song of Songs" — S — Biblical
  (also with orch(R)) PJS
  Set me as a seal upon thine heart.
  My beloved is white and ruddy.
  Whither is thy beloved gone? Come,
  my beloved, let us go forth. By
  night on my bed I sought him. I
  sleep but my heart waketh.
Songs of the rose of Sharon (also with — S — Biblical
  orch(R)) BB
  I am the rose of Sharon and the lily
  of the valley. I sat down under His
  shadow. His left hand is under my
  head. O my dove, that art in the
  clefts of the rock. My beloved is
  mine, and I am his.
Songs of the nativity (cycle of Christmas — med
  songs) HWG
  Behold a virgin shall be with child — Biblical
  That hallowed season — Shakespeare
  Nativity morn — John Milton
  Now begin on Christmas day — Gerard M. Hopkins
  The birds — trad Czech
  Rocking — trad Czech
Stopping by the woods on a snowy evening GAL med — Robert Frost

LANE, Richard
Four songs (also with orch(R) acc) CF — m-S — Mark van Doren
  Mountain house: December. Dunce's
  song. Down dip the branches. Will
  he come back?

Composer, Title and Publisher	Range	Author of Text
LATHAM, William		
The new love and the old (in: <u>Contemporary American songs</u>) S-B	low, high	Arthur O'Shaugh-nessy
LEES, Benjamin		
The angel B&H	med	William Blake
Close all the doors B&H	med	Richard Nickson
Cyprian songs B&H	Bar	Richard Nickson
From what green island. Wake! for the night of shadows. Still is it as it was. Over me like soft clouds.		
The moonlit tree B&H	med	Richard Nickson
Songs of the night B&H	S	Richard Nickson
O shade of evening. A star fell in flames. The enemies. A whisper of rain. Fall to the night wind. On eastern hills.		
LEKBERG, Sven		
Birds singing at dusk (in: <u>Contemporary American songs</u>) S-B	low, high	Li Po
LESSARD, John		
Morning song JC	med	Claire Nicolas
Mother Goose PIC	med	trad
There was an old woman. Doctor Fell. Going to St. Ives. The man in the moon. T'other little tune. Three wise men of Gotham.		
Orpheus MER	med	Shakespeare
Recuerdo JC	med	Edna St. Vincent Millay
Sebastian GEN	med	Claire Nicolas
When as in silk my Julia goes JC	med	Robert Herrick
LEVY, Marvin David		
One person (also with orch acc(R)) B&H	A	Elinor Wylie
LOCKWOOD, Normand		
The golden lady BB	med	Dorothy Lockwood
Joseph, dearest Joseph AMP	med	trad, German
Oh, lady, let the sad tears fall TP	med	Adelaide Crapsey
The snow lay on the ground AMP	med	trad carol
LOEFFLER, Charles Martin		
Five Irish fantasies GS	high	Wm. Butler Yeats
The hosting of sidhe. The host of the air. The fiddler of Dooney. Ballad for the fox hunt. Caitilin ni Vallachain.		
LOMBARDO, Robert		
A song for Morpheus B&H	S	Kathleen Lombardo
LONDON, Edwin		
The bear's song VAL	T	Haida Indian text

Composer, Title and Publisher	Range	Author of Text
LUENING, Otto		
Divine image EBM	med	William Blake
A farm picture AMP	med	Walt Whitman
Here the frailest leaves of me AMP	med	Walt Whitman
Love's secret EBM	med	William Blake
Three songs GS	high	
Auguries of innocence		William Blake
Gliding o'er all		William Blake
Young love		William Blake
MacCOLL, Hugh F.		
Six lyric sketches (Jamaica sketches) SHAW	med	Adèle Kelley
The choice. The net. Protest.		Thompson
Sleep. Spanish madonna. Woman's song.		
Two Keats songs SHAW	med	John Keats
Shed no tear. Ah! woe is me!		
MACDOWELL, Edward		
Eight songs, Op. 47 AMP	med	
Confidence		Johann Bernhoff;
		trans: MacDowell
Folk song		Johann Bernhoff;
		Trans: MacDowell
In the woods		Goethe
Midsummer lullaby		Goethe
The robin sings in the apple tree		Johann Bernhoff;
		trans: MacDowell
The sea		Johann Bernhoff;
		trans: W. D. Howells
Through the meadow		Johann Bernhoff;
		trans: W. D. Howells
The west wind croons		Johann Bernhoff;
		trans: MacDowell
MARTINO, Donald		
Three songs ECS	low, high	James Joyce
Alone (The moon's grey-golden meshes).		
A memory of a player in a mirror at		
midnight (They mouth love's language).		
Tuoto e sciolto (A birdless heaven).		
Zwei Lieder ECS	m-S	Rainer Maria Rilke
1. Die Laute. 2. Aus einer		
Sturmnacht VIII.		
MARTIRANO, Salvatore		
Chansons innocentes AMP	high	e.e. cummings
McDONALD, Harl		
Daybreak EV	med	John Donne
He is gone EV	med, high	Percy B. Shelley
MECHEM, Kirke		
Four songs ECS	Bar	Kirke Mechem
A farewell. The green-blooded fish.		
Inferiority complex. July rain.		

Composer, Title and Publisher	Range	Author of Text
MILLER, Edward J.		
Basho songs (with perc acc) MP	S	Basho
(See also "Percussion")		
MOORE, Douglas		
Come away death (unacc) MIL	b-Bar	Shakespeare
Dear dark head GAL	high	trans from the Irish
		by Sir Samuel
		Ferguson
The dove song (from Wings of a dove) GS	med	Ethan Ayer
I've got a ram (from The devil and	Bar	Stephen Vincent
Daniel Webster) B&H		Benét
Not this alone B&H	med	Pierson Underwood
Now may there be a blessing (from	S	Stephen Vincent
The devil and Daniel Webster) B&H		Benét
Old song CF	med	Theodore Roethke
Silver song (from The ballad of Baby Doe)CHAP	high	John Latouche
Three sonnets of John Donne GS	high	John Donne
Thou hast made me. Batter my heart.		
Death, be not proud.		
Under the greenwood tree CF	high	Shakespeare
MORAVIANS in America		
Ten sacred songs (str orch acc) CFP	S	Biblical
John Antes: Go, congregation, go.		
Jeremiah Dencke: Go ye forth in His		
name. I speak of the things. My soul		
doth magnify the Lord. O be glad, ye		
daughters of His people.		
Johannes Herbst: I will go in the		
strength of the Lord.		
Georg Gottfried Muller: My Savior lies		
in anguish.		
Johann Friedrich Peter: Lead me in Thy		
truth. The Lord is in His holy		
temple.		
Simon Peter: O there's a sight that rends		
my heart.		
Sacred songs (available separately only) B&H	S	
John Antes: And Jesus said: it is finished		Biblical
Loveliest Immanuel		John Antes
Johannes Herbst: I will go in the strength		
of the Lord (Psalm 71)		Biblical
Christian I. Labrobe: How shall a mortal		
song aspire	S or T	Ambrose Serle
John Frederik Peter: The Lord is in His		
holy temple		Biblical
Three sacred songs B&H	S	C.R. von Linzendorf
David Mortiz Michael: I love to dwell		(from Biblical text)
in spirit		
Johann Friedrich Peter: The days of all		
thy sorrow. I will make an everlasting		
covenant.		

Composer, Title and Publisher	Range	Author of Text
MURRAY, Bain		
The pasture (in: Contemporary American Songs) S-B	low, high	Robert Frost
NORDOFF, Paul		
Can life be a blessing AMP	high	John Dryden
Dirge for the nameless AMP	med	Walter Prude
Elegy AMP	med	Elinor Wylie
Embroidery for a faithless friend AMP	med, high	Walter Prude
Fair Annette's song AMP	med	Elinor Wylie
Jour des morts AMP	med	Charlotte Mew
Music I heard with you AMP	med	Conrad Aiken
Song AMP	med	anon
Song of innocence CF	med	William Blake
Songs of Robert Burns TPI	med	Robert Burns
Ay waukin, O. The banks o'Doon. Blythe was she. Bonie wee thing. Ca' the yowes to the knowes. Duncan Gray. For the sake o' somebody. A highland lad by love was born. Highland Mary. I am a bard, of no regard. I am a son of Mars. I hae a wife of my ain. I once was a maid. Lang hae we parted been. Last May a braw wooer. The lea-rig. Let me ryke up to dight that tear. MacPherson's farewell. Mary Morrison. My bonnie lass. My love, she's but a lassie yet. O, that I had never married. O, whistle, and I'll come to ye, my lad. A red, red rose. See the smoking bowl before us. Sir Wisdom's fool. Thou hast left me ever, Jamie. Wandering Willie. Willie Wastle. Wilt thou be my dearie.		
Tell me, Thyrsis AMP	med	John Dryden
There shall be more joy AMP	med	Ford Madox Ford
This is the shape of the leaf AMP	med	Conrad Aiken
Time, I dare thee to discover AMP	med	John Dryden
Willow river AMP	med	M. A. Siefert
OWEN, Richard		
I saw a man pursuing the horizon GEN	med	Stephen Crane
The impulse (from "The Hill Wife") GEN	med	Robert Frost
There were many who went in huddled procession GEN	med	Stephen Crane
Till we watch the last low star GEN	med	Witter Bynner
PANETTI, Joan		
Three songs VAL	med	Lydia Fakundiny
I assure you. I think. What are words?		
PERRY, Julia		
Stabat Mater (with str qrt or str orch) SMPC	A	liturgical
PERSICHETTI, Vincent		
Emily Dickinson songs, Op. 77 EV	med	Emily Dickinson

Composer, Title and Publisher	Range	Author of Text
Out of the morning. I'm nobody. When the hills do. The grass. Harmonium, Op. 50 (song cycle) EV Valley candle. The place of the solitaires. Theory. Lunar paraphrase. The death of a soldier. The wind shifts. The weeping burgher. Six significant landscapes. In the clear season of grapes. Tea. The snow man. Tattoo. Sonatina to Hans Christian. Infanta Marina. Metaphors of a magnifico. Gubbinal. Domination of black. Earthy anecdote. Of the surface of things. Thirteen ways of looking at a blackbird.	high	Wallace Stevens
James Joyce songs, Op. 74 EV Unquiet heart. Brigid's song. Noise of waters.	med	James Joyce
Two Belloc songs EV The microbe. Thou child so wise.	med	Hilaire Belloc

PFAUTSCH, Lloyd

| Lute book lullaby (in: <u>Contemporary American songs</u>) S-B | low, high | William Ballet |

PINKHAM, Daniel

Eight poems ECS Christmas day. Heaven-Haven. Jesu that doth in Mary dwell. Jesus to cast one thought upon. Pied beauty. Spring. Spring and fall. Strike, churl.	Bar	Gerard M. Hopkins
Elegy ECS	med	Robert Hillyer
The faucon BOS	high	anon
The hour glass ECS	high	Ben Jonson
Letters from St. Paul (org or pno; or str octet; or str orch) ECS But of the time and the seasons. Let the word of Christ dwell in you richly. Rejoice in the Lord alway. Wherefore seeing we also are compassed about. Who shall separate us from the love of Christ.	S or T	Biblical
Man that is born of woman (with gtr) ECS	m-S	Biblical
Now the trumpet summons us again (with pno or orch(R)) CFP	high	from the Inaugural Address by John F. Kennedy
A partridge in a pear tree BOS	high	anon
Slow, slow, fresh fount CFP	all voices	Ben Jonson
Song of Jephthah's daughter (cantata) CFP Twilight among the vineyards. My father came as a stranger. What was my sin? With timbrels and dancing. Alas, my daughter (S or Bar). Time is a long valley. I turned to my father. The tidings of my fate. Forever year by year (Lament of the	S	Robert Hillyer

Composer, Title and Publisher	Range	Author of Text
daughters of Israel). (See also "Women's Chorus")		
Three lyric scenes (with str qrt or str orch) BOS Let the florid music praise. Look, stranger, on this island now. Sing agreeably of love.	med	W. H. Auden
Three songs from Ecclesiastes (pno or str qrt acc) ECS Vanity of vanities. Go thy way, eat thy bread with joy. To everything there is a season.	high	Biblical
Two hymns (with fl and gtr) ECS Non vos relinquam orphanos (I will not leave you comfortless). Te lucis ante terminum (To Thee, before the close of day).	S or T	Biblical

PORTER, Quincy

Music when soft voices die MER	med	Percy B. Shelley
Three Elizabethan songs (with pno or fl, ob, bsn, 2 vln, vla, vlc, c-b(R)) YUP The god of love Spring (When daisies pied) When I was young and fair	med	anon Shakespeare anon

POWELL, John

Five Virginian folk songs JF Pretty Sally. The two brothers. The deaf woman's courtship. At the foot of yonder mountain. The rich old lady.	med	trad, USA

POWELL, Mel

Haiku settings GS	med	Four settings to Japanese poems by Basho, Joso, Etsujin, Buson, Issa and Shiki
Two prayer settings (ob and str trio acc) GS Morning hymn Little prayer	T	Gregory the Great Paul Goodman

PRESSER, William

A hymne to God the Father (with vla (or vlc) and pno) TP	high	John Donne
Three epitaphs TP	med	Robert Herrick

RAPHLING, Sam

Anne Rutledge MER	med	Edgar Lee Masters
Cool tombs MER	med	Carl Sandburg
Fog MER	med	Carl Sandburg
Fugue on "Money" (in: Contemporary American songs) S-B	low, high	Richard Armour
Gone MER	med	Carl Sandburg

Composer, Title and Publisher	Range	Author of Text
John James Audubon MER	med	Stephen Vincent Benêt
Lucinda Matlock MER	med	Edgar Lee Masters
Mag MER	med	Carl Sandburg
Pennwit, the artist MER	med	Edgar Lee Masters
Shine! great sun! MER	B	Walt Whitman
Washington monument by night MER	med	Carl Sandburg
READ, Gardner		
At bedtime SMPC	med	Irene Byers
From a lute of jade HE	med	
Ode		Confucius
The river and the leaf		Po Chu-i
Tears		Wang Seng-Ju
It is pretty in the city SMPC	med	Elizabeth Coatsworth
The moon. Op. 23, No. 4 AMP	med	William H. Davies
Nocturne, Op. 48, No. 1 AMP	med	Frances Frost
Piping down the valleys wild GAL	med	William Blake
The unknown god AMP	med	George W. Russell
A white blossom (in: Contemporary American songs) S-B	low, high	Vail Read
RECK, David		
Night sounds (and dream) (with c-b and perc) CPE	S	vocalise
REIF, Paul		
And be my love GEN	high	
The passionate shepherd to his love		Christopher Marlowe
Love under the Republicans (or Democrats)		Ogden Nash
Birches (also with orch(R)) B&H	S or T	Robert Frost
Five finger exercises GEN	med	T. S. Eliot
Lines to a duck in a park. Lines to Mr. Eliot. Lines to Ralph Hodgson, Esqr. Lines to a Persian cat. Lines to a Yorkshire terrier.		
REINAGLE, Alexander		
I have a silent sorrow HE	high	anon
RIEGGER, Wallingford		
The dying of the light, Op. 59 (also with orch(R)) AMP	med, high	Dylan Thomas
Music for voice and flute, Op. 23 AMP	high	vocalise
The somber pine (1902) AMP	med	Egmont Arens
Two bergerettes (1920) PIC	high	anon
Charmant bocage. Toi, dont les yeux.		
Ye banks and braes o'Bonnie Doon (1910) PIC	med	Robert Burns
ROCHBERG, George		
Four songs of Solomon GS	high	Biblical
Rise up, my love. Come, my beloved. Set me as a seal. Behold! thou art fair.		

Composer, Title and Publisher	Range	Author of Text
String quartet No. 2 with soprano (2 vln, vla, vlc) TP		Rainer Maria Rilke; trans: Harry Behn
William Blake songs (with fl, cl, b-cl, hp, cel, vln, vla, vlc(R)) MCA	S	William Blake
ROGERS, Bernard		
Psalm 68 SMPC	Bar	Biblical
ROREM, Ned		
A Christmas carol EV	med	trad
Alleluia HAR	med	liturgical
An angel speaks to the shepherd SMPC	med	Biblical
As Adam early in the morning CFP	med	Walt Whitman
The call SMPC	med	anon, 1500
Cradle song CFP	high	trad, XVI cent
Cycle of holy songs SMPC	med	Biblical
Psalm 134. Psalm 142.		
Psalm 148. Psalm 150.		
Early in the morning CFP	med	Robert Hillyer
Echo's song B&H	S	Ben Jonson
Epitaph SMPC	med	anon, 1500
Flight for heaven (song cycle) MER	Bar	Robert Herrick
To music, to becalm his fever.		
Cherry ripe. Upon Julia's clothes.		
Epitaph. Another epitaph. To the		
willow tree. Comfort to a youth that		
had lost his love. To Anthea, who		
may command him anything.		
For Poulenc (My first day in Paris) ECS	m-S	Frank O'Hara
Four dialogues (2 pno, 4 hands acc) CFP	m-S & T	Frank O'Hara
Subway. The airport. The apart-		
ment. In Spain and in New York.		
From an unknown past (also available for	med	
SATB a cappella) SMPC		
Crabbed age and youth		Shakespeare
Hey nonny no!		anon
The lover in winter plaineth for the spring		anon, 16th cent
The miracle		anon, 16th cent
My blood so red		anon
Suspira		anon
Tears		John Dowland
I am Rose CFP	med	Gertrude Stein
In a gondola CFP	high	Robert Browning
The lordly Hudson MER	med	Paul Goodman
The Lord's prayer CFP	med	Biblical
Lullaby of the woman of the mountain B&H	S	Padriac Pearse
Memory CFP	med	Theodore Roethke
Midnight sun ECS	m-S	Paul Goodman
Mild Mother ECS	med, high	Biblical
(See also "Women's" and "Men's Chorus")		
My papa's waltz CFP	med	Theodore Roethke
O you whom I often and silently come CFP	med	Walt Whitman
Night crow CFP	med	Theodore Roethke
The nightingale B&H	S	anon, c 1500
Philomel HAR	med	Richard Barnefield
Pippa's song CFP	high	Robert Browning

Composer, Title and Publisher	Range	Author of Text
Poems of love and the rain B&H	m-S	
1. Prologue: from The Rain		Donald Windham
2. Stop all the clocks		W. H. Auden
3. The air is the only		Howard Moss
4. Love's stricken "Why"		Emily Dickinson
5. The apparition		Theodore Roethke
6. Do I love you		Jack Larson
7. In the rain-		e.e. cummings
8. Song for lying in bed		Kenneth Pitchford
9. Interlude		Theodore Roethke

(NOTE: From this point in the cycle,
the songs are sung in reverse order
but with differently composed ac-
companiments)
10. Song for lying in bed. 11. In the
rain-. 12. Do I love you. 13. The
apparition. 14. Love's stricken "Why".
15. The air is the only. 16. Stop all
clocks. 17. Epilogue: from The Rain.

A psalm of praise (Psalm 100) AMP	med	Biblical
Rain in the spring B&H	med	Paul Goodman
Requiem SMPC	med	Robert L. Stevenson
The resurrection SMPC	med	Biblical
Root cellar CFP	med	Theodore Roethke
Rondelay CFP	high	John Dryden
Sally's smile CFP	med	Paul Goodman
See how they love me CFP	high	Howard Moss
The silver swan SMPC	high	Ben Jonson
Six songs (with orch acc) CFP	high	
Cradle song		anon, XVI cent
In a gondola		Robert Browning
Pippa's song		Robert Browning
Rondelay		John Dryden
Song for a girl		John Dryden
Song to a fair young lady		John Dryden
Snake CFP	med	Theodore Roethke
Song for a girl CFP	high	John Dryden
A song of David (Psalm 120) AMP	med	Biblical
Song to a fair young lady CFP	high	John Dryden
Spring B&H	high	Gerard M. Hopkins
Spring and fall MER	med	Gerard M. Hopkins
Such beauty as hurts CFP	med	Paul Goodman
Tulip tree ECS	med, high	Paul Goodman
Two songs HAR	med	Elinor Wylie
Little elegy. On a singing girl.		
To you EV	med	Walt Whitman
Visits to Saint Elizabeths (Bedlam) B&H	med	Elizabeth Bishop
The waking CFP	med	Theodore Roethke
What if some little pain HAR	med	Edmund Spenser
Youth, day, old age and night CFP	high	Walt Whitman
SAXE, Serge		
Adonis SMPC	high	Percy B. Shelley
Sonnet SMPC	high	John Keats
Wedded souls SMPC	high	Percy B. Shelley
Why did I laugh tonight SMPC	med	John Keats

Composer, Title and Publisher	Range	Author of Text
SCHIRMER, Rudolph		
Seven songs GS	med	Rudolph Schirmer
Form of wooing. Honey Shun.		
Ianthe. Lullaby. My heart is a		
river. Sound of laughter. Wanderlust.		
SCHULLER, Gunther		
Meditation (in: New vistas in song) EBM	high	Gertrude Stein
SCHUMAN, William		
The Lord has a child TP	med, high	Langston Hughes
Orpheus with his lute GS	med	Shakespeare
SCHWARTZ, Elliott		
Variations (with bsn and perc) GEN	S	vocalise
(See also "Percussion")		
SEEGER, Charles		
The letter (unacc) NME	med	John Hall Wheelock
Psalm 137 (unacc) NME	med	Biblical
SESSIONS, Roger		
Idyll of Theocritus (also with orch(R)) EBM	S	Virgil
On the beach at Fontana (in: New vistas	high	James Joyce
in song) EBM		
(Also published in Cos Cob song		
album B&H med)		
Psalm 140 (with org or orch(R)) EBM	S	Biblical
SHAPIRO, Norman R.		
The fish ECS	S	Ogden Nash
The seagull ECS	S	Ogden Nash
The termite ECS	S	Ogden Nash
SHAW, Clifford		
To you PIC	med	Walt Whitman
SHEPHERD, Arthur		
The fiddlers VAL	med	Walter de la Mare
Seven songs VAL		
Golden stockings	high	Oliver St. John
		Gogarty
Morning glory	high	Siegfried Sassoon
Reverie	med	Walter de la Mare
Serenade (with vla obb)	high	Sacheverell Sitwell
Softly along the road of evening	med	Walter de la Mare
To a trout	med	Oliver St. John
		Gogarty
Virgil	med	Oliver St. John
		Gogarty
Starling Lake VAL	med	Seumas O'Sullivan
Triptych (with str qrt acc) TP	S	Rabindranath Tagore
He it is. The day is no more.		
Light my light.		

Composer, Title and Publisher	Range	Author of Text
SIEGMEISTER, Elie		
American legends EBM	med	
Paul Bunyan		Leo Paris
Nancy Hanks		Rosemary Benét
John Reed		Lewis Allan
Johnny Appleseed		Rosemary Benét
Lazy afternoon (from Ozark set)		Leo Paris
The Lincoln penny		Alfred Kreymborg
Lonely star SMPC	med	Elie Siegmeister
The strange funeral in Braddock TP	Bar	Michael Gold
SMIT, Leo		
Four motets (with vla, 2 fl--<u>or</u>--S & T--	med	anon, German;
rec acc) BB		trans: Sylvia Wright
Wake up, my love. O Katharine,		
dearest. Venus, you and your son.		
O mother, tell me how to die.		
SMITH, Melville		
Three songs VAL	high	Carl Sandburg
Lost. A teamster's farewell. Sketch.		
SMITH, William O.		
Five songs (with vlc) MJQ	med	Kenneth Patchen
Lonesome boy blues. The magical		
mouse. The oldest conversation. My		
pretty animals. What there is.		
STARER, Robert		
Advice to a girl MCA	med	Sara Teasdale
Concertino for vln (or ob, bsn, hn, or	S or Bar	Biblical
trp) & pno MCA		
Dew MCA	med	Sara Teasdale
Evening MCA	high	Hebrew translitera-
		tion & English
My sweet old etcetera MCA	med	e.e. cummings
Silence MCA	med	D.H. Lawrence
To be superior MCA	med	D.H. Lawrence
Two sacred songs SMPC	med	Biblical
Give thanks unto the Lord (Psalm 136)		
Have mercy upon me, Lord (Psalm 31)		
Without him MCA	med	Hebrew translitera-
		tion & English
STERNE, Colin		
Gentle lady PIC	high	James Joyce
My love is in a light attire PIC	med	James Joyce
STILL, William Grant		
Songs of separation MCA	med	Walt Whitman
STRILKO, Anthony		
Canal bank MER	med	James Stephens
Canticle to Apollo MER	med	Robert Herrick
David's harp MER	med	Victor E. Reichert
The fiddler's coin MER	med	Patricia Benton
From autumn's thrilling tomb MER	high	Edgar Bogardus

Composer, Title and Publisher	Range	Author of Text
Little elegy MER	med	Elinor Wylie
Ophelia MER	med	Elinor Wylie
Point Charles MER	med	Ronald Perry
Songs from "Markings" MER	med	Dag Hammarskjold

SWANSON, Howard

Cahoots WEIN	low	Carl Sandburg
A death song MCA	med	Paul Lawrence Dunbar
Four preludes WEIN	high	T.S. Eliot
Ghosts in love WEIN	med	Vachel Lindsay
I will lie down in autumn WEIN	low	May Swenson
In time of silver rain WEIN	high	Langston Hughes
Joy MCA	high	Langston Hughes
The junk man WEIN	high	Carl Sandburg
The Negro speaks of rivers MCA	low	Langston Hughes
Night song WEIN	med	Langston Hughes
Pierrot WEIN	low	Langston Hughes
She saw a grave upon a hill WEIN	low	May Swenson
Snowdunes WEIN	high	May Swenson
Songs for Patricia WEIN	high	Norman Rosten

Darling, those are birds. No leaf
may fall. One day. Goodnight.

Still life WEIN	med	Carl Sandburg
To be or not to be WEIN	high	anon
The valley MCA	low	Edwin Markham

SYDEMAN, William

Four Japanese songs (with 2 vln) ECS	S	from Japanese texts

(See also "Women's Chorus")
In a gust of wind. I passed by the
beach at Tago. The mists rise over
the still pools. When I went out in
the spring meadows.

Jabberwocky (with fl, vlc) ECS	S or T	Lewis Carroll
Lament of Electra (with cham orch(R)) ECS	S	adapted by Sydeman from Greek
Three songs (with vlc) ECS	S or T	Emily Dickinson

Hope is a thing with feathers. I heard
a fly buzz when I died. I taste a
liquor never brewed.

Three songs on Elizabethan texts (with fl) ECS	S or T	
Elegy		Tichborne
The fly		Oldys
A modest love		Dyer
Upon Julia's clothes ECS	Bar	Robert Herrick

TAYLOR, Clifford

Five songs on English texts, Op. 4 AMP	S or T	
1. Rondo, on a favorite cat		Thomas Gray
2. Cherry robbers		D.H. Lawrence
3. On a certain lady at court		Alexander Pope
4. Merchandise		Amy Lowell
5. Fire and ice		Robert Frost

Composer, Title and Publisher	Range	Author of Text
THOMPSON, Randall		
Lullaby from The Nativity according to	S	Biblical
Saint Luke ECS		
My master hath a garden ECS	med	anon
My soul doth magnify the Lord (Magnificat)	S	Biblical
from The Nativity according to Saint		
Luke ECS		
The passenger ECS	Bar	M. A. DeWolfe Howe
Velvet shoes ECS	med	Elinor Wylie
THOMSON, Virgil		
At the spring HWG	med	Jasper Fisher
The bell doth toll SMPC	med	Thomas Heywood
La Belle en dormant (Beauty sleeping) GS	med	Georges Hugnet--
Pour chercher sur la carte des mers.		Eng version: Elaine
(Scanning booklets from ocean resorts)		de Sircay
La première de toutes.		
(My true love sang me no song)		
Mon amour est bon á dire.		
(Yes, my love is good to tell of)		
Partis les vaisseaux.		
(All gone are the ships)		
Consider, Lord SMPC	low	John Donne
English usage GS	med	Marianne Moore
The feast of love (also with cham orch) GS	Bar	anon Latin poem,
		Perviglium Veneris,
		2nd-4th cent A. D.
Four songs to poems of Thomas Campion	m-S	Thomas Campion
(with vla, cl & hp acc) COL		
Follow your saint. There is a garden		
in her face. Rose cheek'd Laura, come.		
Follow thy fair sun.		
Five phrases from the Song of Solomon AME	high	Biblical
Thou that dwellest in the gardens.		
Return, O Shulamite! O, my dove.		
I am my beloved's. By night.		
Five songs from William Blake COL	med	William Blake
The divine image. Tiger! Tiger!		
The land of dreams. The little black		
boy. "And those feet."		
If thou a reason dost desire to know SMPC	med	Sir Francis Kynaston
John Peel SMPC	Bar	John Woodcock
		Graves
Jour de chaleur aux bains de mer SMPC	med	Duchesse de Rohan
Look how the floor of heaven HWG	high	Shakespeare
Mostly about love (song cycle) GS	med	Kenneth Koch
Love song. Down at the docks. Let's		
take a walk. A prayer to St. Catherine.		
My crow Pluto GS	med	Marianne Moore
Pigeons on the grass alas (from Four	Bar	Gertrude Stein
Saints in Three Acts) MER		
Praises and prayers GS	med	
Before sleeping		anon
From the canticle of the sun		St. Francis of Assisi

Composer, Title and Publisher	Range	Author of Text
Jerusalem, my happy home		anon stanzas from Meditations of Saint Augustine
My master hath a garden		anon
Sung by the shepherds		Richard Crashaw
Preciosilla GS	high	Gertrude Stein
Remember Adam's fall HWG	low, high	anon, 15th cent
Shakespeare songs SMPC	med	Shakespeare
Pardon, goddess of the night. Sigh no more, ladies. Take, O take, those lips away. Tell me where is fancy bred. Was this fair face the cause?		
Stabat mater (with pno or str acc) B&H	S	liturgical
Susie Asado (in: Cos Cob song album) B&H	high	Gertrude Stein
The tiger GS	med	William Blake
(See also "Mixed" and "Men's Chorus")		
Tres estampas de niñez SMPC	high	Renya Rivas
Todas las horas. Son amigos de todos. Nadie lo oye como ellos.		
When I survey the bright celestial sphere HWG	med	William Habbington, 17th cent
(See also "Mixed Chorus")		
TRIMBLE, Lester		
Four fragments from The Canterbury Tales	high	Geoffrey Chaucer
(with fl, cl, hpcd (or pno)) CFP		
Prologue. A knyght. A yong squier. The wyf of Biside Bathe.		
Petit concert (with vln, ob, hpcd) CFP	S or T	
Tell me where is fancy bred (The Merchant of Venice)		Shakespeare
Love seeketh not itself to please (Songs of Experience)		William Blake
O, Rose, thou art sick! (Songs of Experience)		William Blake
TURNER, Charles		
Hunting song GS	high	Marcia Bradley
In youth and May GS	med	A. E. Housman
VINCENT, John		
Miracle of the cherry tree (also with orch (R)) MIL	A	trad
WARD, Robert		
As I watched a ploughman ploughing PIC	low, high	Walt Whitman
Ballad (from Pantaloon) GAL	low, high	Bernard Stambler
Rain has fallen all the day PIC	high	James Joyce
Sacred songs for Pantheists (also with orch (R)) GAL	S	
1. Pied beauty		Gerard M. Hopkins
2. Little things		James Stephens
3. Intoxication		Emily Dickinson
4. Heaven-haven (a nun takes the veil)		Gerard M. Hopkins
5. God's grandeur		Gerard M. Hopkins
Sorrow of Mydath PIC	high	John Masefield
Vanished PIC	med	Emily Dickinson

Composer, Title and Publisher	Range	Author of Text
WEBER, Ben		
Concertaria after Solomon, Op. 29 (1949) MM	S	Biblical
Four songs, Op. 40 (with solo vlc acc) NME	S or T	
An immortality		Ezra Pound
Animula Blandula Vagula		Emperor Hadrian; trans: Wallis
The moon		Bhasa; trans: Keith
The vine to the goat		Euenus; trans: Lind
Mourn! Mourn! (in: New vistas in song) EBM	high	John Dowland
WEISGALL, Hugo		
Four songs TP	med, high	Adelaide Crapsey
Dirge. Oh, lady, let the sad tears fall. Old love. Song.		
A garden eastward (also with orch(R)) TP	high	Moses Ibn Ezra; Eng. version: Milton Feist
I looked back suddenly (1943) MER	med	Humbert Wolfe
No more I will thy love importune TP	low, high	anon
Nuptial song, "Be nimble, quick away" TP	high	anon
Soldier songs (1945-1946) MER	med	
The dying airman		anon
The dying soldier		Isaac Rosenberg
Fife tune		John Manifold
Futility		Wilfred Owen
The leveller		Robert Graves
Lord, I have seen too much		Karl Shapiro
My sweet old etcetera		e.e. cummings
Shilow		Herman Melville
Suicide in trenches		Siegfried Sassoon
WOLFE, Jacques		
The news came CF	med	Eric von der Goltz
Three Negro poems GS	low, med	Clement Wood
Debbil-foot. De glory road. Gwine to hebb'n.		
WORK, John W.		
Three glimpses of night (in: Contemporary American songs) S-B	low, high	Frank Davis

MIXED CHORUS (SATB a cappella unless otherwise indicated)

Composer, Title and Publisher	Chorus	Solos	Accompaniment	Author of Text
ADLER, Samuel				
Autumn rain AMP				Judah Stampfer
Behold your God FAM			fl, ob, cl, bsn,	Biblical & trad
1. O Thou that tellest good tidings. 2. Burgundian carol. 3. For unto us a child is born. 4. Never was a child so lovely. 5. Recitative, trio and chorus. 6. Glory to God. 7. Arise, shine. 8. Hallelujah.			hn, trp, trb, hp (or org or pno), perc	
The binding (oratorio) OX		2 S, m-S (m-S also Narr) T, Bar	orch(R)	Biblical
Contrasts MIL				
I. Pastoral.				Robert Hillyer
II. Drum				Langston Hughes
Five choral pictures AB				Robert Sward
The immortals in question. Snow. Marriage. Owl. People glow.				
How precious is Thy loving kindness (Psalm 36) OX		T or S	org or pno	Biblical
I will give thanks (Psalm 9) OX			org	Biblical
Nothing is enough! AMP				Laurence Binyon
Psalm 24 TP			3 trp, 3 trb, tba	Biblical
Psalm 96 GS			org	Biblical
Someone AMP				Walter de la Mare
Strings in the earth AMP				James Joyce
Three encore songs L-G				Humbert Wolfe
Things lovelier. The rose. Queen Victoria.				
Three madrigals L-G				
The pearl				Hans Christian Anderson
The choir boys				Heinrich Heine
Love song				Abraham Reisen; trans: Marie Sypkin
Two Psalm motets L-G			org	Biblical
O Lord, open Thou my lips. The Lord reigneth.				
ALEXANDER, Joseph				
anyone lived in a pretty how town L-G				e.e. cummings
Blessed be God (Psalm 66) MIL			pno or org	Biblical
A new psalm (Dead Sea Scrolls) L-G			pno	Qumran Psalter

Composer, Title and Publisher	Chorus	Solos	Accompaniment	Author of Text
ALTMAN, Ludwig				
Psalm 13 L-G		A solo opt	org or orch	Biblical
AMRAM, David				
Let us remember (cantata) CFP		S, A, T, B	orch(R)	Langston Hughes
A year in our land (cantata) CFP		S, A, T, B	orch(R)	
Prologue				James Baldwin
Spring in the East				John dos Passos
Summer in the West				Jack Kerouac
Autumn in the North				John Steinbeck
Winter in the South				Thomas Wolfe
Epilogue				Walt Whitman
ANTES, John				
Shout ye heavens B&H			org or str with 2 trp (or 2 hn)	Biblical
Surely He has borne our grief (printed with "Go, congregation, go" S aria) B&H		S	str orch	Biblical
Twelve Moravian chorales B&H				
Soul, at this most solemn season				Johann Franck
O lord in me fulfill				Martha Claggett
Resting in the silent grave				Christian I. Latrobe
What splendid rays of truth and grace				Christian Gregor
O deepest grief				Johann Rist
God Holy Ghost, in mercy us preserve				Martin Luther
Precious name of Jesus				Louise von Hayn
In joyful hymns of praise				anon
Christ the Lord, the Lord most glorious				John Miller
For grace I sigh and weep				Ludwig von Zinzendorf
Hark, my soul, it is the Lord				William Cowper
O what a depth of love and boundless grace				Anne Schindler Dober
ANTHEIL, George				
Cabeza de Vaca SHAW			pno or orch	Allan Dowling
Eight fragments from Shelley WEIN				Percy B. Shelley
A dirge. I faint, I perish with my love. I stood upon a heaven cleaving turret. Sonnet to Byron. Tomorrow.				

Composer, Title and Publisher	Chorus	Solos	Accompaniment	Author of Text
To the moon. When soft winds. When the lamp is shattered.				
ARGENTO, Dominick				
Ode to the west wind B&H (See also "Solo Vocal Music")				Percy B. Shelley
ASCHAFFENBURG, Walter				
The 23rd Psalme TP		T	org and/ or ob	George Herbert
AVSHALOMOV, Jacob				
Because your voice GAL				James Joyce
How long, O Lord EBM	A		orch	Biblical
I promise nothing MER				A. E. Housman
Of man's mortalitie PIC				
Hic jacet				Thomas Nashe
In time of plague				Rabelais
Tangle, wrangle, brangle				Sir Walter Raleigh
Now welcome, summer ECS			fl	Chaucer
Threnos ECS				Ezra Pound
1. No more for us the little sighing. 2. What thou lovest well remains.				
Tom o'Bedlam ECS			ob, jingles, tabor	anon, 17th cent
Whimsies ECS				Ogden Nash
1. Tweedledee & Tweedledoom. 2. Raker. 3. Central Park tourney.				
BACON, Ernst				
A Christmas carol PIC			pno or org	Robert Herrick
The Colorado trail L-G		T(opt)	pno	trad
Devilish Mary SHAW			pno, 4 hands	trad
The gamblin' man AMP		B	pno	trad
Golden rules PIC			pno or org	from the Talmud
How many? EBM			pno	trad
John Hardy L-G			pno	trad
Jonah PIC			pno or org	Herman Melville
The last train SHAW			pno, 4 hands	Paul Horgan
The long farewell SHAW			pno	trad
The Lord star MER		B	pno, org or orch(R)	Walt Whitman
Ode to freedom MER			pno	Ralph W. Emerson
Pilgrim hymn GS	unison		pno or org	anon
The robe SHAW			pno	spiritual
Seven canons MER	2-4 pt		pno	
(See also "Women's" and "Men's Chorus")				
Chop-cherry	high, low voices			Robert Herrick
God	SATB			Angelus Silesius

Composer, Title and Publisher	Chorus	Solos	Accompaniment	Author of Text
The little children. Sinai.	high, low voices			from the Talmud
Money. The pelican.	high, low voices			anon
Schools and rules	unison			William Blake
Shouting pilgrim L-G			pno, 4 hands	trad
Waiting PIC				John Burroughs
BAKSA, Robert F.				
The constant lover, Op. 11, No. 1 AB				Sir John Suckling
Madrigals from the Japanese MER	SSATB			from Haiku
The cricket's widow. Now this year goes away. Sudden shower.				
Madrigals from Shakespeare MER				Shakespeare
Blow, blow, thou winter wind. Fancy. Hark, hark, the lark.				
Three madrigals from Shakespeare AB				Shakespeare
Come away, death. O mistress mine. Under the Greenwood tree.				
BALES, Richard				
Lines HWG			pno	Louise Haskins
BARAB, Seymour				
An angel-carol (Christmas) AMP	divisi			George Wither
Merry are the bells B&H				Seymour Barab
The silver swan B&H				anon
Sweet was the song B&H				John Attey (1622) from First Book of Ayres
BARBER, Samuel				
Agnus Dei (transcribed from "Adagio for Strings," Op. 11)GS			org or pno	liturgical
Easter chorale GS			3 trp, 3 trb, 2 hn, tba, timp, org	Pack Browning
Let down the bars, O death GS				Emily Dickinson
A nun takes the veil GS (See also "Women's" and "Men's Chorus")				Gerard M. Hopkins
Prayers of Kierkegaard GS		S, T, B	pno or orch	Soren Kierkegaard
Reincarnations GS Mary Hynes. The				James Stephens

Composer, Title and Publisher	Chorus	Solos	Accompaniment	Author of Text
coolin. Anthony O'Daly.				
Sure on this shining night GS				James Agee
Under the willow tree (from Vanessa) GS				Gian Carlo Menotti
BARLOW, Wayne				
Madrigal for a bright morning JF	SAATB			John R. Slater
BARTOW, Nevett				
A Christmas canticle SHAW			hp, pno or org	Nevett Bartow
A Thanksgiving ex-ultation SHAW (See also "Women's" and "Men's Chorus")			org or pno, 4 hands	Nevett Bartow
Scene on Easter morn-ing SHAW		Narr opt	org	Nevett Bartow
BAUER, Marion				
At the new year, Op. 42 AMP				Kenneth Patchen
China, Op. 38 JF			pno	Boris Todrin
Death spreads his gen-tle wings AMP	divisi			Eunice Prossor Crain
BEADELL, Robert				
Blow, prairie wind AMP	divisi			Robert Beadell
BEATTIE, Herbert				
The burning babe (a Christmas anthem)L-G				Robert Southwell
Six choral settings from the Bible L-G				
Let Thy work appear (Psalm 90)	SAB			Biblical
I will not leave you comfortless (John 14; 18)	SAB			Biblical
Lo, this is our God (Isaiah 25; 9)	SAB			Biblical
O give thanks (Psalm 106)	SAB			Biblical
Truly my soul	SATB			Bay State Psalm Book
Holy, holy, holy	SATB			Bay State Psalm Book
BECK, John Ness				
Canticle of praise TP			pno or org or orch(R) or band(R)	Biblical

Composer, Title and Publisher	Chorus	Solos	Accompaniment	Author of Text
Hymn for Easter day TP Introit. Processional. Upon this rock GS			3 trp, pno or org org or pno; or 3 trp, hn, trb, tba	Charles Wesley (1739) & Biblical Biblical
Visions of St. John TP Prologue. The seven angels and the seven trumpets. The heavenly city.			pno or org; or brass ensemble with hp, pno & perc(R)	Biblical
BEESON, Jack Boys and girls together (a round) B&H				anon
Give the poor singer a penny (a round) B&H				anon
Greener pastures (a round) B&H				anon
Hiccup, Snicup MIL				nursery rhyme
Matthew, Mark, Luke and John MIL				nursery rhyme
A round for Christmas MIL				Biblical
Swan song MIL				nursery rhyme
BENNETT, Robert Russell Epithalamion TP			orch(R)	John Milton
Verses Nos. 1,2,3 TP				Robt. R. Bennett
BERRY, Wallace No man is an island SMPC			pno	John Donne
BENTZ, Cecil Two short poems by Robert Frost L-G Nothing gold can stay. Waspish			pno	Robert Frost
BERGSMA, William Confrontation (book of Job) GAL			pno or orch(R)	Biblical
In a glass of water before retiring CF		S	pno	Stephen Vincent Benét
Let true love among us 2-pt be CF (See also "Women's" and "Men's Chorus")			pno	trad, 13th cent
On the beach at night CF				Walt Whitman
Riddle me this GAL I. Answer: The snow II. Answer: The egg III. Answer: A cow				trad
The sun, the soaring eagle, the turquoise prince, the god GAL		Sp from Ch	pno; pno & perc; brass (2 trp, 2 trb, tba) (brass & perc	text version adapted & prepared by Wm. Bergsma from books 2 & 7 of the

Composer, Title and Publisher	Chorus	Solos	Accompaniment	Author of Text
(See also "Percussion")			parts on rental only	Florentine Codex (c. 1566) by Fray Bernardino de Shagun; trans: Arthur O. Anderson & Charles E. Dibble
BERNSTEIN, Leonard				
Chichester Psalms GS I. Psalms 108 & 100 II. Psalms 23 & 2 III. Psalms 131 & 133			org (incl hp & timp parts); or 3 trp, 3 trb, 2 hp, perc, str(R)	Biblical
Choruses from "The Lark" GS				Jean Anouilh
Kaddish: Symphony No. 3 GS I. Invocation. Kaddish 1. II. Din-Torah. Kaddish 2. III. Scherzo. Kaddish 3. Finale.		Sp(female),orch(R) S solo & boy's choir		Leonard Bernstein
BIALOSKY, Marshall				
A song of degrees TP				Howard Nemerov
There is a wisdom that is woe TP				Herman Melville
BIGGS, John				
Meditabor GS	SSAATTBB			from the Proper Offertory
BILLINGS, William				
An anthem for Thanksgiving MER		S, A, T, B	org or pno	from The Continental Harmony, 1794
Be glad then America MER		T or Bar	pno	from The Continental Harmony, 1794
Bethlehem MER				from The Singing Master's Assistant, 1778
Consonance MER				Dr. Byles
Creation TP				Isaac Watts
David's lamentation GS				Biblical
I am the rose of Sharon GS				Biblical
Jargon MER				William Billings
Jordan EBM				Isaac Watts
Lamentation over Boston MER				from The Singing Master's Assistant, 1778
Modern music L-G				from Psalm-singers Amusement
Morpheus EBM				anon

Composer, Title and Publisher	Chorus	Solos	Accompaniment	Author of Text
Paris EBM				Isaac Watts
Retrospect TP				from The Singing
(See also "Men's				Master's Assistant,
Chorus")				1778
Rose of Sharon L-G				Biblical
The shepherd's carol				from The Suffolk
("Shiloh") S-B				Harmony, 1786
(See also "Men's				
Chorus")				
Three fuguing tunes MER			a cap or pno	Isaac Watts
Two Easter anthems MER				trad
Crucifixion.				
Resurrection.				
A virgin unspotted MER,				from The Singing
L-G				Master's Assistant,
				1778
When Jesus wept MER,				from The New Eng-
L-G				land Psalm Singer,
(See also "Women's"				1770
and "Men's Chorus")				
BINDER, A.W.				
The legend of the Ari	T, b-		pno or org	George Alexander
(Oratorio) GS	Bar			Kohut
BINGHAM, Seth				
Hail to the Lord's an-				Biblical
nointed FLAM				
Missa sancti Michaelis JF				liturgical
Kyrie eleison. Gloria.				
Sanctus. Benedictus.				
Agnus Dei.				
BINKARD, Gordon				
Ad te levavi (from				Biblical
Psalm 25) AMP				
Ave Maria EV				liturgical
Ave Regina caelorum	SSAATB			text from Latin
(Hail, queen of				
heaven) AMP				
The ebb and flow B&H				Edward Taylor
Laetentur caeli HWG			org	liturgical
Madrigal: Eyes of				Gutierre de Cetina
clear serenity AMP				(16th cent); trans:
				Kate Flores
Nativitas est hodie B&H				liturgical
On the shortness of				William Cowper
human life B&H				
Psalm 93 (The Lord is			org	Biblical
King) CFP				
The recommendation B&H				Richard Crashaw
Remember now thy	S		org	Biblical
Creator B&H				

Composer, Title and Publisher	Chorus	Solos	Accompaniment	Author of Text
Third mass and octave day of Christmas WLP Gradual. Alleluia.			org	Biblical
BLACK, Charles				
Christmas-tide (A processional service) JF	SATB & youth choir		org	folk & trad
BOATWRIGHT, Howard				
Canticle of the sun ECS	with 2nd unison chorus, ad lib	S	orch(R)	St. Francis of Assisi; trans: Matthew Arnold
God is our refuge (Psalm 46) ECS				Biblical
Hear my cry, O Lord (Psalm 61) ECS				Biblical
I will lift up mine eyes unto the hills (Psalm 121) ECS				Biblical
Morning hymn ECS				anon, 7th cent
The Passion according to St. Matthew ECS				
Go to dark Gethsemane (descant)			org	melody: PETRA by Richard Redhead, 1853; text: James Montgomery (1771-1854), adapted by H. Boatwright
Ah, holy Jesus, how hast Thou offended				melody: ROUEN, Poitiers Antiphoner, 1746; text: Johann Heermann(1623): trans: Robert Bridges
Who was guilty?				melody: HERZ-LIEBSTER JESU by Johann Crueger (1640); Text: Johann Heermann (1623): trans: Robt. Bridges
For sins of heedless word and deed				melody: JERVAULX ABBEY, French Psalter(1562); text: Wm. Boyd Carpenter (1841-1918)
All praise to Thee				melody: ENGLE-BERG by Charles V. Stanford(1904-); text: F. Bland Tucker, 1938
Alone Thou goest forth, O Lord				THIRD MODE MELODY by

Composer, Title and Publisher	Chorus	Solos	Accompaniment	Author of Text
				Thomas Tallis (1567); text: Peter Abelard(1079-1142) trans: F. Bland Tucker
The royal banners forward go				melody: PUER NOBIS, adapted by M. Praetorius (1609); text: Venantius Honorius Fortunatus, 596
O sacred head sore wounded				melody: PASSION CHORALE by Hans Leo Hassler(1601), adapted by J. S. Bach; text: Paul Gerhardt(1656); trans: Robt. Bridges
When I survey the wondrous cross				melody: GUIDETTI, arr. by Giovanni Guidetti(1582); text: Isaac Watts (1707)
Jesus, all Thy labor vast				melody: SWEDISH LITANY (1697); text: Thomas Benson Pollack(1870)
Sing, my tongue, the glorious battle				melody: DULCE CARMEN, an essay on Church Plain Chant(1782); text: Venantius Honorius Fortunatus, 596
Star in the East (Christmas) ECS				Reginald Heber
BRIGHT, Houston				
August moon SHAW				Wm. Cullen Bryant
Benedictus and hosanna SHAW	SSATBB			liturgical
Come to me, gentle sleep AMP	divisi			Felicia D. Hemans
The days that are no more SHAW				Alfred Lord Tennyson
De profundis (Psalm 130) SHAW				Biblical
Dirge for the dead moths SHAW				Allen E. Woodall
Evening song of the weary AMP	divisi			Felicia D. Hemans
Fall, leaves, fall SHAW	SSAATTBB			Emily Brontë
From "A child's garden of verses" SHAW				R. L. Stevenson

Composer, Title and Publisher	Chorus	Solos	Accompaniment	Author of Text
Autumn fires. Happy thought. The river. Windy nights. Whole duty of children. The house that Jack built SHAW				Mother Goose
I hear a voice a-prayin' SHAW				Houston Bright
Jabberwocky SHAW			pno; or 2 cor, 2 hn, 2 trb, tba, timp, perc (c-b opt)	Lewis Carroll
Kyrie eleison SHAW				liturgical
Lament of the enchantress AMP	divisi			Percy B. Shelley
The lotus dust SHAW				Alfred Lord Tennyson
Never tell thy love AMP				William Blake
Now deck thyself with majesty SHAW			pno; or 3 trp, 2 hn, 3 bar, tba, (c-b opt), timp; or band(R)	Biblical
Rainsong AMP	divisi			Houston Bright
Reflection SHAW				Christina Rossetti
A song in the wind SHAW				Houston Bright
Song of the meadowlark SHAW		S		Houston Bright
Star, moon and wind SHAW				Percy B. Shelley
The stars are the voyager SHAW				Thomas Hood
Summer evening SHAW				Houston Bright
Sunrise alleluias SHAW			pno; or 3 cor, 2 hn, 2 trb, (c-b opt), timp	Houston Bright
Te Deum laudamus AMP	SSATBB			liturgical
Three quatrains AMP Ah, moon of my delight. Ah, with the grape my failing life provide. When thou with shining foot shall pass among the guests.	divisi			Omar Khayyam
Watchman, what of the night SHAW				Biblical
Weep no more, sad fountains AMP	divisi			John Dowland
What can an old man do? SHAW				Thomas Hood
Winter night on the mountain SHAW				Percy B. Shelley
Winter song SHAW				from Mother Goose
BRUBECK, Dave The light in the wilderness (oratorio) SHAW		Bar	org and jazz combo: pno,	Biblical with additional text by

Composer, Title and Publisher	Chorus	Solos	Accompaniment	Author of Text
The temptations (Ch); Forty days (Ch; opt pno solo; org solo); Repent! follow Me (Bar solo; opt pno solo); The sermon on the Mount (Bar solo; Ch; opt pno solo); The Kingdom of God (Bar solo); The great commandment (Bar solo and Ch; opt pno solo); Love your enemies (Bar solo and Ch); Interlude (opt); Fantasia on "Let not your heart be troubled"; What does it profit a man? (Bar solo); Where is God? (Bar solo and Ch); We seek Him (choral interlude; opt pno solo); Peace I leave with you (Bar solo); Let not your heart be troubled (Ch; opt pno solo); Yet a little while (Bar solo and Ch); Praise ye the Lord (Ch).			c-b, dr(improvisational pno solo opt); or orch(R)	Dave & Iola Brubeck
CADMAN, Charles Wakefield				
Joy GS				Elsie Long
CALDWELL, Mary E.				
The little lamb S-B	unison	fl (opt)	org	William Blake
Spring prayer S-B	unison		org	Chas. Hanson Towne
CALVIN, Susan				
The half-moon westers low AMP				A.E. Housman
Words of comfort AMP				Dorothy Parker
CANBY, Edward T.				
The interminable farewell (a canonic joke) AMP				Edward T. Canby
CANNING, Thomas				
Three old nursery rhymes JF				nursery rhymes
Mary had a little lamb. Little Boy Blue. Humpty Dumpty.				
CARPENTER, John Alden				
The home road GS (See also "Women's" and			pno	John A. Carpenter

Composer, Title and Publisher	Chorus	Solos	Accompaniment	Author of Text
"Men's Chorus")				
Song of faith GS			pno, org or orch	John A. Carpenter
Song of freedom GS			pno	Morris H. Martin
When I bring you colored toys GS			pno	Rabindranath Tagore
(See also "Women's Chorus")				
CARR, Albert Lee				
Christo paremus canticum L-G				liturgical
Innocence L-G			pno	Albert Lee Carr
My silks and fine array L-G				William Blake
She dwelt among un-trodden ways L-G				Wm. Wordsworth
Three years she grew in sun and shower L-G			pno	Wm. Wordsworth
CARTER, Elliott				
Heart not so heavy as mine (1938) AMP				Emily Dickinson
Musicians wrestle every- where MER	SSATB		a cap or str orch	Emily Dickinson
To music PIC				Robert Herrick
CARTER, John				
I sing of a maiden S-B				anon, 1500
CHANLER, Theodore				
Four chorales for summer GS				Leonard Feeney
A breeze. The bee. A butterfly. A shower.				
CHIHARA, Paul				
Nocturne for 24 solo voices CPE				vocalise
Psalm 131 EV				Biblical
CHILDS, Barney				
Three carols on old texts L-G				trad
Be merry. Now make we mirth. There is no rose.				
CHRISTIANSEN, Larry A.				
Echo (a madrigal) S-B				Christina Rossetti
CHRISTIANSEN, Paul				
Every man NAK			org or pno	Paul Christiansen
Prayers of steel AUG				Carl Sandburg

Composer, Title and Publisher	Chorus	Solos	Accompaniment	Author of Text
CHAFLIN, Avery				
Lament for April 15th AMP	SSATB			from U. S. Income Tax Instruction
CLARKE, Henry				
Before dawn COL				Gerrish Thurber
Happy is the man (1935) MER			pno or org	Biblical
No man is an island (1951) MCA		Narr	pno	John Donne
CLOKEY, Joseph W.				
A canticle of peace S-B	unison		pno or orch(R)	Biblical
Adoramus Te (Easter cantata) S-B				liturgical
The divine commission (Easter cantata) JF		Narr	org	ancient liturgies & Biblical texts
If I but knew JF	SSATBB			anon
The temple (oratorio) JF		2 S, A, T, B	org or pno or orch(R)	George Herbert
Dedication. Let all the world. The church floor. The windows. The star. King of glory. The grapes. The wine. Come my way. The cross. The altar. Lord Jesus, be Thou near. The echo. The temple. My joy, my life, my crown.				
The word made flesh (A devotion with music on the Incarnation) JF	SATB & youth choir	S, A, T, B 2 Narr	org	
Prelude: Sleepers, wake				
Come, Emmanuel				Latin Advent antiphons
Drop down, ye heavens				Biblical
The day-star				William Dunbar
Eternal light				Miles Coverdale
Nowell				Robert Southwell
Two kings				Christ Church ms, 16th cent
Redemption				anon, 17th cent
To Thee, O Jesu				Sir Walter Raleigh
O love, how broad				Latin hymn, 15th cent
Immortal love				George Herbert
My joy, my life, my crown				George Herbert
Postlude: Christians, awake				

Composer, Title and Publisher	Chorus	Solos	Accompaniment	Author of Text
COHEN, David Four seasons EV				Christopher Mace
COKER, Wilson The dark hills AMP			pno	Edwin Arlington Robinson
CONE, Edwin Excursions BB	SSATBB			Henry David Thoreau
COOPER, David S. 150th Psalm EBM			3 trp, 3 trb, timp, perc, org(R)	Biblical
COPLAND, Aaron Canticle of freedom (1955)(Rev. 1965) B&H			pno or orch	John Barbour
In the beginning(1947) B&H	SSAATTBB	A		Biblical
Lark (1938) ECS		B		Genevieve Taggard
Las Agachadas (1942) (The shake-down song) B&H	SSAATTBB			anon
Old American songs, Set I (1950) B&H			pno or cham orch(R)	
The boatman's dance (arr. Fine)(See also "Men's Chorus")		Bar		minstrel song, 1843
I bought me a cat (arr. Fine) (See also "Women's" and "Men's Chorus")		S, T		trad
Long time ago (arr. Fine) (See also "Women's Chorus")				trad
Old American songs, Set II (1952) B&H			pno or cham orch(R)	
At the river (arr. Wilding-White) (See also "Women's" and "Men's Chorus")				trad
Ching-a-ring-chaw (arr. Fine)(See also "Women's" and "Men's Chorus")				minstrel song
Promise of living "Thanksgiving song" from Tender land B&H	SATBB		pno duet or orch	Horace Everett
Stomp your foot (from Tender land) B&H (See also "Men's Chorus")			pno, 4 hands	Horace Everett

Composer, Title and Publisher	Chorus	Solos	Accompaniment	Author of Text
That's the idea of freedom (from The Second Hurricane) S-B			pno	Edwin Denby
The younger generation (1943) B&H (See also "Women's Chorus")			pno	Ira Gershwin
CORIGLIANO, John				
Fern Hill GS		m-S	pno, hp, str or orch(R)	Dylan Thomas
What I expected was... GS	SSAATTBB		pno or brass choir and perc(R)	Stephen Spender
CORTÉS, Ramiro				
Two songs B&H Slow, slow, fresh fount. To the old, long life.			pno	Ben Jonson
COWELL, Henry				
Ballad of the two mothers SMPC	SSATBB			Elizabeth Harold
Do you doodle as you dawdle CFP	SSAATTBB		pno(drm ad lib)	Henry Cowell
Edson hymns and fuguing tunes, Parts I & II AMP				The Singing Harmonist, 2nd ed., compiled by Lewis Edson, Jr.
Garden hymn for Easter MER			pno	trad
The Irishman lilts AMP (See also "Women's Chorus")			pno	vocalise
Lilting fancy MER				vocalise
The morning cometh MER				T. Chalmers Furnes
Psalm 121 (1953) AMP				Biblical
The road leads into tomorrow AMP	SSAATTBB			Dora Hagemeyer
Supplication CFP	unison		2 trp, 2 trb, org	Henry Cowell
Sweet was the song the Virgin sung AMP			pno	anon
To America AMP	SSAATTB			Dora Hagemeyer
COWELL, Sidney (editor)				
Early American carols MER	SAB			trad
CRANE, Robert				
A crable song TP				William Blake
CRAWFORD, John				
Magnificat ECS			pno or str orch(R)	Biblical

Composer, Title and Publisher	Chorus	Solos	Accompaniment	Author of Text
CRESTON, Paul				
Dedication SHAW from "Isaiah's Prophecy" COL			pno	Arturo Giovannitti Paul Creston
Alleluia				
Glory to God in the highest	SSAATTBB			
O come, O come, Emmanuel				
Sleep, Holy Babe				
While shepherds watched				
Isaiah's Prophecy (A Christmas oratorio) COL		S, A, T, B, Narr	orch(R)	Biblical
Come near, ye nations (Ch). "And there shall come forth a rod"(Prophet). O come, O come, Emmanuel (Ch). "And the angel Gabriel" (Evangelist). The salutation (orch interlude and Evangelist). Magnificat (Mary). "And it came to pass"(Evangelist). While shepherds watched(Evangelist and Ch). Pastoral night (orch). "Glory to God in the highest" (Ch). Shepherd's colloquy (Evangelist and men's Ch). Sleep, holy babe (S and Ch). Star in the East (Evangelist). We three kings (Caspar, Melchior, and Balthazar). Alleluia (Ch).				
Lilium regis, Op. 73 COL			pno	Francis Thompson
Mass of the angels JF Kyrie. Gloria. Credo. Sanctus. Agnus Dei.	unison		org	liturgical
Missa "Adoro Te, " Op. 54 JF Kyrie. Gloria. Credo. Sanctus. Benedictus. Agnus Dei.	SATB, unison or 2 equal		org	liturgical
Missa solemnis, Op. 44 MIL Kyrie. Gloria. Credo. Sanctus. Benedictus. Agnus Dei. (See also "Men's Chorus")			org or orch(R)	liturgical
Psalm XXIII GS		S	pno	Biblical

Composer, Title and Publisher	Chorus	Solos	Accompaniment	Author of Text
Three chorales from Tagore GS Thou hast made me endless. Here is Thy footstool. Where the mind is without fear.				Rabindranath Tagore
DANIELS, Mabel				
Piper, play on! ECS				anon, ancient Greek
A psalm of praise HWG			3 trp, perc, org(R) or pno	Biblical
Salve, festa dies (Hail thee, day of gladness) ECS				Fortunatus, 6th cent
Through the dark the dreamers came ECS (See also "Women's Chorus")			pno	Earl Marlatt
DELANEY, Robert				
John Brown's song ECS			pno or orch	Stephen Vincent Benét
My lady clear ECS	SATBB			anon, 14th cent
Night ECS			pno	William Blake
DELLO JOIO, Norman				
The bluebird CF			pno	Joseph Machlis
A Christmas carol EBM			pno	G. K. Chesterton
A fable CF		T	pno	Vachel Lindsay
The holy Infant's lullaby EBM			pno	Norman Dello Joio
Impropèrium exspectàvit COL				text: from Latin
Jubilant song GS (See also "Women's Chorus")			pno	Walt Whitman
Madrigal CF		S, T, B hn	a cap or pno	Christina Rossetti
The mystic trumpeter GS		S, T, B		Walt Whitman
Prayers of Cardinal Newman CF			pno or org	Roman Missal by John Henry Cardinal Newman
Proud music of the storm EBM			brass ensemble(R) or org	Walt Whitman
Psalm of David CF			pno or orch(R)	Biblical
Somebody's coming CF			pno	Barbara Anderson
Song of affirmation (Cantata) CF		S & Narr	orch or pno	Stephen Vincent Benét
A song of the open road CF		trp	pno	Walt Whitman
Songs of Walt Whitman EBM The dalliance of eagles.			pno or orch(R)	Walt Whitman

Composer, Title and Publisher	Chorus	Solos	Accompaniment	Author of Text
I sit and look out upon the world. Take our hand, Walt Whitman. Tears.				
Sweet Sunny CF			pno	Barbara Anderson
Three songs of Chopin EBM			pno or orch	English versions by Harold Heiberg
The lovers. The ring. The wish. (See also "Women's Chorus")				
To St. Cecilia CF			3 trp, 3 hn, 2 t-trb, b-trb, tba(R) (or pno)	John Dryden
Vigil strange MER			pno,4 hands	Walt Whitman
Years of the modern EBM			brass & perc	Walt Whitman
DENCKE, Jeremiah				
Lord our God HWG			pno or orch	Biblical
DETT, R. Nathaniel				
The ordering of Moses JF		S, A, T, 2B	orch	Biblical & folklore, comp. by R. Nathaniel Dett
DIAMOND, David				
Chorale SMPC	SSAATTBB			James Agee
Prayer for peace SMPC				trad
This is the garden CF				e.e. cummings
This sacred ground SMPC		B	orch(R)	Lincoln's Gettysburg address
Three madrigals SMPC He who hath glory lost. Gentle lady. Bid adieu.				James Joyce
DIEMENTE, Edward				
Magnificat WLP	(2nd choir ad lib:TTB & boy's choir(STTB)		harmonium & org	Biblical
DIEMER, Emma Lou				
Before the paling of the stars EV			pno or org	Christina Rossetti
The bells B&H			pno, 4 hands	Edgar Allen Poe
O give thanks to the Lord (Psalm 107) COL			org	Biblical
Praise of created things COL			pno or org	St. Francis of Assisi
To Him all glory give EV			orch(R)	Dorothy Diemer Hendry
A spring carol EV			pno	William Blake & Song of Solomon
Three madrigals B&H O mistress mine. Take, o take those lips away. Sigh no more, ladies.				Shakespeare

Composer, Title and Publisher	Chorus	Solos	Accompaniment	Author of Text
DINERSTEIN, Norman Cinque laude (laudate Dominum) B&H				liturgical
DIRKSEN, Richard A child my choice HWG				Robert Southwell
Christmas lullaby L-G				Isaac Watts
The nativity HWG			fl or org using fls and light mutations	Christopher Harvey, 17th cent
Psalm for Christmas day HWG				Thomas Pestel
DONATO, Anthony Christmas eve B&H				Jeanne De Lamarter
How excellent is Thy name (Psalm 8) SMPC			org	Biblical
The last supper SMPC				Biblical
Praise ye the Lord B&H				Biblical
The sycophantic fox and the gullible raven MIL			pno	G. W. Carryl
Wheels of autumn B&H				Jeanne De Lamarter
DONOVAN, Richard Forever, O Lord (In aeternum, Domine- Psalms 71, 101, 108, 119) CFP			org	Biblical
DRINKWATER, David Still was the night when Christ was born JF			pno	Biblical
DRUCKMAN, Jacob Four madrigals MER Shake off your heavy trance				Francis Beaumont
The faery beam upon you		S		Ben Jonson
Death, be not proud				John Donne
Corinna's going a-maying				Robert Herrick
DUKELSKY, Vladimir (DUKE, Vernon) Four choruses BB The anniversary. The private dining room. Taboo to boot. Vanity, vanity.			pno	Ogden Nash
Moulin-rouge CF	SSAATTBB	S	pno	Arthur Symons
EDMUNDS, John Come, sweet peace L-G			org or pno	St. George Tucker
Lord God of Hosts L-G			org	Beatrice Quickenden
Twelve choral hymns and carols L-G				

Composer, Title and Publisher	Chorus	Solos	Accompaniment	Author of Text
Children's New Year song				Eng. trad 17th cent
Come, gracious spirit				Simon Brown(1720)
Come, O creator spirit				9th cent; trans: Robert Bridges
God is ascended up on high				Henry Moore, 17th cent
I praised the earth in beauty seen				Reginald Heber, (1827)
Lift up your hearts				H. Montagu Butler (1881)
Love of the Father				11th cent; trans: Robert Bridges
New Christmas carol				Eng. trad
O mother dear, Jerusalem				F.B.P., c. 16th cent
O sons and daughters, let us sing				Jean Tisserand (15th cent); trans: John Mason Neale
Ye messengers of Christ				Mrs. Vokes (1791)
Ye that have spent the silent night				George Gascoigne (1573)
EFFINGER, Cecil				
Forget not my law HWG (See also "Men's Chorus")				Biblical
Four pastorales GS No mark. Noon. Basket. Wood.		ob		Thomas Hornsby Ferril
Glorious day is here HWG			org	Biblical
The invisible fire HWG		S, A, T, B	orch or org	Tom F. Driver
Mary's soliloquy (from cantata, The St. Luke Christmas story) GS			org or pno	Lucy Vessey
Set of three EV Trial by time. This trail. Inner song while watching a square dance.			pno	Thomas Hornsby Ferril
Shepherds in the field MER				Cecil Effinger
Time CF				Percy B. Shelley
ELLSTEIN, Abraham				
Ode to the king of kings (Cantata) MIL		S, Bar (or T)	pno or orch(R)	Samuel H. Dresner
The redemption (oratorio) MIL		Narr, S, T, Bar	pno or orch(R)	Biblical
ELMORE, Robert				
Psalm of redemption JF		A, Bar	org, 3 trp, 3 trb, perc	Biblical
Veni Emmanuel JF			org, hn, trp, trb, tba(R)	medieval hymn
Vocalise GAL			orch(R)	vocalise

Composer, Title and Publisher	Chorus	Solos	Accompaniment	Author of Text

ELWELL, Herbert
  Lincoln: Requiem
    aeternam AMP
		Bar	pno or orch(R)	John Gould
				Fletcher

EPSTEIN, David
  Five scenes MER
    1. Fall yellow (theme
  in yellow). 2. Nocturne
  in a deserted brickyard.
  3. Fog. 4. Wind-scape.
  5. Uplands in May.
				Carl Sandburg

ESCOVADO, Robin
  Four motets AMP
  Ave Maria. Adoramus
  Te, Christe. O salu-
  taris hostia. Ave
  verum corpus.
				liturgical

ETLER, Alvin
  A Christmas lullaby
    (1960) AMP
  Ode to Pothos (1960)
    AMP
  Peace be unto you AMP
	SSATTB			Alvin Etler
				
				Alvin Etler
				
				St. Augustine's
				prayer book

EVETT, Robert
  The mask of Cain--poems
    of the American Civil
    War PIC
  Portent. Youth is the
  time. Shiloh.
				Herman Melville

FELDMAN, Morton
  Chorus and instruments
    CFP
 	
  Christian Wolff in Cam-
    bridge CFP
	mixed
	cham Ch
			hn, tba, perc,
			pno, vln, vlc,
			c-b
				vocalise
				
				vocalise

FERGUSON, Edwin Earle
  I have built an house L-G
  Ye followers of the lamb
    AMP
			org or pno
			pno
				Biblical
				Shaker song

FERRIS, Joan
  Six songs CF
    All day I hear the noise
  of waters. Bright cap
  and streamers. O cool
  is the valley now.
  Strings in the earth and
  air. This heart that flut-
  ters near my heart. Winds
				James Joyce

Composer, Title and Publisher	Chorus	Solos	Accompaniment	Author of Text
of May, that dance upon the sea.				
FETLER, Paul				
All day I hear L-G				James Joyce
April L-G				William Watson
Drum AMP				Langston Hughes
Jubilate Deo (Sing and rejoice) AUG			2 hn, 3 trp, 3 trb	liturgical
Let me walk AMP				Andrew Fetler
Madman's song AMP				Elinor Wylie
Moonwork AMP		S		Andrew Fetler
November night L-G				Adelaide Crapsey
Oread AMP				Hilda Doolittle
Snow towards evening AMP				Melville Cane
Te Deum AUG				liturgical
FINE, Irving				
Alice in wonderland W-7			pno	Lewis Carroll
Lobster quadrille. Lullaby of the duchess. Father William. (See also "Women's Chorus")				
Hour glass (a cycle on Ben Jonson's poems) GS				Ben Jonson
O know to end as to begin	divisi	2 S, 2 A, T, B		
Have you seen the white lily grow?	divisi			
O do not wanton with those eyes		2 S, A		
Against jealousy		S, A		
Lament				
Hour glass	divisi			
FINK, Michael				
Septem angeli (Seven angels) (cantata) ECS			pno, 4-hands or 2 pno, 4-hands, 4 vlc, 2 c-b, timp, perc(R)	Biblical
Te Deum ECS		T or Bar	pno	liturgical
FINNEY, Ross Lee				
Edge of shadow CFP (See also "Percussion")			2 pno, cel, xy, vib, timp, perc	Archibald MacLeish
The martyr's elegy CFP		high voice	orch(R)	Percy B. Shelley
The nun's priest's tale CFP			orch(R)	Geoffrey Chaucer
Pilgrim psalms CF		S, A, T	orch(R), org or pno	Biblical
Psalm XCV (from Pilgrim psalms) CF			org or pno	Biblical

Composer, Title and Publisher	Chorus	Solos	Accompaniment	Author of Text
Psalm CXXXVIII (from Pilgrim psalms) CF			org or pno	Biblical
Spherical madrigals CFP				
When again all those rare perfections meet				Lord Herbert of Cherbury
All-circling point				Richard Crashaw
His body was an orb				John Dryden
On a round ball				John Donne
Nor doe I doubt				Richard Crashaw
See how the earth				Andrew Marvell
Still are new worlds CFP		Sp	orch(R)	text: quotations from Marjorie Hope Nicolson's The Breaking of the Circle
The sun				Kepler
The moist earth				Harvey
Our soules				Christopher Marlowe
Man hath weav'd out a net				John Donne
To ask or search I blame thee not				John Milton
Is every star				Fontenelle
Farre aboven				Henry More
Give me to learn				Akenside
Here are trees				Camus; trans: Justin O'Brien
He...with ambitious aim				John Milton
FLAGELLO, Nicolas Tristis est anima mea MIL			pno	liturgical
FLANAGAN, William Billy in the darbies PIC			pno	Herman Melville
FLETCHER, Grant At the cry of the first bird S-B				Irish trad
FLOYD, Carlisle Death came knocking B&H			pno	Joseph Auslander
The jaybird song (from Susannah) B&H			pno	anon
Two Stevenson's songs B&H	unison		pno	Robert Louis Stevenson
Rain. Where go the boats? (See also "Women's" and "Men's Chorus")				
FONTRIER, Gabriel Three choruses MER				Hilaire Belloc
The false heart.				
Ha'nacker mill.				
Tarantella.	SSAATTBB			

Composer, Title and Publisher	Chorus	Solos	Accompaniment	Author of Text
Three new directions in music GEN				from N. Y. State income tax instructions
Method of accounting				
A new system of water purification				Nathan Fast
256. Biting humans				Dr. Benjamin Spock
FOSS, Lukas				
Behold, I build an house MER			pno or org	Biblical
Cool prayers (from The prairie) GS				Carl Sandburg
Fragments of Archilochos CF		counter-T Sp (male & female)	man, gtr, perc(R)	Archilochos;trans: Guy Davenport
A parable of death CF		T, Narr	orch or cham	Rainer Maria Rilke; trans: Anthony Hecht
The prairie GS		S, A, T, B	orch or pno	Carl Sandburg
Psalms CF			cham or 2 pno	Biblical
FRACKENPOHL, Arthur				
Elegy on the death of a mad dog BB		S	pno, 4-hands	Oliver Goldsmith
Four Shakespearean songs EBM			pno	Shakespeare
The fox, the ape, and the humble bee (from Love's Labor Lost).				
Hey, ho, the wind and the rain (from Twelfth Night)SSATBB				
Lovers love the spring (from As You Like It)				
Never doubt I love (from Hamlet)				
Lovers love the spring EBM			pno	Shakespeare
Make a joyful noise (Psalm 100) EV			org	Biblical
Marches of peace SHAW				John Greenleaf Whittier
Psalm VIII BB			org	Biblical
FREED, Arnold				
Gloria B&H			3 trp, 4 hn, 3 trb, tba & timp(R) or pno	liturgical
Four seasonal madrigals (from The zodiac) B&H				Edmund Spenser
Autumn. Spring. Summer. Winter.				

Composer, Title and Publisher	Chorus	Solos	Accompaniment	Author of Text
FREED, Isadore The whistle and the drum TP			pno, sn-drm	Amelia J. Burr
FRENCH, Jacob The death of General Washington L-G				Jacob French
GABURO, Kenneth Three dedications CF Arid land. Surprise. The cry.			pno	Lorca
GARLICK, Antony Eleven canzonets WLP (See also "Women's" and "Men's Chorus") The early morning The example In the snow It was a perfect day The may tree The moon Night is fallen The night is freezing fast The rain School's out The stream's song	2 equal voices			 Hilaire Belloc Wm. H. Davies Wm. H. Davies Edward Thomas Alfred Noyes Wm. H. Davies Mary E. Coleridge A. E. Housman Wm. H. Davies Wm. H. Davies Lascelles Abercrombie
GEORGE, Earl A ballad of Jesse James SMPC Four American portraits SMPC Thomas Jefferson. John Quincy Adams. Daniel Boone. Abraham Lincoln. Hosanna to the song of David S-B The lamb S-B Laughing song S-B Songs of innocence S-B Introduction: Piping down the valleys. Infant joy. Laughing song. The shepherd.				Wm. Rose Benét Stephen Vincent Benét liturgical William Blake William Blake William Blake
GETTEL, William D. I taste a liquor never brewed CF				Emily Dickinson
GIANNINI, Vittorio A canticle of Christmas COL Canticle of the martyrs HWG		B, Narr B	orch(R) orch(R) or org	Biblical liturgical

Composer, Title and Publisher	Chorus	Solos	Accompaniment	Author of Text
Requiem TP				liturgical
Three devotional motets			org	Isaac Watts
COL				
Christmas. Good Friday. Easter.				
GIDEON, Miriam				
Slow, slow, fresh fount				Ben Jonson
MER				
GILLIS, Don				
The coming of the king		Narr, S, A,	orch(R)	Norman Vincent
(The Christmas story)		T, B		Peale
MIL				
GLASS, Philip				
Haze gold EV				Carl Sandburg
Spring grass EV				Carl Sandburg
Winter gold EV				Carl Sandburg
GOLD, Ernest				
Oh, good sun (from "Three songs on American Indian lyrics")(with hn obb) L-G (See also "Men's Chorus")				trad
GOLDMAN, Richard Franko (editor)				
Landmarks of early American music GS (a collection of 32 compositions, including psalm-tunes, hymns, patriotic songs and marches.)			pno, band or orch or a cap	
GOODMAN, Joseph				
Four Motets EBM				liturgical
Ego sum panis vivus. Panis angelicus. Caligaverunt. Tenebrae factae sunt.				
How beautiful the queen of night TP				Wm. Wordsworth
Laudate Dominum (Psalm 116) AMP		S(ad lib)		Biblical
Love came down at Christmas AB (See also "Women's" and "Men's Chorus")	high or low voices		org	Christina Rossetti
New Brooms TP				Robert Wilson
Song in the wood MER				Thomas Fletcher
Three responsories AB				liturgical
Caligaverunt oculi mei. Jesum tradidit. Tradiderunt me.				

Composer, Title and Publisher	Chorus	Solos	Accompaniment	Author of Text
Thy rebuke hath broken my heart MER				Biblical
GORDON, Philip				
If thou art sleeping, maiden EV				Henry Wadsworth Longfellow
The pasture GS				Robert Frost
Tell me where is fancy bred GS				Shakespeare
GOTTLIEB, Jack				
In memory of... (cantata) B&H		T or S	org	Moses Ibn Ezra
GRAHAM, Robert				
Autumn moon TP	SAB		pno	Li Po
In the Bamboo wood TP	SAB		pno	Jeana Graham
Spring in the gulch TP	SAB		pno	Myra Lockwood Brown
The voices of Christmas (cantata) SMPC			pno or org; str orch(R)	Joan Sistrunk
The wind chimes: dawn, noon, evening TP	SAB		pno	Jeana Graham
The year of our Lord (Christmas cantata)JF		S, A, T, B	org or pno	Jeana Graham
GREEN, Ray				
Adam lay i-bowndyn AME (See also "Men's Chorus")				anon
Care away, away, awayAME (See also "Men's Chorus")				anon
Corpus Christi AME				anon
Hey nonny no (madrigal) AME				trad
Lullay myn lyking AME				anon
GUSTAFSON, Dwight				
Three songs of parting SHAW			pno	Walt Whitman
The dismantled ship.				
Joy, shipmate, joy.				
Now finale to the shore.				
HAGEN, Francis F.				
Fear not, for behold I bring good tidings B&H			org or pno	Biblical
The morning star B&H			org or pno	Biblical
HANNAHS, Roger C.				
Cantata for the Nativity EV	also with treble choir		org	Biblical and 16th cent Eng. carols

Composer, Title and Publisher	Chorus	Solos	Accompaniment	Author of Text
HANSON, Howard				
Cherubic hymn CF			orch(R) or pno	St. John Chrysostom
How excellent Thy name (Psalm 8) CF (See also "Women's Chorus")			org	Biblical
Lament for Beowulf S-B	SSAATTBB		orch(R)	Anglo-Saxon epic: trans: Wm. Morris & A. J. Wyatt
Merry Mount chorus W-7 Praise we the Lord.			orch(R) or pno 4 hands	Richard L. Stokes
Song of democracy CF (See also "Men's Chorus")			orch(R), band or pno	Walt Whitman
Song of human rights CF			pno or orch(R)	Preamble of the Universal Declaration of Human Rights
Songs from "Drum Taps" JF Beat! Beat! Beat! drums! (also published separately) By the bivouac's fitful flame. To thee, old cause.		Bar	orch(R)	Walt Whitman
HARRIS, Roy				
Birds' courting song MIL				Roy Harris
Blow the man down CF		A, B	orch or pno	trad sea ballad
Cindy CF				trad
David slew Goliath AMP	SSAATTBB	T, B, sp	pno	trad
Folk song symphony GS			orch	trad
Fun and nonsense parody AMP	SSATBB	folk	pno	trad
He's gone away GS	SATBB	S, B		trad
If I had a ribbon bow CF				trad
My praise shall never end AMP	SSAATTBB	folk singer	pno	trad
Sanctus GS				liturgical
Song for occupations, on Walt Whitman poem GS	SSAATTBB			Walt Whitman
Symphony for voices, on Walt Whitman poems GS Song for all seas, all ships. Tears. Inscription.	SSAATTBB			Walt Whitman
Walt Whitman suite MIL The year that trembled. To thee, old cause.			str(R) & 2 pno	Walt Whitman

Composer, Title and Publisher	Chorus	Solos	Accompaniment	Author of Text
When Johnny comes marching home GS				trad
HARRISON, Lou Mass (to St. Anthony) PIC			trp, hp, str orch	liturgical
HEIDEN, Bernhard Divine poems of John Donne (1951) AMP				John Donne
In memoriam AMP				Hal Borland (first published as an editorial in the New York Times, Nov. 24, 1963, on the death of President John F. Kennedy)
HEMMER, Eugene Ode to man in space SE			pno	freely borrowed from Robt. Browning by Eugene Hemmer
HERBST, Johannes The people that in darkness wandered HWG			orch or pno	Biblical
HOIBY, Lee Hymn of the Nativity COL		S, B	orch(R) or pno	Richard Crashaw
The offering (from Hymn of the Nativity) COL			pno	Richard Crashaw
O, mistress mine GS				Shakespeare
When that I was and a little tiny boy GS				Shakespeare
HORVIT, Michael A lullaby ECS	SAB			James Agee
HOVHANESS, Alan Ad lyram, Op. 143 CFP	SSAATTBB	S, A, T, B	orch(R)	from Latin text
Alleluia, Op. 158, No. 10 CFP				liturgical
And as they came down from the mountain, Op. 82 CFP		T		Biblical
Glory to God (cantata), Op. 124 CFP		S, A	4 hn, 4 trp, 4 trb, sax, perc, org	Biblical
Glory to man, Op. 167 CFP	SAB		org	John Lovejoy Elliott
The God of glory thundereth, Op. 140 CFP		T or S	org	Biblical
Hear my prayer, O Lord (Psalm 143), Op. 149 CFP	SSATBB		org or pno	Biblical

Composer, Title and Publisher	Chorus	Solos	Accompaniment	Author of Text
Immortality, Op. 134 CFP		S	org or pno	from hymn by Christian F. Gellert; trans: Frances Cox
In the beginning was the word (cantata), Op. 206 CFP		A, B	cham(R)	Biblical
Look toward the sea, Op. 158(cantata) CFP		Bar	trb and org	Biblical
Magnificat, Op. 157 CFP		S, A, T, B	cham orch or org	liturgical (Eng. text: Hugh Ross)
The Lord's prayer, Op. 35 CFP			org or pno	Biblical
Make haste (Psalm 70), Op. 86 CFP				Biblical
Missa brevis, Op. 4 CFP		B	org and str	liturgical
O for a shout of sacred joy, Op. 161 CFP			org or pno	American Colonial hymn
O God, our help in ages past, Op. 137 CFP			org or pno	Isaac Watts
Out of the depths (Psalm 130), Op. 142, No. 3a CFP		S	org or pno	Biblical
Praise ye the Lord, (Psalm 106) AMP				Biblical
Psalm 23, Op. 188a CFP			org or pno; or fl, 2 trp, timp(R)	Biblical
Psalm 28 (Unto Thee I will cry), Op. 162 CFP				Biblical
Psalm 61 (From the end of the earth), Op. 187 CFP				Biblical
Psalm 148 (Praise ye the Lord), Op. 160 CFP				Biblical
Sing aloud (Psalm 81), Op. 68 CFP				Biblical
Thirtieth ode of Solomon, Op. 76 CFP		Bar	trp, trb, str(R)	Biblical
Transfiguration, Op. 82 CFP		T		Biblical
Triptych (excerpts for SATB), Op. 100 AMP				
The beatitudes	divisi		cham orch(R) or pno	Biblical
Easter cantata			cham orch(R) or pno	trad
Prelude (instrumental)				
O Lord (for S solo)				
Mourn, mourn, ye saints		S		
The Lord now is risen (for S solo)				
Jesus Christ is risen today				

Composer, Title and Publisher	Chorus	Solos	Accompaniment	Author of Text
Unto Thee, O God (Psalm 75) AMP				Biblical
Watchman tell us of the night CFP		B	orch or org	John Bowring
Why hast Thou cast us off (Psalm 74) AMP				Biblical
HOWE, Mary				
Great land of mine MER			pno or org	anon
Williamsburg Sunday CF				Katherine G. Chapin
HUNTER, Ralph				
More nursery rhymes L-G			pno	nursery rhymes
Hey diddle diddle. Little Miss Muffet. The Queen of Hearts. Sing a song of sixpence. (See also "Women's Chorus")				
IMBRIE, Andrew				
On the beach at night SHAW			str(R)	Walt Whitman
IVES, Charles				
Harvest home chorales MER			pno or org or 4 trp, 3 trb, tba, c-b, org(R)	
Harvest home				Rev. Henry Alford
Harvest home				Rev. George Burgess
Lord of the harvest				John Hampton Gurney
Lincoln, the great commoner TP (See also "Women's" and "Men's Chorus")			orch(R)	Edwin Markham
Processional: "Let there be light" PIC (See also "Men's Chorus")			4 trp & org; or 4 vln & org; or str orch	John Ellerton
Psalm 24 MER				Biblical
Psalm 67 AMP	divisi			Biblical
They are there! PIC	unison		pno or orch	Charles Ives
JAMES, Philip				
Come, Holy Spirit HWG		S, Bar	org	Isaac Watts
I know a maiden fair HWG				Henry Wadsworth Longfellow
Mass in honor of St. Mark JF				Biblical
Psalm 149 HWG		S	org, brass ad lib	Biblical

Composer, Title and Publisher	Chorus	Solos	Accompaniment	Author of Text
JARRETT, Jack				
Bright cap and streamers L-G			pno	from Chamber Music by James Joyce
Lean out of the window L-G			pno	from Chamber Music by James Joyce
Strings in the earth L-G			pno	from Chamber Music by James Joyce
Go, lovely rose L-G				Robert Herrick
JOHNSON, Alfred				
Mid-winter carol COL				Christina Rossetti
KADERAVEK, Milan				
Talk not to me WLP				Emily Dickinson
KALMANOFF, Martin				
Benjamin Franklin's prayer S-B			pno	Benjamin Franklin
Moo! BB			pno	Robert Hillyer
To music BB			pno	Robert Herrick
Song of peace EV				Biblical
KASTLE, Leonard				
A noiseless patient spider COL				Walt Whitman
Three whale songs from "Moby Dick" COL				Herman Melville
Whispers of heavenly death COL				Walt Whitman
KAY, Ulysses				
Choral triptych AMP 1. Give ear to my words, O Lord. 2. How long wilt Thou forget me, O Lord. 3. Alleluia			pno or org	Biblical
Flowers in the valley CFP				anon
Grace to you, and peace HWG			org	Biblical
Hanover (O worship the King) CFP			org	Sir Robert Grant
How stands the glass around AMP	SSATB			James Wolfe
Like as a father (Psalm 103) CFP				Biblical
A Lincoln letter CFP		B	pno	Ulysses Kay
O praise the Lord (Psalm 117) CFP				Biblical
Sing unto the Lord (Psalm 149) CFP				Biblical
To light that shines MCA SAB			org	Samuel Johnson
What's in a name? MCA SSATB				Helen F. More

Composer, Title and Publisher	Chorus	Solos	Accompaniment	Author of Text
A wreath for waits (Christmas) AMP Noel. Lully, lullay. Welcome yule.				anon
KENNEDY, John Brodbin Alleluia fanfare BI			org or 2 trp, 3 trb	liturgical
A garland B&H To blossoms. To daffodils. The primrose.				Robert Herrick
I'm nobody! Who are you? B&H				Emily Dickinson
KIRK, Theron Carol Service (with 9 lessons) for Christmas JF Prelude		Narr	org or orch(R)	
Once in royal David's city				music: Henry J. Gauntlett; text: Cecil F. Alexander
Mid-winter				music: Gustav Holst; text: Christina Rossetti
1st lesson				text: Genesis iii, 8-15
The Lord at first did Adam make				music & text trad
2nd lesson				text: Genesis xxii, 15-18
Now every child that dwells on earth				music: Harry Farjeon; text: Eleanor Farjeon
3rd lesson				text: Isaiah ix, 2, 6, 7
O little one sweet				music & text: S. Scheit, 1650
4th lesson				text: Micah v, 2-4
O little town of Bethlehem				music: Louis H. Redner; text: Phillips Brooks
5th lesson				text: St. Luke i, 26-33 and 38
Magnificat				music: Theron Kirk; text: Biblical
6th lesson				text: St. Matthew i, 18-25
While shepherds watched				music: "Whole book of Psalms, 1592" text: Nahum Tate
7th lesson				text: St. Luke ii, 8-16

Composer, Title and Publisher	Chorus	Solos	Accompaniment	Author of Text
In dulci jubilo				music: German, 14th cent; text: anon
8th lesson				text: St. Matthew ii, 1 and 2
We three kings of Orient are				music & text: John H. Hopkins
9th lesson				text: St. John i, 1-14
O come all ye faithful				text from Latin
Five Shakespeare songs SHAW				Shakespeare
Blow, blow from As You Like It. Funeral song from Much Ado About Nothing. Marriage song from The Tempest. Over hill, over dale from A Midsummer Night's Dream. Spring from Love's Labor Lost.				
Glory to God (Christmas cantata) JF		S, A, T, B	org or cham orch(R)	Biblical
It was a lover and his lass SHAW				Shakespeare
Hail, O Son of righteousness JF			2 trp, 2 trb, org	William Austin
King David's deliverance JF			2 pno or orch(R)	Biblical
Night of wonder SHAW Overture. On Christmas night. In the winter heaven. As dew in April. I saw a fair maiden. The carol of the shepherds. Pavane. Blessed was she, that maid Marie. I sing the birth. Ringing, ringing. Alleluia.			pno, org & str quintet(R) or str orch(R)	trad
Now let us all sing SHAW			2 trp, 3 trb, timp, pno	Walter A. Rodby
O come, let us sing S-B			pno or 2 trp, 2 trb, timp	Biblical
Song of immortal praise SHAW			pno	Isaac Watts
KLEIN, Lothar Little book of hours L-G Nones. Prime. Sext. Tierce.				Phillip Murray
KLEIN, Phillip G. A lullaby L-G				James Agee

Composer, Title and Publisher	Chorus	Solos	Accompaniment	Author of Text
KOHN, Karl				
Madrigal CF			pno	Robert Chester, 16th cent
Sensus spei CF	SSAATTBB		pno or 2 trp, 2 trb; or 2 trp, hn, trb; or ob, cl, hn, bsn (all on rental)	Biblical
Three descants from Ecclesiastes CF			2 trp, hn, 2 trb, tba(R)	Biblical
KOHS, Ellis B.				
Three songs from the Navajo MER Song of the horse (SATTBB). Song of the rainchant (SATT-BB). Hunting song (SATB).				from The Indian Book; trans: Natalie Curtis
KORN, Peter Jona				
Three Scottish epitaphs MER				Robert Burns
Three songs of autumn B&H				Basil Swift
KORTE, Karl				
Mass for youth GAL Kyrie. Gloria. Credo. Sanctus. Agnus Dei.			org or pno or orch(R)	liturgical
KOSTECK, Gregory				
Love poems from youth WLP		A, T	pno or orch(R)	Gregory Kosteck
KRAEHENBUEHL, David				
Four Christmas choruses AMP	SSATB			
The star song				Robert Herrick
Ideo gloria in excelsis deo				trad
There is no rose				trad, 15th cent
A song against bores				trad, 16th cent
KRAFT, Leo				
Festival song MER				Leo Kraft
A proverb of Solomon MER			pno or orch(R)	Biblical
KRETER, Leo				
Alleluia EBM				liturgical
Gloria in excelsis Deo EBM			pno	liturgical

Composer, Title and Publisher	Chorus	Solos	Accompaniment	Author of Text
KREUTZ, Robert				
Propers for Christmas midnight mass WLP Introit. Gradual and alleluia. Offertory. Communion.	unison		gtr	Biblical
KRUL, Eli				
Alleluia CFP				liturgical
O come, let us sing CFP			org or pno	Biblical
KUBIK, Gail				
Abigail Adams GS			pno	Rosemary Benét
Adam in the garden COL				trad
American folk song sketches SMPC Little bird, little bird. Oh, my liver and my lungs. (See also "Men's Chorus")				trad
Annie Laurie SMPC	SAATTBB			William Douglas
As I went a-walking one fine summer's evening SMPC	SAATTBB			trad
Black Jack Davy SMPC	SAATTBB			trad
Christopher Columbus COL	divisi		pno	Stephen Vincent Benét
Choral scherzos on a well-known tune SMPC Listen to the mocking bird. Wee Cooper O'Fife.				trad
Creep along, Moses SMPC	SSATTBB			trad
Daniel Drew B&H			vlc, c-b or pno	Rosemary and Stephen Vincent Benét
George Washington COL	divisi		pno	Stephen Vincent Benét
In praise of Johnny Appleseed (cantata) COL Over the Appalachian barricade. The Indians worship him but he hurries on. Johnny Appleseed's old age.		B-Bar	cham(R) or 2 pno(R)	Vachel Lindsay
I ride on Old Paint COL				trad, USA
Jeannie with the light brown hair SMPC	SSAATTBB			trad
Lolly too-dum COL				trad, USA
March of the men of Harlech SMPC			pno	old Welsh air
Miles Standish SMPC	SSAATTBB		pno	Stephen Vincent Benét

Composer, Title and Publisher	Chorus	Solos	Accompaniment	Author of Text
A mirror for the sky COL		S, T, B		Jessamyn West
Audubon's creed			pno	
Choral suite No. 1			pno	
Choral suite No. 2				
My Lord's a fore- fended place			pno	
Nancy Hanks GS	SSAATTBB		pno	Rosemary Benét
Oliver de Lancey GS (See also "Men's Chorus")	SSAATTBB		pno	Stephen Vincent Benét
Pioneer women SMPC	SSAATTBB		pno	Phyllis Merrill
P.T. Barnum COL	divisi		pno	Stephen Vincent Benét
Southern ships and settlers SMPC				Stephen Vincent Benét
Theodore Roosevelt SMPC	SSAATTBB			Stephen Vincent Benét
When I was but a maiden COL				trad, USA
Woodrow Wilson SMPC	SSAATTBB		pno	Stephen Vincent Benét
LAHMER, Reuel				
A song of our own L-G			pno	Edwin L. Peterson
LA MONTAINE, John				
The earth is the Lord's (Psalm 24) PJS			orch(R)	Biblical
Holiday greeting (Christmas) S-B			pno	anon, 17th cent
Merry let us part and merry meet again S-B			pno	John La Montaine
Nativity morn (Christmas carol) HWG				John Milton
Sanctuary (cantata) HWG		Bar	org (2 trp & timp opt)	Theodore Ross & Charles Campbell
Te Deum, Op. 35 PJS			orch(R)	liturgical
Wonder tidings (cycle of Christmas carols)HWG		S, A, T, B, Narr		
Part I:				
What tidings bringest thou, messenger?			pno or hp	anon, 15th cent
O magnum mysterium			cym or gong	anon
Hail, comely and clean			pno or hp	The Townely 2nd shepherd's play, 15th cent; trans: John La Montaine
Hail sovereign Savior			pno or hp	The Townely 2nd shepherd's play; trans: La Montaine
Mary's blessing and farewell			pno or hp, org (opt), cym	The Townely 2nd shepherd's play; trans: La Montaine
O worship the King			pno or hp	J. Michael Haydn

Composer, Title and Publisher	Chorus	Solos	Accompaniment	Author of Text
Part II:				
The magi and King Herod			pno or hp, timp, gong or cym	Old Flemish carol; trans: Robert Graves
Lully, lulla			pno or hp	Pageant of the Shearmen and Taylors, 1534
All poor men and humble			pno or hp	Welsh; trans: K. E. Roberts
Wonder tidings			pno or hp	Sussex carol
LATHAM, William				
Flow, O my tears MER				anon, 16th cent
Gloria S-B				liturgical
A prophecy of peace S-B			ob, cl, hn, bsn, or org	Biblical
Psalm 130 S-B			band	Biblical
Psalm 148 S-B			band	Biblical
Te Deum SHAW			org or perc or wind ensemble(R)	liturgical
LAW, Andrew				
Bunker Hill L-G				Nathaniel Niles
LAYTON, Billy Jim				
Three Dylan Thomas poems GS			2 hn, 2 trp, 2 trb	Dylan Thomas
In my craft or sullen art. O make me a mask. Twenty-four years.				
LEES, Benjamin				
Visions of poets (dramatic cantata) B&H		S, T	orch(R)	Walt Whitman
Introduction. Song of the expositions(S solo). O sun of real peace (T solo). Old ages's lambent peaks (SATB). Song of myself (S solo). Soon shall the winter's foil be here (T solo). Song of the broad-ax. (SATB). Scherzo, from Song of myself (S solo). The mystic trumpeter (T, S, SATB).				
LEKBERG, Sven				
Block city NAK				Robt. L. Stevenson
Envoy JF				Francis Thompson
In quiet night S-B				Sven Lekberg
The lamplighter NAK				Robt. L. Stevenson

Composer, Title and Publisher	Chorus	Solos	Accompaniment	Author of Text
O sing unto the Lord a new song S-B			pno	Biblical
Rain song S-B	SSAATB			from the Pueblo
So wondrous sweet and fair GS				Edmund Waller
LEVY, Marvin David				
Alice in Wonderland B&H				Lewis Carroll
During wind and rain B&H			pno	Thomas Hardy
For the time being (Christmas oratorio) B&H		3 S, m-S, T, Bar, B, Narr	orch(R)	W. H. Auden
Part I: Advent. The annunciation.				
Part II: The temptation of St. Joseph. The summons. The vision of the shepherds.				
Part III: At the manger. Massacre of the innocents. Flight into Egypt.				
Our Father (from For the time being) COL			pno	W. H. Auden
Prayer B&H			org or pno	Biblical
LEWIS, John				
The Alexander's fugue MJQ		vocal qrt: S, A, T, B	vib, pno, c-b, drms(R)	vocalise
Canonic fugue XII MJQ (from Musical Offering by Bach)		vocal qrt: S, A, T, B	vib, pno, c-b, drms(R)	vocalise
Dido's lament (from "When I am laid in earth" by Purcell) MJQ		vocal qrt: S, A, T, B	vib, pno, c-b, drm(R)	vocalise
Little David's fugue MJQ		vocal qrt: S, A, T, B	vib, pno, c-b, drm(R)	vocalise
Ricercar a 6 (from Musical Offering by Bach) MJQ		vocal qrt: S, A, T, B	vib, pno, c-b, drm(R)	vocalise
Vendome MJQ		vocal qrt: S, A, T, B	vib, pno, c-b, drm(R)	vocalise
LINN, Robert				
Anthem of wisdom L-G			2 pnos	Biblical
LOCKWOOD, Normand				
All my heart rejoices (Christmas) AMP			pno	Paul Gerhardt
Apple orchards SHAW		S	pno	Walt Whitman
A babe lies in the cradle (Christmas) AMP			pno	trad
A ballad of the North and South AMP		Narr	pno or wind ensemble	Paul Angle and Earl Miers
Part I 1861: Old Abe Lincoln. Dixie. The bonnie blue flag. John				

Composer, Title and Publisher	Chorus	Solos	Accompaniment	Author of Text
Brown's body. Part II 1861: The battle cry of freedom. The girl I left behind me. The yellow rose of Texas. The battle hymn of the Republic. Part III 1862: We are coming, Father Abraham. Kingdom coming. Go down, Moses. Sherman's march to the sea. Dixie. My captain does not answer. The battle hymn of the Republic.				
Carol fantasy AMP	SATBB		orch or pno or org	trad
The closing doxology (Psalm 150) BB			band(R)	Biblical
Cradle song SHAW				Adelaide Crapsey
Elegy for a hero SHAW	SSAATT BBBB			Walt Whitman
Evening hymn SHAW			org	anon
Here 'mongst ass and oxen mild (Christmas) AMP			pno	trad
Hosanna GS				
How far is it to Bethlehem? HAR				
Hymn of paradise SHAW				Dante
I hear America singing SHAW			pno	Walt Whitman
I heard the voice of Jesus SHAW			org	Horatius Bonar
Inscriptions from the Catacombs AUG I. Vivas in Deo. II. Cum sanctis. III. Vivas inter sanctos. IV. Accersitus ab angelis. V. Dulcis anima. VI. Sophronia, Sophronia dulcis, vivas in Deo.				anon
Joseph, dearest Joseph AMP			pno	trad, German
A lullaby for Christmas NAK				John Addington Symonds
Monotone NAK				Carl Sandburg
Open mine eyes that I may see SHAW				Charles H. Scott
Out of the cradle endlessly rocking GS				Walt Whitman
Praise to the Lord (a motet) CFP				liturgical

Composer, Title and Publisher	Chorus	Solos	Accompaniment	Author of Text
Psalm 123 AMP				Biblical
Rejoice in the Lord (Psalm 33) WLP			2 hn, 2 trb, timp	Biblical
Sing unto the Lord a new song (Psalm 96) SHAW				Biblical
The snow lay on the ground (Christmas) AMP			pno	trad
Soe may we sing SHAW			org or pno	from The Bay Psalm Book
LOMBARDO, Robert				
As the hart panteth (Psalm 42) CFP				Biblical
LO PRESTI, Ronald				
Tribute CF			pno or orch(R) or band(R)	Walt Whitman
LOVELACE, Austin C.				
The house in which I dwell JF	unison		org	Thomas Tiplady
Kindly spring again is here JF	unison		org	John Newton
Wake, sons of the earth JF			org	Wm. Watkins Reid
LUENING, Otto				
Alleluia TP				liturgical
Lines from "A song for occupations" CFP				Walt Whitman
Pilgrim's hymn TP (See also "Women's Chorus")	unison or 2-part Ch	a solo voice	pno or org or orch(R)	Howard Moss
LYNN, George				
The Gettysburg address TP		Bar	pno or orch(R)	Abraham Lincoln
MAILMAN, Martin				
Alleluia MIL			band or pno	liturgical
Three madrigals MIL Hark! Hark! the lark! Take, oh take. O mistress mine.				Shakespeare
MANTON, Robert W.				
Summer evening L-G	SATTBB			R.W. Manton
MARTINO, Donald				
anyone lived in a pretty how town (from Portraits) ECS			pno (perc ad lib)	e.e. cummings
MASON, Daniel Gregory				
Long, long night HWG				Robert Burns

Composer, Title and Publisher	Chorus	Solos	Accompaniment	Author of Text
Twilight song JF			pno	Edwin Arlington Robinson
MATTHEWS, Holon				
Two Sandburg songs MER Fog. Lost.			pno	Carl Sandburg
MAYER, William				
Corinna's going a-maying GS				Robert Herrick
The nymph's reply to the passionate shepherd GS				Sir Walter Raleigh
The passionate shepherd to his love GS				Christopher Marlowe
To Electra MER				Robert Herrick
McCOLLIN, Frances				
Welcome, happy morning L-G			org	Venatius Fortunatus; trans: John Ellerton (1868)
McDONALD, Harl				
Builders of America (cantata) EV		Narr	pno or fl, trp, trb, drm	Edward Shenton
God, give us men (cantata) EV			orch(R) or pno	attributed to a bishop of Exeter
Pioneers, O pioneers EV				Walt Whitman
Songs of conquest (a cycle) EV			orch(R) or pno _ad lib_	Phelps Putman
The breadth and extent of man's empire. A complaint against the bitterness of solitude. A declaration for increase of understanding among the peoples of the world. The exaltation of man in his migrations and in surmounting natural barriers.				
McKAY, George F.				
The lark ascending L-G			fl or pno(opt)	George Meredith
Prayer for this house L-G			pno	Louis Untermeyer
A prayer in spring JF		S		Robert Frost
The seer (Choral rhapsody No. 2) JF				Ralph Waldo Emerson
Bacchanal. Mystic song. The scourge. Unto each and unto all.				
Two modern madrigals L-G Mystery Pieta				Archibald MacLeish Vachel Lindsay
Two nonsense songs JF The crumpetty tree. The table and the chair.			pno	Edward Lear

Voice: Mixed Chorus

Composer, Title and Publisher	Chorus	Solos	Accompaniment	Author of Text
McKINNEY, Howard D. (compiler)				
Easter service with 9 lessons & carols JF		Narr	org	Biblical & trad
A mystery for Christmas (in the Medieval manner) JF (See also Women's Chorus")		S, A, T, B	pno	
Nowell				Eng. carol, 15th cent
People, look East				Besancon carol
We shepherds watch				H.D. McKinney
Behold a rose of beauty				Praetorius
You belfries, towers and steeples				carol, 11th cent
Three kings from Eastern lands afar				P. Cornelius
I heard an infant weeping				Corner's Nachtigall
Sweet Babe				Balthasar Musculus
Babe Jesu, lullaby				Corner's Nachtigall
The Son of man (Christmas cantata) JF		Narr	2 trp, 2 trb, fl, org	
Meditation on Veni Emmanuel (instrumental)				
Two kings				music: Joseph Clokey; text: Christ Church ms, 16th cent
Narration				text: trad (Sandys, 1833)
Ad cantum Laetitiae				text: ancient roundelay
Narration				text: Christmas lauds; 6th cent Ambrosian chant
Nativity hymn				music: Dorothy James; text: John Milton
Narration				text: John Milton
Alle gioie pastors				music: Roberta Bitgood; text: Laude Spirituali (1674)
Narration				text: George Herbert
Our lady sat within her bower				music: Austin Lovelace; text: 15th cent carol
Narration				text: anon and John Milton
Hail, O sun of righteousness				music: Theron Kirk; text: Wm. Austin
Narration				text: George Herbert

Composer, Title and Publisher	Chorus	Solos	Accompaniment	Author of Text
Final prayers and benediction				text: adapted from Bishop Hall, G.R. Woodward, Clement of Alexandria, and Thomas à Kempis
MECHEM, Kirke				
Canon law for newly-weds (from _Proverbs_) ECS 1. Hear ye children. 2. Who so findeth a wife. 3. A merry heart. 4. Who can find a virtuous woman? 5. Who hath woe? 6. Hatred stirreth up strife.	3-6 voices			Biblical
Deny it as she will AMP				Kirke Mechem
Epigrams and epitaphs, Op. 13 (21 catches & canons) ECS	2-8 voices			
Five centuries of spring MER				
1. Spring				Thomas Nashe
2. From you have I been absent				Shakespeare
3. Laughing song				William Blake
4. Loveliest of trees				A. E. Housman
5. Spring				Edna St. Vincent Millay
Forsake me not, O Lord, Op. 23 (memorial motet) ECS				Biblical
Give thanks unto the Lord (Psalm 136) CFP				Biblical
Impromptu AMP				Kirke Mechem
In the land of Morgenstern AMP 1. The questionnaire (Die Behoerde). 2. The odor-organ (Die Geruchsorgel). 3. The lattice (Der Lattenzaum).	divisi			Christian Morgenstern; trans: K. Mechem
Let all mortal flesh keep silent ECS				17th cent French melody
Make a joyful noise unto the Lord ECS				Biblical
Moral precept AMP				Kirke Mechem
Rules for behavior, 1787 L-G			pno	18th cent church rules, Williamsburg, Virginia

Composer, Title and Publisher	Chorus	Solos	Accompaniment	Author of Text
The shepherd and his love, Op. 30 ECS			picc, vla, pno	
The passionate shepherd to his love				Christopher Marlowe
The nymph's reply to the shepherd				Sir Walter Raleigh
Seven joys of Christmas ECS (See also "Women's Chorus")				
1. The joy of love		S		trad (English)
2. The joy of bells				French, 16th cent
3. The joy of Mary				trad (German)
4. The joy of children				trad (Burgundian)
5. The joy of the New Year				trad (Japanese)
6. The joy of dance				trad (Spanish)
7. The joy of song				trad (English)
Songs of wisdom (cantata), Op. 14 ECS				Biblical
1. Recitative--I the preacher. 2. The song of Moses. 3. Recitative --Go thy way. 4. A love song. 5. Recitative--Rejoice, O young man. 6. The protest of Job. 7. Recitative--Be not righteous over much. 8. A song of comfort. 9. Recitative--All hath been heard. 10. A song of praise.				
Tourist time (five satirical songs) ECS			pno	
1. Tourist time				F.R. Scott
2. Boston				J.C. Bossidy
3. Cologne				Samuel Taylor Coleridge
4. Texas				K. L. Mechem
5. Rome				E. Lear
The winds of May (a choral cycle) ECS				Sara Teasdale
The tune. Let it be forgotten.				
Over the roofs. (See also "Men's Chorus")	SSAATTBB			
I shall not care. (See also "Women's Chorus")	SSAA			
Song (Love me with all your heart).				
MEKEEL, Joyce White silence CFP				from the Haiku

Composer, Title and Publisher	Chorus	Solos	Accompaniment	Author of Text
MENNIN, Peter				
Christmas story (a cantata) CF		S, T	brass qrt, timp, str	trad
The cycle (Symphony No. 4) CF			orch or 2 pno	Peter Mennin
Settings of four Chinese poems CF Crossing the Han River. The gold threaded robe. In the quiet night. A song of the palace.				Kiang-Han-Fu; trans: Witter Bryner
MEYEROWITZ, Jan				
Eternitie EBM			2 fl, 2 cl, 2 bsn, 2 hn, 2 trp, trb, tba(R)	Robert Herrick
The glory around His head (cantata of the Resurrection) BB				Biblical
New Plymouth cantata BB				J. Meyerowitz
MIDDLETON, Robert				
Winter wakens all my care L-G				anon, 13th cent
MITCHELL, Lyndol				
When Johnny comes marching home CFP (See also "Percussion" and "Band")			pno & drms or wind sym & drm(R)	trad
MOEVS, Robert				
Et Occidentem illustra EBM			orch(R)	text from the Commission of Theodore Frelinghuysen, New York, May 30, 1755, Par. 1.
MOORE, Douglas				
Dedication B&H	SSATBB			Archibald MacLeish
The Greenfield Christmas tree GS			orch(R)	Arnold Sundgaard
MORGAN, Haydn				
Lament and alleluia (cantata) JF Part I. Behold the lamb. The last supper. Now unto us, Lord. Golgotha. Throned upon the awful tree. When I		S, T	pno	Rev. Dr. Gerald R. Johnson

Composer, Title and Publisher	Chorus	Solos	Accompaniment	Author of Text
survey the wondrous cross. Jesus, priceless treasure. Part II. At the tomb. O sons and daughters, let us sing! All hail the power of Jesus' name.				
MORGAN, Henry				
Never weather-beaten sail ECS			pno or orch(R)	Thomas Campion
MULLINS, Hugh				
Follow your saint S-B				Thomas Campion
MURRAY, Bain				
Hopi flute song S-B	SSATBB			trans: Natalie Curtis Burlin
Winds of truth L-G				Bain Murray
MURRAY, Lynn				
"The miracle" (Christmas oratorio) MCA			brass, hp, org, perc(R)	Norman Corwin
NELSON, Paul				
Two madrigals on old English airs B&H Bring us in good ale. Fortune my foe.				trad, 15th cent
How happy the lover CF				John Dryden
In Bethlehem, that noble place B&H				16th cent text
NELSON, Ron				
Choral fanfare for Christmas B&H			org, 3 trp, 3 trb, tba	Gail M. Kurtz
The Christmas story B&H Praise the birth. Glory to God. Let us also go. Slumber now beloved child. Where is this newborn King? In Bethlehem. The prophecy. Let us all thank Thee, God.		Narr, B	3 trp, 3 trb or a cappella	
Fanfare for a festival (All praise to music) B&H			org or pno; or brass (3 trp, 3 trb, tba), timp	Walter A. Rodby
Sleep, little one B&H (See also "Women's" and "Men's Chorus")				Ron Nelson

Composer, Title and Publisher	Chorus	Solos	Accompaniment	Author of Text
Triumphal te deum B&H			org, 3 trp, 3 trb, perc	liturgical
What is man? B&H		Narr, S, Bar	orch(R) or version for 3 trp, 3 trb, tba, timp, perc, org & pno (ad lib) & electronic sequences	Samuel H. Miller
NELSON, Ronald A.				
How far is it to Bethlehem? AUG			org or pno; or fl, cl, trp, 2 vln, vla, vlc	Finnish song; trans: Olav Lee
NEWMAN, Kent A.				
Make a joyful noise to the Lord (Psalm 98) L-G			org	Biblical
NIXON, Roger				
Firwood L-G				John Claire
Swallows TP				R. L. Stevenson
To the evening star MER				William Blake
The wind TP				R. L. Stevenson
PALMER, Robert				
Slow, slow fresh fount PIC				Ben Jonson
PAPALE, Henry				
A choral miscellany WLP	SAB			
Day				William Blake
Follow the gleam				Alfred Lord Tennyson
Full fadom five				Shakespeare
Hey robin				Shakespeare
PARKER, Horatio				
Hora novissima (oratorio) HWG	SSAATTBB	S, A, T, B	orch	Bernard de Morlaix
PELOQUIN, C. Alexander				
The bells B&H			2 pno, 2 c-b, perc	Edgar Allan Poe
PENINGER, David				
A canticle for Easter JF	SATB & youth choir		org	Charles Wesley

Composer, Title and Publisher	Chorus	Solos	Accompaniment	Author of Text
PERLE, George				
Christ is born today B&H				trad French
The miracle of St. Nicholas B&H				trad French
PERSICHETTI, Vincent				
Agnus Dei (from Mass)EV				liturgical
Celebrations EV			pno or wind ensemble (picc, 2 fl, 2 ob, 3 cl, b-cl, 2 bsn, 3 trp, 4 hn, bar, 3 trb, tba, timp, perc)	Walt Whitman
1. Stranger. 2. I celebrate myself. 3. You who celebrate bygones. 4. There is that in me. 5. Sing me the universal. 6. Flaunt out, O sea. 7. I sing the body electric. 8. A clear midnight. 9. Voyage.				
Four cummings choruses EV	SATB or SB		pno	e. e. cummings
dominic has a doll. maggy and milly and molly and may. nouns to nouns. uncles. (See also "Women's" & "Men's Chorus")				
Gloria (from Mass)EV				liturgical
Jimmie's got a goil GS (See also "Women's" & "Men's Chorus")	SA unison & TB unison		pno	e. e. cummings
Mass EV				liturgical
The pleiades EV			trp & str orch	V. Persichetti
Proverb EV				American folklore
Sam was a man GS (See also "Women's" & "Men's Chorus")	SA unison & TB unison			e. e. cummings
Seek the highest EV	SAB		org or pno	Felix Adler
Stabat mater EV			orch(R) or pno	Jacopone da Todi; Eng. version: V. Persichetti
Te Deum EV			orch(R)	liturgical
PETER, Simon				
Behold a sight HWG			orch or pno	Biblical
I will be as the morning dew B&H			org or pno	Biblical
PETERSON, Wayne				
Earth, sweet earth L-G				Gerard M. Hopkins
PFAUTSCH, Lloyd				
Canticle to peace S-B			pno or band	John Greenleaf Whittier
Invocation L-G			org or pno	Reinhold Niebuhr

Composer, Title and Publisher	Chorus	Solos	Accompaniment	Author of Text
I thank you, God L-G				e. e. cummings
Music when soft voices die L-G		S		Percy B. Shelley
A time carol L-G	unison		pno or org	Ilo Orleans
Sing in excelsis gloria S-B		Bar		Osbert Warmingham
Sing praises L-G				Biblical
PHILLIPS, Burrill				
Bucket of water EV			pno	Alberta Phillips
The return of Odysseus GAL		Bar, Narr	pno or orch(R)	Alberta Phillips
Overture. Entrada. Battle piece. Finale.				
PINKHAM, Daniel				
Canticle of praise ECS		S	3 trp, 2 hn, 2 trb, b-trb, tba, perc(R)	Biblical
Christmas cantata (sinfonia sacra) KING			double brass choir or brass qrt & org	Daniel Pinkham
Christmas eve ECS				Robert Hillyer
Easter cantata CFP			4 trp, 2 hn, 3 trb, tba, cel, timp, perc	Biblical
Elegy (Now time has gathered to itself) ECS				Robert Hillyer
Farewell, vain world ECS				Epitaph on tomb of Edward Carter, 1749, Granary Burying Ground, Boston
Festival magnificat CFP			org, brass qrt	liturgical
Five Psalm motets CFP O Lord God. Why art Thou cast down? Thou hast loved rightousness. Open to me the gates of rightousness. Behold, how good and how pleasant.				Biblical
Glory be to God (motet for Christmas day) ECS	SSAATTBB		org (opt)	Daniel Pinkham
God is a spirit ECS			org	Biblical
Henry was a worthy king ECS				anon, English
Jonah (dramatic cantata) ECS		m-S, T, b-Bar	orch(R)	Biblical
Jubilate Deo (Psalm 100) ECS			org	Biblical
Ch I:	unison of treble voices			
Ch II.	SSA			

Composer, Title and Publisher	Chorus	Solos	Accompaniment	Author of Text
Ch III:	SATB			
Lamentations of Jeremiah CFP			2 trp, 2 hn, 2 trb, c-b, timp, perc(R)	Biblical
The leaf ECS				Robert Hillyer
The martyrdon of St. Stephen ECS			gtr	Biblical
Mass of the Good Shepherd ECS	unison		org	Biblical
Mass of the Holy Eucharist (Communion service) ECS	unison		org	Biblical
Mass of the word of God ECS Lord, have mercy (Kyrie eleison). Glory to God (Gloria). I believe in one God (Creed). Holy, Holy, Holy (Sanctus).			org	liturgical
O Lord God (Psalm 94) CFP			org or pno ad lib	Biblical
Open to me the gates of rightousness (Psalm 4) CFP			org or pno	Biblical
Piping Anne and husky Paul ECS				Robert Hillyer
Psalm 24 CFP			brass	Biblical
The reproaches AMP 1. Prologue: Ecce lignum Crucis. 2. First intonation. 3. Refrain: Popule meus. 4. Verse: Quia eduxi te. 5. Refrain: Agios, O Theos. 6. Verse: Quia eduxi te. 7. Verse: Quid ultra. 8. Verse: Ego propter te flagellavi. 9. Verse: Ego te eduxi de Aegypto. 10. Verse: Ego ante te aperui mare. 11. Verse: Ego ante te praeivi. 12. Verse: Ego te pavi manna. 13. Verse: Ego te potavi. 14. Verse: Ego propter te Chananaeorum reges. 15. Verse: Ego dedi tibi. 16. Verse: Ego te exaltavi. 17. Second intonation. 18. Epilogue: Crucem tuam adoramus.			Version A: wind quintet & str quintet (or str orch(R)), with org ad lib Version B: str quintet or quartet or orch(R) with org ad lib Version C: org Version D: a cappella	Liber Usualis; trans: Jean Lunn
Songs of peaceful departure ECS 1. All flesh is grass. 2. Lord, make me to know mine end. 3. Lord, Thou hast put glad-			gtr	Biblical

Composer, Title and Publisher	Chorus	Solos	Accompaniment	Author of Text
ness in my heart.				
Requiem CFP		A, T	2 trp, 2 hn, 2 trb & c-b(R)	liturgical
St. Mark passion CFP		S, T	2 hn, 2 trp, 2 trb, timp, perc, hp, org(R)	Biblical
Stabat mater CFP Adorations, inner life, contemplation, concert		S	cham(R) or org or pno	liturgical
The star-tree carol BOS				Robert Hillyer
Te Deum KING (See also "Women's" & "Men's Chorus")			3 trp, org	John Dryden
Thou hast loved right-eousness (Psalm 45) CFP			org or pno	Biblical
Thy statutes have been my songs ECS	SAB		org	Biblical
Three Lenten poems of Richard Crashaw ECS On the still surviving marks of our Saviour's wounds. Upon the body of our blessed Lord, naked and bloody. O save us then.			str qrt, str orch or pno	Richard Crashaw
Wedding cantata CFP		S or T ad lib	pno or orch(R)	Biblical
Why art thou cast down? (Psalm 42) CFP			org or pno	Biblical
PISTON, Walter Psalm and prayer of David (1958) AMP			fl, cl, bsn, vln, vla, vlc, c-b(R) (or pno)	Biblical
POWELL, John The deaf woman's court-ship, Op. 35, No. 1 JF		m-S, T		trad
Soldier, soldier, Op. 35, No. 2 JF				trad
POZDRO, John All pleasant things L-G				anon
PRESTON, John E. The coming American MIL			org or str orch	Sam Walter Foss
PURVIS, Richard The ballad of Judas Iscariot EV		S, A, T, B	org or pno; or org, vln, 2 hp, cel	Robert Buchanan
Paean of praise (can-tata) JF		Bar	org or 3 trp, 2 trb, timp	Biblical

Composer, Title and Publisher	Chorus	Solos	Accompaniment	Author of Text
The song of Simeon JF			org or 3 trp, 2 trb, timp, hp	setting of Nunc Dimittis
RAPHLING, Sam				
The bells MER				Edgar Allan Poe
Sayings from The people, yes MER			pno	Carl Sandburg
READ, Daniel				
Complaint EBM				Isaac Watts
Mortality EBM				Isaac Watts
Norwalk EBM				Isaac Watts
READ, Gardner				
The golden harp JF				from "The Sacred Harp"
Jesous Ahtonhia, Op. 87 S-B			org	St. Jean de Brebeuf, S.J.(Martyr)
The lamb, Op. 84, No. 3a JF			pno	William Blake
A mountain song JF				Frances Frost
River night L-G			pno	Frances Frost
Song heard in sleep L-G			pno	Wm. Rose Benét
To a skylark, Op. 51 AMP	SSATB			Percy B. Shelley
REED, Alfred				
Choric song: a romantic idyl B&H	SSATBB		band	Alfred Lord Tennyson
A sea dirge FM	SSAATBB			Shakespeare
REICHENBACH, Herman (editor)				
Modern canons (for 2-5 voices) MER (See also "Women's"& "Men's Chorus")				
Marion Bauer: Song of the wanderer (3 voices)				Marion Bauer
Henry Brant: The 3-way canon blues (3 voices)				Henry Brant
Henry Cowell: Air held her breath (4 voices)				Abraham Lincoln
I strove with none (4 voices)				Walter Savage Landor
David Diamond: Three young rats (4 voices)				anon
Anthony Donato: People take care (2 voices)				Anthony Donato
Ross Lee Finney: Words to be spoken (4 voices)				Archibald Mac-Leish
Everett Helm: Dona nobis pacem (3 voices)				liturgical

Composer, Title and Publisher	Chorus	Solos	Accompaniment	Author of Text
George Henry: When a wicked man dieth (4 voices)				Biblical
Philip James: O nightingale (3 voices)				Philip James
Gail Kubik: A sailor, he came to court me (4 voices)				Bill Roberts
Daniel Gregory Mason: The prisoner to the singing bird (4 voices)				John Buxton
Douglas Moore: Western winde (2 voices)				anon, 16th cent
Vincent Persichetti: Should fancy cease (3 voices)				from the Sanscrit
Preface to canons (2 voices)				Herman Reichenbach
Hallelujah, bum again (2 voices)				trad
Quincy Porter: Barnyard cogitations (4 voices)				Ogden Nash
Herman Reichenbach: The shepherd (3 voices)				Christopher Marlowe
Catch (4 voices)				
Randall Thompson: Epigram (3 voices)				Herman Reichenbach
Lines from "The Ancient Mariner" (3 voices)				John Byrom Samuel Taylor Coleridge
Virgil Thomson: Agnus Dei (3 voices)				liturgical
John Verrall: Ah come, sweet night (4 voices)				John Verrall
REYNOLDS, Roger				
Blind men CFP			3 trp, 2 trb, b-trb, tba, perc, pno(R)	Herman Melville
Masks CFP			orch(R)	Herman Melville
RICHARDS, Howard				
Rain L-G				from Chamber Music by James Joyce
Who goes amid the greenwood L-G				from Chamber Music by James Joyce
RICHTER, Marga				
Psalm 91 EV				Biblical
RIEGGER, Wallingford				
Cantata, "In certainty of song," Op. 46 PIC			orch(R) or pno	Catherine Harris

Composer, Title and Publisher	Chorus	Solos	Accompaniment	Author of Text
Easter passacaglia, Op. 32c FLAM	SATB or SAB		org or pno	trad, 17th cent
Evil shall not prevail (Non vincit malitia) BCS (See also "Women's" and "Men's Chorus")	double ch: SSA-SSA; SSA-TBB or TBB-TBB			Wisdom 7:29-30
A Shakespeare sonnet (No. 138), Op. 65 AMP	SSAB		pno or cham orch	Shakespeare
Who can revoke EBM			pno	Catherine Harris
RINGWALD, Roy				
The song of America SHAW		Narr	orch(R) or pno, 4 hands	Texts from various poets, including Bryant, Emerson, Lowell, Longfellow, Whittier, Holmes and Whitman
RINKER, Alton				
American poet's suite SHAW			pno	
Annabel Lee				Edgar Allan Poe
Eldorado				Edgar Allan Poe
The last leaf				Oliver Wendell Holmes
Little Boy Blue				Eugene Field
O captain! My captain!				Walt Whitman
Song portrait of birds SHAW The dodo. The flamingo. The magpie. The nightingale. The ostrich. The penguin. The swan (text by Alton Rinker).				Tom Adair
ROBERTSON, Leroy				
All creatures of our God and King GAL			hn, trp, trb, tba(R)	Biblical
Come, come ye saints GAL			orch(R)	Biblical
The Lord's prayer GAL			str orch(R)	Biblical
ROCHBERG, George				
Psalm 23 TP				Biblical
Psalm 43 TP	SSATB			Biblical
Psalm 150 TP				Biblical
RODBY, Walter				
Mango walk B&H	SAB			Calypso tune
ROGERS, Bernard				
Hear my prayer, O God TP		S, A	org	Biblical
A letter from Pete (cantata) SMPC		S, T	orch(R) or pno	Walt Whitman

Composer, Title and Publisher	Chorus	Solos	Accompaniment	Author of Text
The light of man TP		S, A, Bar	orch(R) or pno	Biblical
Lord God of hosts (Psalm 89) TP		Bar	pno	Biblical
The prophet Isaiah SMPC			orch(R)	Biblical
ROREM, Ned				
The Corinthians CFP				Biblical
Four Madrigals MER				trad
From an unknown past SMPC				
Crabbed age and youth				Shakespeare
Hey nonny no!				anon
The lover in winter plaineth for the spring				anon, 16th cent
The miracle				anon, 16th cent
My blood so red				anon
Suspira				anon
Tears				John Dowland
He shall rule from sea to sea B&H			org	Biblical
Laudemus tempus actum B&H			orch(R)	Ned Rorem
Proper for the votive mass of the Holy Spirit B&H Introit. Gradual. Offertory. Communion.			org	liturgical
The seventieth Psalm HWG			pno or fl, ob, cl, bsn, 2 hn, tba(R)	Biblical
Truth in the night season B&H			org	Biblical
Two psalms and a proverb ECS Behold how good and pleasant it is (Psalm 133); Wounds without cause (Proverbs 23); How long wilt Thou forget me, O Lord? (Psalm 13)			str quintet or pno	Biblical
ROSS, Orvis				
At the gate of the year CFP		Bar	org or pno	M. L. Hoskins
ROY, Klaus George				
Among the maidens ECS SAB				trad Greek
Canticle of the sun, Op. 17 MIL			vla	from St. Francis' Mirror of Perfection; trans: Robert Steele
Lie still, sleep becalmed L-G				Dylan Thomas
Pride goeth before a fall SAB ECS				trad Slovakian
To ashes burns my heart SAB ECS				trad Dutch

Voice: Mixed Chorus

Composer, Title and Publisher	Chorus	Solos	Accompaniment	Author of Text
RUSSELL, John				
The dark hills L-G				Edwin Arlington Robinson
Merry the green L-G				Donald Justice
SACCO, P. Peter				
The snowstorm L-G			pno	Ralph W. Emerson
SANDERS, Robert				
A hymn of the future MER			org	John Addington Symonds
Out of the cradle BB				Walt Whitman
When lilacs last in the dooryard bloom'd BB				Walt Whitman
SCHICKLE, Peter				
After spring sunset (cantata) VAL				based on Japanese poems
The birth of Christ EV		S, 2 Narr	pno	York Cycle of English Mystery plays
Three choruses AB dim/1(a. dominic has a doll. maggie and milly and molly and may.				e.e. cummings
Two prayers EV Grant this to me. Thee I pray.				William Becker
SCHMUTZ, Albert				
Stopping by the woods on a snowy evening L-G				Robert Frost
SCHUMAN, William				
Carols of death TP The last invocation. The unknown region. To all, to each.				Walt Whitman
Choral etude CF				vocalise
Choruses from The Mighty Casey GS				Jeremy Gury
Deo ac veritati TP (See also "Men's Chorus")				Motto of Colgate Univ.
Four canonic choruses GS				
Epitaph				Edna St. Vincent Millay
Epitaph for Joseph Conrad				Countee Cullen
Night stuff				Carl Sandburg
Come not				Alfred Tennyson
Four rounds on famous words TP Beauty. Caution.	SAB			common aphorisms

Composer, Title and Publisher	Chorus	Solos	Accompaniment	Author of Text
Health. Thrift (See also "Women's Chorus")				
A free song (secular cantata No. 2)GS			orch or pno	Walt Whitman
Holiday song GS (See also "Women's" and "Men's Chorus")			pno	Genevieve Taggard
The Lord has a child TP			org or pno	Langston Hughes
Pioneers GS	SSAATTBB			Walt Whitman
Prelude GS		S		Thomas Wolfe
Prologue GS			orch(R) or pno	Genevieve Taggard
Requiescat GS (See also "Women's Chorus")			pno	vocalise
Te Deum (for coronation scene of Shakespeare's Henry VIII)GS				liturgical fragment
This is our time B&H			orch(R) or pno	Genevieve Taggard
SEMMLER, Alexander				
The owl and the pussy-cat AB			pno	Edward Lear
SESSIONS, Roger				
Mass (1956) EBM	unison		org	liturgical
Turn, O libertad (1943) EBM			orch(R) or pno, 4 hands	Walt Whitman
SHALLENBERG, Robert				
Lilacs AP				Walt Whitman
SHAPERO, Harold				
Two psalms SMPC Laude. Jubilate.				Biblical
SHAW, Martin				
O Christ, who hold the open gate GS			org	John Masefield
SHEPHERD, Arthur				
Jolly Wat (canticum nativitatis Christi) MER (See also "Women's" and "Men's Chorus")	2 equal voices	2 solo voices	orch(R) or pno or org	Balliol ms: 15th-16th cent
SHIFRIN, Seymour				
Give ear, O ye heavens (The Song of Moses) CFP	SSAATTBB		org or pno	Biblical

Composer, Title and Publisher	Chorus	Solos	Accompaniment	Author of Text
SIEGMEISTER, Elie				
Abraham Lincoln walks at midnight B&H			orch(R) or pno	Vachel Lindsay
Anne Rutledge SMPC			pno	Vachel Lindsay
The bold fisherman TP				trad sea ballad
Christmas is coming (a cantata of carols) GS		Narr	pno or cham orch(R)	Dorothy de Fer- ranti
I have a dream (cantata) MCA		Bar, Narr	orch(R)	Edward Mabley
I see a land (an Ameri- can cantata) GS		Narr	pno	Hy Zaret, Guy Carryl & trad
John Henry (an Ameri- can saga) CF				trad
Johnny Appleseed MER			pno	Rosemary Benét
The new colossus MER			pno	Emma Lazarus's inscription on Statue of Liberty
Lazy afternoon (from "Ozark Set") EBM (See also "Women's Chorus")			pno	Leo Paris
Song of democracy MER			pno	Elie Siegmeister
This is our land (an Ameri- can cantata) GS		Narr	pno	Rufus Wheeler
SIMEONE, Harry				
All the world's a stage SHAW			pno	Shakespeare
We are the music makers SHAW			pno	Arthur O'Shaughn- essy
SMIT, Leo				
Psalm PIC				Biblical
SMITH, Carlton Sprague (ed.)				
Bay Psalm Book: Psalms 6, 19, 128 CFP				
SMITH, Gregg				
Landscapes GS New Hampshire. Virginia. Usk. Cape Anne. Rannoch, by Glencoe.				T.S. Eliot
Nature (from "Four Concord Chorales") GS			org or pno, 4-hands	Ralph Waldo Emerson
Spirit (from "Four Concord Chorales") GS			org or pno, 4-hands	Ralph Waldo Emerson
SMITH, Russell				
Gloria COL				liturgical

Composer, Title and Publisher	Chorus	Solos	Accompaniment	Author of Text
Service in G COL Kyrie. Responses. Sanctus and Benedictus. Agnus Dei.				liturgical
SOWERBY, Leo				
Behold, O God, our defender HWG			org	Biblical
Canticle of the sun HWG			orch or pno	St. Francis of Assisi; trans: Matthew Arnold
Christians, to the Paschal victim HWG			org	Wipo, c. 1030 A.D.
Except the Lord build the house HWG			org	Biblical
Forsaken of man HWG			orch or pno	Edward Borgers & Biblical
I will lift up my eyes BOS				Biblical
Solomon's garden (cantata) HWG		T	orch(R) and org	Biblical
The throne of God HWG			orch(R)	Biblical
SPIES, Claudio				
In paradisum (motet)EV	SSATB			Claudio Spies
STARER, Robert				
Ariel, visions of Isaiah MCA Woe to Ariel. The earth mourneth. The daughters of Zion are haughty. Fear, and the pit, and the snare. The Lord shall give thee rest. Break forth into joy.		S, B	orch(R) or pno or org	Biblical
Five proverbs on love EBM It is not good to be a single man Love is life's end Love for sweet April To love is a delightful pleasure If you ask what love may be				(Latin text-trad) Phineas Fletcher Giovanni Prati Le Chevalier de Parny Wilhelm Mueller
I wish I were MER				anon
Joseph and his brothers (cantata) MCA		S, T, b-Bar, Narr	orch(R)	Biblical
Kohelet (Ecclesiastes) MCA		S, Bar	orch(R)	Biblical
A Psalm of David TP		S	org or pno; or str orch & 2 trp(R)	Biblical

Composer, Title and Publisher	Chorus	Solos	Accompaniment	Author of Text
Two songs from "Honey and Salt" MCA			pno or 2 trp & 2 trb	Carl Sandburg
Love is a deep and a dark and a lonely.				
The going of time.				
STEVENS, Halsey				
Ballad of William Sycamore GAL			orch(R) or pno	Stephen Vincent Benét
Beatus vir (Psalm 1) MPC				Biblical
Campion suite WLP				Thomas Campion
Night as well as brightest day. There is a garden in her face. Thrice toss these oaken ashes. To music bent. When to her lute Corinna sings.				
Go, lovely rose HME				Edmund Waller
In Te, Domine, speravi (Psalm 31) CFP			org	Biblical
Lady, as thy fair swan MPC				Gerald Bullett
Like as the culver on the barèd bough AMP	SSATB			Sir Edmund Spenser
Magnificat MPC			trp, str orch	Biblical
A New Year carol HME				anon
Praise ye the Lord (Psalm 148) HME				Biblical
Te Deum MPC			2 trp, 2 hn, 2 trb, timp, org	liturgical
The way of Jehovah MPC			org or pno	Biblical
Weepe O mine eyes HME	SSATB			anon, 16th cent
When I am dead, my dearest AMP				Christina Rossetti
STEWART, Kensey D.				
The tide rises, the tide falls L-G				Henry Wadsworth Longfellow
STILL, William Grant				
Rising tide JF	SSATBB		pno or orch(R)	Albert Stillman
Sahdji (a ballet) CF		B, dancers	orch(R)	Richard Bruce & Alain Locke
Victory tide JF			pno or orch(R)	Albert Stillman
STOUT, Alan				
Creator spirit CFP	unison		org or pno	John Dryden
The great day of the Lord CFP			org or pno	Biblical
In principio erat verbum (motet, 1963) CFP	SSAATTBB		4 vln, 2 vla, 2 vlc, c-b	Biblical

Composer, Title and Publisher	Chorus	Solos	Accompaniment	Author of Text
STRILKO, Anthony				
Carol of the animals L-G				Kenneth Grahame
Lines from Shelley L-G				Percy B. Shelley
Nowell MER				Theophile Gautier; trans: Alan Cander
Seven choruses on Elizabethan texts EV				
Autumnus				Joshua Sylvester
Awake mine eyes				anon, c. 1610
A bellman's song				anon, c. 1611
Lullaby				Thomas Dekker
Mary had a pretty bird				anon, c. 1600
Shall I?				anon, c. 1610
Song for a dance				Francis Beaumont
Three cinquains BB	AATB			Adelaide Crapsey
November night. Triad. The warning.				
SUDERBURG, Robert				
Concert mass TP				liturgical
Kyrie. Gloria. Credo. Sanctus. Agnus Dei.				
SUMMERLIN, Ed				
Evensong--a jazz liturgy MJQ			org, a-sax, t-sax, 2 trp, trb, b-trb, gtr (or pno), c-b, drm(R)	liturgical
SYDEMAN, William				
The lament of Electra (cantata) ECS	5 choruses A (SATB) each & each with own cond.		fl, ob, cl, bsn, hn, trp, 2 vln, vla, vlc, timp (instr pts on rental)	W. Sydeman; adapted from Sophocles, Euripides, Aeschylus
TANNER, Peter				
Sing for joy L-G			org	Biblical
TAYLOR, Clifford				
Gloria L-G			org or pno	old Scottish chant
Lettest thou thy servant depart in peace L-G				based on chant by John Blow
Sing to the Lord a new song L-G			org	Biblical
TAYLOR, Deems				
Hearest thou the wind? (from The King's Henchman) COL		Bar	pno	Edna St. Vincent Millay

Composer, Title and Publisher	Chorus	Solos	Accompaniment	Author of Text
THOMPSON, Randall				
Alleluia ECS				liturgical
Americana (five choruses) ECS			orch(R) or pno	articles in The American Mercury
May every tongue. The staff necromancer. God's bottles. Sublime process of law enforcement. Loveli-lines.				
The best of rooms ECS				Robert Herrick
Excerpts from "Requiem" ECS				liturgical
Good tidings to the meek (from Part 2)	SSAATTBB			
The garment of praise (Part 4 complete)	SSAATTBB			
Ye were sometimes darkness (from Part 5)	SSAATTBB			
The Lord shall be unto thee (from Part 5)	SATB			
Thou hast given Him (from Part 5)	SATBB			
Amen, alleluia (fugal finale)	SSAATTBB			
A feast of praise ECS 1. The stars in their watches. 2. Nocturne. 3. God is gone up with a shout.			2 trp, 2 hn, 2 trb, tba, hp	Biblical
"Frostiana" (Seven country songs) ECS			pno or orch	Robert Frost
The road not taken			pno or orch	
The pasture	TTB			
Come in	SSA			
The telephone	SAATTBB		pno or orch	
A girl's garden	SSA			
Stopping by woods on a snowy evening	TBB			
Choose something like a star			pno or orch	
The gate of heaven ECS				Biblical
The last words of David ECS (See also "Men's Chorus")			orch(R) or pno	Biblical
The Lord is my Shepherd (Psalm 23) ECS			pno, org, or hp	Biblical
Mass of the Holy Spirit (Communion service) ECS				liturgical
Kyrie. Gloria(SSAATTBB). Credo. Sanctus(SSAATTBB). Benedictus. Hosanna.				

Composer, Title and Publisher	Chorus	Solos	Accompaniment	Author of Text
Agnus Dei. Nowel ECS (See also "Women's" &"Men's Chorus")			pno	Biblical
Odes of Horace ECS			orch(R)	Horace
O Venus, regina Cnidi Paphique.	SSATTBB			
Vitas hinnuleo me similis, Chloe.				
Montium custos nemorumque, Virgo.				
O fons Bandusiae, splendidior vitro.	SSATBB			
Felices ter.				
Ode to the Virginian voyage ECS			orch(R) or pno	Michael Drayton
The nativity according to Saint Luke (oratorio) ECS			pno or orch(R)	Biblical
The peaceable kingdom ECS				Biblical
Say ye to the righteous				
Woe unto them				
The noise of the multitude				
Howl ye	SSAATTBB			
The paper reeds by the brooks				
But these are they that forsake the Lord	SSAATTBB			
For ye shall go out with joy	SSAATTBB			
Have ye not known?				
Ye shall have a song	SSAATTBB			
Requiem (a dramatic dialogue) ECS 1. Lamentations. 2. The triumph of faith. 3. The call to song. 4. The garment of praise. 5. The leavetaking.	SSAATTBB			Biblical
THOMSON, Virgil				
Agnus Dei (3-pt canon) MER	any 3 voices			liturgical
Crossing Brooklyn ferry B&H	SSATB		pno	Walt Whitman
De profundis WEIN				Biblical
Follow thy fair sun COL				Thomas Campion
Mass GS	unison		pno	liturgical
Mass MCA (See also "Percussion")			perc ad lib	liturgical
Missa pro defunctis HWG			orch(R)	liturgical

Composer, Title and Publisher	Chorus	Solos	Accompani- ment	Author of Text
My Shepherd will supply my need HWG				trad, USA
Saint's procession (from <u>4 Saints in 3 Acts</u>) MER			pno	Gertrude Stein
There is a garden in her face COL				Thomas Campion
Tiger! Tiger! COL (See also "Men's Chorus")				William Blake
Tribulationes civitatum WEIN				liturgical
Scenes from the Holy Infancy MER 1. Joseph and the angel. 2. The wise men. 3. The flight into Egypt.		T, Bar, B		Biblical
When I survey the bright celestial sphere HWG	unison or 1 solo voice			Wm. Habbingdon, 17th cent
THOMSON, William Desert seasons SHAW Winter. Spring. Summer. Autumn.				Edith Hart Mason
TIRRO, Frank P. American jazz mass S-B Kyrie. Glorio. Credo. Agnus Dei. Sanctus and benedictus.			trp, a-sax, bar-sax, c-b, traps	liturgical
TRIMBLE, Lester A cradle song CFP (See also "Women's Chorus")				William Blake
TRUBITT, Allen R. The carol of the bird WLP			pno	Walt Whitman
TUBB, Monte Agnus Dei L-G				liturgical; English text: Monte Tubb
In just-spring L-G				e.e. cummings
VAN VACTOR, David The new light AME		Narr	org or pno	Biblical
VERALL, John A Christmas fantasy TP (See also "Women's Chorus")	SATB or unison or SAB		band(R)	trad

Composer, Title and Publisher	Chorus	Solos	Accompani- ment	Author of Text
VINCENT, John				
"The hallow'd time" MIL				John Vincent (from
The angel's spell.				a Christmas play
Behold the star.				by Richard Hubler)
Glory to God. Sing				
hollyloo. (See also				
"Men's Chorus")				
Three Grecian songs				trans: J.W.
MIL				Mackail
Pans piping				Alcaeus of Messene
Wood music				anon
The garden of Pan				Plato
WADE, Walter				
Arise, my love L-G				Biblical
WAGNER, Joseph				
American ballad set SMPC				Alfred Kreymborg
Ballad of the common man. Ballad of Lincoln penny. Ballad of me- morial days.				
Ballad of brotherhood EV			orch or a cappella	Alfred Kreymborg
Missa sacra COL		S	orch(R)	liturgical
WAGNER, Roger				
Heritage of freedom CF			cham(R) or pno	Joseph Auslander
WAGNER, Thomas				
For the girl with the little bean nose B&H (six unfinished thoughts)	SSATTB			Thomas Wagner
WARD, Robert				
Concord hymn MER				Ralph Waldo Emerson
Earth shall be fair GAL		S (or children's choir)	orch(R) or org	Biblical & "Turn back O man" by Clifford Bax
Hushed be the camps today HWG			pno	Walt Whitman
Sweet freedom's song (A New England chronicle) GAL		S, Bar, Narr	pno or orch(R)	texts compiled by Mary & Robert Ward
It was a great design O, Lord God of my salvation				from Wm. Bradford from 88th Psalm
Come, ye thankful people, come				from Henry Alford, Anna Barbauld, Leonard Bacon
Ballad of Boston Bay				

Composer, Title and Publisher	Chorus	Solos	Accompaniment	Author of Text
Damnation to the Stamp Act				
Epitaphs				from Tyler Page, James Russell Lowell
Let music swell the breeze				from Samuel Francis Smith
That wondrous night of Christmas Eve GAL				Robert Ward
With rue my heart is laden MER				A.E. Housman
WARREN, Elinor Remick				
Abram in Egypt HWG		B	orch(R) or 2 pno	The Dead Sea Scrolls & Book of Genesis
Our beloved land TP			pno or org; or orch(R)	Samuel Bonner
Requiem L-G Introit & Kyrie. Graduale. Dies irae. Offertorium. Hostias. Sanctus. Benedictus. Agnus Dei. Lux aeterna.		m-S, Bar	pno or org; or orch(R)	liturgical
WASHBURN, Robert				
A child this day is born SHAW				trad
WATERS, James				
Psalm 25 TP				Biblical
WEED, Maurice				
The wonder of the starry night L-G				Maurice Weed
WEISGALL, Hugo				
Four choral preludes TP				
God is due praise				Passover Seder hymn
May the words (Psalm 19)				Biblical
Praise be unto God (Psalm 118)				Biblical
When Israel out of Egypt came (Psalm 114)				Biblical
Two liturgical settings TP				
Evening prayer for peace				liturgical
Who is like unto Thee		Bar	pno or org	Union Prayer Book
WHITE, John				
He dawns upon us L-G			org or pno	Biblical
Three choruses from Goethe's Faust GS			pno	Goethe

Composer, Title and Publisher	Chorus	Solos	Accompaniment	Author of Text
The monkey's sonnet.				
The passing of winter.				
The turmoil.				
When brothers dwell in unity L-G			pno or org	Biblical
With Christ to man L-G			org or pno	Francis Kindelmarsh
WIENHORST, Richard				
Missa brevis AMP				liturgical
Kyrie. Gloria.				
Credo. Sanctus and				
benedictus. Agnus Dei.				
Psalm 150 CPH				Biblical
WILLIAMS, David Howard				
Gloria TP				liturgical
WILLIAMS, David McK.				
In the year that King Uzziah died HWG				Biblical
WILLIAMS, Donald				
Silence spoke with your voice CF			pno	Ryah Tumarkin Goodman
WILLIS, Richard				
The drenched land CFP				Kenneth Patchen
WINSLOW, Richard				
The last quarter moon L-G				Jonathan Brooks
WOOLLEN, Russell				
Prayer of St. Francis EV			pno or org	liturgical
WUORINEN, Charles				
The prayer of Jonah MM			str orch(R)	Biblical
YORK, David Stanley				
The four freedoms TP		Bar		James M. Hester
Once to every man and nation TP	divisi		org or band(R) or str orch(R)	James Russell Lowell
(See also "Men's Chorus")				
ZANINELLI, Luigi				
Barbara Frietchie SHAW			sn-drm & b-drm, pno, 4-hands	John Greenleaf Whittier
I know not what the future hath SHAW			pno	John Greenleaf Whittier
Jubilate Deo SHAW	SSAATTBB	S		liturgical
Never seek to tell thy love SHAW				William Blake

Composer, Title and Publisher	Chorus	Solos	Accompaniment	Author of Text
Seasons SHAW			hp or pno or classic gtr	Mary Hallet
Chorale I	SSA			
Chorale II	TBB			
Chorales I & II	SATB			
(in 2 parts each)				
Chorales I & II	SSTBB			
(in 3 parts each)				
Song of hope SHAW			2 trp, 2 trb, tba or org	Angela Morgan
They dreamed of freedom SHAW			sn-drm & timp	Mary Hallet
The voice of the sea SHAW				Arthur Symonds
World hymn SHAW			pno or org	Lois Bailey Wills

WOMEN'S CHORUS (SSA a cappella unless otherwise indicated)

	Chorus	Solos	Accompaniment	Author of Text
ALBRITTON, Sherodd				
Eldorado AB	SA		pno	Edgar Allan Poe
AMRAM, David				
By the rivers of Babylon CFP	SSAA	S		Biblical
BACON, Ernst				
The animals Christmas oratorio TP		Narr	pno	adapted from medieval French poem by Manuel Komroff
The birds BB	SA		pno	trad
Four innocent airs L-G (See also "Men's Chorus")	SA		pno	
Return of spring				Annette Wynne
Where go the boats				Robert L. Stevenson
The schoolboy				William Blake
A cradle song				William Blake
From Emily's diary GS	SSAA	S, A	pno	Emily Dickinson
Nature ECS			pno	Emily Dickinson
1. The mountain. 2. the gentlest mother. 3. A spider. 4. The Arctic flower. 5. With the first arbutus. 6. There came a day. 7. A wind like a bugle. 8. Winter afternoons. 9. The cricket sang. 10. The sea.				
Precept of Angelius Silesius (cycle for 3-6 women's voices) BCS				Johann Scheffer, 17th cent; trans: Paul Carus
1. Prologue. 2. Chorale.				

Composer, Title and Publisher	Chorus	Solos	Accompaniment	Author of Text
3. Sermon. 4. Ground. 5. Air (S solo). 6. Drone (A solo). 7. Chorale. 8. Song (S and A soli). 9. Response. 10. Conclusion.				
Seven canons MER (for contents, see "Mixed Chorus")	2-4 pt		pno	
BARBER, Samuel				
A nun takes the veil GS (See also "Mixed" & "Men's Chorus")	SSAA			Gerard Manly Hopkins
The virgin martyrs GS	SSAA			Helen Waddell
BARTOW, Nevett				
A Thanksgiving exultation SHAW (See also "Men's Chorus")	SA		org or pno, 4-hands	Nevett Bartow
BASSETT, Leslie				
Hear my prayer, O Lord CFP	children's choir		org	Biblical
BEADELL, Robert				
Blow prairie wind AMP	SSAA			Robert Beadell
BEESON, Jack				
I to the hills lift up mine eyes (Psalm 121) MIL				Biblical
BERGSMA, William				
Let true love be among us CF (See also "Mixed" & "Men's Chorus")	SA		pno	trad, 13th cent
BEVERIDGE, Thomas				
O cool is the valley now ECS			pno	James Joyce
O fanciulla (Oh, fresh young girl) ECS		S	pno	Giovanni Prati; trans: Glaser
BIALOSKY, Marshall				
Be music night TP				Kenneth Patchen
Of music and musicians TP				
1. If the king loves music (SSA).				Mencius
2. Feed the musician (SSAA).				George Crabbe
3. Music is the moonlight (SSAA).				Jean Paul Richter

Composer, Title and Publisher	Chorus	Solos	Accompaniment	Author of Text
4. Proverb (SS).				Hindu proverb
BILLINGS, William				
When Jesus wept (a round) MER (See also "Mixed" & "Men's Chorus")	SSAA			from The New England Psalm Singer, 1770
BINGHAM, Seth				
New England woman JF	SA		pno	Joan Murray
BLISS, Milton				
There came a wind like a bugle S-B				Emily Dickinson
BRIGHT, Houston				
Sacred songs for the night SHAW				Houston Bright
Evensong (vespers).				
Nightfall (compline).				
Dawn (matins).				
Sunrise (lauds).				
Thy lovely saints SHAW				Christina Rossetti
Trilogy SHAW	SSAA			
Fall, leaves, fall				Emily Brontë
Rough wind that moanest loud				Percy B. Shelley
The sigh that heaves the grasses				anon
BURT, George				
New Hampshire ("Children's voices in the orchard") AB	SSAA			T.S. Eliot
CADMAN, Charles Wakefield				
The moon behind the cottonwood tree GS				Nellie R. Eberhart
A moonlight song GS			pno	John Proctor Mills
CARPENTER, John Alden				
The home road GS (See also "Mixed" & "Men's Chorus")			pno	John A. Carpenter
The sleep that flits on baby's eyes GS			pno	Rabindranath Tagore
When I bring you colored toys GS (See also "Mixed Chorus")			pno	Rabindranath Tagore
CARTER, Elliott				
The harmony of morning AMP	SSAA		cham orch or pno	Mark van Doren

Composer, Title and Publisher	Chorus	Solos	Accompaniment	Author of Text
CASE, James				
Autumn L-G				Amy Lowell
Petals AMP				Amy Lowell
Summer L-G				Chaucer
CHIHARA, Paul				
Magnificat for treble voices S-B				Biblical
CLARKE, Henry				
Love-in-the-world (1953) MER		T or S	pno	Genevieve Taggard
CLOKEY, Joseph W.				
Breakers off Barranquilla S-B			pno	Willis Knapp Jones
Dusk in the tropics S-B				Willis Knapp Jones
Flower of dreams S-B				David Stevens
How summer came (an Indian legend) JF			orch(R) or pno	Clara Louise Kessler
Miladie--a cavalier suite JF A hopeless plea. April showers. A star. Lines with a rose. Unrequited love. (See also "Men's Chorus")			str orch(R) or pno	Willis Knapp Jones
Night song S-B				J.W. Clokey
A snow legend S-B			pno	Anna Temple
COOPER, David				
Sancta Maria PIC	SSSSAAAA			liturgical
Three poems to children CF				
Lullaby			pno	trad
Overheard on a salt marsh			pno	Harold Monroe
Poor old Jonathan Bing			pno	Beatrice C. Brown
COPLAND, Aaron				
The house on the hill ECS	SSAA		pno	Edwin Arlington Robinson
An immorality (1925) ECS		S	pno	Ezra Pound
Old American songs, Set I (1950) B&H			pno or cham orch(R)	
Long time ago (arr. Straker) (See also "Mixed Chorus")				trad
Simple gifts (arr. Fine) (See also "Men's Chorus")	SA			Shaker song
I bought me a cat (arr. Straker) (See				trad

Composer, Title and Publisher	Chorus	Solos	Accompani-ment	Author of Text
also "Mixed" and "Men's Chorus")				
Old American songs, Set II (1952) B&H			pno or cham orch(R)	
At the river (arr. Wilding-White) (See also "Mixed" & "Men's Chorus")	SA or SSA			trad
Ching-a-ring-chaw (arr. Fine) (See also "Mixed" and "Men's Chorus")				minstrel song
Little horses (arr. Wilding-White) (See also "Men's Chorus")	SA or SSA			trad
What do we plant? (1935) B&H	SA		pno	Henry Abbey
The younger generation (1943) B&H (See also "Mixed Chorus")			pno	Ira Gershwin
CORTÉS, Ramiro				
Missa brevis (Kyrie-Gloria) TP			picc, 2 fl, 2 ob, 2 cl, b-cl, 2 bsn, c-bsn (or c-b)	liturgical
COWELL, Henry				
American muse MER	SA		pno	Stephen Vincent Benét
The Irishman lilts AMP (See also "Mixed Chorus")			pno	trad
The lily's lament EBM			pno	Elizabeth Alan Lomax
Spring at summer's end PIC			pno	Dora Hagemeyer
CRESTON, Paul				
The lambs to the lambs CF			pno or org	Martha Nicholson Kemp
CRIST, Bainbridge				
To a water-fowl CF			pno	Wm. Cullen Bryant
CUMMINS, Richard				
Rise, heart, thy Lord is risen TP	SSAA	A		George Herbert
DANIELS, Mabel				
Dum Dianae vitrea (When Diana's silver light), Op. 38, No. 2 JF				ms. of Benedict-beurn, 1100-1200

Composer, Title and Publisher	Chorus	Solos	Accompaniment	Author of Text
Flower wagon JF			pno	Frances Taylor Patterson
Through the dark the dreamers came ECS (See also "Mixed Chorus")			pno	Earl Marlatt
DELLO JOIO, Norman				
A Christmas carol EBM			pno	G.K. Chesterton
Adieu mignonne, when you are gone CF			pno	Earl of Lytton
Holy infant's child EBM			pno	N. Dello Joio
Jubilant song GS (See also "Mixed Chorus")			pno	Walt Whitman
Song's end EBM			pno	John Payne
Three songs of Chopin EBM (For contents, see "Mixed Chorus")	SA		pno or orch	English version by Harold Heiberg
DIAMOND, David				
All in green went my love SMPC				e.e. cummings
The glory is fallen out of the sky SMPC				e.e. cummings
Young Joseph MER			str orch or pno	Thomas Mann
DIEMER, Emma Lou				
Alleluia CF				liturgical
Four carols (Christmas) EV Carol of the flowers. Come hasten, ye shepherds. Let our gladness know no end. Rejoice thee, O heaven.				trad
Fragments from the mass EBM Kyrie. Gloria. Credo. Sanctus. Agnus Dei.	SSAA			liturgical
The magnificat EBM	SA		pno or org	Biblical
Mary's lullaby B&H			pno	Helen Barkey
The shepherd to his love EBM	SA		fl & pno	Christopher Marlowe
DONATO, Anthony				
Madonna and child B&H				Jeanne DeLamarter
Song for evening SMPC				Jeanne DeLamarter
DONOVAN, Richard				
Chanson of the bells of Osenay GAL			pno	Cale Young Rice
How should I love? MER	SSAA		pno	anon
Hymn to the night JF				H.W. Longfellow

Composer, Title and Publisher	Chorus	Solos	Accompaniment	Author of Text
Songs of nature AMP Dawn. Wind Sings. Yellow lily. Wind of heaven.			pno	Frances Fenton Park
DUKELSKY, Vladimir (DUKE, Vernon) Victorian street ballads CF				anon
She parted with her lover	SSSAA		pno	
The mulberry tree	SSAA		pno	
The dark-haired girl	SSSAA		pno	
The shepherd's holiday	SSAA			
I won't be a nun			pno	
DUSHKIN, Dorothy Three songs CF The old soldier. The prince of sleep. The ship of Rio.			fl, ob, cl, or pno	Walter de la Mare
EDMUNDS, John Three Christmas carols WLP The birth of Christ. High overhead the stars of heaven. Sing we to our Jesus.	SA		pno or org	Beatrice Quickenden
EFFINGER, Cecil Pandora's box GS	children's voices		pno, fl	Cecil Effinger
Shepherds in the field MER	SA			Cecil Effinger
ELMORE, Robert Out of the depths (Psalm 130) EV		Bar or A	pno	Biblical
ETLER, Alvin Under the cottonwood tree AMP	SA			Alvin Etler
Under stars AMP	SSAA			Alvin Etler
FELCIANO, Richard Four poems from the Japanese CPE			5 hp, cel, glock, tam-tam	from the Japanese
FETLER, Paul Now this is the story CF			pno	from "Biographies" by Dorothy Parker

Composer, Title and Publisher	Chorus	Solos	Accompaniment	Author of Text
FINE, Irving				
Alice in wonderland W-7 (For contents, see "Mixed Chorus")			pno	Lewis Carroll
Beautiful soup W-7				Lewis Carroll
The knave's letter W-7				Lewis Carroll
The White Knight's song W-7				Lewis Carroll
FLOYD, Carlisle				
Long, long ago B&H (See also "Men's Chorus")	SA		pno	anon
Two Stevenson songs B&H (See also "Mixed" & "Men's Chorus") Rain. Where go the boats?	SA		pno	R. L. Stevenson
Who has seen the wind B&H (See also "Men's Chorus")	SA		pno	Christina Rossetti
FRACKENPOHL, Arthur				
The natural superiority of men CF			str qrt(R) or cham(R) or pno	Jean Pearson
Three limericks in canon form EBM A diner at Crewe. A boy of Bagdad. A fellow of Perth. (See also "Men's Chorus")	SA		pno	trad
Wait for the sun CF		m-S	pno	Elizabeth E. Flesch
FRANCO, Johan				
Seven songlets WLP			pno	
1. Little boy, full of joy...				William Blake
2. Sport that wrinkled care derides...				John Milton
3. Our hopes like towering falcons...				Matthew Prior
4. O'er the glad waters...				Lord Byron
5. On with the dance...				Lord Byron
6. From toil he wins his spirits light...				Thomas Gray
7. I heard an angel singing...				William Blake
FREED, Isadore				
Island secret CF			pno	Chard Powers Smith
Postscripts--choral suite CF			pno	

Composer, Title and Publisher	Chorus	Solos	Accompaniment	Author of Text
1. No parking				James Alexander Black
2. Paging Emily Post				Milton Pascal
3. Voice of experience				Avery Giles
4. Hist!				W. E. Farbstein
5. A theory in ratios				Kin McNeil
6. The movies				Figenshu
GARLICK, Antony				
Eleven canzonets WLP (For contents, see "Mixed Chorus")	2 equal voices			
Twelve madrigals WLP				
Bright clouds				Edward Thomas
Days too short				Wm. H. Davies, alt
Gorse				Helen Foley
The happy child				Wm. H. Davies
I am tired of the wind				Gordon Bottomley
I love the beginning of all rain				Geoffrey Scott
In September				Francis Ledwidge
The moon				Wm. H. Davies
Northern light				L. A. G. Strong
Over hill, over dale				Shakespeare
Tall nettles				Edward Thomas
Tell me where is fancy bred				Shakespeare
GEORGE, Earl				
A definition L-G	SSAA			e. e. cummings
GERRISH, John				
The falcon AMP	SSAA		pno	trad, 15th cent
A virgin most pure AMP		S, A	pno	trad
GIANNINI, Vittorio				
Two madrigals COL				
Part I: The passionate shepherd to his love			pno and ob solo	Christopher Marlowe
Part II: The nymph's reply to the shepherd			pno and fl solo	Sir Walter Raleigh
GIDEON, Miriam				
How goodly are thy tents MER			pno or org	Biblical
GLASER, Victoria				
Homeric hymn AMP	SSAA			Homer
An idle song ECS				Anna B. True
GOODMAN, Joseph				
Love came down at Christmas AB (See also "Mixed" & "Men's Chorus")	SA		org	Christina Rossetti

Composer, Title and Publisher	Chorus	Solos	Accompani- ment	Author of Text
Three alleluias for Christmas AMP				
1. Alleluia the Lord said unto me				from the Anglican Missal
2. Alleluia! I bring you good tidings				Biblical
3. Let the heavens rejoice				from the Anglican Missal
GRAHAM, Robert				
Autumn bird EV			pno	Witter Bynner
Sing low, my heart EV			pno	anon
The two windows EV			pno	Witter Bynner
GREEN, Ray				
Three choral songs AME Sparrow. Bobolink. Butterflies.				Emily Dickinson
GRIFFES, Charles				
By a lonely forest pathway GS			pno	N. Lenau; trans: Henry G. Chapman
O'er the tarn's un- ruffled waters GS			pno	N. Lenau; trans: Henry G. Chapman
HAINES, Edmund				
Dialogue from the Book of Job (in memorium, November 22, 1963) AB	SSAA	S, A	pno	Biblical
HANSON, Howard				
Children's dance from Merrymount W-7	SSAA		pno, 4 hands	Richard L. Stokes
How excellent Thy name CF (See also "Mixed Chorus")	SSAA		org	Biblical
HARRIS, Roy				
Walt Whitman triptych GS				Walt Whitman
I hear America singing	SSSSA			
An evening lull				
America	SSSAA			
The weeping willow AMP	SSAA	S & folk singer		trad
They say that Susan has no heart for learning AMP			pno	trad
HARRISON, Lou				
A joyous procession and a solemn procession CFP (See also	SA		2 trb, 4 tam, 8 handbells, b-drm, gong(R)	vocalise

Composer, Title and Publisher	Chorus	Solos	Accompaniment	Author of Text
"Men's Chorus")				
HEIDEN, Bernhard				
Two songs of spring AB Easter meditation. Wind (SSAA).				Samuel Yellen
HENDL, Walter				
A village where they ring no bells CF			pno	Basho; trans: H.B. Henderson
Loneliness CF			pno	Hanshin; trans: H.B. Henderson
HENNING, Ervin				
By the rivers of Babylon ECS	SA		pno	Biblical
HOVHANESS, Alan				
Ave Maria (from Triptych), Op. 100, No. 1a AMP	SSAA		2 ob (or trp or cl), 2 hn (or trb), hp or pno	liturgical
Blessed throughout all generations (Omnes generationes from Magnificat, Op. 157) CFP		S	org or pno or orch(R)	liturgical
HOWE, Mary				
Song of palms CF			pno or orch(R)	Arthur O'Shaughnessy
HUNTER, Ralph				
More nursery rhymes L-G (For contents, see "Mixed Chorus")	SSAA		pno	nursery rhymes
IVES, Charles				
Lincoln the great commoner TP (See also "Mixed" & "Men's Chorus")	SSAA		orch(R)	Edwin Markham
KAY, Ulysses				
Christmas carol PIC				Sara Teasdale
Emily Dickinson set MCA				Emily Dickinson
Two Dunbar lyrics MCA				Paul Lawrence Dunbar
KENNEDY, John Brodbin				
Little lamb, who made thee? B&H (See also "Men's Chorus")	SA		pno	William Blake
Sails, robins and butterflies B&H				Emily Dickinson
A spring festival B&H				
The blossom				William Blake

Composer, Title and Publisher	Chorus	Solos	Accompaniment	Author of Text
Song				John Donne
Spring				William Blake
KENT, Richard				
Amaryllis in mortality L-G				Marya Zaturenska
Autumn songs L-G				Emily Dickinson
As imperceptibly as grief. The morns are meeker than they were. The sky is low, the clouds are mean.				
Katy Cruel L-G				trad (folk)
Offering and dedication L-G				Marya Zaturenska
KLEIN, John				
Sentences from Whitman SSAA AMP				Walt Whitman
KOHN, Karl				
Three songs CF	SSAA			
Cupid and my Campaspe				John Lyly
Give me more love				Thomas Carew
Shake off your heavy trance				Francis Beaumont
KORTE, Karl				
Four poems from "Songs of innocence" ECS				William Blake
1. Piping down the valleys (pno). 2. Infant joy. 3. A cradle song (pno). 4. Spring (pno).				
KOUTZEN, Boris				
An invocation MER			pno or orch(R)	John Addington Symonds
KRAEHENBUEHL, David				
A Christmas blessing AMP				anon
I sing of a maiden AMP				anon
Welcome, yule AMP				anon
What cheer? AMP				anon
(Above four songs also listed under "Men's Chorus")				
KUBIK, Gail				
Little bird, little bird SMPC	SSSSAAAA		pno	trad
Peregrine White and Virginia Dare SMPC	SAA			Stephen Vincent Benét

Composer, Title and Publisher	Chorus	Solos	Accompani- ment	Author of Text
KUPFERMAN, Meyer Six spells for the fingers and the hand GEN				Alastair Reid
LATHAM, William Sister, awake (madrigal) MER				anon, 16th cent
LEVY, Ernst Hear, ye children AB (See also "Men's Chorus")	SMA- SMA			Biblical
LOCKWOOD, Normand The birth of Moses MER			pno, fl	Biblical
LONDON, Edwin Five Haiku AMP				from Japanese; trans: Harold G. Henderson
1. Leaves	SSAA			Natsume Sōseki
2. In the moonlight	SSAA			Masaoka Shiki
3. A spring day	SSSSSAAAA			Masaoka Shiki
4. The whale	SSAA			Taniguchi Buson
5. At the year's end	SSAA			Sōin
Four proverbs AB	SSAA	S	2 trp, bsn	Biblical
A Washington miscel- lany AMP I. Promises. II. Time. III. Potatoes.	SSSAA			George Washington
LUENING, Otto If that high world CFP				Lord Byron
Pilgrim's hymn TP (See also "Mixed Chorus")	SA		pno or org or orch(R)	Howard Moss
Vocalise GAL	SSAA			vocalise
LYBBERT, Donald Austro terris influente MER	SSAA		pno	anon (ms. Florence Laurenziana PL. 29.1)
McDONALD, Harl Dirge for two veterans EV	SSAA		pno	Walt Whitman
Evening EV	SSAA		pno	Wm. Ernest Henley
McKAY, George F. The prayer of Fiona MacLeod JF	SSAA			William Sharp
Summer EV			pno	Henry D. Thoreau
Three lullabies (choral suite) JF			pno	Eugene Field

Composer, Title and Publisher	Chorus	Solos	Accompaniment	Author of Text
Heigho, my dearie. The storm king. Hush, little one.				
McKINNEY, Howard D. (compiler)				
A mystery for Christmas (in the Medieval manner) JF (For contents, see "Mixed Chorus")	SA	S, A, Narr	pno	
McLAUGHLIN, Marian				
Autumn fires L-G			pno	R. L. Stevenson
MECHEM, Kirke				
I shall not care (from "The winds of May") ECS	SSAA			Sara Teasdale
Seven joys of Christmas, Op. 25b ECS (For contents, see "Mixed Chorus")				
Sigh no more, ladies ECS			pno	Shakespeare
The winged joy (a love story in 7 parts), Op. 22 ECS			pno	
1. Love is a terrible thing (SSAA).				Grace Fallow Norton
2. The message (SSAA).				Margaret Sackville
3. The cynic (SA).				Theodosia Garrison
4. A farewell (SA-unison).				Harriet Monroe
5. Love came back at fall o'dew (SA).				Lizette Woodworth Reese
6. Red May (SSAA).				Mary F. Robinson
7. You say there is no love (SSAA).				Grace Fallow Norton
Five centuries of Spring (madrigal cycle) ECS				
1. Spring.				Thomas Nashe
2. From you have I been absent.				Shakespeare
3. Laughing song.				William Blake
4. Loveliest of trees.				A. E. Housman
5. Spring.				Edna St. Vincent Millay
MENNIN, Peter				
Bought locks CF			pno	Martial
The people that walked in darkness CF	SSAA		org or pno	Biblical
Tumbling hair CF			pno	e. e. cummings
MEYEROWITZ, Jan				
Two litanies BB				liturgical

Composer, Title and Publisher	Chorus	Solos	Accompaniment	Author of Text
MIDDLETON, Robert				
Three Christmas carols ECS	SA		pno	
1. December.		Narr		from Robert Herrick & Richard Crashaw
2. O! O! O!	SSAA			early mystery poem
3. X and M.				15th cent carol
MOEVES, Robert				
Et nunc, reges ECS			pno or fl, cl, b-cl	Biblical
MOORE, Douglas				
The mysterious cat S-B				Vachel Lindsay
Now may there be a blessing (from The devil and Daniel Webster) B&H		S		Stephen Vincent Benét
Perhaps to dream CF			pno	Stephen Vincent Benét
NELSON, Ron				
Autumn night B&H				Alice Streatch
Sleep, little one B&H (See also "Men's Chorus")				Ron Nelson
Vocalise B&H			pno or hp	vocalise
NOWAK, Lionel				
"Wisdom exalteth her children" BCS	for double ch:S, m-S, A --S, m-S, A			Biblical
PERSICHETTI, Vincent				
Four cummings choruses EV (For contents, see "Mixed Chorus")	SA		pno	e.e. cummings
Hist whist CF				e.e. cummings
Jimmie's got a goil GS (See also "Mixed" & "Men's Chorus")	SA unison		pno	e.e. cummings
Sam was a man GS (See also "Mixed" & "Men's Chorus")	SA unison		pno	e.e. cummings
Spring cantata EV Threes. If the green. Spring is like a perhaps hand. In Just-spring.				e.e. cummings
This is the garden CF				e.e. cummings
Winter cantata EV A copper pheasant. Winter's first drizzle. Winter seclusion. The woodcutter. Gentlest			fl and mar	Haiku; trans: Harold Stewart

Composer, Title and Publisher	Chorus	Solos	Accompaniment	Author of Text
fall of snow. One umbrella. Of crimson ice. The branch is black. Fallen leaves. So deep. The wind's whetstone. Epilogue.				
PFAUTSCH, Lloyd				
Beautiful yet truthful L-G			pno	trad
Five narrative carols S-B			fl, drm(opt)	
1. Adam lay ybounden.				English, 15th cent
2. Coventry carol.				English, 15th cent
3. Torches.				from Spanish
4. O little one.				from German
5. Patapan.				from French
A hymn to him of true love L-G	SSAA			Lloyd Pfautsch
On hearing a symphony of Beethoven L-G		S		Edna St. Vincent Millay
PHILLIPS, Burrill				
Declaratives EV	SSAA		cham orch or pno	
Bells				Tom Boggs
Love				e. e. cummings
Pueblos				trad, USA
The hag CF	SSAA			Robert Herrick
What will love do? CF	SSAA			Robert Herrick
PIKET, Frederick				
The speaking silence AMP				
1. I heard you (SSAA).				Walt Whitman
2. Spell				Emily Brontë
3. So delicious				Ben Jonson
4. When the lamp is shattered (SSAA)				Percy B. Shelley
5. There be none of beauty's daughters				Lord Byron
6. Echo (SSAA)				Christina Rossetti
PINKHAM, Daniel				
Ave Maria AMP	SA			Liber Usualis
Angelus ad pastores ait KING	SSAA		3 trb, tba	Liber Usualis
An Emily Dickinson mosaic CFP	SSAA		pno or cham orch	Emily Dickinson
The brain is wider than the sky. The heart is the capital of the mind. The mind lives on the heart. To be alive. Exhilaration is the breeze. Each life converges to				

Composer, Title and Publisher	Chorus	Solos	Accompaniment	Author of Text
some center.				
Five canzonets AMP	SA			
The blossom				William Blake
Calico pie				trad, English
Daybreak				John Donne
The nut tree				trad, English
Spring				William Blake
If ye love me ECS			org	Biblical
Let us now praise famous men (five motets) ECS 1. The Lord brought forth Moses. 2. The Lord exalted Aaron. 3. David played with lions. 4. Solomon reigned in days of peace. 5. The prophet Elijah arose.	SA			Biblical
Listen to me (five motets) ECS	SA			Biblical
A litany AMP	SS		pno or org	Phineas Fletcher
Mass of the Good Shepherd ECS (See also "Men's Chorus")	unison		org	Biblical
Mass of the Holy Eucharist ECS (See also "Men's Chorus")	unison		org	Biblical
Song of Jephthah's daughter (cantata) CFP (For contents, see "Solo Vocal Music")		S, Bar	pno	Robert Hillyer
Te Deum KING (See also "Mixed" & "Men's Chorus")	SA		3 trp, org	John Dryden
Three Lenten poems of Richard Crashaw ECS			str qrt or str orch or pno	Richard Crashaw
On the still surviving marks of our Saviour's wounds.	SA			
Upon the body of our blessed Lord, naked and bloody.	S & A unison			
O save us then.	SSA			
POWELL, Mel				
Sweet lovers love the spring CF			pno	Shakespeare
PURVIS, Richard				
The road's end EV		S	pno	Theodosia Garrison

Composer, Title and Publisher	Chorus	Solos	Accompaniment	Author of Text
READ, Gardner				
At bedtime SMPC	SSSSAA		pno	Irene Beyers
The magic hour, Op. 60 JF			pno	Nellie Richmond Eberhart
The moon, Op. 23, No. 4a AMP			pno	William H. Davies
Music, Op. 64 CF			pno	Vail Read
Sister, awake, Op. 84, No. 2a JF			pno	Thomas Bateson
The unknown God, Op. 23, No. 2a AMP			pno	George W. Russell
REICHENBACH, Herman (Ed.)				
Modern canons (from 2-5 voices) MER (For contents, see "Mixed Chorus")				
REVICKI, Roberto				
Random thoughts B&H Morn. Paper. Yesterday. Music.				Henry Kirke White
Songs of praise B&H 1. Dominus illuminatis mea. 2. Alleluia.				Biblical
RHODES, Phillip				
Kyrie CFP				liturgical
RIEGGER, Wallingford				
Eternity, Op. 32a FLAM			fl, 2 hn, c-b	Emily Dickinson
Evil shall not prevail (Non vincit malitia) BCS	SSA-SSA			Wisdom 7:29-30
La belle dame sans merci PIC		T	cham orch(R)	John Keats
ROGERS, Bernard				
Faery song TP	SSAA			John Keats
ROREM, Ned				
A far island EV				Kenward Elmslie
Five prayers for the young TP				
A nursery darling				Lewis Carroll
A dirge				Percy B. Shelley
Now I lay me down to sleep				Percy B. Shelley
Fragment: Wine of the fairies				Percy B. Shelley
The Virgin's cradle hymn				Samuel T. Coleridge
Gentle visitations EV				Percy B. Shelley
Mild mother ECS (See also "Men's	unison		pno	Biblical

Composer, Title and Publisher	Chorus	Solos	Accompaniment	Author of Text
Chorus")				
SANDERS, Robert				
An American psalm MER	SSAA		org or fl, 2 vln, vla, vlc, c-b, 2 pno(R)	H.R. Palmer & Rollo Russell
SCHICKELE, Peter				
Carol: I sing of a maiden AB	SSSSAA			anon (Medieval)
Hymn of our Lord EV				Biblical
SCHUMAN, William				
Four rounds on famous words TP				common aphorisms
Beauty. Health. Thrift. Caution.	4-pt 3-pt			
Holiday song GS (See also "Mixed" & "Men's Chorus")			pno	Genevieve Taggard
Prelude GS			pno	Thomas Wolfe
Questions (from "This is our time") B&H	SSAA		fl	Genevieve Taggard
Requiescat GS (See also "Mixed Chorus")	SSAA		pno	vocalise
SCHWARTZ, Paul				
Fog BB			pno	Carl Sandburg
Serenade BB			pno	Robert Hillyer
SHEPHERD, Arthur				
Jolly Wat (canticum nativitatis Christi with a Christmas carol) MER (See also "Mixed" & "Men's Chorus")	2 equal voices	2 solo voices	orch(R) or pno or org	Balliol ms: 15th-16th cent
SIEGMEISTER, Elie				
Lazy afternoon (from "Ozark Set") EBM (See also "Mixed Chorus")			pno	Leo Paris
SMIT, Leo				
Carol EBM				St. Godric, 12th cent
Christmas carol PIC	SA			anon
Love is a sickness BB	SSAA		pno	Samuel Daniel
SMITH, Russell				
Set me as a seal L-G			hn and str trio(R) (opt)	Biblical
Three songs from Emily Dickinson COL				Emily Dickinson

Composer, Title and Publisher	Chorus	Solos	Accompaniment	Author of Text
Heart, we will forget him. We talked as girls do. Spring comes on the world.				
SOWERBY, Leo				
Benedictus es, Domine HWG	SA		org	liturgical
SPIES, Claudio				
Verses from the Book of Ruth TP		S, A Narr	pno	Biblical
STEVENS, Halsey				
Old rhymes for treble voices AMP When good King Arthur ruled this land. Anna Elise. When I was a little boy (SA). Infirtaris.				anon, English & Scotch
O sing unto the Lord a new song (Psalm 98) PIC			pno	Biblical
SYDEMAN, William				
Four Japanese songs ECS (For content, see "Solo Vocal Music")		S		
THOMAS, Alan				
Tender buttons EV Red roses. A sound. A blue coat. This is this dress, aider. Nothing elegant. More. A time to eat. A fire. A red hat. A petticoat. Orange in. A paper. A box. A dog.				Gertrude Stein
THOMPSON, Randall				
Alleluia ECS	SSAA			liturgical
Come in (No. 3 from Frostiana) ECS			pno	Robert Frost
The gate of heaven ECS	SSAA			Biblical
A girl's garden (No. 5 from Frostiana) ECS	SAA		pno	Robert Frost
God's bottles (from "Americana") ECS	SSAA			from leaflet issued by N.W.C.T.U.
The Lord is my shepherd ECS	SSAA		pno or org or hp	Biblical
Now I lay me down to sleep ECS				Percy B. Shelley
Nowel ECS	SSAA		pno	Biblical

Composer, Title and Publisher	Chorus	Solos	Accompaniment	Author of Text
(See also "Mixed" & "Men's Chorus")				
Pueri Hebraeorum ECS	SSAA antiphonal			liturgical
Rosemary ECS 1. Chemical analysis. 2. A sad song. 3. A nonsense song. 4. To Rosemary on the methods by which she might become an angel.	SSAA			Stephen Vincent Benét
Velvet shoes ECS	SA			Elinor Wylie
THOMSON, Virgil				
Agnus Dei (3-pt canon) MER	any 3			liturgical
The morning star HWG				trad
Seven choruses (from Medea) MER	SSAA		perc ad lib	Euripides
Three antiphonal psalms MCA Psalms 123, 133 and 136 (See also "Men's Chorus")	SA			Biblical
TRIMBLE, Lester				
A cradle song CFP (See also "Mixed Chorus")	SSAA		org or pno(opt)	William Blake
VERRALL, John				
A Christmas fantasy TP (See also "Mixed Chorus")	SA or unison		band(R)	trad
WALKER, George				
Gloria--in memorium VAL			org	liturgical
WARREN, Elinor Remick				
The night will never stay L-G			pno	Eleanor Farjeon
WASHBURN, Robert				
Scherzo for spring OX			pno (fl & cl ad lib)	Thomas Nashe
WEIGEL, Eugene				
Four songs VAL To an isle in the water. A drinking song. A cradle song. To a squirrel at Kyle-no-no.				Wm. Butler Yeats
WILLIS, Richard				
Remember CF				Christina Rossetti

Composer, Title and Publisher	Chorus	Solos	Accompaniment	Author of Text
WINSLOW, Richard K.				
Against pride in clothes L-G			pno	Isaac Watts
Huswifery CF			pno	Edward Taylor
ZANINELLI, Luigi				
The world is so full SHAW			fl, ob, cl, bsn(R) or pno	R. L. Stevenson
The swing. Where go the boats? Foreign children. Shadow march. Bed in summer. Rain. The land of Nod. Marching song. The world is so full (happy thought).				

MEN'S CHORUS (TTBB a cappella unless otherwise indicated)

Composer, Title and Publisher	Chorus	Solos	Accompaniment	Author of Text
ARGENTO, Dominick				
The revelation of St. John the Divine B&H Prologue and adoration. The seven seals and seven trumpets. Jubilation and epilogue.	TB	T	3 hn, 2 trp, 2 trb, perc, hp, pno(R)	Biblical
BACON, Ernst				
Four innocent airs L-G (For contents, see "Women's Chorus")	TB		pno	
Seven canons MER (For contents, see "Mixed Chorus")		2-4 pt		
BARBER, Samuel				
A nun takes the veil GS (See also "Mixed" & "Women's Chorus")				Gerard Manly Hopkins
A stop watch and ordnance map GS			4 hn, 3 trb, tba, timp	Stephen Spender
BARLOW, Wayne				
Diversify the abyss TP			pno	Hyam Plutzik
BARTOW, Nevett				
A Thanksgiving exultation SHAW (See also "Women's Chorus")	TB		org or pno, 4-hands	Nevett Bartow
BEESON, Jack				
The bear hunt (or the	TBB		pno	adapted from

Composer, Title and Publisher	Chorus	Solos	Accompaniment	Author of Text
triumph of Feist, the hound dog) MIL				Abraham Lincoln
BERGSMA, William Let true love among us be CF (See also "Mixed" & "Women's Chorus")	TB		pno	trad, 13th cent
BEVERIDGE, Thomas Drop, drop, slow tears ECS			pno	Phineas Fletcher
BILLINGS, William Retrospect MP				from The Singing Master's Assistant, 1778
The shepherd's carol ("Shiloh") S-B				from The Suffolk Harmony, 1786
When Jesus wept (a round) MER (See also "Mixed" & "Women's Chorus")				from The New England Psalm Singer, 1770
BINKERD, Gordon Dum medium silentium B&H				Liber Usualis
Liebeslied (Song of love) B&H				Rainer Maria Rilke; trans: Ludwig Lewisohn
CARPENTER, John Alden The home road GS (See also "Mixed" & "Women's Chorus")			pno	John A. Carpenter
CARTER, Elliott The defense of Corinth MER		Narr	pno, 4-hands	Rabelais
Emblems MER			pno	Allen Tate
CHENOWETH, Wilber Vocalise L-G		S or T	pno	vocalise
CLARKE, Henry No man is an island MCA		Narr	pno	John Donne
Wonders are many (1954) MER		T, B	pno	Sophocles
CLOKEY, Joseph W. Hunting song JF		S and T	pno	Sir Walter Scott
Miladie--a cavalier suite JF (For contents, see "Women's Chorus")	TTB		str orch(R) or pno	Willis Knapp Jones

Composer, Title and Publisher	Chorus	Solos	Accompaniment	Author of Text
COPLAND, Aaron				
Old American songs, Set I (1950) B&H			pno or cham orch(R)	
The boatman's dance (arr. Fine) (See also "Mixed Chorus")		Bar		minstrel song, 1843
I bought me a cat (arr. Fine) (See also "Mixed" & "Women's Chorus")	TBB	T, Bar, B		trad
The dodger (arr. Fine)		Bar		campaign song
Simple gifts (arr. Fine) (See also "Women's Chorus")	TB			Shaker song
Old American songs, Set II (1952) B&H			pno or cham orch(R)	
At the river (arr. Wilding-White) (See also "Mixed" and "Women's Chorus")				trad
Ching-a-ring-chaw (arr. Copland) (see also "Mixed" and "Women's Chorus")				minstrel song
Little horses (arr. Wilding-White) (See also "Women's Chorus")				trad
Song of the guerrillas (1943) B&H		B	orch or pno	Ira Gershwin
Stomp your foot (from Tender land) B&H (See also "Mixed Chorus")			pno, 4-hands	Horace Everett
COWELL, Henry				
Day, evening, night, morning PIC	TTBBB	Falsetto (or boys' voices ad lib)		Paul Laurence Dunbar
Evensong at brookside PIC	TTBBB			Henry Cowell
CRAWFORD, John				
Amour tu es été mon maître ECS	TBB			English versions by John Crawford
All that has life and beauty				Joachim du Bellay
The fairest maid				Clément Marot
Here is the god who looks both ways				Joachim du Bellay
I have lost all that once I was				Clément Marot

Composer, Title and Publisher	Chorus	Solos	Accompaniment	Author of Text
CRESTON, Paul				
The celestial vision, Op. 60 SHAW				
Dante				Dante
Whitman				Walt Whitman
Arjune				from Bhagavad Gita; trans: Sir Edwin Arnold
Missa solemnis, Op. 44 MIL (For contents, see "Mixed Chorus")			orch(R) or org	liturgical
Three chorales from Tagore GS (For contents, see "Mixed Chorus")				Rabindranath Tagore
Two motets, Op. 45 GS Adoro te devote. Salve Regina.			org	liturgical
DELLO JOIO, Norman				
O sing unto the Lord CF	TBB		org	Biblical
DIAMOND, David				
Let us all take to singing SMPC				Herman Melville
The martyr SMPC			orch(R) or a cappella	Herman Melville
DIEMER, Emma Lou				
Three poems FLAM Celery(TTBB). The centipede. Eels.	TTB		pno	Ogden Nash
DONATO, Anthony				
Homesick blues MER				Langston Hughes
DONOVAN, Richard				
Fantasy of American folk ballads JF			orch or pno, 4-hands	trad, USA
Good ale CF			pno	John Still
To all you ladies now at land GAL		T or S	orch	Charles Sackville
EFFINGER, Cecil				
American men HWG				Axton Clark
Fanfare on chow call HWG			brass or pno	army mess call
Forget not my law HWG (See also "Mixed Chorus")			org	Biblical
Shepherds in the field MER	TB			Cecil Effinger

Composer, Title and Publisher	Chorus	Solos	Accompaniment	Author of Text
ELMORE, Robert				
The prodigal son (a sermon in swing)HWG			orch(R)	James Weldon Johnson
ETLER, Alvin				
Onomatopoesis AB			2 cl, b-cl, bsn, 2 trp, hn, trb, perc	vocalise
FAST, Willard S.				
Bread and music AMP				Conrad Aiken
FELCIANO, Richard				
Double alleluia WLP	unison		org & tape	Biblical
FERGUSON, Edwin Earle				
The dark ocean L-G	TTBBB		timp or pno	Robert Hillyer
Upstream L-G			pno	Carl Sandburg
FINE, Irving				
Father William (from Alice in wonderland) W-7				Lewis Carroll
McCord's menagerie MIL Vulture gryphus. Jerboa. Mole. Clam.	TBB			David McCord
FLOYD, Carlisle				
Death came knocking B&H			pno	Joseph Auslander
Long, long ago B&H (See also "Women's Chorus")	TB		pno	anon
Two Stevenson songs B&H Rain. Where go the boats? (See also "Mixed" & "Women's Chorus")	TB		pno	R. L. Stevenson
Who has seen the wind? B&H (See also "Women's Chorus")	TB		pno	Christina Rossetti
FRACKENPOHL, Arthur				
Essays on women CF 1. Pants and paint(unison). 2. The feminine approach to feminine fashions. 3. To my valentine (TTBB). 4. Lady limericks (TBB). 5. The ladies of the garden clubbub (solos & unison). 6. Women sitting firmly on their coats			pno	Ogden Nash

Composer, Title and Publisher	Chorus	Solos	Accompaniment	Author of Text
(solo & unison). 7. A nice girl with a naughty word (TTBB).				
Shepherds, rejoice KING		T or B	3 hn, 3 trb, tba	The Social Harp, 1868
Three limericks in canon form EBM (For contents, see "Women's Chorus")	TB		pno	trad
GARLICK, Antony				
Eleven conzonets WLP (For contents, see "Mixed Chorus")	2 equal voices			
GOLD, Ernest				
Now you are departed (from "Three songs on American Indian lyrics") L-G (See also "Mixed Chorus")			hn obb	trad
GOODMAN, Joseph				
Love came down at Christmas AB (See also "Mixed" & "Women's Chorus")	TB		org	Christina Rossetti
GORDELL, Evan				
A lonely sailor's life (sea chanty) AMP				Robert Confer
GREEN, Ray				
Adam lay i-bowdyn AME (See also "Mixed Chorus")				anon
Care away, away, away AME (See also "Mixed Chorus")				anon
Corpus Christi AME				anon
Sea calm (using 1/4 tones) AME				anon
HANSON, Howard				
Song of democracy CF (See also "Mixed Chorus")			orch(R) or band(R) or pno	Walt Whitman
HARRIS, Roy				
The working man's pride AMP		B, sp		trad, USA

Composer, Title and Publisher	Chorus	Solos	Accompaniment	Author of Text
HARRISON, Lou				
A joyous procession and a solemn procession CFP (See also "Women's Chorus")	TB		2 trb, 4 tam, 8 handbells, b-drm, gong	vocalise
HAUFRECHT, Herbert				
Speak, for you must PIC				Philip Freneau
HOVHANESS, Alan				
To the god who is in the fire, Op. 146 CFP (See also "Percussion")		T	perc(R)	Sh'vet Upanishad, II, 17
HOWE, Mary				
A devotion HWG				John Donne
IMBRIE, Andrew				
Psalm 42 (As the hart panteth) CFP	TBB		org	Biblical
IVES, Charles				
December PIC	unison		picc, 2 cl, 2 hn, 3 trp, 3 trb, tba	Folgore Da San Geminiano-Rossetti
Lincoln, the great commoner TP (See also "Mixed" & "Women's Chorus")			orch(R)	Edwin Markham
Processional: "Let there be light" PIC (See also "Mixed Chorus")			4 trp, org; or 4 vln & org; or str orch	John Ellerton
KALMANOFF, Martin				
Under the wide and starry sky BB			pno	R. L. Stevenson
KAY, Ulysses				
Come away, come away, death PIC	TTB			Shakespeare
Triumvirate PIC Music. The children's hour. Night march.				Ralph Waldo Emerson
KENNAN, Kent				
The unknown warrior speaks HWG				Margery Smith
KENNEDY, John Brodbin				
Little lamb, who made thee? B&H (See also "Women's Chorus")	TB		pno	William Blake

Composer, Title and Publisher	Chorus	Solos	Accompaniment	Author of Text
The shepherd B&H	TBB (boys' voices)			William Blake
To be or not to be B&H	TTB (boys' voices)			anon
KOHN, Karl				
Three Goliard songs CF	TTB			from "The Goliard poets, Medieval Latin songs & satires," 12th cent; trans: Geo. F. Whichers
Exiit diluculo (She goes out with her flock). Stetit puella (There stood a girl). Tempus hoc letitie (Time for gladness).				
KRAEHENBUEHL, David				
A Christmas blessing AMP				anon
I sing of a maiden AMP				anon
Welcome, yule AMP				anon
What cheer? AMP				anon
(Above four songs also listed under "Women's Chorus")				
KRAFT, Leo				
I waited patiently (Psalm 40) MER	TBB			Biblical
KUBIK, Gail				
American folk song sketch SMPC				trad
Hop up, my ladies. Johnny Stiles. (See also "Mixed Chorus")				
A sailor, he came to court me MER				Bill Roberts
John Henry COL				trad, USA
Litany and prayer SMPC			4 hn, 3 trp, 3 trb, tba, perc	Gail Kubik
The monotony song COL				Theodore Roethke
Oliver De Lancey GS	TB	T, B		Stephen Vincent Benét
(See also "Mixed Chorus")				
KURKA, Robert				
Who shall speak for the people? B&H			pno	Carl Sandburg
LEVY, Ernst				
Hear, ye children AB	TBB-TBB			Biblical
(See also "Women's Chorus")				
MASON, Daniel Gregory				
Ode to big business COL				Corinne R. Swain

Composer, Title and Publisher	Chorus	Solos	Accompaniment	Author of Text
MECHEM, Kirke				
Over the roofs (from "The Winds of May") ECS				Sara Teasdale
Three American folk songs, Op. 6 ECS Aunt Rhody. Blue-tail fly (Bar solo). Way-faring stranger.			pno	trad
MEYEROWITZ, Jan				
Two choruses BB Stone, steel, dominions pass. The farms of home.			hn solo	A. E. Housman
MOORE, Douglas				
Simon Legree CF			pno	Vachel Lindsay
NELSON, Paul				
A lullaby BB				James Agee
Thy will be done B&H			3 trp, trb, bar, tba, perc(R)	John Hay
NELSON, Ron				
Behold man B&H				Albert D. van Nostrand
Sleep, little one B&H (See also "Women's Chorus")				Ron Nelson
NOSS, Luther (editor)				
Psalms and hymns of early America AMP Two tunes from the Ainsworth Psalter. Three tunes from the Bay Psalm Book. Two tunes from the Missouri Harmony.	TBB			Biblical
NOWAK, Lionel				
"Wisdom exalteth her children" BCS	TBB-TBB			Biblical
PARKER, Alice				
Psalms of praise L-G (See also "Percussion")	TB		perc ensemble	Biblical
PERSICHETTI, Vincent				
Four cummings choruses EV (For contents, see "Mixed Chorus")	TB		pno	e. e. cummings
Jimmie's got a goil GS	TB unison		pno	e. e. cummings

Composer, Title and Publisher	Chorus	Solos	Accompaniment	Author of Text
(See also "Mixed" & "Women's Chorus")				
Sam was a man GS	TB unison		pno	e. e. cummings
(See also "Mixed" & "Women's Chorus")				
Song of peace EV			pno or org	anon
PFAUTSCH, Lloyd				
Advent carol L-G				Johann Rist, 1651; trans: Catherine Winkworth
Mary of Allendale L-G				Lloyd Pfautsch
PHILLIPS, Burrill				
That time may cease TP			pno	Christopher Marlowe (from The Tragical History of Dr. Faustus)
PINKHAM, Daniel				
Mass of the Good Shepherd ECS	unison		org	Biblical
(See also "Women's Chorus")				
Mass of the Holy Eucharist ECS	unison		org	Biblical
(See also "Women's Chorus")				
Te Deum KING	TB		3 trp, org	John Dryden
(See also "Mixed" & "Women's Chorus")				
PISTON, Walter				
Carnival song AMP	TBB		3 trp, 4 hn, 3 trb, tba	Lorenzo De'Medici
REICHENBACH, Herman (Editor)				
Modern canons (from 2-5 voices) MER				(For authors of texts, see "Mixed Chorus")
(For contents, see "Mixed Chorus")				
RIEGGER, Wallingford				
Evil shall not prevail (Non vincit malitia) BCS	TBB-TBB			Wisdom 7:29-30
(See also "Mixed" & "Women's Chorus")				
ROGERS, Bernard				
Psalm eighteen TP			pno	Biblical
ROREM, Ned				
Mild mother ECS	unison		pno	Biblical
(See also "Women's Chorus")				

Composer, Title and Publisher	Chorus	Solos	Accompaniment	Author of Text
SCHUMAN, William				
Deo ac veritati GS (See also "Mixed Chorus")	TTB			Motto of Colgate University
Holiday song GS (See also "Mixed" & "Women's Chorus")			pno	Genevieve Taggard
Truth shall deliver (Ballad of good advice) GS	TBB			Geoffrey Chaucer (adapted by Marion Farquhar)
SHEPHERD, Arthur				
Jolly Wat (canticum nativitatis Christi with a Christmas carol) MER (See also "Mixed" & "Women's Chorus")	2 equal voices	2 solo voices	orch(R) or pno or org	Balliol ms: 15th-16th cent
SPIES, Claudio				
Proverbs on wisdom EV			org and pno	Biblical
STARER, Robert				
Never seek to tell thy love SMPC				William Blake
STEVENS, Halsey				
Four carols PIC	TBB			
All this night shrill chanticleer				William Austin
As I rode out this enderes night				Coventry Shearman & Tailors Pageant
A virgin most pure				anon
What sweeter music				Robert Herrick
A set of three HME				
She that denies me				Thomas Heywood
The waning moon				anon
Weeping-cross				anon
SWANSON, Howard				
The nightingales WEIN				Robert Bridges
THOMPSON, Randall				
Alleluia ECS	TTBB			
The gate of heaven ECS			band(R)	Biblical
The last words of David ECS (See also "Mixed Chorus")			orch(R) or pno	Biblical
Nowell ECS (See also "Mixed" & "Women's Chorus")			pno	Biblical
The pasture (No. 2 from Frostiana) ECS	TTB		pno	Robert Frost

Composer, Title and Publisher	Chorus	Solos	Accompaniment	Author of Text
Quis multa gracilis (from Odes of Horace) ECS				Horace
Stopping by the woods on a snowy evening (No. 6 from Frostiana) ECS				Robert Frost
Tarantella (Do you remember an inn, Miranda?) ECS			orch(R) or pno	Hilaire Belloc
The testament of freedom ECS 1. The God who gave us life. 2. We have counted the cost. 3. We fight not for glory. 4. I shall not die without a hope.			pno or band(R) or orch(R)	Thomas Jefferson
THOMSON, Virgil Agnus Dei (3-pt canon) MER	any 3 pt			liturgical
Three antiphonal psalms MCA Psalms 123, 133 and 136 (See also "Women's Chorus")	TB			Biblical
Tiger! Tiger! COL				William Blake
VINCENT, John Glory to God (from "The hallow'd time") MIL (See also "Mixed Chorus")				John Vincent (from a Christmas play by Richard Hubler)
WAGNER, Joseph David jazz RBB			pno; opt parts for cl, a-sax, trp, c-b, dr	Joseph Wagner
WASHBURN, Robert Three Shakespearean love songs OX Come away, death. O mistress mine. Sigh no more, ladies.			pno (with hn, opt)	Shakespeare
WUORINEN, Charles Faire, if you expect admiring (madrigal)L-G				Thomas Campion
Super salutem (1964)MM			3 trp, 2 hn, 2 trb, b-trb, tba, perc, pno(R)	Biblical
Turne backe, you wanton flyer (madrigal) L-G				Thomas Campion

Composer, Title and Publisher	Chorus	Solos	Accompaniment	Author of Text
YORK, David Stanley				
Once to every man and nation TP (See also "Mixed Chorus")			org or band(R) or str orch(R)	James Russell Lowell
ZANINELLI, Luigi				
The water is wide SHAW			pno	Luigi Zaninelli

CHORUS WITH INSTRUMENTAL ACCOMPANIMENT
(including full orchestra, chamber orchestra, string orchestra, band and smaller ensembles)

Composer, Title and Publisher	Chorus	Solos	Accompaniment	Author of Text	Duration (min)
ADLER, Samuel					
Behold your God FAM SATB (For contents, see "Mixed Chorus")	SATB		fl, ob, cl, bsn, hn, trp, trb, hp(pno or org), perc	Biblical and trad	25
The binding OX(R)	SATB	2 S, m-S (also Narr), T, Bar	full	Biblical	50
Psalm 24 TP(R)	SATB		3 trp, 3 trb, tba	Biblical	4
ALTMAN, Ludwig					
Psalm 13 L-G(R)	SATB	A(opt)	full	Biblical	5
AMRAM, David					
Let us remember (cantata) CFP(R)	SATB	S, A, T, B	full	Langston Hughes	20
A year in our land (cantata) CFP(R) (For contents, see "Mixed Chorus")	SATB	S, A, T, B			22
ANTES, John					
Shout ye heavens B&H	SATB		2 trp(or 2 hn), str	Biblical	3
Surely He has borne our grief B&H	SATB		str	Biblical	5
ANTHEIL, George					
Cabeza de Vaca SHAW	SATB		full	Allan Dowling	50
ARGENTO, Dominick					
The revelation of St. John the Divine B&H(R) (For contents, see "Men's Chorus")	TB	T	3 hn, 2 trp, 2 trb, perc, hp, pno	Biblical	36

Composer, Title and Publisher	Chorus	Solos	Accompani- ment	Author of Text	Dura- tion (min)
ASCHAFFENBURG, Walter					
The 23rd Psalme TP	SATB	T	ob and/or org	George Herbert	5
AVSHALOMOV, Jacob					
How long, O Lord EBM	SATB	A	full	Biblical	15
Tom O'Bedlam ECS	SATB		ob, jingles, tabor	anon	3
BACON, Ernst					
The Lord-star MER	SATB		full	Walt Whitman	5
BARBER, Samuel					
Easter chorale GS	SAATB		3 trp, 3 trb, 2 hn, tba, timp, org	Pack Browning	3
Prayers of Kierke- gaard GS	SATB	S, T, Bar	full	Soren Kierkegaard	18
A stop watch and an ordnance map GS	TTBB		4 hn, 3 trb, tba, timp	Stephen Spender	6
BECK, John Ness					
Canticle of praise TP(R)	SATB		full or band	Biblical	5
Hymn for Easter day TP Introit. Processional.	SATB		3 trp, pno or org	Chas. Wesley (1739) and Biblical	4
Upon this rock GS	SATB		3 trp, hn, trb, tba	Biblical	3
Visions of St. John TP(R) (For contents, see "Mixed Chorus")	SATB		brass ensem- ble, hp, pno, perc	Biblical	6
BERGSMA, William					
Confrontation (from the Book of Job) GAL(R)	SATB		full	Biblical	26
The sun, the soaring eagle, the turquoise prince, the god GAL(R) (See also "Mixed Chorus" & "Percussion")	SATB	speak- ers from chorus	2 trp, 2 trb, tba, perc(3 players)		10
BERNSTEIN, Leonard					
Chichester psalms GS(R) (For con- tents, see "Mixed Chorus")	SATB		3 trp, 3 trb, hp, perc, str	Biblical	20

Composer, Title and Publisher	Chorus	Solos	Accompaniment	Author of Text	Duration (min)
Kaddish: Symphony No. 3 GS(R) (For contents, see "Mixed Chorus")	SATB & boy's choir	Sp(female), S solo	full	Leonard Bernstein	30
BOATWRIGHT, Howard					
Canticle of the sun ECS(R)	SATB, 2nd unison ch ad lib		full	St. Francis of Assisi; trans: Matthew Arnold	12
BRIGHT, Houston					
Jabberwocky SHAW	SATB		2 cor, 2 hn, 2 trb, tba, timp, perc, c-b(opt), pno(opt)	Lewis Carroll	7.5
Now deck thyself with majesty SHAW	SATB		3 trp, 2 hn, 3 bar, tba, c-b (opt), timp; or band(R)	Biblical	4
Sunrise alleluias SHAW	SATB		3 cor, 2 hn, 2 trb, c-b(opt), timp	Houston Bright	2.5
BRUBECK, Dave					
The light in the wilderness (oratorio)SHAW(R) (For contents, see "Mixed Chorus")	SATB	Bar	org & jazz combo: pno, c-b, dr; or orch	Biblical; additional text by Dave and Iola Brubeck	70
CARPENTER, John Alden					
Song of faith GS	SATB		full	John A. Carpenter	4
CARTER, Elliott					
The harmony of morning (1944) AMP	SSAA		cham	Mark van Doren	9
Musicians wrestle everywhere MER	SSATB		str	Emily Dickinson	4
CLOKEY, Joseph W.					
A canticle of peace S-B(R)	unison		full	Biblical	3.5
How summer came (an Indian legend) JF(R)	SSA		full	Clara Louise Kessler	11
Miladie--a cavalier suite JF(R) (For contents, see "Women's Chorus")	SSA or TTB		str	Willis Knapp Jones	10
The temple (oratorio) JF(R)	SATB	2 S, A, T, B	full	George Herbert	15
COOPER, David S.					
150th Psalm EBM(R)	SATB		3 trp, 3 trb, timp, perc, org	Biblical	3

Composer, Title and Publisher	Chorus	Solos	Accompaniment	Author of Text	Duration (min)
COPLAND, Aaron					
Canticle of freedom (1955) (rev. 1965) B&H	SATB		full	John Barbour	10
Old American songs (Set I, 1950) B&H(R)			cham(orchestrated by composer)		13
The boatman's dance (arr. Fine)	SATB or TTBB	Bar		minstrel song, 1843	
The dodger (arr. Fine)	TTBB	Bar		campaign song	
I bought me a cat (arr. Fine)	SATB or SSA (arr. Straker) or TBB	S, T T, Bar, B		trad	
Long time ago	SATB(arr. Fine) SSA (arr. Straker)			trad	
Simple gifts (arr. Fine)	SA or TB			Shaker song	
Old American songs (Set II, 1952) B&H(R)			cham (orchestrated by composer		12
At the river (arr. Wilding-White)	SATB or SA or SSA or TTBB			trad	
Ching-a-ring-chaw (arr. Fine)	SATB or SSA or TTBB (arr. Copland)			minstrel song	
Little horses (arr. Wilding-White)	SA or SSA or TTBB			trad	
Promise of living (from Tenderland) B&H	SATBB		full	Horace Everett	5
Song of the guerillas (1943) B&H	TTBB	Bar	full	Ira Gershwin	4
CORIGLIANO, John					
Fern Hill GS(R)	SATB	m-S	full	Dylan Thomas	16
What I expected was... GS(R)	SSAATT BB		brass choir and perc	Stephen Spender	6
CORTÉS, Ramiro					
Missa brevis (Kyrie-Gloria) TP(R)	SSA		picc, 2 fl, 2 ob, 2 cl, b-cl, 2 bsn, c-bsn (or c-b)	liturgical	7.5
COWELL, Henry					
Supplication CFP	unison		2 trp, 2 trb, org	Henry Cowell	3.5
CRAWFORD, John					
Magnificat ECS(R)	SATB		str	Biblical	10

Composer, Title and Publisher	Chorus	Solos	Accompaniment	Author of Text	Duration (min)
CRESTON, Paul					
Isaiah's prophecy (a Christmas oratorio) COL(R) (For contents, see "Mixed Chorus")	SATB	S, A, T, B, Narr	full	Biblical	40
Missa solemnis, Op. 44 MIL(R)	SATB or TTBB		full	liturgical	15
DANIELS, Mabel					
A psalm of praise HWG(R)	SATB		str	Biblical	8
DELANEY, Robert					
John Brown's song ECS	SATB		full	Stephen Vincent Benét	13
DELLO JOIO, Norman					
Proud music of the storm EBM(R)	SATB		brass ensemble	Walt Whitman	10
A Psalm of David CF(R)	SATB		full	Biblical	27
Song of affirmation (cantata) CF	SATB	S, Narr	full	Stephen Vincent Benét	42
Songs of Walt Whitman EBM(R) (For contents, see "Mixed Chorus")	SATB		full	Walt Whitman	25
Three songs of Chopin EBM The lovers. The ring. The wish.	SATB or SA		full	English version by Harold Heiberg	6
To Saint Cecilia CF(R)	SATB		3 trp, 3 hn, 2 trb, b-trb, tba	John Dryden	15
Years of the modern EBM	SATB		brass & perc	Walt Whitman	10
DENCKE, Jeremiah					
Lord our God HWG	SATB		full	Biblical	3
DETT, R. Nathaniel					
The ordering of Moses JF	SATB	S, A, T, 2B	full	Biblical & folklore, compiled by R. Nathaniel Dett	60
DIAMOND, David					
The martyr SMPC(R)	TTBB		full	Herman Melville	4
This sacred ground SMPC(R)	SATB	B	full	Lincoln's Gettysburg address	16.5
Young Joseph MER	SSA		str	Thomas Mann	5.5
DIEMER, Emma Lou					
To Him all glory give EV(R)	SATB		full	Dorothy Diemer Hendry	5

Composer, Title and Publisher	Chorus	Solos	Accompaniment	Author of Text	Duration (min)
DONOVAN, Richard					
Fantasy on American folk ballads JF	TTBB		full	trad, USA	12
To all you ladies now at hand GAL	TTBB	T or S	full	Charles Sackville	3.5
DUSHKIN, Dorothy					
Three songs CF (For contents, see "Women's Chorus")	SSA		fl, ob, cl, or pno	Walter de la Mare	6
EFFINGER, Cecil					
Fanfare on chow call HWG	TTBB		brass ensemble	army mess call	2
The invisible fire (oratorio) HWG(R)	SATB	S, A, T, B	full	Tom F. Driver	57
ELLSTEIN, Abraham					
Ode to the King of Kings (cantata) MIL(R)	SATB	S, Bar (or T)	full	Samuel H. Dresner (from Biblical text)	20
The redemption (oratorio) MIL(R)	SATB	Narr, S, T, Bar	full	Biblical	20
ELMORE, Robert					
The prodigal son (a sermon in swing) HWG(R)	TTBB		full	James Weldon Johnson	22
Psalm of redemption JF	SATB	A, Bar	org, 3 trp, 3 trb, perc	Biblical	17
Veni Emmanuel JF(R)	SATB		org, trp, trb, hn, tba	setting of Medieval poem	4
Vocalise GAL(R)	SATB		full	vocalise	4
ELWELL, Herbert					
Lincoln: requiem aeternam AMP(R)	SATB	Bar	full	John Gould Fletcher	25
ETLER, Alvin					
Onomatopoesis AB	TTBB		2 cl, b-cl, bsn, 2 trp, hn, trb, perc	vocalise	15
FELCIANO, Richard					
Four poems from the Japanese CPE	SSA		5 hp, cel, glock, tam-tam	from the Japanese poets	8
FELDMAN, Morton					
Chorus and instruments CFP	SATB		hn, tba, perc, pno, vln, vlc, c-b	vocalise	6

Composer, Title and Publisher	Chorus	Solos	Accompaniment	Author of Text	Duration (min)
FETLER, Paul					
Jubilate Deo (sing and rejoice)AUG	SATB		2 hn, 3 trp, 3 trb	liturgical	4
FINK, Michael					
Septem angeli (seven angels) ECS(R)	SATB		4 vlc, 2 c-b, timp, perc	Biblical	12
FINNEY, Ross Lee					
Edge of shadow CFP	SATB		2 pno, xy, vib, timp, perc	Archibald Mac-Leish	19
The martyr's elegy CFP(R)	SATB	high voice	full	Percy B. Shelley	17.5
The nun's priest's tale CFP(R)	SATB		full	Geoffrey Chaucer	35
Pilgrim psalms CF(R)	SATB		full	Biblical	30
Still are new worlds CFP(R) (For contents, see "Mixed Chorus")	SATB	Sp	full		28
FOSS, Lukas					
Fragments of Archilochos CF(R)	SATB	counter T, Sp (male & female)	man, gtr, perc	Archilochos; trans: Guy Davenport	10
Parable of death CF	SATB	T, Narr	full or cham	Rainer Maria Rilke; trans: Anthony Hecht	32
The prairie GS	SATB	S, A, T, B	full	Carl Sandburg	15
Psalms CF(R)	SATB		cham	Biblical	13
FRACKENPOHL, Arthur					
The natural superiority of men CF(R)	SSA		str qrt or cham	Jean Pearson	14
Shepherds, rejoice KING	TTBB	T or B solos	3 hn, 3 trb, tba	The Social Harp, 1868	4
FREED, Arnold					
Gloria B&H(R)	SATB		3 trp, 4 hn, 3 trb, tba, timp	liturgical	4
GIANNINI, Vittorio					
A canticle of Christmas COL(R)	SATB	B, Narr	full	Biblical	23
Canticle of the martyrs HWG(R)	SATB	B	full	liturgical	15
Two madrigals COL (For contents, see "Women's Chorus")	SSA		pno & solo fl or pno & solo ob	Christopher Marlowe & Sir Walter Raleigh	10

Composer, Title and Publisher	Chorus	Solos	Accompaniment	Author of Text	Duration (min)
GILLIS, Don					
The coming of the King (The Christmas story) MIL(R)	SATB	Narr, S, A, T, B	full	Norman Vincent Peale	26
GOLDMAN, Richard Franko (editor)					
Landmarks of early American music GS (a collection of 32 compositions)	SATB		full or band		
GRAHAM, Robert					
The voices of Christmas (cantata) SMPC(R)	SATB		str	Joan Sistrunk	18
HANSON, Howard					
Beat! beat! drums! (songs from 'Drum Taps") JF(R)	SATB		full	Walt Whitman	8
Cherubic hymn (1950) CF(R)	SATB		full	St. John Chrysostom	10
Lament for Beowulf S-B(R)	SSAATTBB		full	Anglo-Saxon epic; trans: Wm. Morris & A.J. Wyatt	19
Praise we the Lord from "Merry Mount" W-7(R)	SATB		full	Richard L. Stokes	3
Song of democracy (1957-58) CF(R)	SATB or TTBB		full or band	Walt Whitman	12
Song of human rights CF(R)	SATB		full	Preamble of the Universal Declaration of Human Rights	12
Songs from "Drum "Taps" JF(R) (For contents, see "Mixed Chorus")	SATB	Bar	full	Walt Whitman	20
HARRIS, Roy					
Blow the man down CF	SATB	A, B	full	trad sea ballad	9.5
Folk song symphony GS	SATB		full	trad, USA	44
Walt Whitman suite MIL(R) (For contents, see "Mixed Chorus")	SATB		str & 2 pno	Walt Whitman	12
HARRISON, Lou					
A joyous procession and a solemn procession CFP(R)	SA or TB		2 trb, 4 tam, 8 handbells, b-dr, gong	vocalise	6

Composer, Title and Publisher	Chorus	Solos	Accompaniment	Author of Text	Duration (min)
Mass (to St. Anthony) PIC(R)	SATB		trp, hp, str	liturgical	29
HERBST, Johannes					
The people that in darkness wandered HWG	SATB		full	Biblical	3
HOIBY, Lee					
Hymn of the Nativity COL(R)	SATB	S, B	full	Richard Crashaw	26
HOVHANESS, Alan					
Ad lyram, Op. 143 CFP(R)	SSAATT BB	S, A, T, B	full	from Latin	12
Blessed throughout all generations (from Magnificat, Op. 157) CFP(R)	SSA	S	full	liturgical	3
Glory to God (cantata), Op. 124 CFP(R)	SATB	S, A	4 hn, 4 trp, 4 trb, sax, perc, org	Biblical	14
In the beginning was the word (cantata), Op. 206 CFP(R)	SATB	A, B	cham	Biblical	27
Magnificat, Op. 157 CFP(R)	SATB	S, A, T, B	cham	liturgical	28
Missa brevis CFP	SATB	Bar	org and str	liturgical	12
Psalm 23, Op. 188a CFP(R)	SATB		fl, 2 trp, timp	Biblical	14
Thirtieth ode of Solomon, Op. 76 CFP(R)	SATB	B	cham	Biblical	30
Triptych AMP(R)					
1a. Ave Maria	SSAA		2 ob(or trp or cl), 2 hn, (or trb), hp or pno	liturgical	3
2. The beatitudes	SATB		cham	Biblical	9
3. Easter cantata				trad	16
Prelude (instrumental)			cham		
O Lord (S solo)			cham		
Mourn, mourn, ye saints	SATB	S	cham		
The Lord now is risen (S solo)			cham		
Jesus Christ is risen today	SATB		cham		
Watchman tell us of the night CFP	SATB	B	full	John Bowring	5
HOWE, Mary					
Song of psalms CF	SSA		full	A. O'Shaughnessy	13

Composer, Title and Publisher	Chorus	Solos	Accompaniment	Author of Text	Duration (min)
IMBRIE, Andrew					
On the beach at night SHAW(R)	SATB		str	Walt Whitman	12
IVES, Charles					
December PIC	men's unison		picc, 2 cl, 2 hn, 3 trp, 3 trb, tba	Folgore Da San Geminiano-Rossetti	1.5
Lincoln, the great commoner TP(R)	SATB or SSAA or TTBB		full	Edwin Markham	6
Processional: "Let there be light" PIC	SATB or TBB		4 trp & org; or 4 vln & org; or str	John Ellerton	5
They are there! PIC	unison		full	Charles Ives	3
Three harvest home chorales MER(R) (For contents, see "Mixed Chorus")	SATB		cham		4
JAMES, Philip					
General William Booth enters into Heaven W-7	TTBB		trp, trb,perc, 2 pno or pno and org	Vachel Lindsay	7
KENNEDY, John Brodbin					
Alleluia fanfare BI	SATB		2 trp, 3 trb	liturgical	3
KIRK, Theron					
Carol service with 9 lessons for Christmas JF(R) (For contents, see "Mixed Chorus")	SATB	Narr	full		40
Glory to God (Christmas cantata) JF(R)	SATB	S, A, T, B	cham	Biblical	12
Hail, O Son of righteousness JF	SATB		2 trp, 2 trb, org	William Austin	8
King David's Deliverance JF(R)	SATB		full	Biblical	11
Night of wonder SHAW(R) (For contents, see "Mixed Chorus")	SATB		org, pno, str qrt or full	trad	25
Now let us all sing SHAW	SATB		2 trp, 3 trb, timp, pno	Walter A. Rodby	3
O come, let us sing S-B	SATB		2 trp, 2 trb, timp	Biblical	4
KOHN, Karl					
Sensus spei CF(R)	SSAATTBB		2 trp, 2 trb;or 2 trp, hn, trb; or ob, cl, hn, bsn	Biblical	12

Composer, Title and Publisher	Chorus	Solos	Accompaniment	Author of Text	Duration (min)
Three descants from Ecclesiastes CF(R)	SATB		2 trp, hn, 2 trb, tba	Biblical	12
KORTE, Karl					
Mass for youth GAL(R) (For contents, see "Mixed Chorus")	SATB		full	liturgical	20
KOSTECK, Gregory					
Love poems from youth WLP(R)	SATB	A, T	2 fl, 2 cl, 2 trp, 2 hn, vib, hp, cel, pno, perc, 3 vlc	Gregory Kosteck	5
KOUTZEN, Boris					
An invocation TP(R)	SSA		full	John Addington Symonds	3
KRAFT, Leo					
A proverb of Solomon MER(R)	SATB		full	Biblical	5
KUBIK, Gail					
Daniel Drew B&H	SATB		vlc, c-b	Rosemary and Stephen Vincent Benét	3
In praise of Johnny Appleseed (cantata) COL(R) (For contents, see "Mixed Chorus")	SATB	b-Bar	cham	Vachel Lindsay	25
Litany and prayer SMPC	TTBB		3 trp, 4 hn, 3 trb, tba, perc	Gail Kubik	18
LA MONTAINE, John					
The earth is the Lord's (Psalm XXIV) PJS(R)	SATB		full	Biblical	6
Sanctuary (cantata) HWG	SATB	Bar	org, 2 trp, timp	Theodore S. Ross & Charles Atwood Campbell	10
Te Deum PJS(R)	SATB		full	liturgical	7
LATHAM, William					
A prophecy of peace S-B	SATB		ob, cl, bsn, hn	Biblical	5
Psalm 130 S-B	SATB		band	Biblical	3.5
Psalm 148 S-B	SATB		band	Biblical	3.5
Te Deum SHAW(R)	SATB		wind ensemble	liturgical	18
LAYTON, Billy Jim					
Three Dylan Thomas poems GS (For contents, see "Mixed Chorus")	SATB		2 trp, 2 hn, 2 trb	Dylan Thomas	7

Composer, Title and Publisher	Chorus	Solos	Accompaniment	Author of Text	Duration (min)
LEES, Benjamin					
Vision of poets (a dramatic cantata) B&H(R) (For contents, see "Mixed Chorus")	SATB	S, T	full	Walt Whitman	40
LEVY, Marvin David					
For the time being (Christmas oratorio) B&H(R) (For contents, see "Mixed Chorus")	SATB	3 S, m-S, T, Bar, B, Narr	full	W. H. Auden	105
LEWIS, John					
The Alexander's fugue MJQ(R)	vocal qrt (S, A, T, B)		vib, pno, c-b, dr	vocalise	5
Canonic fugue XII from Bach's Musical Offering MJQ(R)	vocal qrt (S, A, T, B)		vib, c-b pno, dr	vocalise	4.5
Dido's lament from "When I am laid in earth" by Purcell MJQ(R)	vocal qrt (S, A, T, B)		vib, c-b, pno, dr	vocalise	5
Little David's fugue MJQ(R)	vocal qrt (S, A, T, B)		vib, c-b, pno, dr	vocalise	4.5
Ricercar a 6 from Bach's Musical Offering MJQ(R)	vocal qrt (S, A, T, B)		vib, c-b, pno, dr	vocalise	6.5
Vendome MJQ(R)	vocal qrt (S, A, T, B)		vib, c-b, pno, dr	vocalise	3.5
LOCKWOOD, Normand					
A ballad of the North and South AMP (For contents, see "Mixed Chorus")	SATB	Narr	wind symphony	Paul M. Angle & Earl Schenck Miers	25
Carol fantasy AMP	SATBB		full	trad	15
The closing doxology (Psalm 150)BB(R)	SATB		band	Biblical	5
Rejoice in the Lord (Psalm 33) WLP	SATB		2 hn, 2 trb, timp	Biblical	8
LOEFFLER, Charles Martin					
Evocation AME(R)	SSA		full	Greek epigrams	11
LONDON, Edwin					
Four proverbs AB	SSA	S	2 trp, bsn	Biblical	5
LO PRESTI, Ronald					
Tribute CF(R)	SATB		full or band	Walt Whitman	5.5

Composer, Title and Publisher	Chorus	Solos	Accompaniment	Author of Text	Duration (min)
LUENING, Otto					
Pilgrim's hymn TP(R)	unison or SA		full	Howard Moss	4
LYNN, George					
The Gettysburg Address TP(R)	SATB	Bar	full	Abraham Lincoln	7
MAILMAN, Martin					
Alleluia MIL	SATB		band	liturgical	4
McDONALD, Harl					
Builders of America (cantata) EV	SATB	Narr	fl, trp, trb, dr	Edward Shenton	8
God, give us men (Cantata) EV(R)	SATB		orch	Text attributed to a bishop of Exeter	5
Songs of conquest (a cycle) EV(R) (For contents, see "Mixed Chorus")	SATB		orch	Phelps Putnam	12
McKINNEY, Howard D. (Compiler)					
The Son of Man (Christmas cantata) JF (For contents, see "Mixed Chorus")	SATB	Narr	2 trp, 2 trb, fl, org		60
MECHEM, Kirke					
The shepherd and his love, Op. 30 ECS(R) (For contents, see "Mixed Chorus")	SATB		picc, vla, pno	Christopher Marlowe & Sir Walter Raleigh	6
MENNIN, Peter					
Christmas story (a cantata) CF	SATB	S, T	cham	trad	24
The cycle (Symphony No. 4)CF	SATB		full	Peter Mennin	23
MEYEROWITZ, Jan					
Eternitie EBM(R)	SATB		2 fl, 2 cl, 2 bsn, 2 hn, 2 trp, trb, tba	Robert Herrick	4
MOEVS, Robert					
Et nunc, reges ECS	SSA		fl, cl, b-cl	Biblical	10
Et Occidentem illustra EBM	SATB		full	The Commission of Theodore Frelinghuysen, New York, May 30, 1755, Paragraph 1	19

Composer, Title and Publisher	Chorus	Solos	Accompaniment	Author of Text	Duration (min)
MOORE, Douglas The Greenfield Christmas tree GS(R)	SATB		full	Arnold Sundergaard	25
MORGAN, Henry Never weather-beaten sail ECS(R)	SATB		full	Thomas Campion	5
MURRAY, Lyn "The miracle" (Christmas oratorio) MCA(R)	SATB		brass, hp, org, perc	Norman Corwin	21
NELSON, Paul Thy will be done B&H(R)	TTBB		3 trp, trb,bar, tba, perc	John Hay	13.5
NELSON, Ron Choral fanfare for Christmas B&H	SATB		org, 3 trp, 3 trb, tba	Gail M. Kurtz	4
The Christmas story B&H (For contents, see "Mixed Chorus")	SATB	Narr, Bar	3 trp, 3 trb or a cappello	Biblical	31
Fanfare for a festival (All praise to music) B&H	SATB		3 trp, 3 trb, tba, timp	Walter A. Rodby	4
Triumphal Te Deum B&H(R)	SATB		org, 3 trp, 3 trb, perc	liturgical	5
What is man? B&H(R)	SATB	Narr, S, Bar	full or version for 3 trp, 3 trb, tba, timp, perc, org & pno (ad lib) & electronic sequences	Samuel H. Miller	50
NELSON, Ronald A. How far is it to Bethlehem? AUG	SATB		fl, cl, trp, 2 vln, vla, vlc	Finnish song; trans: Olav Lee	40
PARKER, Alice Psalms of praise L-G (See also "Percussion")	TB		perc(b-dr, sn-dr, cmb, gong, tri, tam)	Biblical	5
PARKER, Horatio Hora novissima (oratorio) HWG	SSAATT BB	S, A, T, B	full	Biblical	80
PELOQUIN, C. Alexander The bells B&H	SATB		2 pno, 2 c-b, perc	Edgar Allan Poe	10

Composer, Title and Publisher	Chorus	Solos	Accompaniment	Author of Text	Duration (min)
PERSICHETTI, Vincent					
Celebrations EV (For contents, see "Mixed Chorus")	SATB		picc, 2 fl, 2 ob, 3 cl, b-cl, 2 bsn, 3 trp, 4 hn, bar, 3 trb, tba, timp, perc	Walt Whitman	18
The pleiades EV	SATB		trp & str	V. Persichetti	12
Stabat mater, Op. 92 EV(R)	SATB		orch	Jacopone da Todi, 13th cent; English version by Vincent Persichetti	28
Te deum EV(R)	SATB		orch	liturgical	11
Winter cantata EV (For contents, see "Women's Chorus")	SSA		fl, mar	Haiku; trans: Harold Stewart	18
PFAUTSCH, Lloyd					
Canticle to peace S-B	SATB		band	John Greenleaf Whittier	3.5
Five narrative carols S-B (For contents, see "Women's Chorus")	SSA		fl, dr(opt)		7
PHILLIPS, Burrill					
Declaratives EV(R) (For contents, see "Women's Chorus")	SSAA		cham		17
The return of Odysseus GAL(R) (For contents, see "Mixed Chorus")	SATB	Bar, Narr	full	Alberta Phillips	29
PINKHAM, Daniel					
An Emily Dickinson mosaic CFP (For contents, see "Women's Chorus")	SSAA		cham	Emily Dickinson	10
Angelus ad pastores ait KING	SSAA		2 trp(opt), 3 trb, tba, (opt), org(opt)	Liber Usualis	4
Canticle of praise ECS(R)	SATB	S	3 trp, 2 hn, 2 trb, b-trb, tba, perc	Biblical	12
Christmas cantata (Sinfonia sacra) KING	SATB		brass choir I: 2 trp, 2 trb; brass choir II: 2 trp, 2 trb, bar, tba	Daniel Pinkham	9.5
Easter cantata CFP	SATB		4 trp, 2 hn, 3 trb, tba, cel, timp, perc	Biblical	11.5

Composer, Title and Publisher	Chorus	Solos	Accompaniment	Author of Text	Duration (min)
Festival magnificat CFP	SATB		hn (or trb), 2 trp, trb	liturgical	4.5
Jonah (Dramatic cantata) ECS(R)	SATB	m-S, T, b-Bar	full	Biblical	12
Lamentations of Jeremiah CFP(R)	SATB		2 trp, 2 hn, 2 trb, c-b, timp, perc	Biblical	14
Psalm 24 CFP	SATB		2 trp, 2 trb, org	Biblical	3.5
The reproaches AMP(R) (For contents, see "Mixed Chorus")	SATB		Version A: wind quintet; or str quintet; (or str orch) with org ad lib Version B: str quintet or qrt; or full with org ad lib Version C: org Version D: a cappella	Liber Usualis; trans: Jean Lunn	18
Requiem CFP(R)	SATB	A, T	2 trp, 2 hn, 2 trb, c-b	liturgical	15
St. Mark passion CFP(R)	SATB	S, T	2 hn, 2 trp, 2 trb, timp, perc, hp, org	Biblical	30
Stabat mater CFP(R)	SATB	S	cham	liturgical	16
Te Deum KING	SATB, SA or TB		3 trp, org	John Dryden	4.5
Three Lenten poems of Richard Crashaw ECS (For contents, see "Mixed Chorus")	SATB or SSA		str qrt or str orch	Richard Crashaw	5
Wedding cantata CFP(R)	SATB	S, T	full	Biblical	10
PISTON, Walter					
Carnival song AMP	TBB		3 trp, 4 hn, 3 trb, tba	Lorenzo De'Medici	6
Psalm and prayer of David (1958)AMP(R)	SATB		fl, cl, bsn, vln, vla, vlc, c-b	Biblical	8
PRESTON, John E.					
The coming American MIL	SATB		str	Sam Walter Foss	4.5
PURVIS, Richard					
The ballad of Judas Iscariot EV	SATB	S, A, T, B	org, vln, 2 hp, cel	Robert Buchanan	15
Paean of praise (cantata) JF	SATB	Bar	3 trp, 2 trb, timp	Biblical	9
The song of Simeon JF	SATB		3 trp, 2 trb, timp, hp	setting of Nunc Dimittis	4

Composer, Title and Publisher	Chorus	Solos	Accompaniment	Author of Text	Duration (min)
REED, Alfred					
Choric song: a romantic idyl B&H	SSATBB		band	Alfred Lord Tennyson	6
REYNOLDS, Roger					
Blind men CFP(R)	SATB		3 trp, 2 trb, b-trb, tba, perc, pno	Herman Melville	17
Masks CFP(R)	SATB		full	Herman Melville	25
RIEGGER, Wallingford					
La belle dame sans merci PIC(R)	SSA	T	cham	John Keats	15
Cantata: "In certainty of song, " Op. 46 PIC(R)	SATB		full	Catherine Harris	21
Eternity, Op. 32a FLAM	SSA		fl, 2 hn, c-b	Emily Dickinson	4
A Shakespeare sonnet (No. 138), Op. 65 AMP	SSAB	B	cham	Shakespeare	5
RINGWALD, Roy					
The song of America SHAW(R) (For authors, see "Mixed Chorus")	SATB	Narr	full		40
ROBERTSON, Leroy					
All creatures of our God and King GAL(R)	SATB		hn, trp, trb, tba	Biblical	4
Come, come ye saints GAL(R)	SATB		full	Biblical	6
The Lord's prayer GAL(R)	SATB		str	Biblical	4
ROGERS, Bernard					
A letter from Pete (cantata) SMPC(R)	SATB	S, T	full	Walt Whitman	24.5
The light of man TP(R)	SATB		full	Biblical	11
The prophet Isaiah SMPC(R)	SATB		full	Biblical	32
ROREM, Ned					
Laudemus tempus actum B&H(R)	SATB		full	Ned Rorem	6
The seventieth Psalm HWG(R)	SATB		fl, ob, cl, bsn, 2 hn, tba	Biblical	4
Two psalms and a proverb ECS (For contents, see "Mixed Chorus")	SATB	S, A, Bar	2 vln, vla, vlc, c-b	Biblical	6

Composer, Title and Publisher	Chorus	Solos	Accompaniment	Author of Text	Duration (min)
SANDERS, Robert					
An American psalm MER(R)	SSAA		fl, 2 vln, vla, vlc, c-b, 2 pno	H.R. Palmer & Rollo Russell	15
SCHUMAN, William					
A free song (secular cantata No. 2)GS	SATB		full	Walt Whitman	22
Prologue GS(R)	SATB		full	Genevieve Taggard	3.5
This is our time (Secular cantata No. 1) B&H(R)	SATB		full	Genevieve Taggard	30
SESSIONS, Roger					
Turn, O libertad (1943) EBM(R)	SATB		full	Walt Whitman	4
SHEPHERD, Arthur					
Jolly Wat (canticum nativitatis Christi with a Christmas carol) MER(R)	2 equal voices	2 solo voices	orch	Balliol ms: 15th-16th cent	4
SIEGMEISTER, Elie					
Abraham Lincoln walks at midnight B&H(R)	SATB		full	Vachel Lindsay	7
Christmas is coming (a cantata of carols) GS(R)	SATB	Narr	cham	Dorothy de Ferranti	25
SMITH, Russell					
Set me as a seal L-G(R)	SSA		hn, vln, vla, vlc	Biblical	4
SOWERBY, Leo					
Canticle of the sun HWG	SATB		full	St. Francis of Assissi; trans: Matthew Arnold	35
Forsaken of man (cantata) HWG	SATB	T, 3 Bar, 2 B	full	Edward Borgers and Biblical	60
Solomon's garden (cantata) HWG(R)	SATB	T	full and org	Biblical	12
The throne of God HWG(R)	SATB		full	Biblical	33
STARER, Robert					
Ariel, visions of Isaiah MCA(R) (For contents, see "Mixed Chorus")	SATB	S, B	full	Biblical	27
Joseph and his brothers (cantata) MCA(R)	SATB	S, T, b-Bar, Narr	full	Biblical	26

Composer, Title and Publisher	Chorus	Solos	Accompaniment	Author of Text	Duration (min)
Kohelet (Ecclesiastes) MCA(R)	SATB	S, Bar	full	Biblical	24
A Psalm of David TP(R)	SATB	S	str, 2 trp	Biblical	4.5
Two songs from "Honey and Salt" MCA (For contents, see "Mixed Chorus")	SATB		2 trp, 2 trb	Carl Sandburg	6
STEVENS, Halsey					
The ballad of William Sycamore GAL(R)	SATB		full	Stephen Vincent Benét	18.5
Magnificat MPC(R)	SATB		str, trp	Biblical	6
Te Deum MPC	SATB		2 trp, 2 hn, 2 trb, timp, org	liturgical	13
STILL, William Grant					
Rising tide JF(R)	SSATBB		orch	Albert Stillman	2.5
Sahdji (ballet) CF(R)	SATB	B & dancers	full	senario by Richard Bruce & Alain Locke	45
Victory tide JF(R)	SATB		orch	Albert Stillman	2.5
STOUT, Alan					
In principio erat verbum (motet-- 1963) CFP	SSAATTBB		4 vln, 2 vla, 2 vlc, c-b	Biblical	4
SUMMERLIN, Edward					
Evensong--a jazz liturgy MJQ(R)	SATB		org, a-sax, t-sax, 2 trp, trb, b-trb, gtr (or pno), c-b, dr	liturgical	25
SYDEMAN, William					
The lament of Electra (cantata) ECS(R)	5 choruses SATB each & each with own conductor	A	cham	adapted from Sophocles, Euripides, & Aeschylus by W. Sydeman	15
THOMPSON, Randall					
Americana (five choruses)ECS(R) (For contents, see "Mixed Chorus")	SATB		full	from articles in The American Mercury	20
A feast of praise (cantata) ECS	SATB		2 trp, 2 hn, 2 trb, tba, hp	Biblical	15
The gate of heaven ECS(R)	TTBB		band	Biblical	5
The last words of David ECS(R)	SATB or TTBB		full	Biblical	5
The nativity according to St. Luke (oratorio) ECS(R)	SATB		full	Biblical	15

Composer, Title and Publisher	Chorus	Solos	Accompani- ment	Author of Text	Dura- tion (min)
Ode to the Virginian voyage ECS(R)	SATB		full	Michael Drayton	32
Tarantella ECS(R)	TTDB		full	Hilaire Belloc	10
The testament of freedom ECS(R)	TTBB		full or band	Thomas Jefferson	25
THOMSON, Virgil					
Missa pro defunctis HWG(R)	SATB		full	liturgical	45
TIRRO, Frank P.					
American jazz mass S-B (For contents, see "Mixed Chorus")	SATB		trp, a-sax, bar-sax, c-b, traps	liturgical	25
VERALL, John					
A Christmas fantasy TP(R)	SATB or unison		band	trad	6
WAGNER, Joseph					
Ballad of brother- hood EV	SATB		orch	Alfred Kreymborg	4
David jazz RBB	TTBB		pno; cl, a-sax, trp, c-b, dr	Joseph Wagner	12
Missa sacra COL(R)	SATB	S	full	liturgical	4
WAGNER, Roger					
Heritage of freedom CF(R)	SATB		cham	Joseph Auslander	5
WARD, Robert					
Earth shall be fair GAL(R)	SATB	S (or children's choir)	full	Biblical & "Turn back O man" by Clifford Bax	26
Sweet freedom's song (a New England chronicle)GAL(R) (For contents, see "Mixed Chorus")	SATB	S, Bar, Narr	full	texts compiled by Mary and Robert Ward	40
WARREN, Elinor Remick					
Abram in Egypt HWG(R)	SATB	B	orch	The Dead Sea Scrolls & Book of Genesis	21
Our beloved land TP(R)	SATB		full	Samuel Bonner	3
Requiem L-G(R) (For contents, see "Mixed Chorus")	SATB	m-S, Bar	full	liturgical	50
WUORINEN, Charles					
The prayer of Jonah MM(R)	SATB		str	Biblical	11

Composer, Title and Publisher	Chorus	Solos	Accompaniment	Author of Text	Duration (min)
Super salutem (1964) MM(R)	TTBB		3 trp, 2 hn, 2 trb, b-trb, tba, perc, pno	Biblical	4
YORK, David Stanley					
Once to every man and nation TP(R)	SATB or TTBB divisi		str or band	James Russell Lowell	3.5
ZANINELLI, Luigi					
Song of hope SHAW	SATB		2 trp, 2 trb, tba	Angela Morgan	4
The world is so full SHAW(R) (For contents, see "Women's Chorus")	SSA		fl, ob, cl, bsn	Robert Louis Stevenson	12

2. INSTRUMENTAL SOLO

KEYBOARD MUSIC

PIANO, TWO HANDS (including harpsichord)

ADAMS, George
Sonata (1959) CFP

ADLER, Samuel
Capriccio (in: New Music for the Piano)
L-G
Sonata breve OX

ALEXANDER, Joseph
Incantation (in: New Music for the
Piano) L-G
12 bagatelles GEN

AMRAM, David
Sonata CFP

ANTHEIL, George
Prelude in D-minor (in: U.S.A., Vol.
II) MCA
Sonata No. 2 (The airplane) NME
Sonata No. 4 WEIN
Two toccatas GS

AUSTIN, Larry
Piano set in open style CPE
Piano variations MJQ

BABBITT, Milton
Partitions (in: New Music for the
Piano) L-G
Semi-simple variations TP
Three compositions AMP

BACON, Ernst
Flight B&H
The pig-town fling (in: New Music for
the Piano) L-G
Sombrero (in: U.S.A., Vol. I) MCA

BARBER, Samuel
Excursions, Op. 20 GS
Nocturne, Op. 33 GS
Sonata, Op. 26 GS
Souvenirs, Op. 28 (ballet suite; arr.
by composer) GS
Waltz. Schottische. Pas de deux.

Two-step. Hesitation-tango. Galop.

BARTOW, Nevett
Variations and fugue OX

BAUER, Marion
Aquarelle SHAW
A fancy SHAW
Four piano pieces B&H
Chromaticon. Ostinato. Toccata.
Syncope.
From New Hampshire woods GS
White birches. Indian pipes.
Pine-trees.
Turbulence EBM

BAZELON, Irwin
Five pieces WEIN
Sonatina WEIN
Suite for young people PIC
Part I: Little serenade. Christmas
carol. Dance for a tomboy.
Lullaby. Cowboy tune. Prayer.
Part II: Prelude. The clown and
the puppet. Circus parade. The
haunted chateau. Dance of an elf.
Goblins and ghosts.

BEALE, James
Sonata No. 2 GAL

BECKER, John J.
Sound piece, No. 5, "Sonata for
piano" TP

BERGER, Arthur
Intermezzo (in: American Composers
of Today) EBM
Rondo MER
Three bagatelles EBM
Two episodes, 1933 (in: New Music
for the Piano) L-G

BERGSMA, William
Tangents CF
Vol. 1: Fanfare. Prophecies (1st

prophecy; 2nd prophecy). The
animal world (unicorns; fishes;
Mr. Darwin's serenade).
Vol. 2: Masques (1st masque; 2nd
masque). Pieces for Nickie (for
Nickie Happy; for Nickie Angry;
for Nickie Asleep). Fanfare.
Three fantasies HAR

BERKOWITZ, Sol
Syncopations (in: New Music for the
Piano) L-G

BERNSTEIN, Leonard
Four anniversaries GS
For Felicia Montealegre.
For Johnny Mehegan.
For David Diamond.
For Helen Coates.
Five anniversaries GS
For Elizabeth Rudolf.
For Lukas Foss.
For Elizabeth B. Ehrman.
For Sandy Gellhorn.
For Susanna Kyle.

BERRY, Wallace
Eight 20th century miniatures CF
Chorale.   Folk song.   Habanera.
March.   Melody.   Ostinato.
Polka.   Waltz.

BLACKWOOD, Easley
Three short fantasies, Op. 16 GS

BOWLES, Paul
Carretera de Estepona (Highway to
Estepona) EBM
Dance (in: U.S.A., Vol. II) MCA
Huapango No. 1 and 2 SHAW
Six preludes MER
Sonatina EV

BRIGGS, Ralph
Facetious CPI
Toccata CF

BRIGHT, Houston
Four for piano (a short suite) AMP

BRITAIN, Radie
Epiphyllum RBB
Prelude NAK
Torillo RBB

BROWN, Earle
Folio & 4 systems AMP
(also can be played on more than

one piano and/or with various com-
binations of instruments. See also
"Full Symphony")
Perspectives (1952) AMP
Three pieces (1951) AMP

BRUNSWICK, Mark
Six bagatelles (in: New Music for the
Piano) L-G

BURGE, David
Eclipse II CPE

BURT, George
Four short piano pieces VAL

CAGE, John
Amores (1943) CFP
No. I: for prepared piano & 2 perc
No. IV: for prepared piano & 2 perc
(NOTE: For Nos. II and III, see
"Percussion")
Bacchanale (1938) (for prepared piano)
CFP
Dream (1948) CFP
In a landscape (1948) CFP
Metamorphosis (1938) CFP
Music for Marcel Duchamp (1947)
(for prepared piano) CFP
Music for piano 4-19 (1953) CFP
Music for piano 20-36 (1955) CFP
Music for piano 20-36; 37-52 (1955)CFP
Music for piano 69-84 (1956) CFP
(NOTE: All pieces in above four
series of "Music for piano" may be
performed, in whole or in part, by
any number of pianists.)
Music of changes, Vols. I-IV (1951)
CFP
The perilous night (1944) (for pre-
pared piano) CFP
Prelude for meditation (1944) (for pre-
pared piano) CFP
Root of an unfocus (1944) (for pre-
pared piano) CFP
The seasons (ballet in 1 act, 1947)
(piano transcription by composer)
CFP (See also "Full Symphony")
Seven Haiku (1952) CFP
Sonatas and interludes (for prepared
piano) CFP
Two pastorales (1951) (for prepared
piano) CFP
A valentine out of season (1944) (for
prepared piano) CFP

CALABRO, Louis
Diversities EV

Arietta. Blues. Raga.
Sonatina EV
Suite of seven EV
Prelude. Hymn. Pastoral.
Nocturne. Bounce. Blues. Finale.

CARPENTER, John Alden
Diversions: five pieces for piano GS
Danza GS
Impromptu GS
Polonaise Americaine GS
Skyscrapers: a ballet of modern
American life GS
Tango Americaine GS

CARTER, Elliott
Sonata (1945-46) MER

CASTALDO, Joseph
Sonatina HE
Toccata HE

CAZDEN, Norman
Eight preludes B&H
Sonata, Op. 53, No. 3 L-G
Sonatina, Op. 7 NME
Twenty-one evolutions, Op. 4 B&H
Variations, Op. 26 MER

CHADABE, Joel
3 ways of looking at a square CPE

CHANLER, Theodore
Calm (in: U.S.A., Vol. II) MCA
A child in the house MER
Adults conversing. Mooning.
Nagging mother. Quiet moment.
Little dance. Being naughty.
Being sorry. Being good. The
story of the tortoise and the hare.
Night prayers. Sweet dreams.
Three short pieces B&H
Toccata MER

CHOU, Wen-Chung
The willows are new (after Wang
Wei's Yang Kuan) CFP

CLOKEY, Joseph W.
Symphonic piece (with organ) JF

COLE, Ulric
Vignette (I. II. III.) JF

COPLAND, Aaron
The cat and the mouse (1950) B&H
Dance panels (ballet in 7 sections)
B&H (See also "Small or Cham-

ber Orchestra")
Down in a country lane B&H
Fantasy (1957) B&H
Four piano blues (1948) B&H
Freely and poetic. Soft and
languid. Muted and sensuous.
With bounce.
Our town, three excerpts (1940) B&H
Story of our town. Conversation at
the soda fountain. The resting
place on the hill.
Passacaglia (1922) SMPC
Piano Variations (1930) B&H
Rodeo (ballet suite; arr. composer)
(1942) B&H
Buckaroo holiday. Transition.
Corral nocturne. Ranch house
party. Saturday night waltz.
Hoe-down.
Sonata (1941) B&H
Two children's pieces (1936) CF
Sunday afternoon music.
The young pioneers.

CORTÉS, Ramiro
Prelude TP
Suite EV
Sinfonia. Capriccio. Arioso
sentimentale. Finale.

COWELL, Henry
Amerind suite SHAW
The power of the snake. The
lover plays his flute. Deer dance.
Amiable conversation AMP
Anger dance AMP
Antimony AMP
Celtic set GS
Reel. Caoine. Hornpipe.
Dynamic motion AMP
Episode AMP
Fabric AMP
The harp of life AMP
The harper-minstrel sings CF
Irish legends AMP
The tides of Manaunaum. The hero
sun. The voice of Hir.
The Irishman dances CF
The lilt of the reel AMP
Piano music (in one vol.) AMP
Advertisement. Aeolian harp. The
banshee. Episode. Exultation.
Fabric. The tides of Manaunaum.
Tiger. Two-part invention.
Sinister resonance AMP
Six "ings" AMP
Floating. Frisking. Fleeting.
Scooting. Wafting. Seething.

Snows of Fuji-Yama AMP
Square dance tune EBM
What's this AMP

CRAWFORD-SEEGER, Ruth
Four preludes NME
Piano study TP

CRESTON, Paul
Five dances, Op. 1 SHAW
  Daemonic. Primitive idyl.
  Villanella. Sarabande lugubre.
  Tarantella.
Five little dances GS
  Rustic dance. Languid dance.
  Toy dance. Pastoral dance.
  Festive dance.
Five two-part inventions GS
Metamorphoses MIL
Prelude and dance No. 1 MER
Prelude and dance No. 2 SHAW
Seven theses SHAW
Six preludes, Op. 38 MCA
Sonata, Op. 9 SHAW
Three narratives MIL

CRUMB, George
Five pieces for the piano MIL
  Quasi improvisato. Ruvido.
  Notturno. Ruvido. Senza misura.

CURRAN, Alvin
First piano piece CPE

DAHL, Ingolf
Fanfares (in: New Music for the
  Piano) L-G
Sonata seria TP

DE FILIPPI, Amedeo
4th sonatina HE

DE GASTYNE, Serge
Proem EV

DELLO JOIO, Norman
Night song (in: American Composers
  of Today) EBM
Nocturne in E-major CF
Nocturne in F-sharp-minor CF
Prelude: To a young dancer GS
Prelude: To a young musician GS
Sonata No. 1 HAR
Sonata No. 2 GS
Sonata No. 3 CF
Suite GS
Suite from the ballet On stage! GS
  Overture. Scene à deux. Polka.

Pas de deux. Waltz finale.

DIAMOND, David
Alone at the piano, Books 1 & 2 SMPC
Prelude and fugue, No. 4 (in: U.S.A.,
  Vol. II) MCA
A private world (13 pieces for young
  pianists) SMPC
  At the bottom of the sea. Sifting
  and sorting. A private world.
  Under the open sky. Stepping
  stones. A mysterious game.
  Stumbling blocks. A sad story.
  Go-as-you please! Quickened time.
  Melancholy invention. A poetic
  dream. A happy story.
Sonata SMPC
Sonatina MER
Then and now SMPC
The tomb of Melville MCA

DIEMER, Emma Lou
Serenade B&H

DONOVAN, Richard
Suite NME
  Prelude. Hornpipe. Air. Jig.

DUKELSKY, Vladimir (DUKE, Vernon)
Barrel organ barcarolle MCA
Homage to Boston MCA
  Charles River. Boston Common.
  Molly. The poet and his wife.
  Dining at the Ritz. Prokofieff in
  Louisburg Square. Midnight train.
Parisian suite BB
  A morning stroll. An American
  girl. Flowers in the Place
  Madeleine. A spinster on a bicycle.
  Fisherman on the Seine. My
  grocer's dog. Sunday outing. Cafe
  Flore intellectual. An old boule-
  vardier. Lovers, lovers, every-
  where.
Sonata in E-flat major B&H
Sonata, "Souvenir de Venise" BB
Spring, 1931 B&H
Surrealist suite MCA
  Beach and rocks. Cherrystones in
  love. Rhumba danced by a wilting
  telephone. A lady with a chest of
  drawers. The exploding giraffe.
  Epitaph to a melting watch. The
  headless glamour woman. The
  frolicking sardines. Parade of
  paranoics.
Two pieces B&H
  Romance. Rondo.

ELMORE, Robert
 Venite adoremus (festival prelude)
  (with organ) JF

ELWELL, Herbert
 Sonata OX

ENGLE, Lehman
 Sonata B&H

EPSTEIN, Alvin
 Divertimento WLP
 Elegie. Fugue. Toccatina.
 Lied. Burlesque.

EVETT, Robert
 Second sonata PIC

FAITH, Richard
 Legend S-B

FAREWELL, Arthur
 Navajo war dance, No. 2, Op. 29
  MER
 Sourwood mountain GS

FELDMAN, Morton
 Extensions III CFP
 Illusions NME
 Intermission V CFP
 Intersection II and III (graphs) CFP
 Last pieces CFP
 Piano piece 1952 CFP
 Piano piece 1955 CFP
 Piano piece 1956a CFP
 Piano piece 1956b CFP
 Piano piece (1963) CFP
 Three pieces CFP
 Two intermissions CFP
 Vertical thoughts 4 CFP

FINE, Irving
 Music for piano GS
 Prelude. Waltz-gavotte.
 Variations. Interlude-finale.

FINE, Vivian
 Sinfonia and fugato (in: New Music
  for the Piano) L-G

FINK, Michael
 Three lyric pieces ECS
 1. Song. 2. Passacaglia.
 3. Chorale.

FINNEY, Ross Lee
 Fantasy B&H
 Nostalgic waltzes MER

Sonata No. 1 in D-minor NME
Sonata No. 3 in E-minor VAL
Sonata No. 4 in E-major MER
Hymn. Invention. Nocturne.
 Toccata.
Sonata quasi una fantasia CFP

FLAGELLO, Nicolas
 Divertimento (with perc) MP
  (See also "Percussion")
 Episodes GEN
 March. Lullaby. Pulcinella.
 Prelude, ostinato and fugue GEN
 Sonata (1952) GEN
 Three dances GEN
 Abstract dance. Ceremonial
 dance. Tarantella.

FLANAGAN, William
 Sonata PIC

FLOYD, Carlisle
 Episodes B&H
 Vol. I: First lyric piece. Second
  lyric piece. Scherzino. Third
  lyric piece. Fourth lyric piece.
  Marching hymn. An ancient air.
  Arietta. Lullaby. Chorale.
  Ballad. Pavane. Serenade.
 Vol. II: Fanfare. Waltz. Pro-
  cessional. Siciliano. Dialogue.
  Bagatelle. Jig. Night song.
  Caprice. Impromptu. Morning
  song. Dance.
 Sonata (1958) B&H

FONTRIER, Gabriel
 Little suite GEN

FOSS, Lukas
 Fantasy rondo GS
 Four two-voiced inventions GS
 Scherzo ricercato (1953) CF

FREED, Isadore
 Five pieces (1928-30) AMP
 Intrada and fugue SHAW
 Pastorales AMP
 Prelude, canzonet, and caprice EV
 Sonata (1933) AMP

FULEIHAN, Anis
 Air and fugue on white keys SMPC
 Around the clock SMPC
 Dancing SMPC
 Fifteen short pieces CF
 Madrigal. Canon. Motet.
 Rhythmic episode. Slow waltz.

Five-eight. Invention. Scherzino.
Formula. Conversation. Ameri-
can incident. Plaintive waltz.
Toccatino. Reflection. Major-
minor.
Five tributes SMPC
Prelude. Minuet. Gavotte.
Sicilienne. Capriccio.
From the Aegean SMPC
Serenade. Tango. Sicilienne.
Greek dance.
Fugue CF
Harvest chant GS
Sonata No. 1 SMPC
Sonata No. 2 SMPC
Sonata No. 4 SMPC
Sonatina No. 1 MCA
Sonatina No. 2 MCA
To the young prince (in: U.S.A.,
Vol. I) MCA
Twilight mood SMPC

GEORGE, Earl
Three rounds CF

GERSHWIN, George
Preludes W-7
Rhapsody in blue (original solo) W-7

GIANNINI, Vittorio
Prelude and fughetta TP
Sonata for pianoforte COL
Variations on a cantus firmus EV
Moderato (var. 1-10). Aria (var.
11-12). Taccata (var. 13-22).
Interlude (var. 23-24).

GIANNINI, Walter
Modal variations AME
Sonatina AME

GIDEON, Miriam
Canzona NME
Piano suite No. 3 (in: New Music
for the Piano) L-G

GOLDMAN, Richard Franko
Aubades MER
Etude on white keys MER
The Lee rig MER
Sonatina MER

GOTTSCHALK, Louis Moreau
Album for the piano GS
Bamboula. Le bananier. The
banjo. Berceuse. The last hope.
Marche de nuit. Miserere du
Trovatore. Ojos Criollos. Poète

mourant. Printemps d'amour
mazurka. Réponds-moi.
Album of piano music TP
The banjo. Ricordati. Bamboula.
Le bananier. Pasquinade. The
last hope. L'union-concert.
Paraphrase on American national
airs.
Souvenir de Porto Rico (Marche des
Gibaros) TP

GOULD, Morton
Americana (five mood sketches) CF
Corn cob (barn dance). Indian
nocturne. Hillbilly. Night song.
Music hall.
Pavanne MIL
Rag - blues - rag (in: New Music
for the Piano) L-G
Sonatina MIL

GREEN, Ray
Dance set AME
An American bourée. An American
pastoral. An American rigaudon.
Dance theme and variations AME
Festival fugues (an American toccata)
AME
Prelude promenade. Holiday fugue.
Fugal song. Prelude pastorale.
Jubilant fugue.
Short sonatas (A-major, C-major,
D-major, F-major) AME
Sonata brevis AME
Twelve inventions AME

GRIFFES, Charles T.
Fantasy pieces GS
Barcarolle. Notturno. Scherzo.
Roman sketches GS
Clouds. Fountain of Acqua Paola.
Nightfall. White peacock.
Sonata GS
Three preludes CFP
Three tone-pictures GS
The lake at evening. The vale of
dreams. Night winds.

GRIFFIS, Elliot
Arabesque RBB
Canticle RBB
Chaconne RBB
Dialogue RBB
Invention RBB
Nocturne RBB
Sonata CF
The palace. The lake.
The goblins. The fête.

Transmutations RBB

GRUENBERG, Louis
Jazz masks, No. 2, Op. 30a TP
Polychromatics, Op. 16 TP

HAIEFF, Alexei
Five pieces B&H
Four juke box pieces B&H
Waltz. March. Nocturno. Polka.
Gifts and semblances B&H
For and about Aaron. Two
ostinati. To hang on a Christmas
tree. Sirocco-porto ercole.
Notes of thanks CHAP
Canzonetta sporca. Minsky's sans
souci. Love song Italienne.
Chanteuse. Echo berceuse.
Finalino.
Saints' wheel (variations on a circle
of fifths) CHAP
Sonata CHAP
Three bagatelles (pno or hpcd or
ob and bsn) BB

HALL, Richard
Etude CFP

HANSON, Howard
Clog dance, Op. 13 CF
Three miniatures CF
Reminiscence. Lullaby. Longing.

HARADA, Higo
Sketch, Op. 7, HE

HARRIS, Roy
American ballads CF
Streets of Laredo. Wayfaring
stranger. The bird. Black is the
color of my true love's hair. Cod
liver ile.
Little suite GS
Bells. Sad news. Children at
play. Slumber.
Piano suite MIL
Occupation. Contemplation.
Recreation.
Sonata, Op. 1 AMP
Toccata CF

HARRISON, Lou
Prelude and sarabande (1937) MER
Six cembalo sonatas (1935-1940) NME
Suite CFP
Prelude. Aria. Conductus.
Interlude. Rondo.

HARTLEY, Walter S.
Sonata for flute and harpsichord TP
(See also "Flute")

HAUBIEL, Charles
American rhapsody CPI
Ariel EBM

HAUFRECHT, Herbert
Etudes in blues (1951) AMP
Capriccio. Dialogue. Nocturne.
Quasi ostinato. Toccata.
Three nocturnes AMP

HEIDEN, Bernhard
Sonata No. 2 (1952) AMP

HELM, Everett
Brasiliana suite CF
I would flee thee. Pardon, Emilia.
Taccata Brasileira.
Sonata brevis HAR
New horizons (12 pieces for piano) GS
By way of introduction. Pastorale.
Three-legged dance. Fugue.
Bitonal study. Dialogue. Canon.
Abstraction. Soliloquy. Dreams.
Nocturne. Hommage a Scarlatti.

HELPS, Robert
Image (in: New Music for the Piano)
L-G
Portrait CFP
Recollections CFP
1. In memorian. 2. Interlude.
3. Epilogue.
Three etudes CFP

HOIBY, Lee
Capriccio on five notes B&H
Five preludes GS
Toccata GS

HOPKINSON, Francis
Seven songs for the harpsichord MA

HOVHANESS, Alan
Achtamar PIC
Allegro on a Pakistan lute tune (in:
New Music for the Piano) L-G
Artinis (Urarduan: Sun god), Op. 39
CFP
Bardo sonata, Op. 192 CFP
Bare November day (hpcd or org),
Op. 210 CFP
Dark river and distant bell (clav, pno
or hpcd), Op. 212 CFP

Do you remember the last silence?,
Op. 152 CFP
Fantasy, Op. 16 CFP
Fantasy on an Ossetin tune, Op. 85,
No. 6 PIC
5 visionary landscapes, Op. 214
CFP
Haiku, Nos. 1-3, Op. 113 CFP
(Nos. 4, 5 for piano & perc--
see "Percussion")
Hymn to a celestial musician, Op.
111, No. 3 PIC
Invocations to Vahaken CFP
No. 1 for piano; Nos. 2-5 for
piano and perc (See "Percussion")
Jhala, Op. 103 PIC
Lake of Van sonata, Op. 175 CFP
Macedonian mountain dance, Op.
144, No. 1 CFP
Madras sonata, Op. 176 CFP
Mazert Nman Rehani (Thy hair is
like a basil leaf) CFP
Mountain dance, No. 2 CFP
Mystic flute CFP
Orbit No. 2, Op. 102, No. 2 PIC
Pastoral No. 1, Op. 111, No. 2 PIC
Poseidon sonata, Op. 191 CFP
Shalimar, Op. 177 (suite) CFP
Fantasy. 1st interlude. Jhala of
the fountains. 2nd interlude.
Jhala march. Rain Jhala. 3rd
interlude. Jhala of the waterfall.
Sonata, Op. 145 CFP
Sonata ricercare, Op. 12 CFP
Passacaglia. Mirror fugue.
Fugue.
Sonatina, Op. 120 CFP
Suite, Op. 96 CFP
Three preludes and fugues, Op. 10
CFP
Toccata and fugue, Op. 6 CFP
Twelve Armenian folk songs, Op.
43 CFP
Two ghazals, Op. 36 CFP
Two pieces CFP
Farewell to the mountains.
Vanadour.

IMBRIE, Andrew
Sonata VAL

INCH, Herbert
Nocturne CF

IVES, Charles
Anti-abolitionist riots in the 1830's
and 1840's TP
Some south-paw pitching MER

Sonata No. 1 PIC
Sonata No. 2, "Concord" AMP
Emerson. Hawthorne.
The Alcotts. Thoreau.
Three-page sonata MER
Twenty-two and three protests NME

JACOBI, Frederick
Introduction and toccata SHAW
Moods (in: U.S.A., Vol. I) MCA
Prelude in E-minor SHAW
Sonatina for harpsichord CFP
Toccata SHAW

JOHNSON, Hunter
Sonata MER

JOHNSON, Lockrem
Chaconne, Op. 29 MER

JOHNSTON, Ben
Celebration (orchesis) MM
Knocking piece (for piano interior: 2
players) CPE

JONES, Charles
Three pieces MER

KALMAN, Charles
New York impressions GEN

KAPP, Richard
Simple etudes for advanced beginners
GEN

KAY, Ulysses
Four inventions MCA
Ten short essays MCA

KENNAN, Kent
Three preludes GS
Two preludes (in: New Music for the
Piano) L-G

KERR, Harrison
Four preludes AMP
Sonata No. 2 B&H

KIM, Earl
Two bagatelles (in: New Music for
the Piano) L-G

KIRCHNER, Leon
Little suite MER
Prelude. Song. Toccata. Fantasy.
Sonata (1948) AMP

KLEIN, John
Gotham suite AMP
Queen's minuet. Bronx bourée.
Brooklyn boogie. Manhattan
pavane. Richmond gavotte.

KOCH, Frederick
Anniversary toccata TP

KOHN, Karl
Five bagatelles CF
Five pieces CF
Rhapsody CF

KOHS, Ellis
Piano variations MER
Toccata (pno or hpcd) MER
Variations on L'Homme armé MER

KORN, Peter Jona
Eight bagatelles B&H
Sonata No. 1 B&H

KOUTZEN, Boris
Eidolons GEN
Sonatina (1931) GEN

KRAEHENBUEHL, David
Variations for two AMP

KRAFT, Leo
Allegro giocoso (in: New Music for
the Piano) L-G

KUBIK, Gail
Celebrations and epilogue (1938-50)
SMPC
Autumn rites. Birthday piece.
Joy ride. "Wedded bliss." A
gay time. Poem. 4 planes,
40 men: an elegy. Movies--
Saturday night. Epilogue.
Sonata SMPC
Sonatina MER

KUPFERMAN, Meyer
Little sonata (1947) GEN
Partita for piano GEN
Praeludium. Arioso. Toccata.
Recitative (1947) GEN
Sonata on jazz elements GEN
Variations GEN

KURKA, Robert
For the piano MER
Sonata CHAP
Sonatina, Op. 6 WEIN

LADERMAN, Ezra
Sonata No. 1 OX
Sonata No. 2 OX

LA MONTAINE, John
Fuguing set CF
Prologue. Fugue in G. Pastorale.
Fugue in D. Cadenza. Fugue in C.
Six dance preludes, Op. 18 BB
Toccata BB
Twelve relationships (a set of
canons) PJS

LAYTON, Billy Jim
Three studies, Op. 5 GS

LEE, Dai-Keong
Sonatina MIL
Three preludes B&H

LEES, Benjamin
Fantasia (1954) B&H
Kleidoscopes (1959) (ten pieces)B&H
Six ornamental etudes B&H
Sonata breve (1956) B&H
Sonata No. 4 B&H
Toccata SHAW

LESSARD, John
Little concert (suite) GEN
Prelude. Dance. Lullaby.
March. Pastoral. Procession.
Mask MER
New worlds for the young pianist,
Vols. I and II GEN
Toccata in four movements (pno or
hpcd) GEN

LEWIS, John
Jazz themes with improvisations SF

LIEBERSON, Goddard
Pieces for advanced children or
retarded adults MIL
I. Five songs without Mendelssohn:
Whistling boy on horseback. The
same boy, five years later, in
Paris. My neighbor studies voice.
My father plays pizzicato. An
aimless walk in the woods.
II. Six technical studies (which will
teach you nothing): Prelude.
Melody for the left hand. Melody
for the right hand. Minor seconds. Safe on third. In fifth
form.
III. Eight studies in musicology
(which will teach you a great deal):

Mozart without one mistake. How
to handel a Bach violin solo.
How to be a Soviet composer.
The piano in the distance playing
Chopin. Shostakovitch's vacation
on a collective farm. Liszt, my
children (and you will hear an
enharmonic change). Aaron
Copland shakes hands with Abraham Lincoln. Tschaikovsky's
last waltz.

LLOYD, Norman
Episodes EV
Sonata MER
Three scenes from memory EV

LOCKWOOD, Normand
Lyric arabesque TP

LOMBARDO, Robert
Laude, fuga e cavatina CFP

LUENING, Otto
Eight preludes NME
Two inventions MER

LUNETTA, Stanley
Piano music CPE

LYBBERT, Donald
Sonata brevis CFP

MacCOLL, Hugh
Noël sketches SHAW
Pedal points on C, F, C-sharp,
F-sharp, D, G, A, D-sharp,
A-flat, B. Noël.

MacDOWELL, Edward
Bluette in E-flat major, Op. 46,
No. 8 AMP
Elfin dance, Op. 46, No. 5 AMP
Etude de concert, Op. 36 CF
Four little poems, Op. 32 (rev. 1906)
AMP
The brook. The eagle.
Moonshine. Winter.
Intermezzo, Op. 10, No. 4 CF
Modern suite, No. 1, Op. 10 AMP
Prelude. Intermezzo.
New England idyls, Op. 62 GS, KAL
An old garden. Mid-summer.
Mid-winter. With sweet lavender.
In deep woods. Indian idyl. To
an old white pine. From Puritan
days. From a log cabin. The
joy of autumn.

Praeludium, Op. 10, No. 1 CF
Scotch poem, Op. 31, No. 2 CF
Sea pieces, Op. 55 GS, KAL
To the sea. From a wandering
iceberg. A.D. 1620. Starlight.
Song. From the depths. Nautilus.
In mid-ocean.
Second suite, "Indian" AMP
Legend. Love song. In war time.
Dirge. Village festival.
Select piano pieces CFP
Op. 37: Les orientales--Danse
Andalouse. Op. 51: Woodland
sketches--to a wild rose; in
autumn; from "Uncle Remus;" a
deserted farm; by a meadow brook.
Op. 55: Sea pieces--Anno Domini
1620; song. Op. 61: Fireside
tales--an old love story; of sala-
manders; by smoldering embers.
Op. 62: New England idyls.
Sonata No. 1, "Tragica" KAL
Sonata No. 2, Op. 50, "Eroica" AMP
Sonata No. 3, Op. 57, "Norse" KAL
Sonata No. 4, Op. 59, "Keltic" KAL
Twelve virtuoso studies, Op. 46 AMP
Novelette. Moto perpetuo. Wild
chase. Valse triste. Improvisa-
tion. Elfin dance. Burlesque.
Bluette. Traeumerei. March wind.
Impromptu. Polonaise.
Witches' dance, Op. 17, No. 2 CF
Woodland sketches, Op. 51 AMP
To a wild rose. Will o' the wisp.
At an old trysting place. In
autumn. From an Indian lodge.
To a water lily. From Uncle
Remus. A deserted farm. By a
meadow brook. Told at sunset.

MAILMAN, Martin
Petite partita MIL
Prelude. Invention. Arietta.
Toccatina. Chorale. Dance.

MARTIRANO, Salvatore
Cocktail music MCA

MASON, Daniel Gregory
Color contrasts (in: U.S.A., Vol. II)
MCA
Country pictures, Op. 9 AMP
Vol. 1: Cloud pageant. Chimney
swallows.
Vol. 2: At sunset. The whippoor-
will. The quiet hour. Night wind.
Three preludes EBM

MAURY, L.
Wind-sweep TP

MAYER, William
Sonata CF

McKAY, George Frederick
Dance suite No. 2 TP
Explorations, Vols. I and II JF

MENNIN, Peter
Five pieces (1949) CF
Prelude. Aria. Variation-
canzona. Canto. Toccata.
Sonata CF

MILANO, Robert
Toccata MER

MILLER, Jacques
Impromptu in E-flat minor MER

MOEVS, Robert
Fantasia sopra un motivo (1951) AMP
Sonata (1950) AMP

MOORE, Douglas
Prelude TP
Suite CF
Prelude. Reel. Dancing school.
Barn dance. Air. Procession.

MUCZYNSKI, Robert
Fables GS
Six preludes, Op. 6 GS
Sonatina AMP
Suite, Op. 13 GS
Festival. Flight. Vision.
Labyrinth. Phantom. Scherzo.
A summer journal, Op. 19 GS
Morning promenade. Park scene.
Midday. Birds. Solitude.
Night rain. Jubilee.

MYROW, Frederic
Theme and variations MIL

OVERTON, Hall
Polarities No. 1 (in: New Music
for the Piano) L-G

PALMER, Robert
Three epigrams PIC
Three preludes PIC
Three preludes VAL
Toccata ostinato EV

PANETTI, Joan
Cavata for piano (1965) AB

PERLE, George
Interrupted story TP
Short sonata TP
Six preludes (in: New Music for the
Piano) L-G
Sonata, Op. 27 SMPC

PERSICHETTI, Vincent
Parades EV
Poems (2 vols.) EV
Vol. I: Unroll the flicker's rousing
drum. Soft is the collied night.
Gather for festival bright weed
and purple shell. Wake subtler
dreams, and touch me nigh to
tears. Ravished lute, sing to her
virgin ears. Whose thin fraud I
wink at privily.
Vol. II: And warm winds spilled
fragrance. To whose more clear
than crystal voice. Sleep, weary
mind. Dust in sunlight. Make
me drunken with deep red torrents
of joy.
Serenade No. 2 EV
Tune. Strum. Pluck.
Serenade No. 7 EV
Walk. Waltz. Play. Sing.
Chase. Sleep.
Sonata No. 3 EV
Sonata No. 4 EV
Sonata No. 5 EV
Sonata No. 6 EV
Sonata No. 7 EV
Sonata No. 8 EV
Sonata No. 9 EV
Sonata No. 10 EV
Sonata No. 11 EV
Sonatinas (1-6) EV
Variations for an album MER

PHILLIPS, Burrill
Five various and sundry EV
Dialogue. Tide-mark. The
traveler. Music at night.
Jubilation.
A set of three informalities GS
Blues. Scherzo. Sonatina.
The chatterer TP
Three divertimenti EV
Fancy dance. Homage to
Monteverdi. Brag.
Toccata EV

PINKHAM, Daniel
Partita for hpcd CFP
Toccata. Andante. Fugue.
Three inventions. Canons.
Interlude and rondo. Fantasia.
Recitativo. Scherzo and trio.
Envoi.

PISTON, Walter
Improvisation (in: U.S.A., Vol. I) MCA
Passacaglia MER

PORTER, Quincy
Sonata CFP

POWELL, Mel
Etude (in: New Music for the Piano)
L-G

PREVIN, Andre
Impressions MCA

RAPHLING, Sam
Five forecasts MCA
Novelty suite MIL
Fugue. Blues. Workout.
Sonata No. 1 MIL
Sonata No. 3 EM
Sonata No. 5 GEN
Sonatina No. 1 MER
Sonatina No. 2 GEN
Twenty-four etudes, Vols. I and II
GEN

READ, Gardner
Capriccio, Op. 27, No. 3(in: U.S.A.,
Vol. II) MCA
Poem, Op. 20 JF

REIF, Paul
Seven musical moments GEN
1. Pensive. 2. Impatient.
3. Friendly. 4. Fickle.
5. Sleepy. 6. Laughing.
7. Heroic.

REUNING, Sanford H.
Fantasy for toy drums and piano MP
(See also "Percussion")

REYNOLDS, Roger
Epigrams and evolution CFP
Fantasy for pianist CFP

RIEGGER, Wallingford
Blue Voyage, Op. 6 GS

Four tone pictures, Op. 14 CFP
Prelude. Angles and curves.
Wishful thinking. Grotesque.
New and old (12 pieces for piano)B&H
The augmented triad. The major
second. The tritone. The twelve
tones. Shifted rhythm. Twelve
upside down. Seven times seven.
Chromatics. Tone clusters.
Dissonant counterpoint. Polytonality.
Fourths and fifths.
New dance, Op. 18 AMP
Petite etude, Op. 62 TP
Toccata, Op. 38 (No. 12 from New
and old) B&H

ROCHBERG, George
Arioso TP
Bartokiana TP
Nach Bach, fantasy for hpcd or
pno TP
Sonata-fantasia TP
Twelve bagatelles TP
(See also "Full Symphony Orchestra")

ROREM, Ned
Barcarolles CFP
A quiet afternoon PIC
The little boy lost. The little boy
found. Lonesome waltz. The
tiny tin dancers. Near the strange
garden. A trick. Evening rainbow.
Sonata No. 2 B&H
Sonata No. 3 CFP
Toccata CFP

RUBINSTEIN, Beryl
Arabesque CF
Caprice CF
Gigue CF
Guitarre CF
Nocturne CF

RUGGLES, Carl
Evocations (four chants) (revised,
1954) AME

RUSSELL, Armand
Sonata (with perc) MP
(See also "Percussion")

SCHICKLE, Peter
In my nine lives EV
Three folk settings EV

SCHIFRIN, Lalo
Jazz piano sonata MJQ

SCHRAMM, Harold
  Bharata sangita (Indian music) MCA

SCHUMAN, William
  Three piano moods TP
    Lyrical. Pensive. Dynamic.
  Three-score set GS
  Voyage GS
    Anticipation. Caprice. Realization.
    Decision. Retrospection.

SESSIONS, Roger
  From my diary EBM
  Sonata No. 1 AMP
  Sonata No. 2 EBM
  Sonata No. 3 EBM

SHAPERO, Harold
  Sonata in F-minor SMPC
  Three sonatas GS
  Variations in C-minor SMPC

SHAW, Arnold
  Mobiles: 10 graphic impressions EBM

SHEPHERD, Arthur
  Eclogue TP
  Exotic dance OX
  Gigue fantasque TP
  In mood ostinato TP
  Lento amabile TP
  Sonata No. 2 OX

SHIFRIN, Seymour
  Four cantos NME
  Trauermusik CFP

SIEGMEISTER, Elie
  American sonata EBM
  From my window CHAP
    1. Housewives' chatter. 2. Boy
    and girl. 3. Kids playing tag.
    4. Sunday afternoon. 5. Jitterbug.
    6. Moon on the pavement.
    7. Parade.
  Serenade CHAP
  Sonata No. 2 MCA
  Sunday in Brooklyn EBM
    Prospect Park. Sunday driver.
    Family at home. Children's story.
    Coney Island.
  Toccata in flight (from "Airplane
    suite") EBM

SKILTON, Charles Sanford
  Five miniatures CF
  Three Indian dances CF
  War dance CF

SMIT, Leo
  Fantasy, "The farewell" BB
  Rural elegy B&H
  Rondel for a young girl. Toccata-
    breakdown. Hymn.
  Seven characteristic pieces BB
    Prelude. Gigue. Pastorale.
    Arietta. Impromptu. Scherzino.
    Ostinato.
  Sonata in one movement MIL
  Variations in G-major B&H

SMITH, Hale
  Evocation CFP

SMITH, Julia
  Sonatina TP

SMITH, Leland
  Four etudes TP

SOWERBY, Leo
  Toccata MER

SPAULDING, Albert
  Berceuse CF
  Intermezzo CF
  Prelude CF
  Rhapsody CF

SPIES, Claudio
  Impromptu EV
  Three intermezzi EV

STARER, Robert
  Fantasia TP
  Five caprices SMPC
  Five preludes MCA
  Lullaby for Amittai MCA
  Prelude and toccata MCA
  Seven vignettes MCA
  Sketches in color MCA
    Purple. Shades of blue. Black
    and white. Bright orange. Grey.
    Pink. Crimson.
  Sonata MCA
  Sonata No. 2 MCA
  Three Israeli sketches MCA

STERNS, Peter Pindar
  Partita (1961) AMP

STEVENS, Halsey
  Eight Yugoslavian folk songs PIC
  Fantasia WLP
  Five Portuguese folk songs PIC
  Four bagatelles WLP
  Lyric piece TP

Partita (for pno or hpcd) PIC
Seventeen piano pieces WLP
  Another waltz. Bellsounds.
  Chaconne. Erratic rhythms. For
  the left hand alone. Finale. From
  a Roman sketch book. Hommage à
  Fréderic Chopin. Hommage à
  Muzio Clementi. Hommage à
  Arthur Honegger. Invention.
  Legato and staccato. Night pro-
  cession. Night song. Palindrome
  II. Prelude. Study in Hemiola.
Ritratti per pianoforte WLP
  Intrada. Arietta. Tema con
  quatro variazioni.
Sonata No. 3 AME
Sonatina No. 1 WLP
Sonatina No. 2 WLP
Sonatina No. 5 WLP
Sonatina No. 6 WLP
Study in Bulgarian rhythms WLP

STILL, William Grant
  Marionette (in: U.S.A., Vol. I) MCA
  Seven traceries JF
    Cloud cradles. Mystic pool.
    Muted laughter. Out of the silence.
    Woven silver. Wailing dawn. A
    bit of wit.

STRAIGHT, Willard
  Structure for piano B&H

SUBOTNICK, Morton
  Prelude No. 4 for piano and electronic sounds (1966) AMP

SWANSON, Howard
  Sonata WEIN

SYDEMAN, William
  Sonata ECS
  Variations for piano MCA

TALMA, Louise
  Alleluia in form of toccata CF
  Pastoral prelude CF
  Six etudes GS
  Sonata No. 1 CF

TAYLOR, Deems
  The smugglers CF

THOMSON, Virgil
  Day dream CF
  Eccentric dance CF
  Etudes CF
    Set 1: Repeating tremolo (fanfare).

Tenor lead (madrigal). Fingered
fifths (canon). Fingered glissando
(Aeolian harp). Double glissando
(waltz). For the weaker fingers
(music-box lullaby). Oscillating
arm (spinning song). Five-finger
exercise (portrait of Briggs
Buchanan). Parallel chords
(tango). Ragtime bass.
    Set 2: With trumpet and horn.
Pivoting on the thumb. Alternat-
ing octaves. Double sevenths.
The harp. Chromatic major
seconds (the wind). Chromatic
double harmonies (portrait of
Sylvia Marlowe). Broken arpeg-
gios (the waltzing waters).
Guitar and mandoline.
Filling station (ballet) B&H
Five two-part inventions EV
Portraits MER
  Album 1: Bugles and birds (Pablo
  Picasso). With fire and drums
  (Minna Curtis). An old song
  (Carrie Settheimer). Tango lulla-
  by (Mlle. Alvarez de Toledo).
  Solitude (Lou Harrison). Barca-
  rolle (Georges Hugnet). Fugue
  (Alexander Smallens). Alterna-
  tions (Maurice Grosser).
  Album 2: Aria (Germaine Hugnet).
  Portrait of R. Kirk Askew. In
  a bird cage (Lise Deharme).
  Catalan Waltz (Ramon Senabre).
  Five finger exercise (Leon Koch-
  nizky). Sea coast (Constance
  Askew). Meditation (Jere Abbott).
  Fanfare for France (Max Kahn).
  Album 3: Cantabile (Nicolas de
  Chatelain). Toccata (Mary Wid-
  ney). Pastoral (Jean Ozenne).
  Prelude and fugue (Agnes Rindge).
  The dream world (Peter Rose-
  Pulham). The bard (Sherry Man-
  gan). Souvenir (Paul Bowles).
  Canons with cadenza (Andre
  Ostier).
  Album 4: Tennis (Henry McBride).
  Hymn (Josiah Marvel). Lullaby
  which is also a spinning song
  (Howard Putzel). Swiss waltz
  (Sophie Tauber-Arp). Poltergeist
  (Hans Arp). Insistences (Louise
  Crane). The hunt (A.E. Austin,
  Jr.). Wedding music (Jean
  Watts).
Ragtime bass (available also in
  simplified version) CF

Sonata No. 4 EV
Tenor lead CF

TRAVIS, Roy
Five preludes TP

TRIMBLE, Lester
Five episodes MCA

VERRALL, John
Autumn sketches VAL
Four pieces for piano GAL
Prelude. Lament. Dance.
Toccata.
Ten sketches and miniatures VAL
Prelude I. Canons. Intermezzo.
Fughetta I. Allegretto. Prelude II.
Fughetta II. Arietta. Fugue.
Bizarria.

WAGNER, Joseph
Dance divertissement EBM
Four miniatures SMPC
Preface. Sarabande. Berceuse.
March.
Pastorale and toccata SMPC
Sonata in B-minor SMPC

WARD, Robert
Lamentation MER

WEBER, Ben
Fantasia (variations) EBM
Five bagatelles MER
Humoreske (in: New Music for the
Piano) L-G
New adventure TP
Three pieces, Op. 23 AMP

WEISGALL, Hugo
Graven images No. 3 TP
Sine nomine

WERLE, Frederick
Sonata brevis No. 2 BB
Toccata BB

WOLFF, Christian
For pianist CFP
For piano I CFP
For piano II CFP
Suite for prepared piano CFP

WUORINEN, Charles
Piano variations MM

YARDUMIAN, Richard
Chromatic sonata EV

Passacaglia, recitative and fugue EV
Prelude and chorale EV
Three preludes EV
Wind. Sea. Sky.

PIANO, FOUR HANDS
(*one piano; all others 2 pianos)

AITKEN, Hugh
*Four pieces, 4-hands EV

ANDRUS, Donald
Imbrications (with perc) AP
(See also "Percussion")

BACON, Ernst
The burr frolic AMP

BACON, Ernst and Otto Luening
Coal scuttle blues AMP

BARBER, Samuel
*Souvenirs, Op. 28 (ballet suite) GS
Waltz. Schottische. Pas de deux.
Two-step. Hesitation-tango.
Galop.

BEREZOWSKY, Nicolai
Fantasy, Op. 9 AMP

BERNSTEIN, Leonard
Age of anxiety (Symphony No. 2) GS

BOWLES, Paul
Night waltz AME
Sonata GS

BROWN, Earle
Available forms II (2-piano reduction
by composer) AMP
(See also "Full Symphony")
Folio and 4 systems for 2 or more
pianos and/or various instruments)
AMP

CAGE, John
A book of music for 2 prepared
pianos (1944) CFP
Experiences I (duo for 2 pno, 1945-48)
CFP
Three dances (1945) for 2 prepared
pianos CFP

CAZDEN, Norman
Stony hollow JS
(See also "Full Symphony")

CHADABE, Joel
Diversions CPE

CHANCE, John Barnes
Introduction and capriccio B&H
(See also "Band")

CHANLER, Theodore
Second joyful mystery (a fugue) AMP

CLOKEY, Joseph W.
The hill country FLAM
My old home town. The river
hills. Summer evenings.
Symphonic piece (with organ) JF

COPLAND, Aaron
Billy the kid (1938) (arr. composer)
B&H
The open prairie. Street in a
frontier town. Celebration dance.
Billy's death. The open prairie
again.
Danzon Cubano (1942) B&H
Hoe-down and Saturday night waltz
from "Rodeo" B&H
Waltz from Billy the Kid (1938) (arr.
composer) B&H

CORIGLIANO, John
Kaleidoscope GS

COWELL, Henry
Celtic set GS
Reel. Caoine. Hornpipe.

DELLO JOIO, Norman
Aria and toccata CF
*Family album EBM
Five images EBM
Suite from ballet "On Stage" EBM

DIAMOND, David
Concerto SMPC

DONOVAN, Richard
Adventure TP

DOUGHERTY, Celius
Music from seas and ships GS
Banks of the Sacramento. Sea-
calm. Mobile Bay.
Sonata No. 3 CF

DUKELSKY, Vladimir (DUKE, Vernon)
*Concerto in C TP

ELMORE, Robert
Venite adoramus (Festival prelude)
(with organ) JF

FELDMAN, Morton
Intermission VI (for 1 or 2 pianos,
4 hands) CFP
Ixion (summerspace--a ballet) (for 2
pianos (graph)) CFP
Piano (Three hands) CFP
*Piano CFP
Projection 3 for 2 pianos CFP
Two pianos CFP
Vertical thoughts 1 for 2 pianos CFP

FREED, Isadore
Carnival TP
Hard times TP

FULEIHAN, Anis
Toccata SMPC
Introduction. Variations.
Interlude. Fugue.

GERSHWIN, George
An American in Paris (arr. Gregory
Stone) W-7
Concerto in F W-7
Cuban overture (arr. Gregory Stone)
W-7
Preludes (arr. Gregory Stone) W-7
Rhapsody in blue W-7
Second rhapsody W-7

GIDEON, Miriam
*Hommage à ma jeunnesse TP
Sonatina TP

GOLDMAN, Richard Franko
Le bobino (burlesque in 3 scenes)
SMPC
Overture. Entr'acte. Le jazz cold.

GOULD, Morton
Dialogues CHAP
Recitative and chorale. Embellish-
ments and rondo. Dirge and
meditation. Variations and coda.
(See also "String or Chamber Or-
chestra with Solo")
Interplay (arr. composer) MIL

GRAHAM, Robert
*Shepherd's suite EV

GREEN, Ray
Dance sonata AME
Jig for a concert AME

HAIEFF, Alexei
Sonata CHAP

HAUBIEL, Charles
Suite passecaille HE
  Allemande. Gavotte.
  Menuet. Sarabande.

HEIDEN, Bernhard
*Sonata (1946) AMP

HEMMER, Eugene
Introduction and dance AME

HOVHANESS, Alan
Child in a garden CFP
Ko-ola-u, Op. 136 CFP
Mihr NME
Vijag CFP

IVES, Charles
From the steeples and the mountains
  (with trp, trb, bells or chimes) PIC
Three quarter-tone pieces CFP

JACOBI, Frederick
Concertino EV

KOUTZEN, Boris
Sonatina GEN

KUPFERMAN, Meyer
Sonata GEN

KURKA, Robert
*Dance suite, Op. 29 WEIN
  Prelude. Furiante. Polka.
  Waltz. Finale.

LA MONTAINE, John
Sonata, op. 25 EV

LEES, Benjamin
Sonata B&H

LUENING, Otto and Ernst Bacon
Coal scuttle blues AMP

LYBBERT, Donald
Movement CFP

MacDOWELL, Edward
Polonaise, Op. 46, No. 12 AMP

MASON, Daniel Gregory
Divertimento, Op. 26a CF
  March. Fugue.
  Prelude and fugue (with organ) JF

Scherzo CF

MEYEROWITZ, Jan
Homage to Hieronymus Bosch BB
St. John on Patmos. The prodigal
son. Ecce homo.

MOSS, Lawrence
*Omaggio EV

PALMER, Robert
Sonata PIC

PERSICHETTI, Vincent
Concertino EV
*Concerto EV
*Serenade No. 8 EV
Sonata, Op. 13 MCA

PHILLIPS, Burrill
*Serenade SMPC

PHILLIPS, Donald
Concerto in jazz MIL
  (See also "Full Symphony with Solo")

RAPHLING, Sam
Square dance EM
Square dance (from "American album")
  MER

RIEGGER, Wallingford
Canon and fugue, Op. 33c FLAM
The cry, Op. 22 (for 1 or 2 pianos,
  4 hands) PIC
Evocation, Op. 17 (for 1 or 2 pianos,
  4 hands) PIC
Finale from the "New Dance" AMP
Scherzo, Op. 13a PIC
Variations, Op. 54a (1954) AMP

ROREM, Ned
Sicilienne SMPC

RUSSELL, Robert
*Places GEN

SCHICKLE, Peter
The civilian barber (overture) EV
  (See also "Full Symphony")

SHAPERO, Harold
*Sonata MIL

SHIFRIN, Seymour
*The modern temper CFP

SMITH, Julia
American dance suite TP
Lost my partner. Negro lullaby.
Chicken reel.

STARER, Robert
Concerto for piano and winds MCA
(See also "Full Symphony with
Solo" and "Band")
Fantasia concertante MCA
The fringes of a ball (waltz var. on
theme by William Schuman) TP

TALMA, Louise
Four-handed fun CF

THOMSON, Virgil
Synthetic waltzes EV

TOWNSEND, Douglas
*Four fantasies on American folk
songs CFP
Follow the drinking gourd. The
New River train. Johnny has gone
for a soldier. Two in one.

WEAVER, Powell
Exultation (pièce symphonic) (with
organ) JF

WEISGALL, Hugo
Fugue and romance (1939) MER

WOLFF, Christian
*Duet I CFP
Duo for pianists I CFP
Duo for pianists II CFP

WOOLLEN, Russell
*Sonata for piano duet SMPC

PIANO, SIX HANDS

FELDMAN, Morton
Extensions IV (for 3 pianos) CFP
Two pieces (for 3 pianos) CFP

PIANO, EIGHT HANDS

DAHL, Ingolf
Quodlibet on American folk tunes
(for 2 pianos) CFP
("The fancy blue devil's breakdown")
featuring tunes such as: Boston

fancy; Deep blue sea; The devil's
dream; Old fiddler's breakdown;
California Joe; Old Zip Coon.

FELDMAN, Morton
Piece for four pianos CFP

ORGAN

ADLER, Samuel
Toccata, recitation and postlude OX
Two meditations MER
Arioso. Pastorale.

ATWELL, Richard
Christmas suite ABP
The shepherds. The angel Gabriel.
The chorus of angels.

BAILEY, Parker
Toccata, ricercata, finale HWG

BARBER, Samuel
Chorale prelude on "Silent night"
from Die Natale, Op. 37 GS
Toccata festiva (with vln, vlc, trp,
timp) (also for org and pno) GS
Wondrous love, Op. 34 (variations on
a shapenote hymn) GS

BARLOW, Wayne
Voluntaries on the hymn of the week
(3 sets of preludes, 1963, 1964,
1966) CPH

BECKLER, Stanworth
Three pieces for organ and brass
(3 trp, 4 hn, 3 trb, bar, tba) KING

BERLINSKI, Herman
The burning bush HWG
Processional MER
Three preludes for festivals MER

BIELAWA, Herbert
Fantasy on "Nicaea" SHAW

BIGGS, John
Aria and toccata WIM

BINGHAM, Seth
Agnus Dei, Op. 36, No. 2 JF
Baroques GAL
Bells of Riverside, Op. 36, No. 5 JF
Concerto for brass and organ (3 trp,
3 trb, perc, sn-drm) HWG

Fantasy in C HWG
The good shepherd GAL
Night sorrow, Op. 36, No. 4 JF
Passacaglia, Op. 40 JF
Pastoral psalms (suite) CF
Unto the hills. Forgotten graves.
Black cherries. Voice of the
tempest. Beside still waters.
Pastorale, Op. 16 HWG
Pioneer America, Op. 26 (2nd
organ suite) HWG
Prelude and fugue in C-minor HWG
Prelude and fughetta in F, Op. 36,
No. 1 JF
Prelude and fughetta on "St. Kevin"
GAL
Roulade HWG
Sonata of prayer and praise HWG
Prelude. Rapid lyric. Christmas
meditation. Finale. (with optional
solos in "Christmas meditation" for
S, A and T voices)
Suite, Op. 25 GS
Toccata on Leoni JF
Ut queant laxis CFP

BINKERD, Gordon
Andante AMP
Arietta AMP
Cantilena GAL

BLANCHARD, Robert
Preludio festivo HWG

BROWN, Rayner
Fugue and prelude WIM
Liturgical fugue WIM
Preludes WIM
Toccata WIM

BURNHAM, Cardon
Festival chorale with brass (3 trp,
4 hn, 2 trb, tba) KING

CARR, Benjamin
Andante HWG
Aria ABP

CASE, James H.
Sonnet HWG
Ye men of Galilee HWG

CHADWICK, George W.
Elegy HWG
Fantasia in E-flat HWG
Suite in variation form HWG

CHAPMAN, Roger
Festival overture CFP

CLAFFLIN, Avery
Three pieces HWG
Moissac. Silvacane. Albi.

CLOKEY, Joseph W.
Ballade in D HWG
Cantabile from "Symphonic fantasy"
HWG
Cathedral prelude JF
Fantasy on a mountain song JF
Legend HWG
Partita in G-major (with pno) HWG
Symphonic piece (with pno) JF
Three mountain sketches HWG
Canyon walls. Jagged peaks.
Wind in the pine trees.
A wedding suite JF

COPLAND, Aaron
Episode (1941) HWG
Preamble for a solemn occasion
(1950) B&H

COPLEY, R. Evan
Chorale toccata on "Lasst uns
erfreuen" HWG
Out of the depths HWG

COWELL, Henry
Hymn and fuguing tune No. 14 (1962)
AMP
Prelude AMP
Processional HWG

CRESTON, Paul
Fantasia, Op. 74 COL
Rapsodia breve, Op. 81 (for pedals)
COL
Suite, Op. 70 COL
Prelude. Prayer. Toccata.

DELAMARTER, Eric
Intermezzi HWG
Nocturnes HWG
The fountain. Nocturne at sunset.
Nocturne at twilight.
Toccatino HWG

DELLO JOIO, Norman
Antiphonal fantasy (with brass and
str) EBM
Laudation EBM

DIEMER, Emma Lou
Fantasie OX

Toccata OX

DIRKSEN, Richard
Prelude on "Urbs beata" HWG

DONATO, Anthony
Two pastels MER

DONOVAN, Richard
Paignion HWG
Two chorale preludes TP

EFFINGER, Cecil
Prelude and fugue HWG

ELKUS, Jonathan
Three medieval pieces MER

ELMORE, Robert
Humoresque GAL
Meditation on "Veni Emmanuel" with
brass (2 trp, 2 trb) JF
Night of the star GAL
Night song JF
Retrospection JF
12 interludes EV
Two choral preludes EV
1. Supplication on Arcadelt "Ave
Maria" 2. Triumph on "St.
Theodulph" by Teschner
Two pieces HWG
Air. Canone: trio all'ottava.
Venite adoramus (festival prelude)
(with pno) JF

ETLER, Alvin
Prelude and toccata AMP

GEHRENBECK, David
Carol prelude on "Venite adoramus"
HWG

GILL, Milton
Toccata HWG

GOODMAN, Joseph
Fantasia on the hymn tune "Windsor"
TP
Fantasy (1968) AB

GROOM, Lester
Gothic fanfare ABP
Processional march on "St. Dunstan's"
ABP

HAIGH, Morris
Fantasia on a Lutheran chorale (with
b-hn) SHAW

HAINES, Edmund
Promenade, air and toccata JF

HALL, Arthur
Toccata in C-sharp WIM

HARRIS, Roy
Fantasy with brass (2 trp, 2 trb,
timp) AMP

HARTLEY, Walter
Prelude and fanfare TP

HAUBIEL, Charles
Vox cathedralis HE

HERBERT, Paul
Four contrasts for organ CF
Ballade. Consolation. Triumphal
march. Toccata.

HOVHANESS, Alan
Bare November day (or for hpcd or
pno), Op. 210 CFP
Dark river and distant bell (or for
clav or hpcd) CFP
Dawn hymn CFP
Sonata (with fl) CFP
Sonata (with ob) CFP
Sonata (with 2 ob) CFP
Sonata (with trp) CFP

IVES, Charles
Variations on America MER

JACOBI, Frederick
Prelude HWG
Three quiet preludes HWG

JAMES, Phillip
Alleluia toccata CF
Dithyramb HWG
Ostinato HWG
Pantomime HWG
Passacaglia on a Cambrian bass CF
Pastorale SMPC
Solemn prelude SMPC
Sonata No. 1 HWG

JOHNS, Donald
Organ mass WIM
Partita on a Passion chorale WIM
Three chorale preludes WIM
Three meditations WIM

KAY, Ulysses
Two meditations HWG

KELLER, Homer
Fantasy and fugue HWG

KING, Robert
Prelude and fugue with brass (2 cor,
trb, bar) KING

KOHN, Karl
The day is done, the sun is setting
(chorale-prelude) CF

KOHS, Ellis
Capriccio MER
Passacaglia (with pno) HWG
Three chorale preludes on Hebrew
hymns TP

KOUTZEN, Boris
Sonnet MER

KRAPF, Gerhard
Second organ sonata, for Thanks-
giving JF

KREMMER, Rudolph
Three fantasies for organ EV

KUBIK, Gail
Quiet piece HWG

LAMB, Hubert
Toccata VAL

LA MONTAINE, John
Even song HWG
Processional HWG

LAZAROF, Henri
Lamenti WIM

LOCKWOOD, Normand
Concerto for organ and brass (2 trp,
2 trb) AMP

LOVELACE, Austin C.
By waters still JF
Song of consecration TP

LUENING, Otto
Fantasia CFP

MANOOKIN, Robert
Hymn prelude on "Dennis" WIM

MARTIN, Gilbert M.
Intercession WIM

MASON, Daniel Gregory
Chorale prelude on Lowell Mason's
tune "Dort" JF
Chorale prelude on Lowell Mason's
tune "Wesley" JF
Passacaglia and fugue HWG
Prelude and fugue (with pno) JF

MASON, Lowell
A joyous prelude ABP

MATTHEWS, Thomas J.
Two Christmas preludes WIM

McKAY, George F.
Benedictions CF
Canzone celesti MER
Contemplations ABP
Elegiac poem TP
Evocations CF
Four poetic images CF
Lament for Absalom WIM
Meditations ABP
Nativity trilogy TP
Poems of exultation CF
Sing, choir of angels JF
In remembrance JF
Sonata mistica WIM
Sonata No. 1 UWP
Suite on Easter hymns JF
Suite on 16th century hymn tunes
HWG
Meditation over an ancient hymn
tune. Rondolet. Aire varie.
Choeur celeste. Cortege joyeux.
Three miniatures JF
Three pastoral preludes JF
On a Norwegian folk hymn. On an
American folk hymn. Green fields
and meadows.
Wedding music MER
A wedding procession WIM

MEANS, Claude
Chorale prelude on "Sawley" HWG

MERRITT, Charles
Variations on "Gott des Himmels"
ABP

MOORE, Douglas
Dirge (passacaglia) HWG

OWEN, Harold
Overture dans le style Français WIM

PARKER, Horatio
Concerto for organ HWG

PERSICHETTI, Vincent
Chorale prelude: drop, drop slow tears EV
Shimah B'Koli (Psalm 130), Op. 89 EV
Sonata EV
Sonatine (pedals alone) EV

PFAUTSCH, Lloyd
Three choral preludes HWG
Heinlein. St. Flavian. Windsor.

PINKHAM, Daniel
Concertante (with 2 trp, t-trb, b-trb, perc) CFP
Concertante (with cel and prec) CFP
Aria. Scherzo. Elegy.
(See also "Percussion")
Five voluntaries for organ manuals ECS
Four short pieces for manuals ECS
Prelude. Aria. Interlude. Ostinato.
Pastorale on "The Morning Star" GAL
Revelations ECS
Pastorale. Litany. Toccata.
Signs in the sun (for 2 organs) CFP
Sonata No. 1 for organ and strings ECS
(See also "String Quartet" and "String or Chamber Orchestra with Solo")
Sonata No. 2 for organ and strings ECS
(See also "String Quintet" and "String or Chamber Orchestra with Solo")
Suite ECS
Introduction. Epitaph. Morning song. Toccata.

PISTON, Walter
Chromatic study on the name of Bach HWG
Partita (with vln and vla) AMP
Prelude. Sarabande. Variations. Burlesca.

POLIFRONE, Jon
Chorle prelude WIM

PORTER, Quincy
Canon and fugue HWG
Prelude and wedding march HWG
Toccata, andante and finale HWG

PRESSER, William
Four preludes TP

PURVIS, Richard
Divinum mysterium MCA
St. Francis suite JF
Ascription. Canticle of the sun. Earth carol. Hymn to the moon.
Seven chorale preludes CF
Three pieces JF
Prayer for peace. Elegy. Capriccio (on the notes of the cuckoo).
Trio of contrasts FLAM

READ, Daniel
Trumpet tune for Advent ABP

READ, Gardner
Eight preludes on old Southern hymns (from The Sacred Harp) HWG
My soul forsakes her vain delight. Thou man of grief, remember me. David, the king, was grieved and moved. On Jordan's stormy banks I stand. Alas! and did my Savior bleed. Fight on, my soul. Do not I love Thee, O Lord. Once more, my soul, the rising day.
Little pastorale GAL
Passacaglia and fugue in D-minor HWG
Six preludes on old Southern hymns (from The Sacred Harp) HWG
By Babel's streams we sat and wept. How happy are the souls above. Though the morn may be serene. Hail! ye sighing sons of sorrow. Mercy, O thou son of David. Hark! the jubilee is sounding.
Suite for organ, Op. 81 W-7
Preamble. Scherzo. Aria. Toccata.

REINAGLE, Alexander
Allegro (Sonata in E) WWN

RIEGGER, Wallingford
Canon and fugue, Op. 33b FLAM

ROBERTS, Myron J.
Homage to Pèrotin HWG
In memoriam HWG
Litany HWG
Prelude and trumpetings HWG

ROGERS, Bernard
Miniature suite TP
Second suite TP

ROREM, Ned
  Pastorale SMPC

SCHAFFER, Robert
  Paschal triptych with brass (3 trp,
    4 hn, 3 trb, bar, tba, perc) KING

SCHMIDT, William
  Allegro breve WIM

SCHWARTZ, Elliott
  Memorial 1963 (with pno) GEN
  (See also "Band")

SELBY, William
  Fugue in D AMP

SESSIONS, Roger
  Chorale (1938) HWG
  Three chorale preludes (1925) EMB

SHATTO, Charles
  Poem WIM

SIMONDS, Bruce
  Dorian prelude OX
  Prelude on "Iam sol recedit igneus"
    OX

SMITH, Kent
  Toccata WIM

SMITH, Russell
  Three chorale preludes HWG
  Forty days and forty nights.
  St. Flavian. Windsor.

SOWERBY, Leo
  Ad perennin vitae fontem HWG
  Ballade (with E-hn or vla or vln
    or cl) HWG
  Bright, blithe and brisk HWG
  Canon, chacony, and fugue HWG
  Capel HWG
  Carillon HWG
  Charter house HWG
  Chorale prelude on "Palisades" HWG
  Classic concerto (with pno) HWG
  Comes autumn time BOS
  Concert piece (with pno) HWG
  Festival musick (with 2 trp, 2 trb,
    timp) HWG
  Fanfare. Chorale. Toccata on
  "A. G. O."
  Jubilee HWG
  Medieval poem (with pno) HWG
  Organ music for the church year CFP
  Advent: Veni, veni, Emmanuel.

Christmas: In dulci jubilo.
  Lent: Aus der Tiefe.
  Passiontide: Passion chorale.
  Easter: O filii et filiae.
  Whitsuntide: Veni, Creator, spiritus.
  Pageant of autumn HWG
  Postludium super "Benedictus es,
    Domine" HWG
  Praeludium super "Benedictus sit,
    Domine" HWG
  Prelude on "Malabar" HWG
  Prelude on "Non nobis, Domine" HWG
  Poem (with vla) HWG
  Requiescat in pace HWG
  Rhapsody HWG
  Sinfonia brevis HWG
  Sonatina HWG
  Song 46 HWG
  Suite OX
  Chorale and fugue. Air with
  variations. Fantasy for flute stops.
  March.
  Symphony in G-major OX
  Three pieces CFP
  Fugue. Interlude. Toccata.
  Toccata HWG
  Two sketches HWG
  Fancy-free. Nostalgic.
  Wedding processional HWG
  Whimsical variations HWG

STEVENS, Halsey
  Improvisation on "Divinim mysterium"
    PIC
  Three short preludes PIC

STILL, William Grant
  Elegy WIM

STONE, Don
  Two pieces WIM
  Interlude on "Veni Emmanuel."
  Procession.

STOUT, Alan
  Serenity (with vlc or bsn) CFP

STRILKO, Anthony
  Tranquil music for organ MER

SWANN, Frederick L.
  The Agincourt hymn (Dunstable) GS

THOMSON, Virgil
  Fanfare HWG
  Pange lingua GS
  Pastorale on Christmas plainsong
    HWG

WAGENAAR, Bernard
Eclogue HWG

WAGNER, Joseph
Classical variations CF

WEAVER, Powell
Copper country sketches HWG
Passacaglia (Iron mountain).
Scherzo (Laughing water).
Toccata (The lake).
Exultation (Pièce symphonic) (with
    pno) JF

WEBER, Ben
Closing piece TP

WUORINEN, Charles
Evolutio MM

YON, Pietro A.
American rhapsody JF
Arpa notturna JF
Concert study GS
Concerto Gregoriano (with pno) JF
Echo JF
Humoresque--L'organo primitivo JF
Hymn of glory JF
Minuetto antico e musetta JF
Rapsodia Italiana JF
Second concert study GS
Sonata cromatica (seconda) JF
Sonata romantica (terza) JF

YOUNG, Gordon
Organ voluntaries TP
    Antiphon. Bachiana. Carillon.
    Interlude. Offertorium. Morning
    hymn. Paean. Praeludium.
    Psalm. Soliloquy.
Petite trio for organ TP
Seven tone poems JF

YOUNG, Michael E.
Prelude and fugue No. 3 WIM

ACCORDION

DIAMOND, David
Introduction and dance SMPC
Sonatina SMPC

HOVHANESS, Alan
Suite, Op. 166 CFP

MARIMBA

ROGERS, Bernard
Mirage SMPC

STRING MUSIC
(with piano unless otherwise indicated)

VIOLIN

ALEXANDER, Joseph
Nocturne and scherzo GEN

AMRAM, David
Sonata CFP
Sonata (unacc) CFP

BACON, Ernst
Buncombe County, N.C., of an
    afternoon AMP
Holbert's cove GS

BARATI, George
Sonata CFP
Two dances PIC

BARBER, Samuel
Canzone (transcribed from 2nd mov
    of pno concerto, Op. 38) GS

BAUER, Marion
Fantasia quasi una sonata GS

BENNETT, Robert Russell
Hexapoda (five studies in jitteroptera)
    CHAP
    Gut-bucket Gus. Jane shakes her
    hair. Betty and Harold close their
    eyes. Jim jives. --till dawn Sunday.
A song sonata CHAP
Suite (1945) CHAP
    Warm up. Serenade. March.
    Blues. Hoe down.

BENSON, Warren
Miniature suite MCA

BERRY, Wallace
Duo CF
Trenody (unacc) SMPC

BLACKWOOD, Easley
Sonata, Op. 7 GS

BRITAIN, Radie
Prison NAK

BROWN, Raynor
Prelude and fugue (with org) WIM

CADMAN, Charles Wakefield
Sonata in G JF

CAGE, John
59 1/2" for a string player (1953)
(unacc) CFP
Nocturne (1947) CFP
Six melodies (1950) CFP

CARPENTER, John Alden
Sonata GS

COLE, Ulric
Sonata TP

COPLAND, Aaron
Celebration dance from Billy the
kid (1938) B&H
Hoe-down from Rodeo (1942) B&H
Nocturne (1926) AMP
Sonata (1943) B&H
Ukelele serenade (1926) AMP

CORIGLIANO, John
Sonata GS

CORTÉS, Ramiro
Elegy EV

COWELL, Henry
Homage to Iran CFP
How old is song? PIC
Hymn and fuguing tune No. 16 CFP
Sonata AMP
Suite AMP

CRESTON, Paul
Suite GS
Prelude. Air. Rondo.

CRUMB, George
Night Music II MIL

CURRAN, Alvin
Thursday afternoon (unacc) CPE

CYTRON, Samuel
Suite (unacc) SMPC

DELLO JOIO, Norman
Colloquies EBM
Fantasia on a Gregorian theme CF
Variations and capriccio CF

DIAMOND, David
Canticle EV
Chaconne SMPC
Perpetual motion EV
Sonata GS
Sonata (unacc) SMPC

DONATO, Anthony
Precipitations MER
Fog. Snow. Rain. Hail.

DUKELSKY, Vladimir (DUKE, Vernon)
Capriccio Mexicano MCA
Sonata in D-major COL

ELLSTEIN, Abraham
Haftorah MIL

ERICKSON, Robert
Duo TP

FELDMAN, Morton
Extensions I CFP
Piece CFP
Projection IV (graph) CFP
Vertical thoughts 2 CFP

FETLER, Paul
Three pieces TP
Essay. Air. Caprice.

FINE, Irving
Sonata W-7

FINNEY, Ross Lee
Fantasy in two movements (unacc)
CFP
Statement and variation.
Development and conclusion.
Fiddle-doodle-ad (eight American
folk tunes) GS
Rosin the bow. Rye whiskey.
Wayfaring stranger. Cotton eye
Joe. Rippytoe Ray. The nightin-
gale. Oh, lovely appearance of
death. Candy girl.
Sonata No. 2 AME
Sonata No. 3 VAL

FLANAGAN, William
Chaconne PIC

FOSS, Lukas
Composer's holiday GS
Dedication HAR
Early song HAR

FULEIHAN, Anis
Four preludes SMPC

GIANNINI, Vittorio
Sonata (unacc) COL

GILLIS, Don
Retrospection MIL

GOLDMAN, Richard Franko
Sonata MER

GOULD, Morton
Suite CHAP
Warm-up. Serenade. March.
Blues. Hoe down.

GREEN, Ray
Duo concertante AME

GRIFFIS, Eliot
Sonata in G-major HE

HADLEY, Henry
Suite ancienne, Op. 101 CF
Prelude. Minuetto.
Air plaintif. Gigue.

HAIEFF, Alexei
Three pieces AMP
Air. Polka. Ritornel.

HARRIS, Roy
Dance of spring (2nd mov from vln
    sonata) MIL
Fantasy (1st mov from vln sonata)
    MIL
Four charming little pieces MIL
Mood. Afternoon slumber song.
Summer fields. There's a charm
about you.
Melody (3rd mov from vln sonata)
    MIL
Toccata (4th mov from vln sonata)
    MIL

HARRISON, Lou
Concerto in slendro (with cel, 2
    tackpianos, perc) CFP
(See also "Percussion")

HAUBIEL, Charles
Epochs HE
Asymmetry. En saga.
Nocturne. Symmetry.
Gothic variations HE
Nuances HE
Fear. Gentle. Jocose.

Plaintive. Still.
Sonata in D-minor HE

HEIDEN, Bernhard
Sonata (1954) AMP

HELM, Everett
Sonata AMP

HOVHANESS, Alan
Duet (with hpcd), Op. 122 CFP
Prelude. Haiku. Aria.
Kirgiz suite, Op. 73, No. 3 CFP
Oror (lullaby), Op. 1 CFP
Saris CFP
Shatakh PIC
Suite (with pno & perc), Op. 99 CFP
(See also "Percussion")
Prelude. Pastoral. Allegro.
Pastoral. Canon. Allegro.
Three visions of St. Mesrob, Op.
    198 CFP
Celestial mountain. Celestial bird.
Celestial alphabet.
Varak, Op. 47 CFP
Yeraz (unacc) MIL

HOWE, Mary
Sonata CFP

IMBRIE, Andrew
Impromtu SHAW

IVES, Charles
Largo PIC
Sonata No. 1 PIC
Sonata No. 2 GS
Autumn. In the barn. The revival.
Sonata No. 3 NME
Sonata No. 4 (Children's day at the
    camp meeting) AMP

JACOBI, Frederick
Ballade CF
Impressions from the Odyssey VAL
Three preludes CF

JONES, Charles
Sonatina CFP

KIRCHNER, Leon
Duo MER
Sonata concertante MER

KOHN, Karl
Song (or for clarinet) CF

KOHS, Ellis
Sonatine MER

KOUTZEN, Boris
Holiday mood GEN
Melody with variations GEN
Nocturne MCA
Pastoral and dance GEN

KRAEHENBUEHL, David
Diptych AMP
Canzona di Dionigi.   Partita
d'Apollone.

KUBIK, Gail
Soliloquy and dance SMPC
Sonatina COL

KUPFERMAN, Meyer
"Pierrot" GEN
Three pieces (unacc) GEN

KURKA, Robert
Sonata, Op. 5 (unacc) WEIN
Sonata, Op. 23, No. 3 WEIN

LADERMAN, Ezra
Portraits (unacc) OX
Sonata OX

LEE, Dai-Keong
Incantation and dance GS

LEE, Noel
Dialogues TP

LEES, Benjamin
Invenzione (unacc) B&H

LLOYD, Norman
Three pieces AMP
Declaration.   Ballad.   Dance.

LOEFFLER, Charles Martin
Partita GS
Intrada.   Sarabande.   Divertisse-
ment.   Finale des tendres adieux.
Peacocks GS

LUENING, Otto
Elegy (unacc) CFP
Manana B&H

MacCOLL, Hugh
Suite in A-major SHAW
Sonata.   Promenade.   Ecossaise.

MARTINO, Donald
Fantasy variations ECS

MASON, Daniel Gregory
Sonata in G-minor, Op. 5 GS

MECHEM, Kirke
Five duets, Op. 4 ECS

MENNIN, Peter
Sonata concertante (1956) CF

MOORE, Douglas
Down East suite CF
(See also "Full Symphony")

NEMIROFF, Isaac
Sonata No. 2 TP

NOWAK, Lionel
Sonata (unacc) NME

PERLE, George
Solo partita for violin & viola TP
(See also "Viola")
Prelude--vla
Allemande--vln
Courante--vla
Sarabande--vln
Finale--vln

PERSICHETTI, Vincent
Masques EV
Sonata (unacc) EV

PINKHAM, Daniel
Serenade (with hpcd) RDR

PISTON, Walter
Sonata (1939) AMP
Sonatina (with hpcd or pno) B&H

PORTER, Quincy
Four pieces MER
Pastorale.   Scherzando.
Melody.   Rondo.
Sonata No. 2 CFP

POWELL, John
From a loved past, Op. 23a GS
Natchez-on-the-hill (3 Virginian
country dances) GS
Sonata Virginianesque, Op. 7 GS

RAPHLING, Sam
Sonata No. 3 GEN

READ, Gardner
Six intimate moods, Op. 35 CF
Serious. Whimsical. Amorous.
Coquettish. Wistful. Hysterical.

RIEGGER, Wallingford
Sonatina, Op. 39 EBM
Whimsy, Op. 2 AMP

ROCHBERG, George
La bocca della verità TP

ROGERS, Bernard
Sonata TP

ROREM, Ned
Mountain song SMPC
Sonata CFP

SCHULLER, Gunther
Recitative and rondo AMP

SESSIONS, Roger
Duo (1942) EBM
Sonata (1953) (unacc) EBM

SHAPERO, Harold
Sonata SMPC

SHIFRIN, Seymour
Konzertstuck (unacc) CFP

SMITH, David Stanley
Sonata TP

SOKOLOFF, Noel
Epithalamium PIC

SOWERBY, Leo
Poem (with org) HWG
Suite BOS
Gavot. Rigadoon.
Sarabande. Jig.

STARER, Robert
Introduction and hora SMPC
Little suite MCA
Variants SMPC

STEVENS, Halsey
Sonatina No. 3 (1959) HME
Suite (1954) (unacc) HME

STILL, William Grant
Pastorela W-7
Suite MCA
African dancer. Mother and
child. Gamin.

SWANSON, Howard
Nocturne WEIN

TERRY, Frances
Sonata TP

THOMSON, Virgil
Sonata No. 1 B&H
Three portraits TP
Barcarolle: portrait of Georges
Hugnet; In a bird cage: portrait
of Lise Deharme; Tango lullaby:
portrait of Mlle. Alvarez de Toledo

TURNER, Charles
Serenade for Icarus GS

VARDI, Emmanuel
Suite on American folk songs GS
The unconstant lover. I will and
I must get married. The wayfar-
ing stranger. On the banks of the
old Pee Dee.

WAGNER, Joseph
Sonata No. 2 MIL

WARD, Robert
Sonata No. 1 PIC

WEBER, Ben
Sonata da camera, Op. 30 B&H

WEINER, Stanley
Seven caprices, "Homage to violin-
ists" (unacc) AMP

WHITE, Paul
Sonata EV

WOLFF, Christian
Duo for violinist and pianist CFP

YARDUMIAN, Richard
Monologue (unacc) EV

VIOLA

AMRAM, David
The wind and the rain CFP

AVSHALOMOV, Jacob
Sonatine MER
Two bagatelles MER

BABBITT, Milton
Composition for viola and piano AMP

BACON, Ernst
Koschatiana MCA

BARATI, George
Cantabile e ritmico PIC

BARNETT, David
Ballade, Op. 16 OX

BAUER, Marion
Sonata (alternate version for cl) TP

BERGSMA, William
Fantastic variations on theme from
"Tristan" GAL

BLACKWOOD, Easley
Sonata EV

BROWN, Raynor
Sonata (with organ) WIM

BRUNSWICK, Mark
Fantasia (unacc) VAL

CAGE, John
59 1/2" for a string player (1953)
(unacc) CFP

CARTER, Elliott
Elegy PIC
Pastorale (alternate versions for
E-hn and cl) NME

COLGRASS, Michael
Theme and variations for 4 drums
and viola PM
(See also "Percussion")

COOLEY, Carlton
Concertino HE
Etude suite (unacc) HE
Prelude. Scherzo. Theme
Russe. Rondino spiccato.

COWELL, Henry
Hymn and fuguing tune No. 7 PIC

CRESTON, Paul
Homage, Op. 41 GS
Suite, Op. 13 (1938) SHAW
Prelude. Caprice. Air.
Tarantella.

DAHL, Ingolf
Divertimento TP
Sinfonia. Barcarolle. Variations.
Finale and coda.

DUKE, John
Melody in E-flat EV
Suite (unacc) VAL
Aria. Scherzo. Cadenza. Finale.

ETLER, Alvin
Sonata (with hpcd) AMP

FUCHS, Lillian
Sonata pastorale (unacc) AMP

GREEN, Ray
Concertante AME

HARRIS, Roy
Soliloquy and dance GS

HEIDEN, Bernhard
Sonata (1959) AMP

HOVHANESS, Alan
Chahagir, Op. 56a (unacc) BB

JACOBI, Frederick
Fantasy CF

LONDON, Edwin
Sonatina VAL

McBRIDE, Robert
Workout AMP

PALMER, Robert
Sonata PIC

PERLE, George
Solo partita for violin and viola TP
(For contents, see "Violin")
Sonata (unacc) SMPC

PERSICHETTI, Vincent
Infanta marina EV

PISTON, Walter
Interlude B&H

PORTER, Quincy
Duo (1957) (with hp or hpcd) AMP
Poem VAL
Speed etude VAL
Suite (unacc) VAL

202 Catalog of Published Concert Music by American Composers

READ, Gardner
Poem, Op. 31a CF

RICHTER, Marga
Aria and toccata MIL

SCHICKELE, Peter
Windows: 3 pieces for viola (or
flute or clarinet) and guitar
(1966) AB

SCHMIDT, William
Sonata in two movements WIM

SHULMAN, Alan
Suite (unacc) SHAW

SMITH, Julia
Two pieces TP
Nocturne. Festival piece.

SOLLBERGER, Harvey
Composition MM

SOWERBY, Leo
Poem (with org) HWG

STEVENS, Halsey
Serenade (also for clarinet) MER
Suite (also for clarinet) CFP
Three Hungarian folk songs GAL

TRIMBLE, Lester
Duo CFP

VAN de VATE, Nancy
Sonata TP

VARDI, Emmanuel
Suite on American folk songs GS
The unconstant lover. I will and
I must get married. The wayfar-
ing stranger. On the banks of
the old Pee Dee.

VERRALL, John
Sonata No. 2 CFP

WARD, Robert
Arioso GAL
Tarantelle GAL

WARREN, Elinor Remick
Poem CF

WEINER, Stanley
Sonata (unacc) CFP

VIOLONCELLO

BACON, Ernst
Koschatiana MCA

BARATI, George
Triple exposure (unacc) CFP

BARBER, Samuel
Sonata, Op. 6 GS

BAZELON, Irwin
Five pieces WEIN

BLACKWOOD, Easley
Fantasy, Op. 8 GS

BROWN, Earle
Music for cello and piano AMP

CAGE, John
59 1/2" for a string player (1953)
(unacc) CFP

CARTER, Elliott
Sonata (corrected ed. 1966) AMP

CHILDS, Barney
Interbalances III (with opt other
instruments, up to five) TP

COPLAND, Aaron
Waltz and celebration dance (from
Billy the kid) (arr. composer)
B&H

COWELL, Henry
Gravely and vigorously (unacc) AMP
Hymn and fuguing tune No. 9 (1950)
AMP

CRESTON, Paul
Homage GS
Suite GS
Prelude. Scherzino.
Cantilena. Tarantella.

CRUMB, George
Sonata (unacc) CFP
Fantasia. Tema pastorale con
variazioni. Toccata.

DELLO JOIO, Norman
Duo concertato GS

DIAMOND, David
Sonata NME

Sonata (unacc) SMPC

DUKE, John
Melody in E-flat-major EV

ENGEL, Lehman
Sonata TP

FELDMAN, Morton
Durations II CFP
Intersection IV CFP
Projection I CFP

FINNEY, Ross Lee
Sonata No. 2 in C-major VAL

FOSS, Lukas
Capriccio GS

FREDRICKSON, Thomas
Allegro TP

FREED, Isadore
Passacaglia COL

FULEIHAN, Anis
Recitative and scilienne GS
Rhapsody CF
Three pieces SMPC
Prologue. Interlude. Epilogue.

GIANNINI, Vittorio
Psalm 130 (or for contra-bass) COL

GRUENBERG, Louis
Poème, Op. 19 TP

HADLEY, Henry
Danse ancienne, Op. 92, No. 13 CF
Élegie, Op. 36 GS
From "Suite ancienne" CF
Air plaintif. Gigue.

HAIEFF, Alexei
Sonata CHAP

HARRISON, Lou
Suite (with hp) PIC
Chorale. Pastorale. Interlude.
Aria.

HAUBIEL, Charles
Sonata in C-minor HE

HOVHANESS, Alan
Suite, Op. 193 CFP
Yakamochi (unacc) CFP
Prelude. Jhala. Intermezzo.

Tremolando glissando. Requiem.

INCH, Herbert
Sonata CF

KERR, Harrison
Study (unacc) TP

KOUTZEN, Boris
Concert piece (also for vlc, str qrt
or str orch) MER

KUBIK, Gail
Serenade CHAP

KUPFERMAN, Meyer
Evocation (1951) GEN
Four pieces GEN

KURKA, Robert
Sonatina WEIN

LA MONTAINE, John
Sonata Op. 8 EV

LEWIN, David
Classical variations on a theme by
Schoenberg UCP

MARTINO, Donald
Parisonatina al'Dodecafonìa (unacc)
ECS

MENNINI, Louis
Sonatina B&H

PARRIS, Robert
Fantasy and fugue (unacc) CFP

PERLE, George
Hebrew melodies (unacc) NME
Psalm 93. Cantillation.

PERSICHETTI, Vincent
Vocalise, Op. 27 EV

PORTER, Quincy
Poem VAL

RAMSIER, Paul
Divertimento concertante on a theme
of Couperin (also with orch(R)) GS
(See also "Double Bass")
Theme. Barcarolle. March.
Dirge. Recitative. Valse cine-
matique. Toccata Barocca
(passacaglia).

REED, H. Owen
  Concerto in C-major HE

RHODES, Phillip
  Three pieces (unacc) CFP

RIEGGER, Wallingford
  Whimsy, Op. 2 AMP

ROREM, Ned
  Mountain song SMPC

SCHICKELE, Peter
  Bellshadows AB

SCHULLER, Gunther
  Fantasy, Op. 19 (unacc) BB

SESSIONS, Roger
  Six pieces EBM

SHULMAN, Alan
  Suite (unacc) SHAW

SMITH, David Stanley
  Sonata, Op. 59 GS

STEVENS, Halsey
  Hungarian children's songs PIC
  Intermezzo, cadenza and finale PIC
  Sonata PIC
  Sonata (unacc) CFP
  Sonatina (or for bsn) HME
  Three pieces (or for bsn) CFP

STOUT, Alan
  Serenity (with org) CFP

SWANSON, Howard
  Suite WEIN
    Prelude.   Pantomime.
    Dirge.   Recessional.

SYDEMAN, William
  Sonata (unacc) CFP

TWEEDY, Donald
  Sonata MCA

WAGENAAR, Bernard
  Sonatina CF

WARD, Robert
  Arioso GAL
  Tarantelle GAL

WEBER, Ben
  Dance (unacc) NME

WUORINEN, Charles
  Duuiensela MM

GUITAR

BODA, John
  Introduction and dance TP

DOUBLE BASS

AUSTIN, Larry
  Bass (a theater piece in open style
    for c-b, tape and stroboscope) CPE

CHILDS, Barney
  Sonata (unacc) MM

FISHER, Stephen
  Concert piece (unacc) CFP

GIANNINI, Vittorio
  Psalm 130 (or for vlc) COL

LUENING, Otto
  Sonata (unacc) GAL

MOROSS, Jerome
  Sonatina CHAP

PERLE, George
  Monody II (unacc) TP

PHILLIPS, Peter
  Sonata MM

RAMSIER, Paul
  Divertimento concertante on a theme
    of Couperin (also with orch(R)) GS
    (For contents, see "Violoncello")

SHULMAN, Alan
  Three sketches MCA

STEVENS, Halsey
  Arioso and etude AME
  Sonatina giocoso CAM

SYDEMAN, William
  For double bass alone MM

TUTHILL, Burnet
  Concerto (with pno or orch(R)) CF

WUORINEN, Charles
Concert for double bass (unacc) MM

WOODWIND MUSIC
(with piano unless otherwise indicated)

HARP

ADLER, Samuel
Introduction and capriccio SMPC

BARATI, George
Prisma PIC

CAGE, John
In a landscape (1948) CFP

CRESTON, Paul
Lydian song COL

FOX, Charles
Ancient dance (after Ravel) SMPC

HOVHANESS, Alan
Nocturne, Op. 20, No. 2 CFP
Sonata, Op. 127 CFP
Two sonatas, Op. 110 CFP

McDONALD, Harl
Suite from childhood EV

PERRY, Julia
Homunculus C.F. (with perc) SMPC

SALZEDO, Carlos
Sonata (with pno) TP

SCHULLER, Gunther
Fantasy AMP

STARER, Robert
Prelude PIC

STEVENS, Halsey
Prelude PIC
Six Slovakian folksongs PIC
Sonatina PIC

WAGENAAR, Bernard
Four vignettes EV

VIBRAHARP

JACKSON, Milt
Jazz themes with improvisations SF

FLUTE

ADLER, Samuel
Flaunting (unacc) (with opt picc or
a-fl) TP

ALEXANDER, Joseph
Sonata GEN

AMRAM, David
Overture and allegro (unacc) CFP

ANTHEIL, George
Sonata WEIN

AVSHALOMOV, Jacob
Disconsolate muse AMP

BACON, Ernst
Burnt cabin branch BB

BAILEY, Parker
Sonata, Op. 3 CF

BARAB, Seymour
Sonatina B&H

BARBER, Samuel
Canzone (transcribed from 2nd mov
of pno concerto, Op. 38) GS

BENNETT, Robert Russell
A flute at dusk (unacc) CHAP

BRANT, Henry
Mobiles (unacc) JS

BRICCETTI, Thomas
Sonata, Op. 14 MM

BUDD, Harold
The edge of August CPE

CHOU, Wen-Chung
Cursive CFP
Three folk songs (with harp) CFP

COHN, James
Baroque suite (also for ob or sax)
EM
Allemande. Courante. Sarabande.
Gavotte. Gigue.

CORTÉS, Ramiro
Elegy PIC

COWELL, Henry
Two-bits CF
1. A tuneful bit.
1. A blarneying bit.

CRAWFORD-SEEGER, Ruth
Diaphonic suite (1930) (unacc) NME

DAHL, Ingolf
Duettino concertante for flute and
percussion AB
(See also "Percussion")
Variations on a Swedish folktune
(unacc) TP

DELANO, Jack
Sonatina PIC

DORAN, Matt
Four short pieces (unacc) WIM

EFREIN, Laurie
Attraction (unacc) AB

FINK, Michael
Sonata da camera WIM

FLAGELLO, Nicolas
Burlesca (with gtr) GEN

FREED, Isadore
Scherzino CF

FULEIHAN, Anis
Pastoral sonata SMPC

GIANNINI, Vittorio
Sonata COL

GILLIS, Don
North Harris (from Four scenes
from yesterday) B&H
Three short pieces MIL
Frolic. Calculation.
Social whirl.

GOLD, Ernest
Sonatina GS

GOLDMAN, Richard Franko
Divertimento SHAW
Two monochromes (unacc) SHAW

GREEN, Ray
Dance energies (unacc) AME

HANSON, Howard
Serenade, Op. 35 (1945) CF
(See also "String or Chamber Or-
chestra with Solo")

HARRISON, Lou
First concerto for flute and percus-
sion CFP
(See also "Percussion")

HARTLEY, Walter
Four sketches TP
Sonata for flute and harpsichord TP

HAUBIEL, Charles
Nuances HE
Still.   Fear.   Gentle.
Plaintive.   Jocose.

HEIDEN, Bernhard
Sonatina (1958) AMP

HELM, Everett
Sonata B&H

HIBBARD, William
Portraits ECS

HOIBY, Lee
Pastoral dances GS

HOVHANESS, Alan
The burning house overture, Op. 185a
(with perc acc) CFP
(See also "Percussion")
Dance of the black-haired mountain
storm (from Wind Drum), Op. 183a
(with perc acc) CFP
(See also "Percussion")
Sonata (unacc), Op. 118 CFP
Sonata (with org) Op. 121 CFP

JACOBI, Frederick
Night piece and dance B&H

KENNAN, Kent
Night soliloquy CF
(See also "Strings with Voice, Winds
and/or Percussion;" "String or
Chamber Orchestra with Solo" and
"Band")

KERR, Harrison
Suite B&H
Prelude.   Dance.
Recitative.   Toccata.

KOHN, Karl
Encounters (also for piccolo) CF
Three pieces CF

KOUTZEN, Boris
Nocturne MCA

KUBIK, Gail
Nocturne GS

KUPFERMAN, Meyer
Music from "Hallelujah the hills"
(also for rec and hpcd) GEN
Romanza. Scherzetto. Baroque
fantasy. Divertimento. Rococo
air. Valse de neige. Variations.

LADERMAN, Ezra
Duet (with dancer) BB

LA MONTAINE, John
Sonata (unacc), Op. 24 BB

LATHAM, William
Fantasy concerto JS
Sonata No. 2 (with pno or hpcd) JS
(See also "Oboe" and "Recorder")

LEVY, Burt
Orbs with flute AP

LONDON, Ed
Song and dance MJQ

LUENING, Otto
Second suite (unacc) COL
Lyric scene. Intermezzo.
Song. Finale.

MARTINO, Donald
Quodlibets for flute MM
Studio. Arietta. Burla.

McKENZIE, Jack
Pastorale (with perc) MP
(See also "Percussion")

MILLER, Edward
Song for recorder (or fl) MM

MUCZYNSKI, Robert
Sonata, Op. 14 GS

NIXON, Roger
Nocturne TP

PERLE, George
Monody I (unacc) TP

PERSICHETTI, Vincent
Little recorder book (treble) EV
Parable for solo flute EV
Serenade No. 10 (with hp) EV

PHILLIPS, Burrill
Four figures in time EV
Pantomine. A quiet field.
Stilt march. Racing rhyme.
Three nostalgic songs TP

PINKHAM, Daniel
Duet (also for rec with hpcd) ECS
Eclogue (with hpcd and offstage
handbells) ECS

PISTON, Walter
Sonata AMP

POLIN, Claire
Structures (unacc) EV

PRESSER, William
Prelude and dance TP
Rondo for piccolo and piano TP

RAPHLING, Sam
Warble for lilac-time EM

READ, Gardner
Threnody W-7

REYNOLDS, Roger
Ambages (unacc) CFP
Mosaic CFP

REYNOLDS, Verne
Sonata CF

RIEGGER, Wallingford
Suite, Op. 8 (unacc) NME

ROGERS, Bernard
Soliloquy CF
(See also "String or Chamber Or-
chestra with Solo")

ROREM, Ned
Mountain song SMPC

SCHICKELE, Peter
Windows: 3 pieces for flute (or
viola or clarinet) and guitar (1966)
AB

SCHMIDT, William
Septigrams (with perc) WIM
(See also "Percussion")

208   Catalog of Published Concert Music by American Composers

Introduction. Quartal blues.
Syncophrases. Polyjazz. Im-
provisatorial variant. The
percussive rondo. Finale.

SCHWARTZ, Elliott
Sonata GEN

SOLLBERGER, Harvey
Music for flute and piano MM

STARER, Robert
Recitation SMPC

STEVENS, Halsey
Sonatina BB
Sonatina piacevole (also for a-rec)
(with pno or hpcd) PIC

THOMSON, Virgil
Sonata (unacc) EV

TOWNSEND, Douglas
Dance-improvisation and fugue
(S-Rec, or picc, or fl, and pno)
CFP

TUTHILL, Burnet
Flute song SMPC

ULRICH, E.J.
Sonatina (unacc) TP

WATSON, Walter
Essay for flute SHAW

WEBER, Ben
Nocturne TP

WESTERGAARD, Peter
Divertimento on discobbolic fragments AB

WIDDOES, Lawrence
Sonatina TP

WIGGLESWORTH, Frank
Lake music (unacc) MER

WUORINEN, Charles
Variations A 2 MM
Variations (unacc) MM

OBOE

ADLER, Samuel
Oboration (with opt E-hn) TP

ALEXANDER, Joseph
Movement BI

BARLOW, Wayne
Winter's passed CF
(See also "String or Chamber
Orchestra with Solo")

BROWN, Rayner
Sonata (with org) WIM

CHILDS, Barney
Five little sound pieces TP
Oboe piece for Jackson Maclow AMP

COHN, James
Baroque suite (also for fl or sax) EM
(For contents, see "Flute")

COPLAND, Aaron
Quiet city B&H

COWELL, Henry
Three ostinati with chorales MER

CRAWFORD-SEEGER, Ruth
Diaphonic suite (unacc) (1930) NME

DIERCKS, John
Sonata TP

ETLER, Alvin
Introduction and allegro (1952) AMP

GILLIS, Don
Courthouse Square (from Four Scenes
from Yesterday) B&H

HANSON, Howard
Pastorale CF

HOLLINGSWORTH, Stanley
Sonata, Op. 2 GS

HOVHANESS, Alan
Sonata, Op. 171 (with org) CFP

KAY, Ulysses
Brief elegy MCA

LATHAM, William
Sonata No. 1 JS

Sonata No. 2 (with pno or hpcd) JS
(See also "Flute" and "Recorder")

PINKHAM, Daniel
Duet (or with rec or fl and hpcd)
ECS

PISTON, Walter
Suite ECS
Prelude. Sarabande. Minuetto.
Nocturne. Gigue.

PRESSER, William
Sonata TP

RAPHLING, Sam
Pastorale EM
Sonata JS

RIEGGER, Wallingford
Duos, Op. 35 NME

ROCHBERG, George
La bocca della verita TP

ROREM, Ned
Mountain song PIC

SCHULLER, Gunther
Sonata MM

SCHWARTZ, Elliott
Sonata (unacc) GEN

SMITH, David Stanley
Sonata TP

STARER, Robert
Recitation SMPC

STILL, William Grant
Incantation and dance CF

SYDEMAN, William
Variations (with hpcd) ECS

TUTHILL, Burnet
Sonata, Op. 24 JS

WUORINEN, Charles
Composition for oboe and piano MM

ENGLISH HORN

CARTER, Elliott
Pastoral NME

CHILDS, Barney
Four involutions (unacc) TP

LATHAM, William
Sonata No. 2 JS

PRESSER, William
Passarumbia TP

SOWERBY, Leo
Ballad (with org and with alternate
parts for vla, vln and cl) HWG

TROWBRIDGE, Luther
Quietude HE

CLARINET

ADLER, Samuel
Clarinon (with opt E-flat cl and/or
b-cl) TP

ALEXANDER, Joseph
Sonata GEN

AUSTIN, Larry
Current CPE

AVSHALOMOV, Jacob
Sonatine MER
Two bagatelles MER
Inquietude. Pipe dream.

BACON, Ernst
Okefenokee BB

BARLOW, Wayne
Lyrical piece CF

BAUER, Marion
Sonata (alternate version for vla) TP

BERNSTEIN, Leonard
Sonata W-7

BODA, John
Sonatina TP

BRANT, Henry
Ice age (with glock or xy and pno)
NME

BROWN, Rayner
Prelude and fughetta (for b-cl) WIM
Sonata (with org) WIM

CAGE, John
Sonata (unacc) CFP

CARTER, Elliott
Pastorale NME

CHILDS, Barney
Sonata (unacc) TP

COWELL, Henry
Three ostinati with chorales MER

CRESTON, Paul
Suite SHAW
Scherzoso. Pastorale. Toccata.

CROLEY, Randell
Trittico (unacc) TP

CUSTER, Arthur
Bagatelle MIL

DELLO JOIO, Norman
Concertante CF

DIAMOND, Arline
Composition for clarinet (unacc) TP

DORAN, Matt
Seven pieces (unacc) WIM
Sonata WIM

EAGLES, Moneta
Two sketches CHAP
Scherzino. Soliloquy.

ELLSTEIN, Abraham
Chassidic dance MIL

ETLER, Alvin
Sonata (1952) AMP

FINK, Michael
Caprices WIM
Cafe. In between. Excursion.

GILLIS, Don
From a winter's dream (from Four
Scenes from Yesterday) B&H

GORDON, Philip
Sonatina TP

GOULD, Morton
Guajira (popular dance) CHAP

HEIDEN, Bernhard
Sonatina AMP

HOVHANESS, Alan
Lament, Op. 25 (unacc) CFP

KLEINSINGER, George
Street corner concerto CHAP

KOHN, Karl
Song (or for vln) CF

KOHS, Ellis
Sonata MER

KOUTZEN, Boris
Melody with variations GEN
Pastoral and dance GEN

KRAFT, Leo
Ballad TP

KUPFERMAN, Meyer
Four on a row GEN

LADERMAN, Ezra
Serenade (unacc) BB

LATHAM, William
Five atonal studies JS
Sonata No. 2 JS

LA VIOLETTE, Wesley
Suite (unacc) WIM

MARTINO, Donald
B, a, b, b, it, t ECS
A set for clarinet MM
Strata for bass clarinet (unacc) AP

McKAY, George F.
Moods: three expressive pieces TP
Wistful. Blues. Playful.
Sonata MER
Two dance scenes TP
Grotesque dance. Fantastic dance.

MILANO, Robert
Four arabesques (unacc) MER
Prologue. Etude.
Dialogue. Dithyramb.

MOORE, Michael
Ragtime and variations on an Irish
theme WIM

OWEN, Harold
Twelve concert etudes WIM

Fantasia. Air. Sarabande. Invention. Prelude. Adagio
sostenuto. Sonatina. Canon.
(can be performed as a solo, as
a duet with another performer, or
as a duet with pre-recorded tape--
one performer plays both parts).
Allegresse (after Telemann).
Elegy. Ritornello. Theme and
four variations.

PARRIS, Herman
Nocturne ad burlesca HE

PERLE, George
Three sonatas (unacc) TP

PINKHAM, Daniel
Etude ECS

PRESSER, William
Fantasy TP

RAPHLING, Sam
Lyric prelude (for b-cl) EM

REED, Alfred
Afro EBM
Guaracha EBM
Haitian dance EBM
Hora EBM
March variations EBM
Pastorale EBM
Rahoon EBM
Sarabande EBM
Scherzo fantastique EBM
Serenata EBM

REED, H. Owen
Scherzo MIL

ROCHBERG, George
Dialogues TP

RUSSELL, Armand
Pas de deux for clarinet and
percussion MP
(See also "Percussion")

SCHICKELE, Peter
Windows: 3 pieces for clarinet (or
viola or flute and guitar (1966) AB

STARER, Robert
Dialogues MCA
Recitation SMPC
Serenade SMPC

STEVENS, Halsey
Four short pieces (or for hn) COR
Serenade (or for vla) TP
Sonata (or for hn) CAM
Suite (or for vla) CFP

SYDEMAN, William
Duo SMPC
Sonata (unacc) CFP

TROWBRIDGE, Luther
Quietude HE

TUTHILL, Burnet
Concerto EV
Fantasy sonata, Op. 3 CF

WAGNER, Joseph
Rhapsody B&H
Sonatina B&H

WEBER, Ben
Concertino B&H

ZAMBARNO, Alfred
Neapolitan tarantella SHAW

SAXOPHONE

BENNETT, David
Moderne CF

CHILDS, Barney
Sonatina (unacc) TP

COHN, James
Baroque suite (or for flute or clarinet) EM
(For contents, see "Flute")

COWELL, Henry
Air and scherzo AMP

CRESTON, Paul
Sonata, Op. 19 SHAW
Suite SHAW (E-flat alto sax)
Scherzoso. Pastorale. Toccata.

DORAN, Matt
Lento and allegro WIM

HARTLEY, Walter
Duo for saxophone and piano TP
Poem (1967) TP

HEATH, Jimmy
Jazz themes with improvisations SF

HEIDEN, Bernhard
Sonata AMP

JACOBI, Frederick
Sonata BI

LANE, Richard
Suite B&H
Prelude. Song. Conversation.
Lament. Finale.

RAPHLING, Sam
Pastorale (for E-flat alto sax) EM

RUSSELL, Armand
Particles BI

SCHMIDT, William
Sonata WIM
Sonatina WIM
March. Sinfonia. Rondoletto.
Ten contemporary etudes (unacc) WIM

STILL, William Grant
Romance BI

TUTHILL, Burnet
Concerto for tenor sax and piano
SMPC

ZAMBARNO, Alfred
Neopolitan tarantella SHAW

BASSOON

ADLER, Samuel
Bassoonery (with opt contra bassoon)
TP

ALEXANDER, Joseph
Patterns BI

BACON, Ernst
The woodchuck BB

CASCARINO, Romeo
Sonata B&H

CHILDS, Barney
Sonata TP

COHN, Arthur
Declamation and toccata EV

Hebraic study EV

ETLER, Alvin
Sonata AMP

GILLIS, Don
Brushy Creek (from Four Scenes
from Yesterday) B&H

KOHS, Ellis
Sonatina MER

PERLE, George
Three inventions (unacc) TP

PHILLIPS, Burrill
Concert piece CF
(See also "String or Chamber Or-
chestra with Solo" and "Band")

PRESSER, William
Partita TP
Suite TP

ROGERS, Bernard
Soliloquy No. 2 EV

SCHMIDT, William
Fantasy on an American spiritual
WIM

SCHWARTZ, Elliott
Romance GEN

SMITH, David Stanley
Caprice CF

STEVENS, Halsey
Sonatina No. 1 (or vlc) HME
Three pieces (or vlc) CFP

STOUT, Alan
Serenity (with organ) CFP

RECORDER

LATHAM, William
Sonata No. 2 (with pno or hpcd) JS
(See also "Flute" and "Oboe")
NOTE: For music for recorder en-
sembles, see 'Instrumental Ensembles:
Woodwinds--duos, trios, and
quartets ")

HARMONICA

HOVHANESS, Alan
Seven Greek folk dances, Op. 150
CFP
1. The Selybrian Syrtos.
2. Sweet-basil Green.
3. Karagouns. 4. Tsaconian
dance. 5. Pastoral. 6. Sousta.
7. Hassapiko.

BRASS MUSIC
(with piano unless otherwise indicated)

TRUMPET OR CORNET

ANTHEIL, George
Sonata WEIN

BENNETT, Robert Russell
Rose variations CHAP

BENSON, Warren
Prologue EBM

BERNSTEIN, Leonard
Rondo for Lifey GS

CHILDS, Barney
Interbalances IV (with opt Narr) TP

COWELL, Henry
Triad PIC

CROLEY, Randell
Variazioni (unacc) TP

FRACKENPOHL, Arthur
Sonatina GS

GOEB, Roger
Lyric piece MER

GOLDMAN, Edwin Franko
Concert waltz TP
Introduction and tarantelle MER
Scherzo SHAW

HOLMES, Paul
Sonata SHAW

HOVHANESS, Alan
Prayer of Saint Gregory (with pno
or org acc) SMPC

Sonata (with org), Op. 200 CFP

KENNAN, Kent
Sonata W-7

KENNEDY, John Brodbin
Gloria (festive piece with org) B&H

KNIGHT, Morris
Introduction and allegro TP

LATHAM, William
Suite for trumpet TP
(See also "Band")

MAYER, William
Concert piece B&H

PERSICHETTI, Vincent
The hollow men EV

SANDERS, Robert
Square dance GAL

SHAPERO, Harold
Sonata (trp in C) SMPC

SOWERBY, Leo
Fantasy (with org) HWG
Sonata W-7

STARER, Robert
Invocation MIL
(See also "String or Chamber Or-
chestra with Solo")

STEVENS, Halsey
Sonata CFP

THOMSON, Virgil
At the beach CF
(See also "Band")

TROWBRIDGE, Luther
Alla marcia HE

TUTHILL, Burnet
Scherzo W-7
Sonata, Op. 29 W-7

WEBBER, Lloyd
Suite in F-major MIL

WHITE, Donald
Sonata KING

FRENCH HORN

ADAMS, Leslie
Largo AMP

ADLER, Samuel
Sonata KING

BACON, Ernst
Song after the rain BB

BASSETT, Leslie
Sonata KING

BENSON, Warren
Soliloquy EBM

BERNSTEIN, Leonard
Elegy for Mippy I GS

CAZDEN, Norman
Sonata, Op. 33 JS

CHILDS, Barney
Variations for David Racusen TP

DIERCKS, John
Fantasy TP

DONATO, Anthony
Sonata W-7

GOWER, Albert
Three short pieces (for bar) TP

HADDAD, Don
Sonata SHAW

HEIDEN, Bernhard
Sonata AMP

HOLMES, Paul
Serenade SHAW

HUGHES, Mark
Sonata TP

KORN, Peter Jona
Concertino B&H
Sonata, Op. 18 B&H

KURKA, Robert
Ballad WEIN

McKAY, George F.
Three pastoral scenes GS
A mountain serenade. Evening

horizon. Way down yonder in a
hollow log.

PORTER, Quincy
Sonata W-7

PRESSER, William
Fantasy on hymn tune "The moulder-
ing vine" TP
Rondo (for bar) TP

RAPHLING, Sam
Concert studies (unacc) EM
Sonata. Variations.
Introduction and workout.
Sonata (also called "Rhapsody")
(with pno or ob and str) COL
(See also "String or Chamber
Orchestra with Solo")

READ, Gardner
De profundis (hn or trb, with org)
KING
Poem, Op. 31a CF

SANDERS, Robert
Sonata in B-flat major KING

SCHULLER, Gunther
Nocturne MIL

STEVENS, Halsey
Four short pieces (or for cl) COR
Sonata (or for cl) CAM
Sonata KING

ULRICH, E.J.
Sonata TP

WOLFF, Christian
Duet II CFP

TROMBONE

ALEXANDER, Joseph
Sonata GEN

AUSTIN, Larry
Changes (for trb and tape) CPE

BASSETT, Leslie
Sonata KING

BENSON, Warren
Aubade EBM

BERNSTEIN, Leonard
Elegy for Mippy II (unacc) GS

BODA, John
Sonatina KING

CHILDS, Barney
Sonata (unacc) TP

COKER, Wilson
Concerto TP
(See also "Band")

COWELL, Henry
Hymn and fuguing tune No. 13 AMP

CRESTON, Paul
Fantasy, Op. 42 GS

DAVISON, John
Sonata SHAW

DRUCKMAN, Jacob
Animus I (for trb and tape) MCA

GILLIS, Don
Dialogue MIL

HENRY, Otto
Passacaglia and fugue (for b-trb)
KING

HOVHANESS, Alan
Mysterious horse before the gate,
Op. 215 (with prec) CFP
(See also "Percussion")
O world CFP

HUTCHISON, Warner
Sonatina CF

JACOBI, Frederick
Meditation W-7

LUENING, Otto
Sonata GAL
Introduction. Dance.
Hymn. March.

McKAY, George F.
Sonata W-7

McKENZIE, Jack
Song for trombone and percussion
MP
(See also "Percussion")

RAPHLING, Sam
Lyric prelude EM

READ, Gardner
De profundis (trb or hn, with org)
KING

ROY, George Klaus
Sonata KING
Aria. Interludio. Passacaglia.

SANDERS, Robert
Sonata in E-flat major W-7

SHUMAN, Davis
Three gymnastics (unacc) WEIN

STEVENS, Halsey
Sonatina PIC

TANNER, Paul
Aria WIM
(See also "Band")

TOWNSEND, Douglas
Chamber concerto No. 2 (pno or str
qrt acc) MER

TUTHILL, Burnet
Fantasy piece, Op. 10, No. 2 CF

WATSON, Walter
Sonatina SHAW

TUBA

ALEXANDER, Joseph
Requiem and coda (for euphonium
and pno) BI

BENSON, Warren
Arioso EBM

BERNSTEIN, Leonard
Waltz for Mippy III GS

DIERCKS, John
Variations on a theme of Gottschalk
TP

HADDAD, Don
Suite SHAW

HARTLEY, Walter
Sonata (1967) TP
Suite (unacc) EV

HOLMES, Paul
  Lento SHAW

PERSICHETTI, Vincent
  Serenade No. 12 (unacc) EV
    Intrada. Arietta. Mascherata.
    Capriccio. Intermezzo. Marcia.

PRESSER, William
  Suite (unacc) TP

RECK, David
  Five studies (unacc) CFP

SCHMIDT, William
  Serenade WIM

SOWERBY, Leo
  Chaconne CF

STEVENS, Halsey
  Sonatina (b-tba) PIC

3. INSTRUMENTAL ENSEMBLES

STRING ENSEMBLES

DUOS

CHAPMAN, Roger
Music for two cellos   2 vlc
CFP
Overture. Dialogue.
Dance. Aria. Finale.

CRAWFORD-SEEGER, Ruth
Diaphonic suite AB   2 vlc; or vla,
                   vlc (or bsn,
                   vlc; or ob, vlc;
                   or 2 cl)

ETLER, Alvin
Duo VAL   vln, vla

FELDMAN, Morton
Extensions V CFP   2 vlc

GABURO, Kenneth
Ideas and transforma-   vln, vla
   tions No. 1 TP

GIANNINI, Walter
Sonata AME   vln, vlc

HASLAM, Herbert
Haiku set TP   vla, vlc

KOUTZEN, Boris
Sonata GEN   vln, vlc

KUPFERMAN, Meyer
Available forms GEN   any 2 instru-
                   ments

LADERMAN, Ezra
Duo OX   vln, vlc

MOEVS, Robert
Variazioni sopra una   vln, vlc
   melodia EBM

NIXON, Roger
Four duos TP   vln, vla

PERLE, George
Solo partita TP   vln, vla

PHILLIPS, Durrill
Conversations SMPC   vln, vla
Dialogues SMPC   vln, vla

PISTON, Walter
Duo AMP   vla, vlc

PORTER, Quincy
Duo VAL   vln, vla
Duo (1957) AMP   vla, hp

RIEGGER, Wallingford
Variations, Op. 57 AMP   vln, vla

ROCHBERG, George
Duo concertante TP   vln, vlc

SCHWARTZ, Elliott
Sonata GEN   vln, c-b
Three short scenes AB   2 vlc

STARER, Robert
Duo PIC   vln, vla

STEVENS, Halsey
Bicinia HME   2 vln
Five duos CFP   2 vlc
Seven duets HME   vln, vlc
                   (or vla)
Twelve Slovakian folk-   2 vln
   songs GAL

SYDEMAN, William
Duo CFP   vln, vlc

TOWNSEND, Douglas
Duo CFP   2 vla

WOLFF, Christian
Duo CFP   2 vln

TRIOS
(vln, vlc, pno unless otherwise indicated)

ADLER, Samuel
Trio OX

217

AMRAM, David
Dirge and variations CFP

ANTES, John
Three trios, Op. 3 B&H   2 vln, vlc

BEACH, Mrs. H.H.A.
Trio, Op. 150 HE

BOATWRIGHT, Howard
Trio VAL   2 vln, vla

COPLAND, Aaron
Vitebsk (1929) B&H

COWELL, Henry
Seven paragraphs CFP   vln, vla, vlc
Trio CFP

DIAMOND, David
Trio SMPC

DONOVAN, Richard
Terzetto VAL   2 vln, vla
Trio B&H

ERB, Donald
String trio AP   vln, electric
                        gtr, vlc
FELDMAN, Morton
Four instruments CFP   vln, vlc, pno
                        (and chimes)
FINE, Irving
Fantasia MIL   vln, vla, vlc

FINNEY, Ross Lee
Trio CF

GILLIS, Don
Silhouettes MIL

HARRIS, Roy
Trio NME

HARRISON, Lou
Trio CFP   vln, vla, vlc

HAUBIEL, Charles
Romanza HE
Trio in D-minor HE   vln, vla, vlc

HEIDEN, Bernhard
Trio (1956) AMP

HEILMAN, William Clifford
Trio, Op. 7 TP

HOVHANESS, Alan
Trio, Op. 3 CFP
Trio, Op. 201 CFP   vln, vla, vlc

IMBRIE, Andrew
Trio SHAW

IVES, Charles
Trio PIC

JENKINS, John
Seven fantasies TP   2 vln, vlc

KIRCHNER, Leon
Trio AMP

MARTINO, Donald
Trio ECS   vln, vla (or
                          cl), pno
McDONALD, Harl
Trio in G-minor EV

McKAY, George Frederick
Suite MM   2 c-b, pno

MECHEM, Kirke
Trio, Op. 9 ECS

MOORE, Douglas
Trio GAL

MORRIS, Harold
Trio No. 2 TP

NOWAK, Lionel
Diptych VAL   2 vln, vlc (or
                          vla)
PERSICHETTI, Vincent
Serenade No. 3 SMPC
Trio SMPC

PISTON, Walter
Partita AMP   vln, vla, org
  Prelude. Sarabande.
  Variations. Burlesca.
Trio AMP

PORTER, Quincy
Divertimento VAL   2 vln, vla

RIEGGER, Wallingford
Trio, Op. 1 AMP

ROCHBERG, George
Trio TP

ROGERS, Bernard
Trio SMPC   vln, vla, vlc

SCHUMAN, William
  Amaryllis: variations for vln, vla, vlc
    string trio (with 3 S
    voices at ending or with
    alternate ending for
    string trio) TP

SMITH, Julia
  Trio--Cornwall TP

STEVENS, Halsey
  Trio for strings COR   vln, vla, vlc
  Three pieces HME   3 vln

STOESSEL, Albert
  Suite antique TP   2 vln, pno

THOMPSON, Randall
  Trio ECS   3 c-b; or 3 vla;
                                 or 3 vlc
VERALL, John
  Trio VAL   2 vln, vla

QUARTETS
(2 vln, vla, vlc unless otherwise indicated)

ADLER, Samuel
  Fourth string quartet MIL

AMRAM, David
  String quartet CFP

BABBITT, Milton
  Quartet No. 2 (1954) AMP

BARBER, Samuel
  Quartet, Op. 11 GS
  Serenade, Op. 1 GS

BASSETT, Leslie
  Five pieces GAL

BEREZOWSKY, Nicolai
  String quartet, Op. 16 B&H

BERGSMA, William
  Quartet No. 2 HAR
  Quartet No. 3 CF

BERRY, Wallace
  String quartet No. 2 EV

BEZANSON, Philip
  String quartet TP

BLACKWOOD, Easley
  Quartet No. 1 TP
  Quartet No. 2 GS

BOYKAN, Martin
  String quartet VAL

BRUNSWICK, Mark
  Two movements for
    string quartet TP

CAGE, John
  Quartet in four parts
    (1949) CFP

CARPENTER, John Alden
  Quartet for four stringed
    instruments GS

CARTER, Elliott
  Elegy PIC
  Quartet No. 1 (1951) AMP
  Quartet No. 2 (1959) AMP

COPLAND, Aaron
  Quartet (1950) B&H   vln, vla, vlc,
                                          pno
  Two pieces (1928) B&H
  Lento molto. Rondino.

COWELL, Henry
  Mosaic quartet (1935) AMP
  Movement for string
    quartet (1934) AMP
  Quartet No. 1 (1916) AMP
  Quartet No. 4 ("United
    Quartet") CFP
  Quartet No. 5 CFP

CRESTON, Paul
  Quartet, Op. 8 SHAW

CUSTER, Arthur
  Colloquy TP
  Exposition. Debate.
  Resolution. Epilogue.

DELAMARTER, Eric
  Foursome MIL   3 vln, vla
  String quartet No. 2
    in F MIL

DENNY, William
  Quartet No. 2 B&H

DIAMOND, David
  Concerto (1936) SMPC
  Sinfonia. Capriccio.

Aria. Scherzo-finale.
Quartet No. 1 (in one
  movement) SMPC
Quartet No. 2 SMPC
Quartet No. 3 SMPC
Quartet No. 4 SMPC
Quartet No. 5 SMPC
Quartet No. 6 SMPC
Quartet No. 8 SMPC

DONATO, Anthony
Quartet in E-minor TP

DRUCKMAN, Jacob
String quartet No. 2 MCA

DUKELSKY, Vladimir (DUKE, Vernon)
String quartet in C COL

ELSTON, Arnold
String quartet (1961) UCP

ETLER, Alvin
String quartet No. 2 (1965)
  AB

FELDMAN, Morton
Structures CFP
Three pieces CFP

FINE, Irving
Quartet CF

FINNEY, Ross Lee
Quartet No. 1 B&H
Quartet No. 4 TP
Quartet No. 6 CFP
Quartets No. 7 & 8 VAL

FISHER, Stephen
String quartet No. 1 MJQ

FOSS, Lukas
Quartet No. 1 in G-major
  (1947) CF

FRACKENPOHL, Arthur
Suite for strings GS   (c-b ad lib)

FREED, Isadore
Triptych TP   vln, vla, vlc,
                          pno
FULEIHAN, Anis
Quartet No. 1 SMPC
Quartet No. 2 SMPC

GIANNINI, Vittorio
Quartet AME

GOLD, Ernest
Quartet No. 1 TP

GORDON, Philip
Fiddling for fun GS
(See also "String
  Orchestra")

GREEN, Ray
Five epigrammatic
  portraits AME

GRIFFES, Charles T.
Two sketches based on
  Indian themes GS

GRUENBERG, Louis
Four indiscretions,
  Op. 20 TP

HADLEY, Henry
Quartet, Op. 132 GS

HAIEFF, Alexei
Quartet No. 1 B&H

HANSON, Howard
Quartet in one move-
  ment, Op. 23 AME

HARRIS, Roy
Quartet No. 3 (four
  prelude and fugues) MIL
Three variations on a
  theme GS

HARRISON, Lou
Suite No. 2 MER
(See also "String
  Orchestra")

HAUBIEL, Charles
Echi classici HE

HELLER, James
Quartet, Op. 1 GS
Three aquatints for
  string quartet TP

HELM, Everett
String quartet No. 2 AMP

HILLER, L.A., Jr.
Illiac suite TP

HOVHANESS, Alan
Quartet, Op. 8 CFP

IMBRIE, Andrew
Quartet No. 2 SHAW
Quartet No. 3 SHAW

IVES, Charles
Quartet No. 1 PIC
Fugue. Prelude.
Offertory. Postlude.
Quartet No. 2 PIC
Scherzo PIC

JACOBI, Frederick
Quartet on Indian
themes TP
Quartet No. 2 TP
Quartet No. 3 AME

JOHNSTON, Ben
Nine variations AP

JONES, Charles
Quartet (1944) MER

KERR, Harrison
Quartet B&H

KIRCHNER, Leon
Quartet (1949) MER
Quartet No. 2 (1958) AMP

KOHS, Ellis
Quartet (1940) MER

KORTE, Karl
Second quartet for
strings GAL

KOUTZEN, Boris
Quartet No. 2 GEN

KROLL, William
Four bagatelles GS
Four characteristic
pieces GS
Little march. Magyar.
The ancient. Cossack.

KRUL, Eli
Quartet CFP

LADERMAN, Ezra
String quartet No. 2 OX

LA MONTAINE, John
String quartet, Op. 16 PJS

LEES, Benjamin
Quartet No. 1 B&H

Quartet No. 2 B&H

LIEBERSON, Goddard
String quartet OX

LOCKWOOD, Normand
Quartet No. 3 TP
Six serenades MER

LOEFFLER, Charles Martin
Music for four stringed
instruments TP

MARTINO, Donald
Sette canoni enigmatici
(also for 4 cl or for
quartet for mixed in-
struments) ECS

MASON, Daniel Gregory
Intermezzo, Op. 17 NME
Quartet on Negro themes,
Op. 19 TP
Serenade TP

McKAY, Neil
String quartet No. 1 KAL

MECHEM, Kirke
String quartet ECS

MENNIN, Peter
Quartet No. 2 (1951) CF

MOEVS, Robert
String quartet EBM

MOORE, Douglas
Quartet CF

OVERTON, Hall
Quartet No. 2 GAL

PALMER, Robert
Quartet TP   vln, vla, vlc,
                          pno
PERLE, George
Quartet No. 3 NME

PERSICHETTI, Vincent
Third string quartet EV

PINKHAM, Daniel
Sonata No. 1 ECS   2 vln, vlc, org
(See also "String or
Chamber Orchestra
with Solo")

PISTON, Walter
Quartet No. 1 (1933) AMP
Quartet No. 2 GS
Quartet No. 3 B&H
Quartet No. 4 AMP
Quartet No. 5 AMP

PORTER, Quincy
Quartet No. 3 CFP
Quartet No. 4 B&H
Quartet No. 6 CFP
Quartet No. 7 VAL
Quartet No. 8 VAL

POWELL, Mel
Filigree GS (R)

REYNOLDS, Roger
Quartet No. 2 CFP

RIEGGER, Wallingford
Introduction and fugue,   4 vlc
Op. 69 AMP
Prelude, Op. 69 AMP
Quartet No. 1, Op. 30
AMP
Quartet No. 2, Op. 43
AMP
Romanza, Op. 56a AMP

RILEY, John
Quartet No. 2 VAL

ROCHBERG, George
Quartet No. 1 TP
String quartet (with
soprano) TP
(See also "Solo Vocal
Music")
String quartet No. 1 TP

ROSEN, Jerome
Quartet No. 1 B&H

RUBENSTEIN, Beryl
Passe-pied CF

SCHULLER, Gunther
Fantasy quartet MJQ   4 vlc
Quartet for double   4 c-b
basses ABE
Quartet No. 1 TP
String quartet No. 2 AMP

SCHUMAN, William
Quartet No. 2 B&H
Sinfonia. Passacaglia.
Fugue.

Quartet No. 3 TP
Introduction and fugue.
Intermezzo. Rondo
variations.
Quartet No. 4 GS
String quartet No. 8 TP

SEARCH, Frederick
Quartet in E-minor HE

SESSIONS, Roger
Quartet No. 1 in E-
minor (1936) EBM
Quartet No. 2 (1951) EBM

SHAPERO, Harold
Quartet No. 1 SMPC

SHEPHERD, Arthur
Quartet in E-minor TP

SHIFRIN, Seymour
Quartet (1949) AMP

SMITH, David Stanley
Quartet in E-flat-major,
Op. 57 OX
Quartet, Op. 46 TP
Quartet No. 6 in C-
major TP

SOWERBY, Leo
Serenade in G-major TP

STARER, Robert
Elegy MCA
(See also "String
Orchestra")
Quartet (1947) MER

STILL, William Grant
Danzas de Panama SMPC
Tamborito. Mejorana
y Socovan. Punto.
Cumbia y congo.

TAYLOR, Deems
Lucrece, Op. 21 COL

THOMPSON, Randall
Quartet No. 1 in D-
minor ECS

THOMSON, Virgil
Quartet No. 1 B&H
Quartet No. 2 B&H

TRIMBLE, Lester
String quartet No. 1 (1950)
TP

VERALL, John
Quartet No. 2 VAL
Quartet No. 3 TP
Quartet No. 4 TP

VINCENT, John
Quartet MIL

WAGENAAR, Bernard
Quartet No. 3 TP

WARD, Robert
First string quartet GAL

WASHBURN, Robert
Suite OX
(See also "String
Orchestra")

WEINBERG, Henry
Movement for string
quartet (1959) AP

WILSON, George Balch
Quartet in G-major TP

WOLFF, Christian
Summer CFP

YANNATOS, James
Five epigrams AMP

QUINTETS
(2 vln, vla, vlc, pno unless otherwise
indicated)

CARPENTER, John Alden
Quintet GS

COLE, Ulric
Quintet TP

DIAMOND, David
Night music SMPC   2 vln, vla, vlc,
                          acdn

FELCIANO, Richard
Aubade CPE   vln, vla, vlc,
                          hp, pno

FINNEY, Ross Lee
String quintet CFP   2 vln, vla,
  I. Introduction.   2 vlc
     Statement 1.

Episode 1. Statement 2.
Episode 2.
II. Intermezzi: nocturne,
capriccio, restatements,
conclusion.

GIANNINI, Vittorio
Quintet COL

GILLIS, Don
Three sketches B&H   2 vln, vla,
Enchantment.   vlc, c-b
Whimsy. Day dreams.

HARRIS, Roy
Quintet GS
Passacaglia. Cadenza.
Fugue.

HOLDEN, David
Music for piano and
strings TP

HOVHANESS, Alan
Quintet, Op. 9 CFP

IVES, Charles
Hallowe'en (from Three
outdoor scenes) AMP
In re con moto et al PIC
Largo risoluto No. 1 PIC
Largo risoluto No. 2 PIC

JACOBI, Frederick
Hagiographa AME
Three Biblical narra-
tives: Job; Ruth;
Joshua.

KENNAN, Kent
Quintet GS

KOUTZEN, Boris
Concert piece MER   solo vlc and
(See also "String &   str qrt
Chamber Orchestra
with Solo")

LEOFFLER, Charles Martin
Quintet in one move-   3 vln, vla,
ment GS   vlc

PALMER, Robert
Quintet CFP

PERSICHETTI, Vincent
Quintet EV

PETER, Johann F.
Six quintets ("Salem"   2 vln, 2 vla,
quintets) CFP   vlc

PINKHAM, Daniel
Sonata No. 2 ECS   2 vln, vla,
(See also "String or   vlc, org
Chamber Orchestra
with Solo")

PISTON, Walter
Quintet AMP

RANCY, James
Four pieces for guitar   gtr, 2 vln, vla,
quintet MJQ (R)   vlc, c-b

RIEGGER, Wallingford
Quintet, Op. 47 AMP

ROBERTSON, Leroy
Quintet in A-minor TP

SESSIONS, Roger
Quintet (1958) EBM   2 vln, 2 vla,
                             vlc

SMITH, David Stanley
Quintet, Op. 56 OX

VINCENT, John
Consort MIL

WALDROP, Gid
Pressures B&H   2 vln, vla,
                             vlc, c-b

WEBER, Ben
Serenade B&H   2 vln, vla,
                             vlc, c-b

SEXTETS, OCTETS AND LARGER
ENSEMBLES

COPLAND, Aaron
Nonet B&H   3 vln, 3 vla,
(See also "String   3 vlc
Orchestra")

DIAMOND, David
Nonet SMPC   3 vln, 3 vla,
                             3 vlc

FULEIHAN, Anis
Divertimento SMPC   2 vln, 2 vla,
                             2 vlc

HALL, James
Pieces for guitar and   gtr, 2 vln, 2
strings MJQ (R)   vla, vlc, c-b

HOLDEN, David
Music for piano and   2 vln, 2 vla,
strings TP   vlc, pno

KOHS, Ellis
Chamber concerto MER   solo vla, 4
                             vln, 2 vla, 2
                             vlc, c-b

LEWIS, John
Sketch for double   soli: vib, pno,
quartet MJQ (R)   c-b, dr; 2 vln,
                             vla, vlc

PISTON, Walter
Sextet for stringed in-   2 vln, 2 vla,
struments AMP   2 vlc

RUGGLES, Carl
Angels AME   4 vln, 2 vlc
(See also "Brass
Sextet")

SCHULLER, Gunther
Conversations MJQ (R)   2 vln, vla, vlc,
                             c-b, vib, pno,
SEARCH, Frederick   perc, dr
Sextet TP   2 vln, 2 vla,
                             2 vlc
SHULMAN, Alan
Suite miniature SHAW   8 vlc

STRINGS WITH VOICE AND/OR
WINDS, PERCUSSION

ALEXANDER, Joseph
Three pieces for   fl, cl, trp,
eight GEN   vln, vlc, c-b,
                             pno, perc

AMRAM, David
Discussion CFP   fl, vlc, pno,
                             perc

Shakespearean concerto   ob, 2 hn, 2
CFP (R)   vln, vla, vlc,
                             c-b
Three songs for Marl-   hn, vlc
boro CFP

AUSTIN, Larry
A broken consort MJQ(R)   fl, cl, hn,
                             trp, pno, c-b,
                             perc

BABBITT, Milton
All set AMP(R)   a-sax, t-sax,
                             trp, trb, c-b,
                             pno, vib, perc

Composition for four instruments NME	fl, cl, vln, vlc
BARATI, George	
Quartet CFP	hpcd, fl, ob (or E-hn), c-b (or vlc)
BARBER, Samuel	
Dover Beach GS	med voice, 2 vln, vla, vlc; text: Matthew Arnold
Toccata festiva GS	org, vln, vla, vlc, trp, timp
BAUER, Marion	
Concertino B&H	ob, cl, 2 vln, vla, vlc
BEREZOWSKY, Nicolai	
Theme and variations fantastique B&H	cl, 2 vln, vla, vlc, pno
BERGER, Arthur	
Three poems of Yeats NME (For contents, see "Solo Vocal Music")	med voice, vlc, fl, cl
BERGSMA, William	
Pastorale and scherzo HAR	fl, 2 vla
BLACKWOOD, Easley	
Concertino GS	vln, vla, vlc, fl, ob
Un voyage à Cythère, Op. 20 GS(R)	S; picc (also 2nd fl), fl, ob (also E-hn), 2 cl, bsn, trp, hn, trb, c-b text: Charles Baudelaire
BOATWRIGHT, Howard	
Black is the color OX	m-S, vln text: trad
Cock Robin OX	m-S, rec text: trad
Gypsy laddie OX	m-S, 2 melody instruments text: trad
One morning in May OX	S, vln text: trad
Quartet OX	cl, vln, vla, vlc
BROWN, Rayner	
Concertino WIM	hp, 2 trp, trb, hn, tba
Trio WIM	fl, cl, vla

BUDD, Harold	
III for double ensemble CPE	quartet: fl, cl, vlc, vib; jazz trio: trp, c-b, drms
BURGE, David	
Aeolian music BCM	fl, cl, vln, vlc, pno
CAGE, John	
Six short inventions (1933) CFP	vln, 2 vla, vlc, a-fl, cl, trp
CARTER, Elliott	
Sonata AMP	fl, ob, vlc, hpcd
CHILDS, Barney	
Jack's new bag CPE (See also "Percussion")	fl, trp, trb, pno(2 players), perc I: 2 timp, 2 tom-toms, 2 temple blocks, gong, cym, sn-drm, tri); perc II: (jazz drum set), vla, vlc, c-b
Take 5 (chance music: any 5 instruments-- string, wind, perc, toy) CPE	
CHOU, Wen-Chung	
Suite CFP	fl, ob, cl, bsn, hn, hp
Three folk songs CFP	hp, fl
Yü Ko CFP	vln, fl, E-hn, b-cl, trb, perc
COKER, Wilson	
Concertino TP	bsn, vln, vla, vlc
COPLAND, Aaron	
Sextet (1937) (cham version of Short Symphony) B&H (See also "Full Symphony")	2 vln, vla, vlc, cl, pno
COWELL, Henry	
Persian set CFP(R)	2 vln, c-b, picc (or fl), cl, gtr (or man), pno
Toccanta B&H(R)	S voice (vocalise), vlc, fl, pno (or orch)

CRAWFORD-SEEGER, Ruth
Diaphonic suite AB   bsn, vlc;or ob, vlc; or vla, vlc; or 2 cl

CRESTON, Paul
Partita, Op. 12 (1937) MCA   fl, vln (or 2 vln), pno

DAHL, Ingolf
Concerto a tre B&H   vln, vlc, cl

DELLO JOIO, Norman
Antiphonal fantasy on a theme of Vicenzo Albrici EBM(R)   3 trp, 4 hn, 3 trb, tba, org, 2 vln, vla, vlc, c-b
Lamentation of Saul CF(R)   Bar; fl, ob, cl, vla, vlc, pno text adapted from the play "David" by D.H. Lawrence
Trio CF   vlc, fl, pno

DIAMOND, David
Quintet CF   vln, vla, vlc, fl, pno
Quintet SMPC   2 vla, 2 vlc, cl

DONATO, Anthony
Drag and run HE   2 vln, vlc, cl

DONOVAN, Richard
Music for six CFP   ob, cl, trp, vln, vlc
Serenade NME   pno, ob, vln, vla, vlc

DORAN, Matt
Trio WIM   fl, vlc, pno

DUKELSKY, Vladimir (DUKE, Vernon)
Etude MCA   vln, bsn

DUSHKIN, Dorothy
Quintet for Amanda (for young people) VAL   vln, vla, vlc, ob, fl (or cl)

ETLER, Alvin
Concerto for clarinet (1962) AMP   cl; 3 trp, 3 trb, 2 c-b, 3 perc
Duo VAL   ob, vla(or vln or fl and cl)
Quartet VAL   vla, ob, cl, bsn
Sextet AMP   ob, cl, bsn, vln, vla, vlc
Sonata VAL   vla, ob, cl

FELDMAN, Morton
de Kooning CFP(R)   hn, perc, pno, vln, vlc
Durations I CFP   vln, vlc, a-fl, pno
Durations III CFP   vln, tba, pno
Durations IV CFP   vln, vlc, vib
Durations V CFP   vln, vlc, hn, vib, hp, pno (or cel)
Eleven instruments CFP   vln, vlc, fl, a-fl, hn, trp, bass trp, trb, tba, vib, pno
For Franz Kline CFP   S(vocalise), vln, vlc, hn, chimes, pno
Four songs to e.e. cummings CFP   S, vlc, pno
Intervals CFP(R)   Bar (vocalise), vlc, trb, vib, perc
Ixion (Summerspace-- a ballet) CFP   3 fl, cl, hn, trp, trb, pno, vlc, c-b(graph)
Journey to the end of night CFP   S, fl, 2 cl, bsn
Numbers CFP   vln, vlc, c-b, fl, hn, trb, tba, perc, pno(cel)
The O'Hara songs CFP   b-Bar; vln, vla, vlc, chimes, pno; text: John O'Hara
Projection 2 CFP   vln, vlc, fl, trp, pno
Projection 5 CFP   3 vlc, 3 fl, trp, 2 pno
Rabbi Akiba CFP   S, fl, hn, E-hn, trp, trb, tba, pno, perc, cel, vlc, c-b
The Straits of Magellan CFP   fl, hn, trp, amplified gtr, hp, pno, c-b (graph)
Two instruments CFP   vlc, hn
Two pieces CFP   vln, vlc, fl, a-fl, hn, trp
Two pieces for clarinet and string quartet CFP   cl, 2 vln, vlc, vla
Vertical thoughts 3 CFP   S (vocalise, fl, hn trp, trb, tba, pno (cel), perc, vln, vlc, c-b
Vertical thoughts 5 CFP   S (vocalise), vln, tba, perc, cel

FINE, Vivian
The great wall of
China NME — med voice; fl, vlc, pno; text: Franz Kafka

Four songs NME
(For contents, see
"Solo Vocal Music")

FINNEY, Ross Lee
Divertissement BCM — pno, cl, vln, vlc

FISHER, Stephen
Music for 9 instru-
ments MJQ(R) — cl, bsn, hn, trp, trb, tba, vln, vlc, c-b

FLAGELLO, Nicolas
Burlesca GEN — fl, gtr

FLANAGAN, William
Good-bye my fancy PIC — S, fl, gtr (or pno); text: Walt Whitman

FOOTE, Arthur
Night piece S-B — fl, 2 vln, vla, vic, c-b

FOSS, Lukas
Echoi CF — vlc, cl, pno, perc
Elytres CF — solo fl, 2 solo vln, 3 distant vln(or vln groups), perc, hp, vib, pno

FULEIHAN, Anis
Quintet SMPC — hn, str qrt

GABURO, Kenneth
Line studies MCA — vla, fl, cl, trb

GOODMAN, Joseph
Trio AMP — fl, vln, pno

GRAVES, William
Song for St. Cecilia's
day (cantata) CF(R) — solo voice, cl, str qrt, pno; text: W.H. Auden

GREEN, Ray
Holiday for four AME — vla, cl, bsn, pno
Fugal introduction.
Prairie blues.
Festive finale.

HABER, Louis
Six miniatures GEN — fl, vln
March. Intermezzo.
Barcarolle. South
American dance.

Prelude. Perpetual
motion.
Trio GEN — fl, vln, pno

HANSON, Howard
Pastorale, Op. 38
CF — solo ob; hp, vln, vla, vlc, c-b

HARRIS, Arthur
Four pieces for three
instruments BB — fl, 2 ob or E-hn, 2 cl, or 2 vln, vla

HARRIS, Roy
Abraham Lincoln walks
at midnight (a can-
tata of lamentation)
AMP — m-S; vln, vlc, pno; text: Vachel Lindsay
Concerto, Op. 2 AMP — 2 vln, vla, vlc, cl, pno

HARRISON, Lou
Air from Rapunzel PIC — high voice; fl, vln, vla, vlc, hp, pno; text: Wm. Morris
Alma redemptoris
mater (1951) PIC — Bar; vln, trb, tack-pno; text: liturgical
Concerto CFP(R)
(See also "Percus-
sion") — vln, perc orch

HAUBIEL, Charles
In the French manner
HE
In praise of dance HE — fl, vlc, pno
Masks
Specters. Fauns. — vln, vlc, ob, pno
Witches.
Partita
Minuet. Pavane. — vln, vlc, ob, pno
Gigue.

HEIDEN, Bernhard
Quintet (1952) AMP — 2 vln, vla, vlc, hn
Serenade (1955) AMP — vln, vla, vlc, bsn
Notturno. March.
Intermezzo. Scherzo.
Epilogue.

HELM, Everett
Concerto for five solo
instruments AMP(R) — vln, fl, ob, bsn, trp; perc, str orch
(See also "String or
Chamber Orchestra
with Solo")

HOSMER, James
Rhapsody MM   fl, str (or pno)

HOVHANESS, Alan
The flowering peach   cl, a-sax,
(music for Clifford   timp, tam-tam,
Odets' play) AMP   vib, glock, hp,
1. Overture. 2. Lift-   cel
ing of voices & build-
ing of the Ark. 3. In-
termezzo. 4. Rain.
5. Love song. 6. Sun
& moon. 7. Rainbow
hymn. (See also
"Percussion")
Hercules CFP   S, vln; text:
       A. Hovhaness
Koke no Niwa (Moss   hp, E-hn (or
garden), Op. 181 CFP   cl), perc
(See also "Percus-
sion")
O lady moon (in: New   high voice, cl,
Vistas in Song)EBM   pno; text:
       Lafcadio Hearn
Overture CFP   trb, 2 vln, vla,
       vlc
Quartet No. 1, Op. 97   fl, ob, vlc,
CFP   hpcd(or pno)
Quartet No. 2, Op. 112   fl, ob, vlc,
CFP   pno
Sextet, Op. 164 CFP(R)   2 vln, vla, vlc,
       a-rec, hpcd
       (pno or org)
Symphony No. 16, Op.   2 vln, 2 vla,
202 CFP(R)   vlc, c-b, hp,
       timp, perc
Upon enchanted ground,   vlc, fl, giant
Op. 90, No. 1 CFP   tam-tam, hp

IVES, Charles
Allegretto sombreoso   3 vln, fl, E-hn,
PIC   pno
Chromâtimelôdtune   ob, cl, bsn,
(1913) (reconstructed   trp, hn, trb,
and completed by   tba, 3 vln, vla,
Gunther Schuller   vlc, c-b, sn-dr,
(1962) MJQ(R)   chimes, pno
Largo PIC   vln, cl, pno

JOHNSON, J. J.
Perceptions MJQ(R)   soli: trp, c-b,
Ballade. Blue   drm; 4 fl, 6 ob,
mist. Fantasia.   4 cl, 2 bsn, 2
       hp, timp

JOHNSTON, Ben
Duo MM   fl, c-b

KANITZ, Ernest
Notturno VAL   fl, vln, vla

KAY, Ulysses
Brief elegy MCA   2 vln, vla,
       vlc, ob
KENNAN, Kent
Night soliloquy CF   2 vln, vla,
       vlc, c-b, fl,
       pno
KERR, Harrison
Trio NME   vlc, cl, pno

KIRCHNER, Leon
Concerto (1960) AMP(R)   soli: vln, vlc;
       fl, ob, cl, bsn,
       hn, 2 trp, 2
       trb, timp, 3
       perc
Toccata AMP(R)   solo winds:
       ob, cl, bsn,
       trp, hn, trb,
       perc, cel, str
KOHN, Karl
Capriccio CF   fl, cl, hp,
       vlc, pno
KOHS, Ellis B.
Legend AMP   solo ob, 2
       vln, vla, vlc,
       c-b
KORN, Peter Jona
Aloysia serenade,   vla, vlc, fl
Op. 19 B&H
KOUTZEN, Boris
Music AMP   a-sax, bsn,
       vlc
KRAEHENBUEHL, David
Variations for two   any combina-
AMP   tion
KUBIK, Gail
Divertimento No. 2   vla, 2 fl, ob,
COL   cl, bsn, trp,
       trb, pno
KUPFERMAN, Meyer
Infinities thirteen BCM   fl, picc, a-fl,
       cl, b-cl, vln,
       vla, pno
LAYTON, Billy Jim
Divertimento, Op. 6   vln, vlc, cl,
GS(R)   bsn, trb,
       hpcd, perc
LESSARD, John
Trio JC   fl, vln, pno

LEWIS, John
The Milanese story
MJQ(R)   fl, t-sax, gtr,
pno, c-b, drm,
2 vln, vla, vlc

LEWIS, Peter
Septet MER   fl, cl, bsn, vln,
vla, vlc, pno

LEWIS, Robert Hall
Music for twelve
players TP(R)   fl (picc), cl,
bsn, hn, trp,
trb, vib, glock,
xy, pno, hp,
vln, vlc, c-b

LIPSCOMB, Helen
Design TP   cl, 2 vln, vla,
vlc

LUNETTA, Stanley
Quartet (1965) CPE   fl, vln, vib,
c-b

MARTINO, Donald
Cinque frammenti MM   ob, c-b
Quartet ECS   cl, vln, vla,
vlc
Trio ECS   vln, cl (or
vla), pno

MASON, Daniel Gregory
Pastorale COL   pno, vln, cl
Three pieces TP   2 vln, vla, vlc,
Sarabande. Elegy.   fl, hp
Caprice.

McBRIDE, Robert
Quintet GS   2 vln, vla,
vlc, ob

MECHEM, Kirke
Divertimento ECS   fl, vln, vla,
vlc

MOORE, Douglas
Quintet CF   2 vln, vla,
vlc, cl

MORAN, Robert
Four visions TP   fl, hp, 2 vln,
vla, vlc

THE MORAVIANS
Ten sacred songs CFP   S; 2 vln, vla,
(For contents, see   vlc, org; texts:
"Solo Vocal Music")   Biblical

MORYL, Richard
Improvisations BCM   fl, cl, vln, vlc
and electronic
amplification

NEMIROFF, Isaac
Variations to a theme   fl, ob, vlc (or
MM   bsn)

PALMER, Robert
Quintet SMPC   cl, vln, vla,

vlc, pno

PERRY, Julia
Pastoral SMPC   2 vln, 2 vla,
2 vlc, fl
Stabat mater SMPC   A; 2 vln, vla,
(See also "String or   vlc (or str
Chamber Orchestra   orch); text:
with Solo")   liturgical

PERSICHETTI, Vincent
Serenade No. 6 EV   vla, vlc, trb

PINKHAM, Daniel
Three lyric scenes BOS   med voice;
(For contents, see   2 vln, vla, vlc
"Solo Vocal Music")   text: W. H.
(See also "String or   Auden
Chamber Orchestra
with Solo")
Three songs from Ec-   high voice;
clesiastes ECS   2 vln, vla,
(For contents, see   vlc (or pno);
"Solo Vocal Music")   text: Biblical

PISTON, Walter
Divertimento for nine   2 vln, vla, vlc,
instruments AMP   c-b, fl, ob,
cl, bsn
Partita AMP   vln, vla, org
Quintet AMP   2 vln, vla, vlc,
fl
Suite AMP   vla, ob, cl

PORTER, Quincy
Little trio VAL   fl, vln, vla
Quintet AB   cl, 2 vln, vla,
vlc
Three Elizabethan   med voice; fl,
songs YUP(R)   ob, bsn, 2 vln,
(For contents, see   vla, vlc, c-b
"Solo Vocal Music")

POWELL, Mel
Improvisation GS   cl, vla, pno
Miniatures for baroque   fl, ob, vln,
ensemble (tonality   vla, vlc,
studies) GS   hpcd
Two prayer settings   T; ob, vln,
GS(R)   vla, vlc
(For contents, see
"Solo Vocal Music")

PRESSER, William
Passacaglia HE   cl, hn, vln,
vla, vlc
Rhapsody on a peace-   vln, hn, pno
ful theme TP

RECK, David
Number 1 for 12   fl, cl, t-sax,
  players MJQ(R)   hn, gtr, vib,
                         pno, 3 perc,
                         vla, c-b
REYNOLDS, Roger
Acquaintances CFP   fl, c-b, pno
Quick are the mouths   ob, 3 fl, 3 vlc,
  of earth CFP   trp, trb, b-trb,
                         pno, 2 perc
ROCHBERG, George
Blake songs MCA(R)   S; fl, cl, b-cl,
  (For contents, see   hp, cel, vln,
  "Solo Vocal Music")   vla, vlc
Contra mortem et   fl, cl, vln,
  tempere TP   pno
Serenata d'estate   fl, hp, gtr,
  (summer night)   vln, vla, vlc
  MCA(R)
String quartet No. 2   S; 2 vln, vla,
  with soprano TP   vlc; text:
                         Rainer Maria
                         Rilke; trans:
                         Harry Behn
Summer serenade   fl, vln, vla,
  MCA   vlc, hp, gtr

ROGERS, Bernard
Allegory TP   2 fl, mar, 2
                         vln, vla, vlc,
                         c-b
Ballade SMPC   pno, vla, bsn

ROREM, Ned
Eleven studies for   fl (or picc), ob
  eleven players B&H   (or E-hn), cl,
  Prelude. Alegretto.   C-trp, perc,
  Bird call. The diary. vln, vla, vlc,
  Contest. Invention   pno, hp, xy
  for battery. In mem-
  ory of my feelings.
  Fugato. Elegy.
  Presto. Epilogue.
Lovers (a narrative in   hpcd, vlc, ob,
  ten scenes) B&H   perc
  1. 53 Harp Street.
  2. Before. 3. Murmur-
  ing of her past. 4.
  During. 5. Later. 6.
  While he sleeps. 7.
  Bridge of the arts.
  8. After. 9. The Bridge
  of Sighs. 10. Harp
  Street again.
Mourning scene from   med voice; 2
  Samuel CFP   vln, vla, vlc;
                         text: Biblical
Trio CFP   fl, vlc, pno

ROSEN, Jerome
Sonata B&H   vlc, cl

SCHICKELE, Peter
Windows AB   vla, gtr (or
                         fl and cl)
SCHIFRIN, Lalo
Ritual of sound MJQ(R)   fl, cl, b-cl,
                         hn, 2 trp, trb,
                         tba, gtr, vib,
                         2 c-b, perc
SCHMIDT, William
Sonata breve WIM   fl, cl, vla

SCHULLER, Gunther
Abstraction AMP   sax, gtr, 2
                         vln, vla, vlc,
                         2 c-b, perc
Adagio AMP   fl, vln, vla,
                         vlc
Chromâtimelôdtune   ob, cl, bsn,
  (originally written   trp, hn, trb,
  by Charles Ives in   tba, 3 vln, vla,
  1913 and recon-   vlc, c-b, sn-
  structed by Schuller   dr, chimes,
  in 1962) MJQ(R)   pno
Conversations for   2 vln, vla,
  jazz qrt & str qrt   vlc, vib, pno,
  AMP   perc, c-b
Movements for flute   fl, vln, vla,
  and strings AMP   vlc, c-b
Trio AMP   ob, hn, vla

SCHWARTZ, Elliott
Concert piece for 10   fl (picc), ob,
  players AB(R)   cl(b-cl), bsn,
                         hn, perc, vln,
                         vla, vlc, c-b
Music for oboe, trum-   ob, trp, vlc
  pet, cello GEN
Quartet GEN   ob, vln, vla,
                         vlc
Serenade GEN   fl, c-b, perc
  (See also "Percus-
  sion")
Soliloquies BCM   fl(picc), cl,
                         vln, pno
Texture (1966) AB   fl, ob, cl, bsn,
                         hn, trp, trb,
                         2 vln, vla, vlc,
                         c-b
Trio GEN   fl, cl, vlc
Trio GEN   fl, vlc, pno
Variations GEN   S; bsn, perc
  (See also "Percus-   vocalise
  sion")

SHEPHERD, Arthur
Serenade MER — high voice with vla obb; text: Sacherer-all Sitwell

Triptych TP
(For contents, see "Solo Vocal Music") — S; 2 vln, vla, vlc; text: Rabindranath Tagore

SHIFRIN, Seymour
Serenade CFP — ob, cl, hn, vla, pno

SMIT, Leo
Four motets BB
(For contents, see "Solo Vocal Music") — med voice; vla, 2 fl (or S & T-rec); text: anon, German; trans: Sylvia Wright

Quintet BB — fl, vln, vla, vlc, hp

Trio BB — fl, vla, hp

SMITH, John Shaffer
Quintet CF — ob(or cl), 2 vln, vla, vlc

SMITH, William O.
Elegy for Eric MJQ — fl(a-sax), cl (b-sax), trp, trb, vib, vln, c-b, dr

Five songs MJQ
(For contents, see "Solo Vocal Music") — med voice, vlc

Four pieces MJQ — vln, cl, pno
Quartet MJQ — cl, vln, vlc, pno

SOLLBERGER, Harvey
Chamber variations for 12 players MM(R) — fl, a-fl(picc), ob, cl(b-cl), bsn, 2 perc, vln, vla, vlc, c-b, pno

Solos for violin and five instruments MM(R) — solo vln; fl, cl, hn, c-b, pno

SOWERBY, Leo
Ballad HWG — E-hn (or cl, or vln, or vla), org

STARER, Robert
Concertino MCA — S; vln (or ob or trp), pno
or
Bar; vln (or bsn or trb), pno; text: Biblical

STEVENS, Halsey
Quintet HME — fl, vln, vla, vlc, pno
Pastoral. Scherzo. Threnody. Fugue. Epilogue.

SUBOTNICK, Morton
Serenade No. 1 MM(R) — fl, vlc, vib, man, pno
Serenade No. 3 BCM(R) — fl, cl, vln, pno, tape

SYDEMAN, William
Concerto da camera AMP(R) — solo vln, 2 trp, perc
(See also "Percussion")
Duo CFP — cl, c-b
Music CFP(R) — fl, gtr, vla, perc
Trio MM — fl, vln, c-b

THOMPSON, Randall
Suite ECS — vla, ob, cl

THOMSON, Virgil
Four songs to poems of Thomas Campion COL — m-S; vla, cl, hp
(For contents, see "Solo Vocal Music")
Ondine (incidental music) COL — fl, perc, cel, hp, vlc, c-b; 2 vln, vla, vlc
Serenade SMPC — vln, fl
Sonata da chiesa (1926) B&H — vla, cl, hn, trp, trb
Stabat mater B&H — S; 2 vln, vla, vlc; text: liturgical

TOWNSEND, Douglas
Chamber concerto No. 2 MER — trb(or bar), 2 vln, vla, vlc
8 x 8, variations on a theme by Milhaud CFP — s-rec (or picc or fl), trp, (or cl or ob), vlc, pno

TRIMBLE, Lester
Nonet CFP — fl, ob, cl, bsn, 2 vln, vla, vlc, c-b
Petit concert CFP — S or T; hpcd, vln, ob
(For contents, see "Solo Vocal Music")

VAN VACTOR, David
Quintet TP — 2 vln, vla, vlc, fl

WAGNER, Joseph
Serenade SMPC   vln, vlc, ob
Prelude. Pastorale.   (or fl or cl)
Nocturne. Burlesque.
Theme and variations   vln, vlc, fl,
SMPC   cl

WEBER, Ben
Four songs, Op. 40   S or T, vlc
NME
(For contents, see
"Solo Vocal Music")

WESTERGAARD, Peter
Variations for six   fl (picc), cl
players AB   (b-cl), vln, vlc,
                       pno, perc
WIGGLESWORTH, Frank
Duo TP   ob, vla (cl)

WILDER, Alec
Horn o'plenty MJQ   4 hn, gtr, pno
                       (hpcd), c-b, dr
WOLFF, Christian
Nine CFP   2 vlc, fl, cl,
                       hn, trp, trb,
                       cel, pno
Trio I CFP   vlc, fl, trp

WUORINEN, Charles
Bearbeitungen ueber   fl (picc), cl(b-
das Glogauer   cl), vln, c-b
Liederbuch (1961)
MM
Chamber concerto for   vlc; fl, ob, cl,
cello and 10 players   bsn, 2 perc,
MM   pno, vln, vla,
                       c-b
Chamber concerto for   fl; gtr, hp,
flute and 10 players   hpcd, pno, cel,
MM   xy, vib, ob, 2
                       perc
Chamber concerto for   ob; tba, hp,
oboe and 10 players   pno, 6 perc,
MM   c-b
Composition for violin vln; 2 ob, b-cl,
and 10 instruments   2 hn, 2 trb,
MM   perc, pno, c-b
Concertante III MM   solo hpcd; ob,
                       vln, vla, vlc
Into the organ pipes and picc, cl, sax,
steeples MM   timp, 2 pno, 2
                       vla, 2 vlc, c-b
Octet MM   ob, cl, hn, trb,
                       vln, vlc, c-b,
                       pno
Trio No. 1 MM   fl, vlc, pno
Trio No. 2 MM   fl, vlc, pno

Turetzky pieces MM   fl, cl, c-b

WOODWIND ENSEMBLES

DUOS AND TRIOS

ALEXANDER, Joseph
A brace of duets GEN   cl(b-cl), bsn

AMRAM, David
Trio CFP   sax, hn, bsn

BARAB, Seymour
Pastorals GAL   3 rec (SAA
                       or SAT)
Six pieces for three   3 rec (SAT)
recorders B&H
Divisions for soprano.
Pavane. Divisions
for alto. Ballet.
Divisions for tenor.
Fugue.
Sonatina B&H   3 fl
BAUER, Marion
Duo CFP   ob, cl
Prelude. Improvisa-
tion. Pastoral.
Dance.

BAVICCHI, John
Six duets OX   fl, cl

BEESON, Jack
Sonata canonica GAL   2 rec (AA)

BERGER, Arthur
Duo CFP   ob, cl

BERRY, Wallace
Two canons EV   2 cl

BIGGS, John
Tre canzoni WIM   3 cl

CAGE, John
Music for wind instru- duo (ob, hn);
ments (1938) CFP   trio (fl, cl,
                       bsn)
CAZDEN, Norman
Ten conversations,   2 cl
Op. 34 KAL

COPLAND, Aaron
As it fell upon a day S; fl, cl;
(1923) B&H   text: Richard

Barnefield

CORTÉS, Ramiro
Divertimento PIC   fl, cl, bsn

COWELL, Henry
Three pieces AMP   3 rec (SSA)
1. Pelog.
2. Birthday piece.
3. Jig.

CRAWFORD-SEEGER, Ruth
Diaphonic suite AB   2 cl

DANIELS, Mabel
Three observations for   ob (or fl), cl,
   woodwinds CF   bsn
Ironic. Canonic.
Tangonic.

DAVENPORT, LaNoue
Variations on "The   3 rec (SAT)
   Ravens" AM

DIAMOND, David
Partita SMPC   ob, bsn, pno

DONATO, Anthony
Three pieces for 3   3 cl
   clarinets TP
Autumn mood.
Overcast.
The twister.

DORAN, Matt
Sonatina WIM   2 fl

DUKELSKY, Vladimir (DUKE, Vernon)
Trio (Theme &   fl, bsn, pno
   variations) B&H

ELKUS, Jonathan
Five sketches AME   2 cl, bsn
Intrada. Alla polacca.
Notturno. Burlesca.
Recitativo-capriccio.

ETLER, Alvin
Duo VAL   ob, cl
Music for three   3 rec (SAT)
   recorders AMP
Alla marcia (SAT);
Allegro gioioso (AAT);
Andante (SAT); Pen-
sieroso (SAT); Scherzo
capriccio (AAT).
Suite (1960) AMP   fl, ob, cl
Prelude. Musette.
Pavane. Finale.

Three pieces GAL   3 rec (AAT)

GOEB, Roger
Suite PIC   fl, cl, ob

GOULD, Elizabeth
Disciplines EV   ob, cl, bsn

HAIEFF, Alexei
Three bagatelles BB   ob, bsn
(See also "Piano,
Two Hands")

HAUBIEL, Charles
To Apollo HE   3 fl
In the Dorian mode.
In the Lydian mode.
In the Phrygian mode.
Pastoral WIM   ob, bsn

HOSMER, James
Four flute duos MM   2 fl

HOVHANESS, Alan
Prelude and fugue CFP   fl, bsn
Prelude and fugue,   ob, bsn
   Op. 13 CFP
Sonata CFP   2 ob, org
Suite, Op. 21 CFP   E-hn, bsn
Suite CFP   ob, bsn

JOHNSON, Hunter
Serenade VAL   fl, cl (with
                           pno arr)
KATZ, Erich
A miniature suite AM   2 rec (AA)
Santa Barbara suite   3 rec (SAT)
   AMP
Six cantus firmus   3 rec (SAT)
   settings (with voice
   ad lib) AMP
Three movements GAL   3 rec (SAT)

KAY, Ulysses
Suite MCA   fl, ob
Prelude. Air.
Minuet. Gigue.

KOCH, John
Songs and dances GAL   3 rec (SAT)

KOHS, Ellis
Night watch MER   fl, hn, kettle-
                           drums
KRAEHENBUEHL, David
Variations for two AMP   any two com-
                           binations

KRAFT, Leo
Little suite TP   2 cl

KUBIK, Gail
Little suite HAR   fl, 2 cl
Prelude. Plaintive
song. Canon.

KUPFERMAN, Meyer
Available forms GEN   cl, bsn (or
                           trp, trb)
Duo divertimento GEN   cl, bsn
Four charades GEN   fl, cl

LONDON, Ed
Trio MJQ   fl, cl, pno

LYBBERT, Donald
Trio CFP   cl, bsn, hn

MECHEM, Kirke
Trio ECS   ob, cl, bsn

MILLER, Edward
Three pieces MM   3 rec (or 3 cl)

MOEVS, Robert
Duo AMP   ob, E-hn

MUCZYNSKI, Robert
Fragments SHAW   fl, cl, bsn
Waltz. Solitude.
Holiday. Reverie.
Exit.

NEMIROFF, Isaac
Perspectives MM   fl, ob, bsn

NIXON, Roger
Four duos TP   fl (ob), cl

PERSICHETTI, Vincent
Serenade No. 13 EV   2 cl

PISTON, Walter
Three pieces (1926)   fl, cl, bsn
NME

POWELL, Laurence
Trio sonata No. 4 GAL   2 rec (SA),
                           pno
PRESSER, William
Five duets TP   ob, bsn
Suite TP   3 fl

RAPHLING, Sam
Duograms EM   2 ob
Prelude and toccata EM   fl, bsn

Sonatina EM   fl, cl
Suite in modern style   3 ob
EM
Variations EM   fl, cl

RIEGGER, Wallingford
Duos, Op. 35 NME   fl, cl (or fl,
                           ob)
Music BOS   2 fl (or voice
                           & fl)
SCHICKELE, Peter
Windows AB   fl, cl

SCHMIDT, William
Prelude and fugue WIM   fl, cl, bsn

SCHULLER, Gunther
Duo sonata BB   cl, b-cl

SCHWARTZ, Elliott
Four studies GEN   2 cl

SHERMAN, Elna
Suite "For an Oriental   3 rec (SAT)
bazaar" AMP

SMITH, William O.
Five pieces MJQ   fl, cl

SOLLBERGER, Harvey
Two oboes troping MM   2 ob
Two pieces for 2   2 fl
flutes MM

STARER, Robert
Serenade SMPC   3 cl

STERN, Robert
A little bit of music   2 cl
VAL

STEVENS, Halsey
Five duos PIC   fl, cl
Trio for winds CAM   fl, cl, bsn

STILL, William Grant
Miniatures OX   fl, ob, pno
I ride an old paint.
Adolorido. Jesus is
a rock in a weary
land. Yaravi. A
frog went a-courtin'.

SYDEMAN, William
Music for oboe and   ob, cl
clarinet SMPC

TEPPER, Albert
Suite MCA   cl, bsn

TOWNSEND, Douglas
Ballet suite CFP   3 cl
Overture. Song.
Scherzo.

TUTHILL, Burnet
Intermezzo CF   3 cl
Sonatine in canon TP   fl, cl
Scherzo CF   3 cl
Trio JS   3 cl

WASHBURN, Robert
Three pieces for 3   fl, cl, bsn
woodwinds OX
Prelude and fugue.
Passacaglia.
Invention.

WEAVER, Thomas
Seven dialogues SHAW   fl, cl

WIGGLESWORTH, Frank
Duo TP   ob, cl (vla)

WOOLLEN, Russell
Sonatina AMP   3 rec (AAT)

QUARTETS
(fl, ob, cl, bsn unless otherwise indicated)

BABBITT, Milton
Quartet AMP

BARAB, Seymour
Quartet B&H   4 cl

BENNETT, Robert Russell
Rondo capriccioso   4 fl
CHAP

BERGER, Arthur
Quartet in C-major
CFP

CABLE, Howard
Wind song CHAP   4 cl

CACAVAS, John
Romantica JS   4 cl

CARTER, Elliott
Canonic suite (1955)   4 cl (or 4
AMP   a-sax)
Eight etudes and a
fantasy AMP
Suite AMP   4 a-sax
Fanfare. Nocturne.
Tarantella.

CASSEDAY, A. L.
Quartet in G-minor BI   4 sax

CAZDEN, Norman
No. 6 round dance,   4 cl
Op. 40 JS
Plainfield square, Op.   4 rec (SATB)
40a AMP

COWELL, Henry
Sailor's hornpipe PIC   4 sax

DAHL, Ingolf
Serenade B&H   4 fl
Alla marcia.
Cadenza. Canon.
Pas de quatre.
Alla marcia.

DAVENPORT, LaNoue
A day in the park   4 rec (SATB)
(children's suite)
AMP
1. Arrival.
2. Dance.
3. Carrousel.

DONATO, Anthony
Pastorale and dance GS   4 cl

DONOVAN, Richard
Quartet VAL

ERICKSON, Frank
Petite suite CF   4 cl

FULEIHAN, Anis
Humoristic preludes
Nos. 1, 2, 3 SMPC
(Published separately)

GREEN, Ray
Four conversations AMP 4 cl

HARRIS, Arthur
Diversion BB

HELM, Everett
Woodwind quartet AMP

HENNING, Ervin
Badinage TP

HOVHANESS, Alan
Divertimento, Op. 61,   4 cl (or ob, cl,
No. 5 CFP   hn, bsn)
Prelude. Fantasy.
Canzona. Canon.
Aria. Fugue.

JONES, Charles
Lyric waltz suite CFP

KADERAVEK, Milan
Introduction and   4 sax
allegro TP

KRAEHENBUEHL, David
Variations AMP   3 cl, b-cl

KURKA, Robert
A little suite (based on
Moravian folk songs)
WEIN
Jack, Jack... Why are
you so sad, little girl?
Grove, grove, green
grove. There'll be a
war, there will. Katy,
come to church. What
did you do?

LINN, Robert
Quartet WIM   4 sax
Prelude and dance WIM   4 sax

LUNETTA, Stanley
Free music CPE

MARSHALL, Jack
The goldrush suite   4 sax (also arr
SHAW   for woodwind
Sweet Betsy from   ensemble)
Pike. The days of
'49. California stage
coach. Used up man.
What was your name
in the States? Lousey
miner. Joe Bowers
and California bank
robbers.

MARTINO, Donald
Sette canoni enigmatici   4 cl (or str qrt;
ECS   or qrt of mixed
                           instruments)

McKAY, George Frederick
On a pastoral theme TP 4 cl

MOROSS, Jerome
Sonatina CHAP   4 cl

NEMIROFF, Isaac
Four treble suite MM   2 fl, 2 cl, (or
                           fl, ob, 2 cl)
Variations to a theme   fl, ob, bsn
MM   (or vlc)

OWEN, Harold
Chamber music WIM   4 cl

PRESSER, William
Waltz and scherzo KSM   4 sax

REYNOLDS, Roger
Four etudes CFP   2 fl, a-fl,
                           picc
RIEGGER, Wallingford
Three canons, Op. 9
NME
I. 3-part canon with   fl, ob, b-cl,
bsn obb   bsn
II. Canon in unison   fl, b-cl
III. Double canon   picc, ob,
                           b-cl, bsn

SCHICKELE, Peter
Seven bagatelles EV
Three-legged march.
Serenade. Walking
piece. Country song.
Game. City song.
River.

SCHMIDT, William
Suite WIM   4 sax

SCHUMAN, William
Quartettino PIC   4 cl; or 4 bsn;
Ostinato. Nocturne.   or 4 sax
Waltz. Fughetta.

SOLLBERGER, Harvey
Grand quartet for flutes 4 fl
MM

STEIN, Leon
Suite KSM   4 sax

STEVENS, Halsey
Two pieces HME   4 cl

STONE, Don
Introduction, air and   4 rec (SAAT)
country dance GAL

SUMMERS, Stanley
Allegro breve WIM   4 cl

TOWNSEND, Douglas
8 x 8, variations on a   s-rec (or picc
theme by Milhaud   or fl), cl (or
CFP   ob), bsn, pno

TUTHILL, Burnet
Divertimento CF

WEISGALL, Hugo
Graven images TP
1. Lines.
2. Pastorale.

WUORINEN, Charles
Sonatina NME

QUINTETS
(fl, ob, cl, bsn, hn, unless otherwise
indicated)

AITKEN, Hugh
8 studies for wind
quintet EV

BARBER, Samuel
Summer music, Op.
31 GS

BARROWS, John R.
March for woodwind
quintet GS

BENSON, Warren
Marche SHAW

BEREZOWSKY, Nicolai
Suite No. 2 MIL
Suite, Op. 11 MIL

BERGSMA, William
Concerto GAL

BRIGHT, Houston
Three short dances
SHAW

CAGE, John
Music for wind in-
struments (1938)
CFP
Duo (ob, hn);
Quintet (fl, ob, cl,
hn, bsn);

Trio (fl, cl, bsn)

CALABRO, Louis
Divertimento EV

CARTER, Elliott
Quintet AMP

CAZDEN, Norman
Three constructions,
Op. 38 KAL

COKER, Wilson
Quintet TP

COWELL, Henry
Ballad AMP
Suite MER

CRAWFORD-SEEGER, Ruth
Suite for woodwind
quintet AB

DAHL, Ingolf
Allegro arioso MM

DIAMOND, David
Quintet SMPC

DIEMER, Emma Lou
Quintet B&H

DIERCKS, John
Quintet TP

DUKELSKY, Vladimir (DUKE, Vernon)
Nocturne CF

ETLER, Alvin
Quintet No. 1 (1955) AMP
Quintet No. 2 (1957) AMP

FINE, Irving
Partita B&H
Romanza MIL

GERSHWIN, George
Promenade CHAP

GILLIS, Don
Suite No. 1 ("The fable
of the tortoise and
hare") MIL
They're off. Br'er
rabbit dreams. And
Mr. Tortoise wins
the race.
Suite No. 2 ("Three

sketches") MIL
Self-portrait. Shadows.
Sermonette (Southern
style).
Suite No. 3 ("Gone with
the woodwinds") MIL
Five-piece combo.
"Take five" blues.
A frolic in B-bop major.

GIUFFRE, James
Clarinet quintet No. 1   5 cl
MJQ

GOEB, Roger
Prairie songs PIC
Evening. Dance.
Morning.
Quintet No. 1 PIC
Quintet No. 2 PIC
Suite PIC   2 fl, ob, 2 cl

GOODMAN, Joseph
Quintet (1954) AB

GREEN, Bernard
Idyl (cl solo, with
4 cl) B&H

HADDAD, Don
Blues au vent SHAW
Encore "1812" SHAW

HAUBIEL, Charles
Five pieces HE
Flowingly. In five-
eight. Canon. In
seven-eight. With
animation.

HAUFRECHT, Herbert
A woodland serenade
(1955) BB
Pastorale. Nocturne.
Rondo.

HEIDEN, Bernhard
Quintet (1965) AB
Sinfonia AMP

HEINEMAN, John
Views CPE   3 cl, basset
                         hn (or t-sax),
                         vib
HOSMER, James B.
Fugue in C W-7

HOVHANESS, Alan
Quintet, Op. 159 CFP

JACOBI, Frederick
Scherzo CF

JAMES, Philip
Suite in four move-
ments CF
Praeludium. Gavot
and drone. Intro-
spection. Variations
and fugue.

KAUFMAN, Walter
Partita SHAW

LESSARD, John
Partita for wind
quintet GEN

LINN, Robert
Quintet WIM

LONDON, Ed
Quintet MJQ

LUENING, Otto
Fuguing tune AMP

MARTINO, Donald
Concerto ECS

MASON, Daniel Gregory
Divertimento W-7
March. Fugue.

McBRIDE, Robert
Jam session HE

McKAY, George F.
Joyful dance MER

MOORE, Douglas
Quintet CF

MUCZYNSKI, Robert
Movements, Op. 16
SHAW

PARRIS, Herman
Woodwind miniatures
HE

PERSICHETTI, Vincent
Pastoral, Op. 31 GS

PISTON, Walter
Quintet (1956) AMP

PORTER, Quincy
Divertimento CFP

POWELL, Mel
Divertimento for five
winds CF

PRESSER, William
Minuet, sarabande and
gavotte TP

READ, Gardner
Scherzino SMPC

REED, Alfred
Five dances for five   5 cl
clarinets EBM
Afro. Guaracha.
Hoe down. Hora.
Sarabande.

REIF, Paul
Wind spectrum--five
short movements GEN

REYNOLDS, Roger
Gathering CFP
Quintet MCA

RIEGGER, Wallingford
Quintet, Op. 51 AMP

SCHULLER, Gunther
Quintet AMP
Suite MM
Prelude. Blues.
Toccata.

SOWERBY, Leo
Quintet HWG

SYDEMAN, William
Quintet No. 2 MM

VERRALL, John
Serenade MER
Overture. Nocturne.
March. Rondo.

WASHBURN, Robert
Suite EV

WHITE, Donald H.
3 for 5 (a set of moods for
woodwind quintet) SHAW

WILDER, Alec
Quintet No. 3 GS

WUORINEN, Charles
Movement for wind
quintet TP

ZANINELLI, Luigi
Dance variations SHAW
Theme. Duet. Waltz.
Polka. March.

SEXTETS, OCTETS AND LARGER
ENSEMBLES

ADLER, Samuel
Music for eleven OX   2 fl, ob, cl,
(See also "Percus-   b-cl, bsn,
sion")   5 perc

ANDERSON, Leroy
Suite of carols MIL   picc, 2 fl, 2
Angels in our fields.   ob, Eng-hn,
O sanctissima.   2 bsn, c-bsn,
O come, O come   3 cl, E-flat
Emmanuel. O come,   a-cl, B-flat
little children. Cov-   b-cl, B-flat
entry carol. Patapan.   c-b (c-bsn &
     c-b cl parts
     may be played
     by bsn & b-cl)

BRANT, Henry
Angels and devils MCA fl orch

CACAVAS, John
Two miniatures EV   cl choir: 4
     b-flat cl, a-
     cl, b-cl

CAZDEN, Norman
Six discussions, Op.   various mixed
40 JS   wind ensem-
     bles

DONATO, Anthony
Cowboy reverie B&H   fl, E-flat cl,
     ob, 3 B-flat cl,
     E-flat alto cl,
     B-flat bass cl,
     2 A-sax, B-flat
     tenor sax, E-
     flat bar sax, 2
     bsn, 4 hn, 3 B-
     flat cor, 2 trp,
     3 trb, bar,
     basses, c-b,
     timp, drums

ERICKSON, Frank
Variants GS   picc, 2 fl, 2 ob,
                            2 bsn, 8 cl,
                            4 sax
HILL, Edward Burlingame
Sextet TP   fl, ob, cl, hn,
                            bsn, pno
MICHAEL, David Moritz
Parthia VI B&H   2 cl, 2 hn, 2 bsn

SCHICKELE, Peter
Monochrone EV   8 fl

THOMSON, Virgil
Barcarolle MER   fl, ob, E-hn,
                            cl, b-cl, bsn

MIXED WOODWINDS, BRASS, VOICE,
KEYBOARD, AND/OR PERCUSSION

AMRAM, David
Trio CFP   t-sax, bsn, hn

BECKLER, Stanworth
Three pieces for organ   3 trp, 4 hn, 3
  and brass KING   trb, bar, tba,
                            org
BERRY, Wallace
Divertimento EV   fl, cl, ob, bsn,
(See also "Percus-   hn, pno, perc
sion")

BINGHAM, Seth
Concerto for brass   org, 3 trp, 3
  and organ HWG   trb, perc, sn
                            drm
BLACKWOOD, Easley
Un voyage à Cythère,   S, picc (or 2nd
  Op. 20 GS(R)   fl), fl, ob (also
(See also "Solo   E-hn), 2 cl, bsn,
  Vocal Music")   trp, hn, trb,
                           c-b; text: Chas.
                           Baudelaire
BOWLES, Paul
Music for a farce WEIN   cl, trp, perc,
                            pno
BRANT, Henry
Ice age NME   cl, glock (or
                            xy), pno
BRIGHT, Houston
Prelude and fugue in   pic, 2 fl, 2 ob,
  F-minor SHAW   E-flat cl, 3 B-
                            flat cl, E-flat
                            alto cl, b-cl, 2
                            c-b cl, 2 bsn, 3
                            hn, 3 cor, 2 trp,

                            4 sax, bar hn,
                            3 trb, str bass,
                            timp, drm
BURNHAM, Cardon
Festival chorale KING   3 trp, 4 hn, 2
                            trb, tba, org
CHANCE, John Barnes
Introduction and capric-   5 fl, picc, 4 cl,
  cio for piano and 24   4 hn, 4 trb, 4
  winds B&H   tba, 2 bar, pno

CHOU, Wen Chung
Chamber concerto CFP   2 fl, E-hn, 2
                            cl, bsn, hn,
                            trp, trb, tba,
                            perc, pno
Seven poems of T'ang   T voice; fl
  Dynasty NME   (picc), ob, cl,
                            bsn, trp, hn,
                            trb, pno, perc;
                            texts: Chinese
                            poets of 8th &
                            9th cent; trans:
                            Louise Varèse
Three folk songs CFP   hp, fl

COPLAND, Aaron
As it fell upon a day   high voice, fl,
  (1923) B&H   cl; text:
                            Richard Barn-
                            efield
COWELL, Henry
Vocalise CFP   S; fl, pno

DIAMOND, David
The mad maid's song   med voice, fl,
  SMPC   hpcd; text:
                            Robt. Herrick
Vocalises SMPC   high voice, vla

DRUCKMAN, Joseph
Dark upon the harp   m-S, 2 trp, hn,
  TP(R)   trb, tba, perc
                            Biblical

DUKELSKY, Vladimir (DUKE, Vernon)
Nocturne CF   fl, ob, cl, hn,
                            bsn, pno
ELMORE, Robert
Meditation on Veni   org, 2 trp,
  Emmanuel JF   2 trb
ETLER, Alvin
Concerto for clarinet   cl; 3 trp, 3
  (1962) AMP(R)   trb, 2 c-b,
                            perc

FELDMAN, Morton
Journey to the end of S voice, fl, cl,
  night CFP b-cl, bsn

FLAGELLO, Nicolas
Concertino for piano, pno, 2 trp, 4
  brass and timpani hn, 2 trb, 2 b-
  GEN trb, tba, timp

FOSS, Lukas
For twenty-four winds 3 fl, 3 ob, 4 cl,
  CF(R) 3 bsn, 4 trp, 3
  hn, 3 trb, tba
GABOR, Harley
Voce II AP med or high
  voice, fl, perc;
  text: from a
  Japanese Haiku
  poem

GREEN, Ray
Three pieces for a fl, 2 cl, 2 trp,
  concert AME trb, perc, pno
March. Quiet song.
Piece to end.

GRUENBERG, Louis
Creation, Op. 23 TP fl, cl, bsn, hn,
  trp, perc, vla,
  pno

HAIGH, Morris
Fantasia on a Lutheran 6 hn, org
  chorale SHAW

HARRIS, Roy
Fantasy AMP org, 2 trp, 2
  trb, timp

HARTLEY, Walter
Duet TP fl, tba

HILL, Edward Burlingame
Sextet TP fl, ob, cl, bsn,
  hn, pno

HOVHANESS, Alan
Khaldis, Op. 91 KING pno, 4 trp,
  perc

IVES, Charles
From the steeples and bells or chimes),
  the mountains PIC 2 pno, trp, trb
Scherzo: Over the picc, cl, bsn
  pavements PIC (or sax), trp,
  3 trb, cmb,
  drm, pno

KENNAN, Kent
Night soliloquy CF fl solo; 3 fl, 5
  ob, bsn, 3 hn,
  2 trp, 2 trb,
  tba, c-b, timp,
  perc, pno

KING, Robert
Prelude and fugue 2 cor, trb,
  KING bar, org

KURKA, Robert
The good soldier picc, fl, ob,
  Schweik suite E-hn, cl, b-
  WEIN(R) cl, bsn, c-
  bsn, 3 hn, 2
  trp, trb, sn-
  drm, timp
Polka & waltz (from picc, fl, ob,
  Good soldier E-hn, cl, b-cl,
  Schweik) WEIN bsn, c-bsn, 3
  trp, 2 hn, trb,
  timp, sn-drm
LAZAROF, Henri
Octet AMP(R) fl, ob, 2 cl,
  bsn, trp, hn,
  trb

LEES, Benjamin
Three variables B&H ob, cl, bsn,
  hn, pno

LESSARD, John
Octet for wind in- fl, cl, 2 trp,
  struments GEN 2 hn, bsn, trb

LOCKWOOD, Normand
Concerto for organ org; 2 trp,
  and brass AMP 2 trb

MAYER, William
Essay for brass and fl, ob, cl, bsn,
  winds B&H 2 trp, trb, 2
  hn, tba, perc
  (opt)
McPHEE, Colin
Concerto CFP(R) 4 picc, 3 ob,
  3 cl, 3 c-bsn,
  4 trp, 3 hn, 3
  trb, tba, timp,
  perc, hp, pno,
  c-b
Concerto for pno & pno solo, 2 fl,
  wind octette AMP ob, cl, bsn,
  trp, hn, trb
MICHALSKY, Donal R.
Trio concertino WIM fl, ob, hn

PERSICHETTI, Vincent
Serenade No. 1 EV fl, ob, cl, bsn,
  Prelude. Episode. 2 hn, 2 trp,
  Song. Interlude. trb, tba
Dance.

PINKHAM, Daniel
Concertante CFP 2 trp, t-trb,
  Canzona. Procession. b-trb, org,

Plaint.	perc
PRESSER, William	
Sonatina TP	trb, bsn (or bar), pno
REED, H. Owen	
Symphonic dance MIL	fl, ob, cl, bsn, hn, pno
RIEGGER, Wallingford	
Concerto for piano & wind quintet, Op. 53 AMP	pno solo; fl, ob, cl, hn, bsn
Music for voice and flute, Op. 23 AMP	high voice, fl vocalise
ROCHBERG, George	
Black sounds TP(R)	2 fl, ob, 2 cl, 2 hn, 2 trp, 2 trb, tba, pno (cel), perc
ROREM, Ned	
Sinfonia CFP(R)	picc, 2 fl, 2 ob, E-hn, 3 cl, b-cl, 2 bsn, c-bsn, 2 hn, perc
SCHAFFER, Robert	
Paschal triptych KING	3 trp, 4 hn, 3 trb, bar, tba, perc, org
SCHIFRIN, Lalo	
Gillespiana MJQ(R)	soli: a-sax(or fl), trp, pno, c-b, dr; 4 trp, 4 hn, 4 trb, tba, 3 perc
SCHULLER, Gunther	
Double quintet AMP	fl, ob, cl, hn, bsn, 2 trp, trb, tba
Ornette Coleman: collections of his compositions edited and transcribed by Schuller SF	a-sax, trp, b-dr
SCHWARTZ, Elliott	
Divertimento GEN	cl, hn, pno
Humoresque. Dirge. Dance. Variations.	
Trio GEN	fl, cl, pno
Variations GEN	S, bsn, perc
(See also "Percussion")	
SOWERBY, Leo	
Festival musick HWG	2 trp, 2 trb, timp, org
Fanfare. Chorale. Toccata on "A.G.O."	

SUBOTNICK, Morton	
Serenade No. 2 MM	cl, hn, pno, perc
TRIMBLE, Lester	
Four fragments from the "Canterbury Tales" CFP (For contents, see "Solo Vocal Music")	high voice, fl, cl, hpcd (or pno); text: Geoffrey Chaucer

BRASS ENSEMBLES

DUOS, TRIOS AND QUARTETS

ADDISON, John	
Divertimento, Op. 9 GAL	2 trp, hn, trb
ALEXANDER, Joseph	
Trio of duets SMPC	trp, trb
BASSETT, Leslie	
Quartet KING	4 trb
BERGSMA, William	
Suite CF	2 trp, trb, bar
BERNSTEIN, Leonard	
Fanfare for Bima GS	trp, hn, trb, tba
BEZANSON, Philip	
Diversion for brass trio VAL	trp, hn, trb
BIALOSKY, Marshall	
Two movements KING	trp, hn, trb
BODA, John	
Quartet TP	2 trp, hn, trb
BRIGHT, Houston	
Legend and canon AMP	2 trp, hn, trb, (or 2 trp, 2 trb)
BUTTS, Carroll M.	
Suite for trombones SHAW	4 trb
CALABRO, Louis	
Ceremonial march EV	2 trp, 2 trb, timp, b-dr, sn-dr
CAZDEN, Norman	
Three directions, Op. 39 AMP	2 cor (or trp), 2 bar (or trb)

CHAPMAN, Roger
Suite of three cities CFP 4 trb
Fanfare. Extensity.
Diversity. Eccentricity.

COWELL, Henry
Hymn and fuguing tune,   3 hn
No. 12 AMP
Sailor's hornpipe PIC   4 sax

CROLEY, Randell
Sonata TP   trp, trb, pno

DIERCKS, John
Figures on china TP   hn, trb, tba
Quartet TP   2 trp, hn, trb

DONAHUE, Robert
Five pieces TP   2 trp, 2 trb
Parallel organum.
Lied. Estampie.
Chant. Accents.

DONATO, Anthony
Sonatine GS   3 trp
Suite KING   2 trp, hn, trb

FRACKENPOHL, Arthur
Quartet KING   2 cor, trb, bar

GILLIS, Don
Sonatina No. 2 B&H   4 cor

GOLDMAN, Richard Franko
Duo TP   2 tba

HAINES, Edmund
Toccata KING   2 trp, 2 trb, (or
                            2 trp, hn, bar)
HARMON, Robert
Pasacalle WIM   3 trp

HARRIS, Arthur
Theme and variations   4 hn
SHAW

HAUBIEL, Charles
Anthenaeum suite HE   trp, hn, trb
Minuet in Dorian mode.
Allemande in Aeolian
mode. Courante in
Mixolydian mode. Air
in Ionian mode. Gavotte
in Melodic-harmonic
mode. Sarabande in
Phrygian mode. Gigue
in Lydian mode.

HOVHANESS, Alan
Sharagan and fugue   2 trp, hn, bar
KING

HUGHES, Mark
Divertimento TP   trp, hn, trb

KAY, Ulysses
Brass quartet PIC   2 trp, trb,
Fantasia. Arioso.   b-trb
Toccata.
Serenade No. 2 MCA   4 hn
Prelude. Arietta.
Toccata. Fantasy.
Epilogue.
Three fanfares MCA   4 trp

KELLER, Homer
Quartet KING   2 trp, hn, trb

KING, Robert
French suite KING   trp, bar

KLEIN, John
Sonata AMP   2 trp, 2 trb

KNIGHT, Morris
Cassation TP   trp, hn, trb
Six brass quartets   2 trp, 2 trb
(each in one move-
ment) TP

KROEGER, Karl
Sonata breve TP   trp, hn, trb

KUPFERMAN, Meyer
Available forms GEN   trp, trb (or
                            cl, bsn)
LO PRESTI, Ronald
Miniature SHAW   2 trp, hn, trb
Second suite SHAW   4 hn
Intrada. Arioso.
Finale.

MAREK, Robert
Trio KING   trp, hn, trb

MAYER, William
Country fair B&H   2 trp, trb

McCARTY, Patrick
Recitative and fugue   4 trb
KING

McKAY, George Frederick
Moderato e cantabile CF 4 hn
Molto religioso CF   4 hn
Prelude CF   4 hn

Two pieces for brass 2 trp, 2 trb
quartet TP

McMULLEN, Patrick
Three movements for 2 trp
two trumpets SHAW

MUCZYNSKI, Robert
Trio GS 3 trp

PARRIS, Herman
Seven moods EV 2 trp, hn, trb
What? March of the
drunken clowns.
Flirt. Spiritual.
Saddened. Religion.
That's all.

PHILLIPS, Burrill
Prelude EV trp I, trp II
(or hn), 2 trb
Trio EV 2 trp
Trio KING 3 trp

PINKHAM, Daniel
Fanfare, aria and echo 2 hn, timp
CFP
(See also "Percus-
sion")

PRESSER, William
Five southern songs trp, hn, 2 trb
HE
Sonatina TP trb, bar(or
bsn), pno
Suite TP 3 trp
Waltz and scherzo 4 sax
SMPC

RAPHLING, Sam
Concert suite KING 4 trp
Dance suite EM 2 trp
Prelude and toccata trp, trb
KING
Sonatina EM 2 trb

RAYMOND, Lewis
Short suite WIM hn, 2 trp, trb
March. Nocturne.
Dance. Finale.

REYNOLDS, Verne
Short suite KING 4 hn
Toccata. Recitativi.
Ricercata.

RIEGGER, Wallingford
Movement, Op. 66 PIC 2 trp, trb, pno

SANDERS, Robert
Scherzo and dirge AMP 4 trb
Suite KING 2 trp, 2 trb
Sonatina. Folk-
song. March.
Trio KING trp, hn, trb

SCHULLER, Gunther
Duets OX 2 hn

SCHWARTZ, Elliott
Essays (1966) AB trp, trb

SMITH, Frank
Three chorale settings trp I, trp II
KING (hn), trb I (hn),
trb II (bar)
STARER, Robert
Dirge TP 2 trp, 2 trb

TANNER, Paul
Imitation WIM 3 trb
Larghetto WIM 3 trb
A study in texture WIM 4 trb

WALKER, Richard
Badinerie AMP 2 trp, hn, trb

WHITE, Donald H.
Serenade No. 3 SHAW 2 trp, hn, trb
Recitative. Arioso.
Whimsy.

QUINTETS
(2 trp, hn, trb, tba, unless otherwise
indicated)

ADLER, Samuel
Five movements KING
Toccata. Chorale.
Scherzo. Intermezzo.
Gigue.

AMRAM, David
Fanfare and proces-
sional CFP

BAZELON, Irwin
Brass quintet B&H 2 trp, hn, t-
trb, b-trb
CHEETHAM, John
Scherzo WIM

CROLEY, Randell
Disquisition: cyclic
chorale TP

DAHL, Ingolf
Brass quintet W-7
Choral fantasy.
Intermezzo. Fugue.

EAST, Michael
Desperavi AMP

ETLER, Alvin
Quintet for brass in-
struments (1965) AMP
Sonic sequence (1967) AB

EWALD, Victor
Symphony for brass
choir KING

FRACKENPOHL, Arthur
Brass quintet EV

HARTLEY, Walter
Quintet TP

HAUFRECHT, Herbert
Suite for brass quintet
AMP
Intrada. Ceremonial.
Passacaglia. Fugue.

HEIDEN, Bernhard
Four dances (1967) AB

KUBIK, Gail
Celebrations COL

LOCKWOOD, Normand
Concerto for organ and   org; 2 trp,
brass AMP   2 trb

LO PRESTI, Ronald
Suite for five trumpets   5 trp
SHAW

MOSS, Lawrence
Music for five TP

REYNOLDS, Verne
Music for five trumpets   5 trp
KING
Suite for brass quintet
MCA

SANDERS, Robert
Quintet in B-flat major   2 trp (or cor),
MER   hn, 2 trb (or
                          bar)

SCHMIDT, William
Suite No. 1 WIM
Variations on a Negro
folk song WIM

SCHULLER, Gunther
Five pieces for five   5 hn
horns ABE
Music for brass
quintet AMP

SCHWARTZ, Eliott
Three movements GEN

STARER, Robert
Five miniatures for
brass quintet SMPC

STEVENS, Bernard
Two improvisations on   2 trp, 2 trb,
folk songs GAL   b-trb

SWANSON, Howard
Soundpiece WEIN

WHEAR, Paul
Invocation and study   2 trp, hn, trb,
KING   bar (or trb)

ZANINELLI, Luigi
Designs for brass   2 trp, 2 trb,
quintet SHAW   b-trb

ZINDARS, Earl
Quintet KING

SEXTETS

CAZDEN, Norman
Suite, Op. 55 AMP   2 trp, hn, bar,
                          trb, tba

COWELL, Henry
Tall tale MER   2 cor (or trp),
                          hn, 2 trb (or
                          bar), tba

DAHL, Ingolf
Music for brass in-   2 trp, hn, 2
struments W-7   trb, tba (ad
                          lib)

FLAGELLO, Nicolas
Lyra GEN   3 C-trp, t-
                          trb, b-trb, hn

HANNA, James
Song of the redwood   2 trp, 2 hn,
tree KING   2 trb, timp

HARTLEY, Walter
Suite TP   6 tba

KAUFMANN, Walter
Passacaglia and   2 trp, hn, 2
  capriccio SHAW   trb, tba

KROEGER, Karl
Canzona I TP   2 trp, 2 hn,
                           trb, tba
Canzona II TP   2 trp, hn, bar,
                           trb, tba
Canzona III TP   3 trp, 3 trb

LUENING, Otto
Entrance and exit   3 trp, 3 trb,
  music CFP   cym

LYBBERT, Donald
Praeludium CFP   3 trp, 3 trb,
  (See also "Percus-   perc
  sion")

PHILLIPS, Burrill
Piece for six trom-   4 trb, 2 b-trb
  bones KING

PRESSER, William
Suite TP   6 tba

RAPHLING, Sam
Little suite EM   3 trp, 3 trb

RUGGLES, Carl
Angels AME   4 trp, 2 trb
  (See also "String   (all muted)
  Sextets")

SIEGMEISTER, Elie
Sextet MCA   2 trp, 2 trb,
                           hn, tba, perc

VERRALL, John
Suite TP   2 trp, hn, bar,
Prelude. Fugue.   trb, tba
Ballade. Scherzo.
Antiphon.

WHITE, Donald H.
Diversions COL   2 trp, 2 trb,
                           hn, tba

LARGE ENSEMBLES

ADLER, Samuel
Concert piece KING   3 trp, 2 hn, 3
                           trb, 2 bar,

tba, timp
Divertimento KING   3 cor, 3 hn, 3
                           trb, 2 bar, tba
Praeludium KING   2 trp, 2 hn, 2
                           trb, bar, tba,
                           timp
ANDERSON, Leroy
Suite of Christmas   4 trp, 4 hn, 3
  carols MIL   trb, b-trb, bar,
While by my sheep.   tba
In dulci jubilo. Lo,
  how a rose e'er
  blooming. I saw
  three ships. From
  heaven high I come
  to you. We three
  kings of Orient are.
  March of the kings.

BEADELL, Robert
Introduction and   3 trp, 3 hn, 3
  allegro KING   trb, bar, tba,
                           timp
BEREZOWSKY, Nicolai
Suite MIL   2 trp, 2 hn,
Fanfare & gallop.   2 trp, tba
  Lullaby. Valse.
  Rondo.

BEYER, Howard
Suite KING   3 trp, 4 hn, 3
                           trb, timp

BOTTJE, Will Gay
Symphonie allegro   6 trp, 4 hn, 3
  KING   trb, bar, tba,
                           perc
BROWN, Rayner
Prelude and fugue WIM   4 trp, 4 hn, 4
                           trb, bar, tba,
                           timp, perc
CALABRO, Louis
Ceremonial march EV   2 trp, 2 trb,
                           perc
CHOU, Wen-Chung
Soliloquy of a Bhiksuni   trp solo, 4 hn,
  CFP   2 trb, b-trb,
  (See also "Percus-   tba, 3 perc,
  sion")   timp

COBINE, Albert
Vermont suite KING   4 trp, 3 hn, 4
                           trb, bar, tba

COHN, Arthur
Music for brass in-   4 trp, 2 trb,
  struments SMPC   b-trb

COLGRASS, Michael
Concertino for   3 trp, 3 trb,

timpani MP (See also "Percus- sion")	tba, timp, 2 perc	HARRIS, Albert Theme and variations KING	8 hn
COPLAND, Aaron Fanfare for common man B&H	3 trp, 4 hn, 3 trb, tba, drm, tam-tam	HARTLEY, Walter Sinfonia TP	5 trp, 4 hn, 3 trb, bar, tba
COWELL, Henry Fanfare for the forces of the Latin Ameri- can Allies B&H	3 trp, 2 hn, 3 trb, perc	HARTMEYER, John Negev (tone poem for brass) KING	3 trp, 3 hn, 3 trb, bar, tba, timp
Rondo CFP	3 trp, 2 hn, 3 trb	HAUFRECHT, Herbert Symphony for brass and timpani B&H	3 trp, 4 hn, 3 trb, tba, timp
De JONG, Conrad Three studies WIM	3 trp, 3 trb, tba	Dona nobis pacem. Elegy. Jubilation. (See also "Percus- sion")	
DeLONE, Peter Introduction and capriccio SHAW (See also "Percus- sion")	2 trp, 2 hn, 2 trb, tba, timp, perc	HIBBARD, William Variations for brass nonet MJQ	3 hn, 3 trp, 3 trb
De YOUNG, Lynden Divertissement KING	4 trp, 4 hn, 3 trb, bar, tba, timp, sn-dr, cym	HOGG, Merle Concerto for brass KING	3 trp, 3 hn, 3 trb, bar, tba, timp
DIAMOND, David Ceremonial fanfare SMPC (See also "Percus- sion")	4 trp, 6 hn, 3 trb, tba, timp, perc	HOLMES, Paul Suite SHAW Prelude. Chorale. Dance.	3 trp, 4 hn, 3 trb, tba
DIEMER, Emma Lou Declamation for brass and percussion EV (See also "Percus- sion")	4 trp, 2 hn, bar, 2 trb, tba, timp	JESSON, Roy Variations and scherzo KING	4 cor, 3 hn, 3 trb, bar, tba, timp, sn-drm
DIERCKS, John Mirror of brass TP	2 trp, 2 hn, 2 trb, tba	JOHNSON, J.J. Poem for brass MJQ	trp, trb solo; 6 trp, 4 hn, 3 trb, 2 bar, tba, c-b, perc
FLAGELLO, Nicolas Chorale and episode GEN	2 trp, 4 hn, 2 trb, b-trb, tba	KING, Robert D. Prelude and fugue KING	2 trp, 2 hn, 2 trb, bar, tba
GIUFFRE, James The pharaoh MJQ	4 hn, 6 trp, 3 trb, 2 tba, bar, timp	Seven conversation pieces KING	4 trp, 3 trb, 2 bar, tba
GOLDMAN, Richard Franko Hymn for brass choir KING	4 trp, 4 hn, 3 trb, bar(or trb), tba, timp, c-b (ad lib)	LEWIS, John The comedy MJQ	pno solo; 4 hn, 4 trp, 2 trb, tba, c-b, dr
		Fanfare I and II MJQ	4 hn, 4 trp, 2 trb, tba, dr
		The golden striker MJQ	pno solo; 4 hn, 4 trp, 2 trb, tba, c-b, dr

Three little feelings
MJQ

soli: trp, trb;
4 hn, 6 trp, 3
trb, 2 tba, bar,
c-b, dr.

MARKS, James
Introduction and pas-
sacaglia KING

3 cor, 3 hn, 3
trb, bar, tba,
timp

Music for brass and
timpani KING
(See also "Percus-
sion")

3 cor, 4 hn, 3
trb, bar, tba,
timp

McKAY, George F.
Bravura prelude AMP

4 trp, 4 hn, 4
trb, 2 bar, tba

MEYEROWITZ, Jan
Short suite BB

3 hn, 3 trp,
2 trb, b-tba

MUCZYNSKI, Robert
Allegro deciso SHAW

2 trp, 2 hn,
trb, tba, timp

NOVY, Donald
Sonatina KING

3 trp, 3 hn,
3 trb, timp

OSBORNE, Willson
Two ricercari KING

2 trp, 2 hn,
trb, bar (or
trb), tba

PARRIS, Herman
Four rhapsodies EV

3 trp, 4 hn,
3 trb, tba

PARRIS, Robert
Lamentations and
praises CFP

3 trp, 2 hn, 3
trb, tba, 3
timp, 2 perc

PISTON, Walter
Fanfare for the fight-
ing French B&H

3 trp, 4 hn, 3
trb, tba, perc,
timp

PRESSER, William
Passacaglia and fugue
TP

3 trp, 4 hn, 3
trb, bar, tba,
timp, perc

Research for brass
choir TP

3 trp, 3 hn, 3
trb, 2 bar, tba

READ, Gardner
Choral and fughetta
KING

4 trp, 4 hn, 3
trb, bar, tba

Sound piece KING

4 trp, 4 hn, 3
trb, bar, 2 tba,
timp, perc

REED, H. Owen
Fanfares 4 MIL

2 trp, 2 trb, 3
hn, 3 bar, 3
tba, sn-drm,
b-dr

REYNOLDS, Verne
Prelude and allegro
KING

3 trp, 4 hn, 3
trb, 2 bar, tba,
timp

Theme and variations
KING

3 trp, 3 hn, 3
trb, bar, tba,
timp

RIEGGER, Wallingford
Music for brass choir,
Op. 45 MER(R)

10 trp, 4 hn,
10 trb, 2 tba,
timp, cmb

Nonet, Op. 49 AMP

3 trp, 2 hn,
3 trb, tba

ROY, Klaus George
Tripartita, Op. 5
KING

3 cor, 2 hn,
3 trb, 2 bar,
tba

SCHULLER, Gunther
Lines and contrasts
AMP

16 hn

Symphony for brass
and percussion
SHAW
(See also "Percus-
sion")

6 trp, 4 hn, 3
trb, bar, 2 tba,
perc, timp

SCOTT, Wayne
Rondo giojoso KING

3 trp, 4 hn, 4
trb, bar, tba,
timp, dr

SHAHAN, Paul
Leipzig towers KING

4 trp, 4 hn, 4
trb, bar, tba,
perc

Spectrums KING

4 trp, 4 hn, 4
trb, bar, tba,
timp, dr

SHULMAN, Alan
Top brass, "Six
minutes for twelve"
SHAW

4 trp, 4 hn,
3 trb, tba

TAYLOR, Corwin H.
Inscriptions in brass
GS
Pro patria. In
memorium. Gloria
in excelsis.

3 cor, 4 hn,
3 trb, bar,
tba, timp,
perc

THOMSON, Virgil
Fanfare for France
B&H

3 trp, 4 hn,
3 trb, perc

TULL, Fisher
  Soundings for brass   3 trp, 3 hn, 4
    and percussion   trb, 2 bar,
  SHAW   timp, perc
  (See also "Percus-
  sion")

TURNER, Godfrey
  Fanfare, chorale, and   3 trp, 4 hn,
    finale B&H   2 trb, tba

WAGNER, Leonard
  Fanfare, scherzo and   8 trp, 4 hn, 4
    allegro KING   trb, 2 bar, 2
                               tba, perc
WARD, Robert
  Fantasia GAL   3 trp, 4 hn, 2
                               trb, bar, tba,
                               timp
WERLE, Frederick
  Variations and fugue   3 trp, 2 trb,
    BB(R)   b-trb, tba

WINTER, Paul
  Festival fanfare CFP   3 trp, 3 trb,
                               b-tba, timp
WOOLLEN, Russell
  Triptych, Op. 34   4 trp, 2 hn,
    CFP   3 trb, tba

ZINDARS, Earl
  The brass square   4 cor, 4 hn,
    KING   3 trb, tba,
                               timp, cmb

4. CONCERT JAZZ

JAZZ COMBOS

BUDD, Harold
III for double ensemble CPE — fl, cl, vlc, vib, jazz trio (trp, c-b, perc set)

ELLIS, Donald
Improvisational suite No. 1 MJQ — trp, pno, double a-sax (opt), c-b, dr

GIBBS, Michael
Melanie MJQ — gtr, vib, c-b, dr

Six improvisatory sketches MJQ — vib, pno, c-b, dr

GIUFFRE, James
Finé MJQ(R) — cl (t-sax, b-sax), gtr, vib, pno, 2 c-b, dr

Fun MJQ — cl, vib, pno, c-b, dr

Passage to the veil MJQ — cl, trb, pno, c-b, dr

Suspensions MJQ(R) — fl, 2 sax, hn (trp opt), trp, trb, gtr, vib, pno, c-b, dr

JOHNSON, J. J.
Turnpike MJQ(R) — fl, cl, t-sax, bsn, hn, trp, hp(gtr opt), pno, c-b, dr

LEWIS, John
Bel (belkis) MJQ — t-sax, trp, trb, pno, c-b, dr

Django MJQ — t-sax, trp, trb, pno, c-b, dr

Django (arr. by Gunther Schuller) MJQ — fl, cl, t-sax, bsn, hn, trb (trp), hp(pno), c-b, dr

Exposure MJQ — fl, cl, bsn, hn, vib, pno, hp, c-b, dr

Little David's fugue MJQ(R) — fl, cl, t-sax, bsn(t-sax), hn (a-sax), trb (trp), hp(pno), c-b, dr

Milano MJQ — t-sax, trp, trb, pno, c-b, dr

N. Y. 19 MJQ — t-sax, trp, trb, pno, c-b, dr

Original sin (2 excerpts) MJQ — vib, pno, c-b, dr

Polchinella MJQ — vib, pno, c-b, dr

The queen's fancy (arr. by Gunther Schuller) MJQ(R) — fl, cl, t-sax, bsn, hn, trb, hp, c-b, dr

Sketch for double quartet MJQ — vib, pno, perc, c-b, 2 vln, vla, vlc

Sun dance MJQ — fl, cl, t-sax, bsn(b-sax), hn (a-sax), trb, hp(gtr), c-b, dr

Two degrees east, two degrees west MJQ — t-sax, trp, trb, pno, c-b, dr

McFARLAND, Gary
Night float MJQ(R) — a-sax, t-sax, b-sax, hn, trp, gtr, pno, c-b, dr

SCHIFRIN, Lalo
Dionysos MJQ(R) — fl(cl), gtr, c-b, dr

Mount Olive MJQ(R) — fl(double a-sax), gtr, pno, c-b, dr

SCHULLER, Gunther
Abstractions MJQ — solo a-sax; gtr, 2 vln, vla, vlc, 2 c-b, dr

Densities I MJQ — cl, vib, hp, c-b

Night music MJQ — b-cl, gtr, c-b, dr

Progression in tempo (3rd mov. of "Concertino") MJQ — soli: vib, pno, c-b, dr; fl, cl, gtr, str qrt

Twelve by eleven MJQ — fl, cl, t-sax, hn, trb, vib, pno, hp, c-b, dr

250

Variants on a theme by   fl, a-sax
  John Lewis (Django)   (double on fl),
  MJQ   vib, gtr, pno,
   2 vln, vla, vlc,
   2 c-b, dr

BIG BAND CONCERT JAZZ

CURNOW, Robert
  Passacaglia KSM   10 brass and
   5 sax
GIUFFRE, James
  Affinity MJQ(R)   4 sax, hn, trp,
   trb, 3 c-b, dr
Finé MJQ(R)   fl, cl(a-sax),
   b-sax, hn, 3
   trp, trb, pno,
   c-b, dr
Motion-eterne MJQ(R)   3 sax, hn, 3
   trp, trb, pno,
   c-b, dr
Pharoah MJQ(R)   6 trp, 4 hn, 3
   trb, 2 bar, tba,
   timp
Quest MJQ(R)   3 sax, hn, 3
   trp, trb, pno,
   c-b, dr
JACKSON, Milt
  Ralph's new blues   soli: vib, pno,
  MJQ(R)   c-b, dr; 2 a-
   sax, 2 t-sax,
   b-sax, 4 trp,
   3 trb, gtr
JOHNSON, J.J.
  El Camino Real MJQ(R)   trb solo; 5 sax,
   2 hn, 4 trp, 3
   trb, c-b, dr
Poem for brass   solo trp & trb;
  MJQ(R)   6 trp, 4 hn, 3
   trb, 2 bar, tba,
   c-b, perc
Sketch for trombone   solo trb; 5 sax,
  and orchestra MJQ(R) 2 hn, 3 trp, hp,
   c-b, dr
LEVITT, Rod
  Breathin' easy AMP   2 a-sax, 2 t-
   sax, bar-sax,
   4 trp, 4 trb,
   gtr, pno, c-b,
   dr
El general AMP   2 a-sax, 2 t-
   sax, bar-sax,
   4 trp, 4 trb,
   gtr, pno, c-b,
   dr

The lost soul AMP   2 a-sax, 2 t-
   sax, bar-sax,
   4 trp, 4 trb,
   gtr, pno, c-b,
   dr
Safari AMP   2 a-sax, 2 t-
   sax, bar-sax,
   4 trp, 4 trb,
   gtr, pno, c-b,
   dr
Speedway AMP   2 a-sax, 2 t-
   sax, bar-sax,
   4 trp, 4 trb,
   gtr, pno, c-b,
   dr
LEWIS, John
  Animal dance MJQ(R)   soli: vib, pno,
   c-b, dr; 2 a-
   sax, 2 t-sax,
   b-sax, 4 trp,
   3 trb, gtr
Django MJQ(R)   soli: vib, pno,
   c-b, dr; 2 a-
   sax, 2 t-sax,
   b-sax, 4 trp,
   3 trb, gtr
Excerpts from ("The   solo pno; 4
   comedy") MJQ(R)   trp, 4 hn, 2
  Fanfare I. Spanish   trb, tba, c-b,
   steps. Polchinella.   perc
  La cantatrice.
  Piazza Navona.
  Fanfare II.
The golden striker   solo pno; 4
  MJQ(R)   trp, 4 hn, 2
   trb, tba, c-b,
   perc
Home MJQ(R)   soli: vib, pno,
   c-b, dr; 2 a-
   sax, 2 t-sax,
   b-sax, 4 trp,
   3 trb
MUTCHLER, Ralph
  Concerto grosso for
   jazz combo and
   symphonic band
   KSM
POWELL, Morgan
  Sirhmrej for jazz   5 trp, 3 trb,
   ensemble AP   b-trb, tba, 3
   sax, b-cl, gtr,
   pno, c-b, perc
SCHIFRIN, Lalo
  Study in rhythm MJQ(R)   4 sax, hn, 4
   trp, 2 trb, pno,
   c-b, dr

The web MJQ(R)   fl(or t-sax), 2
                          cl, hn, 4 trp,
                          2 trb, pno,
                          c-b, dr

SCHULLER, Gunther
Night music MJQ(R)   solo cl; 4 sax,
                          b-cl, 4 trp, 3
                          trb, gtr, pno,
                          c-b, dr

Passacaglia MJQ(R)   soli: vib, pno,
                          c-b, dr; 2 fl,
                          ob, 2 cl, 5 sax,
                          b-sax, 2 hn, 5
                          trp, 4 trb, tba,
                          perc

When the saints go   5 sax, 2 hn, 4
   marchin' in MJQ(R)   trp, 3 trb, tba,
                          c-b, dr

SEIBERT, Bob
A roarin' borealis   8 brass and
   KSM   5 sax

5. PERCUSSION

ADLER, Samuel
Music for eleven OX

2 fl, ob, cl, b-cl, bsn, 5 perc

ANDRUS, Donald
Imbrications AP

2 pno and perc (glock, vib, cel, pno, str)

ANTHEIL, George
Ballet méchanique (rev. 1952) SHAW(R)

glock, large and small airplane propeller sounds, gong, cmb, woodblock, military dr, tri, tam, large and small electric bells, t-dr, b-dr, 2 xy, 4 pno

AUSTIN, Larry
The maze (a theater piece in open style) CPE

3 perc, dancer, tapes, projections

BARTLETT, Harry
Four holidays for three percussionists MP
  I. New Year's eve.
  II. Washington's birthday.
  III. Fourth of July.
  IV. Cuban Christmas

1. vib, xy, susp cmb; 2. double dr with timbales, hi-hat, cowbell, bells, woodblock, ratchet, pistol; 3. 2 kettle dr, susp cmb, tri, claves, sleighbells, noisemakers

BAZELON, Irwin
Short symphony (testament to a big city) B&H(R)

full symphony with emphasis on percussion: dr, gongs, cowbells, woodblocks, maracas, xy, glock

BENSON, Warren
Polyphonies for percussion MCA(R)
  (See also "Band")
Streams MCA
Symphony for drums CFP(R)
Invocation. Contemplation.
Declaration.
  (See also "Band")
Three pieces for percussion quartet GS
Trio for percussion MP

winds, brasses, timp, perc, str

percussion ensemble
soli: 4 timp, perc (5 players); wind symphony

1. 3 tom-toms, tri; 2. tri, woodblock, cmb; 3. maracas, gong, b-dr

BERG, Sidney
Hollida MP
Rolling rhythm MP
Rumbling along MP
South American capers (duet) MP
The victor MP

sn-dr
sn-dr
sn-dr
sn-dr
sn-dr

BERGAMO, John
Four pieces for timpani MP

timp

BERGSMA, William
The sun, the soaring eagle, the
   turquoise prince, the god GAL(R)
   (See also "Mixed Chorus")

SATB with pno and perc (bongos, maracas, woodblock, whip, ratchet, tri,
cmb, sn-dr, t-dr, b-dr, glock, xy,
vib, whistle); text adapted and prepared by William Bergsma from books
2 and 7 of the Florentine Codex
(c. 1566) by Fray de Shagun; trans:
Arthur O. Anderson and Charles E.
Dibble

BERRY, Wallace
Divertimento EV
   (See also "Mixed Winds, Brass
   Voice, Keyboard and/or Percus-
   sion")

fl, cl, ob, bsn, hn, pno, perc

BEVERSDORF, Thomas
Symphony for winds and percussion
   SMC
   (See also "Band")

BRANT, Henry
Ice age NME

cl, glock (or xy), pno

BRITTON, Mervin
First quartet MP

1. tri; 2. susp cmb; 3. tam;
4. b-dr

One over three MP

1. tam; 2. bells; 3. 2 kettle dr;
4. b-dr

Snare drum duet No. 1 MP
Solo piece for timpani and piano MP

sn-dr
timp, pno

BRODKORB, Wayne
Duet for snare and bass drums MP

sn and b-dr

BUGGERT, Robert
Introduction and fugue MP

1. mar, pno; 2. sn-dr; 3. tom-
tom; 4. bongo dr; 5. large tom-
tom; 6. xy, woodblock; 7. maracas;
8. t-dr, tri; 9. susp cmb; 10. timp,
chimes; 11. b-dr, gong

CAGE, John
Amores (1943) CFP
   No. II: Trio for 9 tom-toms, pod
      rattle
   No. III: Trio for 7 woodblocks
   (For "Amores, No. I and IV,"
      see "Piano, Two Hands")
Cartridge music (1960) CFP
Credo in US (1942) CFP
First construction in metal (1939) CFP

Forever and sunsmell (1942) CFP

Imaginary landscape No. 3 (1942) CFP
March (imaginary landscape No. 2)
   (1942) CFP
Quartet (1935) CFP

duet for cmb, pno duet and pno trio
perc qrt, including pno
for perc sextet with assistant (5 graduated thundersheets and string pno)
med voice and perc duo; text: e.e.
cummings
perc sextet
perc quintet

for any perc instruments

She is asleep (1943) CFP

4 tom-toms with addition of duet for voice and perpared pno

CAGE, John and Lou Harrison
Double music for percussion
   quartet CFP

water buffalo bells, sistrums, Japanese temple gongs, tam-tams, muted gongs, graduated cowbells, brake dr

CALABRO, Louis
Ceremonial march EV

2 trp, 2 trb, timp, b-dr, sn-dr

CARTER, Elliott
Recitative and improvisation AMP

4 timp (1 player)

CHILDS, Barney
Jack's new bag CPE
  (See also "Strings with Voice
  and/or Winds, Percussion")

Music for bass drum AMP
Music for a celebration AMP

fl, trp, trb, pno (2 players), perc 1: 2 timp, 3 tom-toms, 2 temple blocks, cmb, sn-dr, tri; perc 2: jazz dr set; vla, vlc, c-b
for 3 performers
picc, dr

CHOU, Wen-Chung
Soliloquy of a Bhiksuni CFP(R)

solo trp; 4 hn, 3 trb, tba, perc ensemble (3 players: timp, b-and sn-dr, tri, tam, susp cmb, gong)

COHN, Arthur
Quotations in percussion (6 or more
  players) MIL
    Part I: ...as if it were some
    strange incantation--D.H.
    Lawrence.
    A divine nimbus exhales--
    Walt Whitman.
    All roads, howsoe'er they
    diverge--Ambrose Bierce.
    Part II: Pray, what is lighter
    than the wind?--anon.
    My coffin shall be black--
    James Joyce.

(instrumentation: Metal: cowbells, cmb, gongs, anvil or steel pipe, tamtam, tri; Glass: cracked glass (in a tin or glass container), susp drinking glass; Wood: castanets, claves, woodblocks; Membrane: b-dr, bongoes, sn-dr, tam, timbales, tom-toms; Assorted: sand paper blocks, porcelain cups or bowls, cat's meow (or imitation), susp cocoanut shells, pod rattle, stone plate, washboard)

COLGRASS, Michael
Chamber piece for percussion quintet
  MP

Concertino for timpani MP
  (See also "Large Brass Ensembles")
Percussion music MP

Six allegro duets for percussion L-G
Six unaccompanied solos for snare
  drum L-G
Theme and variations for 4 drums
  and viola MP
  (See also "Viola")
Three brothers MP

4 timp-toms, 3 high, 3 med and 3 low, tom-toms, cmb, xy, tri, b-dr, 2 timp, tam-tam
3 trp, 3 trb, tba, timp, 2 perc

4 temple blocks, 4 toy dr, high and deep tom-toms

1. bongo dr; 2. timp; 3. sn-dr; 4. cowbell; 5. 3 tom-toms; 6. tam; 7. susp cmb; 8. maracas; 9. timp

COWELL, Henry
Concerto for percussion and full

8 timp, 4 stands of perc, glock, vib,

orchestra CFP(R)
Ostinato pianissimo for percussion
band NME

Set of five: five movements for
violin, percussion and piano CFP(R)

gongs, mar, temple blocks; full orch
2 string pno, 8 rice bowls, xy, 2
woodblocks, 2 bongoes, 3 dr, 3 gongs,
tam, guiro

CRUMB, George
Night music I MIL

voice, pno (cel), perc; text: Garcia
Lorca

CURRAN, Alvin
Home-made CPE

fl, S (vocalise), c-b, perc, (vib, xy,
tri, cowbells, cmb, woodblocks, bongoes, tom-toms, sn-dr, congo dr,
b-dr)

DAHL, Ingolf
Duettino concertante for flute and
percussion AB

D'ANGELO, James
Toccata for solo percussionist MP

2 tom-toms, snare, timbales, 2 cmb,
tri

De LONE, Peter
Introduction and capriccio for brass
and percussion SHAW
(See also "Large Brass Ensembles")

De PUE, Wallace E.
Toccatina MIL

2 dr, pno

DIAMOND, David
Ceremonial fanfare SMPC
(See also "Large Brass Ensembles")

4 trp, 6 hn, 3 trb, tba, timp, perc

DIEMER, Emma Lou
Declamation for brass and percus-
sion EV
(See also "Large Brass Ensembles")
Toccata for marimba (unacc) MP

4 trp, 2 hn, bar, 2 trb, tba, timp,
sn-dr, susp cmb

mar

DOTSON, James R.
Count-down SMPC

sn-dr and practice pad

EDDY, Murl
Quartet MP

1. claves; 2. castagnets; 3. bongoes;
4. maracas

FARBERMAN, Harold
Concerto COL(R)
Evolution BB(R)
"N.Y. Times--Aug. 30, 1964" GEN

Progressions BB(R)
Variations BB(R)
Variations on a familiar theme BB(R)

solo timp; orch
perc ensemble with S and hn
S, pno and perc; text: N.Y. Times,
ed. of Aug. 30, 1964
fl and perc
perc ensemble with pno
perc ensemble

FELCIANO, Richard
Glossolalia (speaking with tongues)
WLP(R)

Bar or dramatic T; org, perc: vib,
whip, glock, woodblock, 2 timp, xy,

FELDMAN, Morton
The King of Denmark CFP

chimes, tom-toms, bongoes, temple
blocks, sn-dr, mounted ratchet, 2
susp cmb, gongs; electronic tape;
text: Biblical (Psalm 150)

solo perc and perc ensemble

FINNEY, Ross Lee
Concerto for percussion solo and
orchestra CFP(R)
(See also "Full Symphony with Solo")
Edge of shadow CFP
(See also "Mixed Chorus")
Three studies in four CFP

SATB, 2 pno, xy, vib, timp, perc;
text: Archibald MacLeish
perc (3 players), timp

FITT, Robert
Mallets in wonderland MIL

perc ensemble: 1. vib, xy, bells,
chimes, cmb; 2. sn-dr, tom-tom;
3. tom-toms, sn-dr, b-dr, mar

FITZ, Richard
Chamber sonata MP

1. gong, tri, cmb, snare, chimes;
2. 4 timbales, 2 tri, cmb; 3. 4 tom-
toms, tri, mar, gong; 4. gong, 4
timp-toms, cmb, vib; 5. 4 cowbells,
4 timp, tri; 6. bells, b-dr, xy

Duet for 2 snare drums MP

2 sn-dr

FLAGELLO, Nicolas
Divertimento for piano and percus-
sion MP
(See also "Piano, Two Hands")

1. pno; 2. cmb, xy, vib, bells,
chimes, b-dr, tom-toms, snare, tri;
3. b-dr, cel, vib, bells, cmb, tam;
4. snare, cmb, tri, b-dr, tam-tam,
tom-toms, b-dr with pedal; 5. 5 timp,
tam-tam

FRAZEUR, Theodore
Rondo for marimba and piano MP

mar, pno

FULEIHAN, Anis
Accent on percussion SMPC

GABOR, Harley
Voce II AP
(See also "Solo Vocal Music")

med or high voice, fl, perc: vib, xy,
wind chimes; text: from Haiku

GAUGER, Thomas
Snare drum solo No. 1 MP

sn-dr

GOLDENBERG, Morris
6/8 etude MP
Rim shot march MP

sn-dr
sn-dr

GOODMAN, Saul
Ballad for dance MIL
Canon for percussion MIL

solo for 4 timp and susp cmb
perc ensemble: timp, xy, bells, tam-
tam, dr, mar, chimes, sn-dr, field
dr, tri, temple blocks, bongoes, tom-
toms

Dance patterns for 4 percussionists MIL bongoes, sn-dr, field dr, timp, claves

Introduction and allegro for 3 solo
  timpanists MIL
Off we go for 4 percussionists MIL
Scherzo for percussion MIL
Theme and variations for 4 percus-
  sionists MIL

GORDON, David
Bali MP

1. s-rec; 2. vib; 3. xy; 4. xy,
glock; 5. mar; 6. mar, 2 steel
plates; 7. pno, cel; 8. timp; 9.
timbales, blocks; 10. 2 gongs, 2
Korean cmb

GRAEFFE, Didier
Scherzo for 4 timpani and piano MP

4 timp, pno

GRANT, Phil
Chasing the beat for percussion
  quartet MER

2 sn-dr, cmb, b-dr

HANNA, James
Fugue and chorale MP

1. sn-dr; 2. sn-dr, cmb; 3. timp;
4. pno

HARRISON, Lou
Canticle No. 1 MP

1. tam or sist, 3 woodblocks, 3 high
bells; 2. rattle, 3 dragon's mouths,
3 large gongs; 3. rattle, 3 claybells,
cowbells, rasp or guiro; 4. windbell,
tri, cmb, dr, tam-tam, thundersheet;
5. dr, 3 gongs, 3 low dr

Canticle No. 3 MP

1. ocarina (or fl); 2. iron pipes, 5
woodblocks; 3. 5 brake dr, 3 brake
dr muted, xy, maracas, 5 temple
blocks, elephant bell; 4. gtr; 5. 6
water buffalo bells, box, sistrum;
6. 5 muted cowbells, tam-tam, 5
teponazli; 7. snare, b-dr, 5 tom-
toms, large elephant bell

Concerto CFP(R)
Concerto in slendro CFP
First concerto for flute and percus-
  sion (2 players) CFP
Fugue MP

vln; perc orch
vln solo; cel, 2 tackpianos, perc
blocks, rattles, gongs, drm, bells

claves, maracas, metalaphones, 5
cowbells, meditation bells, 5 brake dr,
washtub, bell-coils, b-dr, 2 gongs,
cmb, 3 tri

A joyous procession and a solemn
  procession CFP(R)
Song of Queztecoatl MP

tams, great gong, chimes, bells

1. 5 blocks, 5 dragon's mouths, 5
bells, sistrums, maracas; 2. 5 susp
brake dr, 5 muted brake dr, 5 cowbells, rattle; 3. sn-dr, guiro, wind-
glass, tri, gong, tam-tam; 4. 5 tom-
toms, b-dr

HARRISON, Lou and John Cage
Double music for percussion quartet
  CFP

water buffalo bells, muted brake dr,
sistrums, sleighbells, thundersheet,
temple gongs, tam-tam cowbells, gongs

HART, William
Concert piece for timpani duet MP — 2 timp

HARTWEG, Jerry
Snare drum solo MP

HAUFRECHT, Herbert
Symphony for brass and timpani B&H — 3 trp, 4 hn, 3 trb, tba, timp
(See also "Large Brass Ensembles")

HILLER, Lejaren
Machine music TP — pno, perc, 2-channel tape recorders

HODKINSON, Sidney
Drawings: set No. 1 MP — perc quartet (1. sn-dr, t-dr, b-dr, 3 cmb; 2. 3 tom-toms; 3. 2 bongoes, 3 tri; 4. 3 timp)

HOPKINS, Matthew
Statement for percussion EV — sn-dr, t-dr, b-dr, xy, vib, susp cmb, timp

HOVHANESS, Alan
The burning house overture, Op. 185a CFP — fl and perc (4 players: 1. timp; 2. timp, glock; 3. b-dr, xy, mar; 4. giant tam-tam, mar)

Dance of the black-haired mountain storm (from Wind Drum, a dance drama), Op. 183a CFP — fl and perc (3 players), timp, xy, dr

Fantasy on Japanese wood prints, Op. 211 CFP(R) — xy; full orch
(See also "Full Symphony with Solo")

The flowering peach (music for Clifford Odets' play) AMP — cl, a-sax, timp, tam-tam, vib, glock, hp, cel
(For contents, see "Strings with Voice and/or Winds, Percussion")

Haiku CFP — (Nos. 2-5 for pno and perc)

Invocations to Vahaken CFP — (Nos. 2-5 for pno and perc)

Koke no Niwa (Moss garden), Op. 181 CFP — E-hn (or cl), perc, timp, hp, glock, mar

Mysterious horse before the gate CFP — trb and perc (glock, 2 vib, chimes, tam-tam)

October mountain, Op. 135 CFP(R) — suite for perc sextet: timp, 2 dr, tam-tam, 2 mar, glock, cel

Pilate (opera in 1 act) CFP(R) — perc (5 players: 1. glock, a-gong; 2. vib, t-gong; 3. vib, b-dr; 4. chimes; 5. giant tam-tam), 3 fl, 3 trb, male Ch
(See also "Opera")

Sextet CFP — vln, perc

Suite, Op. 99 CFP — vln, pno, cel, xy, tam-tam, perc
(For contents, see "Violin")

Symphony for metal orchestra No. 17 CFP(R) — 6 fl, 3 trb, perc (6 players: 1. glock; 2. vib; 3. vib; 4. chimes; 5. giant tam-tam)

To the god who is in the fire, Op. 146 CFP(R) — TTBB Ch, T solo, perc: 2 mar, timp, pedal timp in F, t-dr without snares, b-dr, tam-tam; text: Sh'vet
(See also "Men's Chorus") — Umpanishad, II, 17

Upon enchanted ground CFP(R) — tam-tam, fl, vlc, hp

Wind drum (opera--dance drama in
1 act) CFP(R)
(See also "Opera")

timp, perc, fl, hp, str, unison Ch,
B or A solo, dancer (solo or group)

HUSTON, Scott
Suite for solo timpanist GS

timp

IVERSON, Cole
Contrarhythmic ostenato MP

1. 4 timp; 2. tri, side dr; 3. pno;
4. cmb, b-dr; 5. t-dr, sn-dr;
6. xy, vib

JOHNSTON, Ben
Knocking piece CPE

for pno interior (2 players)

JONES, D.
Sonata for 3 unaccompanied kettledrums CFP

KOZINSKI, David
Project percussion TP

timp, pno and 13 perc instruments
(cmb, tam, castanets, tri, sn-dr,
gourd, woodblock, bongoes, gong, b-
dr, xy, glock, chimes)

KRAFT, William
Momentum for 8 percussionists SMPC
Morris dance WIM
Suite for percussion MIL
Fanfare. Andante. Ostinatos.
Toccata. Cadenze.
Theme and variations WIM

perc solo
perc qrt

perc qrt and narrated commentary on
music for percussion

KUBIK, Gail
Gerald McBoing Boing SMPC
(See also "String or Chamber
Orchestra with Solo")

Narr, pno, perc solo

LAMBRO, Phillip
Dance barbaro MP

1. b-dr, 2 conga dr; 2. timp;
3. low tom-tom, timp; 4. 3 tuned
dr, snare; 5. bongo dr, timp bowl;
6. claves, cmb; 7. tam, snare,
gong; 8. maracas, bongo dr

LANG, Philip J.
Trumpet and drum MIL(R)
(See also "Band")

solo trp; sn-dr (or pno or band acc)

LEPRE, Robert
Snare drum solo No. 1 MP

sn-dr

LO PRESTI, Ronald
Sketch MP

1. xy; 2. mar, cel; 3. timp;
4. snare, susp cmb, tri; 5. b-dr,
tam-tam, cmb; 6. pno

LYBBERT, Donald
Praeludium CFP

3 trp, 3 trb, perc (2 players)

MARKS, James
Music for brass and timpani KING

3 trp, 4 hn, 3 trb, bar, tba, timp

(See also "Large Brass Ensembles")

MATHIS, Judy M.
Impressionato MP   1. conga; 2. bongoes; 3. cowbell;
    4. sn-dr

McKENZIE, Jack
Introduction and allegro for percus-
sion ensemble MP
Nonet MP   1. bongo dr; 2. small conga;
    3. large conga dr; 4. gourd, b-dr;
    5. cowbell, tam-tam; 6. susp cmb;
    7. maracas, claves; 8. 4 tom-toms;
    9. marimbula, tom-tom

Pastorale for flute and percussion   4 small dr, susp cmb, tam-tam
MP
(See also "Flute")
Song for trombone and percussion MP   trb, vibes, timp, snare, 2 tom-toms,
(See also "Trombone")   tam-tam
Three dances MP   1. 8 tom-toms; 2. woodblock, 2 tri,
   I. Samba. II. Tango. III. Bolero.   tam, sn-dr; 3. timp

McPHEE, Colin
Tabuh-Tabuhan AMP(R)   full symphony with timp, perc, hp,
    cel, xy, mar, glock, 2 pno

MILLER, Edward J.
Basho songs for soprano and per-   S, bells, maracas, temple blocks,
cussion MP   vibes, xy, cmb, gongs
(See also "Solo Vocal Music")

MILLER, Malloy
Prelude for percussion (two rituals)   1. glock; 2. xy; 3. cmb, whip, tri;
MP   4. tom-tom, snare, woodblock;
    5. b-dr, susp cmb; 6. timp

MISSAL, Joshua
Hoe-down! MP   1. hi-hat cmb, block, 2 tom-toms;
    2. b-dr with attached cmb; 3. xy;
    4. bells; 5. timp; 6. snare; 7. pno

MITCHELL, Lyndol
When Johnny comes marching home   SATB; pno dr; also wind sym and
CFP   dr(R); text: trad
(See also "Mixed Chorus" and "Band")

MORAN, Robert
Bombardments No. 2 CFP   perc ensemble
Interiors CFP   perc ensemble

MUCZYNSKI, Robert
Three designs for three timpani GS   3 timp

NELSON, Oliver
Concerto CFP(R)   xy, mar, vib; wind sym
(See also "Band")

OLSON, Donovan
Sextet MP   1. tam; 2. claves; 3. tri; 4. b-dr
    with cmb; 5. t-dr; 6. sn-dr

PARCHMAN, Gen
Symphony for percussion EV   sn-dr, maracas, bongoes, vibraharp,
                                              glock, guiro, timp
PARKER, Alice
Psalms of praise L-G   men's chorus and perc (b-dr, sn-dr,
                                              cmb, gong, tri, tam); text: Biblical
PARRIS, Robert
Concerto for 5 kettledrums CFP(R)

PASCHKE, Richard
Duet for snare and bass drums (with   sn-dr, b-dr, cmb
  cmb) MP

PAYSON, Albert
Quartet MP   1. 2 sn-dr, vib; 2. timbales, tom-
                                              tom, chimes; 3. 3 tom-toms, susp
                                              cmb; 4. 4 kettle dr, tam-tam
Snare drum solo No. 1 MP   sn-dr

PETERS, Mitchell
A la nanigo KSM   cowbells, cmb, tri, bongoes, tom-
                                              toms, tam, 3 timp, temple blocks,
                                              b-dr, woodblock
Etude No. 1 KSM   4 tom-toms
Etude No. 2 KSM   sn-dr, 2 tom-toms
Scherzo KSM   3 timp
Study in 5/8 KSM   sn-dr, tam, cmb, tom-toms, casta-
                                              nets, b-dr, field dr
PINKHAM, Daniel
Concertante CFP   org, cel, timp, tri, glock, tam-tam,
                                              gongs, cmb, woodblock, sn-dr
Fanfare, aria and echo CFP   2 hn, timp

PLANCHART, A.E.
Divertimento for percussion trio MP   1. timp, sn-dr; 2. sn-dr, tom-tom,
                                              temple blocks; 3. temple blocks,
                                              gong, tri, cmb
PRICE, Paul
Exhibition snare drum No. 1 MP   sn-dr
Invention for 4 percussion players   1. sn-dr, xy, susp cmb; 2. 3 tom-
  MP   toms, tri, block; 3. b-dr, tam-tam,
                                              castagnets; 4. tam, claves, susp cmb
Six bass drum solos (published   b-dr
  separately) MP
Twelve timpani solos (published   timp
  separately) MP

RAMEY, Phillip
Sonata for 3 timpani (unacc) MP   3 timp

REUNING, Sanford H.
Fantasy for toy drums and piano MP   pno, 4 toy dr, cmb
  (See also "Piano, Two Hands")

REYNOLDS, Roger
The emperor of ice cream CFP(R)   8 voices, perc, pno, c-b
The wedge CFP(R)   2 fl, 2 trp, 2 trb, perc, c-b, pno

ROREM, Ned
  Lions (a dream) (1963) B&H   full sym; perc: timp, tri, castagnets,
                                    tam, tam-tam, gong, sn-dr, xy, vib,
                                    glock, cmb, t-dr, woodblock, 5
                                    temple blocks, bongoes, chimes;
                                    combo: a-sax, A "set": sn-dr, b-dr,
                                    cmb, pno, c-b

ROSEN, Jerome
  Elegy for solo percussion MP   glock, vibes, mar, chimes, tri, 8
                                    cmb, gong, cowbells, temple blocks,
                                    woodblock, 2 snares, 3 tom-toms,
                                    conga, dumbeg, 2 b-dr, timp

ROSS, Don
  Easy 2/4 percussion quintet MP   tri, cmb, snare, b-dr, timp

RUSSELL, Armand
  Pas de deux for clarinet and per- susp cmb, tom-tom, tri, snare
    cussion MP
    (See also "Clarinet")
  Percussion suite MP   1. 5 blocks, glock, xy; 2. 4 tom-
    Toccata. Nocturne. Scherzo.   toms, tri, cmb, gong, 5 temple
                                    blocks; 3. sn-dr, tri, b-dr, 4 tom-
                                    toms, 2 wood blocks, susp cmb
  Sonata for percussion and piano MP 4 tom-toms, tri, claves, woodblock
    (See also "Piano, Two Hands")

RUSSELL, William
  Fugue TP   perc, pno
  Three dance movements TP   perc, pno
    Waltz. March. Fox trot.

SCHMIDT, William
  Septigrams WIM   fl, pno, perc

SCHULLER, Gunther
  Symphony for brass and percussion 6 trp, 4 hn, 3 trb, bar, 2 tba, perc,
    SHAW   timp
    (See also "Large Brass Ensembles")

SCHWARTZ, Elliott
  Serenade GEN   fl, c-b, perc
  Variations GEN   S, bsn, perc
    (See also "Solo Vocal Music")

SHIFRIN, Seymour
  Concerto for trumpet, percussion
    and wind orchestra CFP(R)
    (See also "Band")

SHOAFF, Truman
  Quintet in five MP   1. tam, tri; 2. blocks, bells;
                                    3. susp cmb, cowbell, 2 tom-toms;
                                    4. woodblock, sn-dr; 5. b-dr,
                                    ratchet, blocks

SILVERMAN, Alan
  Contest snare drum solo No. 1 MP sn-dr

SIWE, Thomas
Duet for timpani and snare drum MP
Sextet MP   1. claves; 2. bongo dr; 3. maracas;
                                             4. timbales; 5. woodblock, cowbell;
                                             6. timp

SMITH, Warren
Introduction and samba MP   1. cmb, gong, cowbell; 2. bongo dr;
                                             3. congo dr; 4. sn-dr; 5. 3 tom-
                                             toms; 6. timbales

SOMERS, Harry
Symphony for woodwinds, brass and
    percussion CFP(R)
(See also "Band")

SONGER, Lewis
Crab-canon for 3 percussion MP   1. sn-dr; 2. bongoes; 3. 4 small dr

STARER, Robert
Night music for percussion (6 play-   dr, gong, cmb, xy, glock, chimes,
    ers) MIL   cel, timp

STERN, Robert
Adventures for one MP   4 timp, cmb, bongoes, timbales, vib

STRANG, Gerald
Percussion music for three players   cmb, 5 temple blocks, bells, anvil
    TP

SYDEMAN, William
Concerto da camera AMP(R)   solo vln; 2 trp, perc (glock, xy,
                                             blocks, ratchet, chimes, tri, cmb,
                                             gong, bongoes, sn-dr, b-dr, timbales)

THOME, Joel
Drums on the 'phone MP   1. sn-dr, tri; 2. sn-dr, woodblock

THOMSON, Virgil
Mass for 2-part chorus and per-   text: liturgical
    cussion MCA

TULL, Fisher
Soundings for brass and percussion   3 trp, 3 hn, 4 trb, 2 bar, timp, perc
    SHAW
(See also "Large Brass Ensembles")

TUTHILL, George
Snare drum solo MP   sn-dr

ULRICH, E.J.
Suite No. 1 (unacc) MP   mar

WUEBOLD, Edward B., Jr.
Fantasy for timpani and piano MP   timp, pno

WUORINEN, Charles
Invention for percussion quintet MP   1. cel; 2. xy, glock; 3. vib, chimes;
                                             4. b-dr, timp; 5. pno
Prelude and fugue MP   1. 5 blocks; 2. cmb, gong; 3. 2 sn-
                                             dr, gong; 4. 3 pedal timp

6. ORCHESTRA

STRING ORCHESTRA   Duration*   Duration
                              (min)   (min)

ADLER, Samuel   string quartet, Op. 11)GS
Concertino GS   7   Serenade, Op. 1 GS   10
Elegy TP(R)   7
Four early American tunes GS   6.5   BAZELON, Irwin
Chester. Yankee Doodle.   Adagio and fugue WEIN(R)   5
Down Derry down. The
riflemen's song at Bennington.   BEREZOWSKY, Nicolai
                                           Sextet-concerto for string   16
AMRAM, David   orchestra AMP(R)
Autobiography CFP(R)   8
                                           BERGER, Arthur
ANDERSON, Leroy   Three pieces AMP   10
Suite of carols MIL   11.5   Prelude. Aria. Waltz.
Pastores a Belén. It
came upon a midnight   BILLINGS, William
clear. O, little town of   Chester CF   4
Bethlehem. Bring a
torch, Jeanette, Isabella.   CACAVAS, John
Wassail song.   Montage CHAP   5

ANTHEIL, George   CADMAN, Charles Wakefield
Serenade WEIN(R)   15   American suite HE   7
                                           Indian. Negro. Old
BALES, Richard   fiddler.
Music of the American   19
Revolution PIC   CALABRO, Louis
Suite No. 1: Washington's   9   Ten short pieces EV   8.5
march. Minuet danced   Choral. Dance. Berceuse.
before General Washing-   Bounce. Song. In the
ton. Brandywine quick-   nursery. Walking. De-
step. Beneath a weeping   serted street. Melody.
willow's shade. The   Finale.
toast (to Washington).
Suite No. 2: General Bur-   10   CARTER, Elliott
goyne's march. Minuet.   Elegy (1943) PIC   5
Gavotte. Delia. Yankee
Doodle with quicksteps.   CHADWICK, George W.
                                           Rip Van Winkle overture CF(R)   5
BARATI, George
Chamber concerto CFP(R)   23   COPLAND, Aaron
(See also "Small or   Hoe-down (from Rodeo)   3.5
Chamber Orchestra")   (1942) B&H
                                           Nonet for strings B&H   18
BARBER, Samuel   (See also "Large String
Adagio for strings (from   7.5   Ensembles")

*Approximate

265

Duration (min)

The pied piper (1951) (ballet   17
  in one act) B&H(R)
  (See also "String or Cham-
  ber Orchestra with Solo,"
  Concerto (1948) for clarinet)
Two pieces (1928) B&H(R)   11
  Lento molto. Rondino.

COWELL, Henry
  Ballad (1954) AMP   4
  Ensemble (1925; rev. 1956)   8
    AMP
  Hymn and fuguing tune No. 2   7
    AMP

CRESTON, Paul
  Gregorian chant (from String 6.5
    quartet, Op. 8) SHAW

DAHL, Ingolf
  Variations on a theme by   10
    C. P. E. Bach (1967) AB

DELAMARTER, Eric
  Serenade near Taos COL(R)   13

DELLO JOIO, Norman
  Air for strings EBM   4
  Meditations on Ecclesiastes   22
    CF(R)

DIAMOND, David
  Elegy in the memory of   7
    Maurice Ravel SMPC
  Rounds EV   12

ELMORE, Robert
  Three colors AMP   13
    Green. Blue. Orange.

FINE, Irving
  Notturno (with hp) B&H   14.5
  Serious song BB(R)   9

FINNEY, Ross Lee
  Slow piece VAL   6

FLAGELLO, Nicolas
  Concerto for strings GEN   24

FOOTE, Arthur
  Suite in E-major S-B   11
    Prelude. Pizzicato. Fugue.

Duration (min)

FORST, Rudolf
  Adagio (from the quartet) EM   4
  Threnody EM   4

FRACKENPOHL, Arthur
  Scherzo (from Symphony No.   4
    2 for Strings) CF
  Star Lake suite B&H   6
  Suite for strings (based on   7
    American folk songs) GS
    Union train. Shenandoah.
    Fiddle-de-dee. Every
    night when the sun goes in.
    A-rovin'.

FULEIHAN, Anis
  Divertimento SMPC   9
    Entrance. Serenade.
    Chorale. Fugue.

GIANNINI, Vittorio
  Concerto grosso EV   13
  Prelude and fugue CHAP   10.5

GILLIS, Don
  Three sketches for strings   8.5
    B&H
    Enchantment. Whimsy.
    Day dreams.

GLASS, Philip
  Arioso No. 2 EV   4

GORDON, Philip
  Fiddling for fun GS   6
  Three preludes for string   7
    orchestra BI
  Two moods EV   6

GOULD, Morton
  Spirituals MIL   17.5
    Deep river. Go down,
    Moses. Nobody knows the
    trouble I've seen. Some-
    times I feel like a mother-
    less child. Swing low,
    sweet chariot.

GUTCHE, Gene
  Symphony No. 5 GAL(R)   22

HARRIS, Roy
  Prelude and fugue GS   14

	Duration (min)		Duration (min)

HARRISON, Lou
Suite for symphonic strings 20
CFP(R)
Estampie. Chorale. Double
fugue. Ductia. Lament.
Canonic variations. Little
fugue. Round. Nocturne.
Suite No. 2 MER 17
(See also "String Quartet")

HAUBIEL, Charles
Miniatures EV 8.5
A mystery. Madonna. Gaiety.
Shadows. Snowflakes. Festival.

HAUFRECHT, Herbert
Square set (1941) AMP 10
Reel. Clog dance. Jig time.

HEIDEN, Bernhard
Concertino AB(R) 18

HELM, Everett
Concerto for string orchestra 15
CFP
Symphonie AMP 19

HERRMANN, Bernard
Sinfonietta BB 7.5

HILL, Edward Burlingame
Sinfonietta B&H(R) 16.5

HOIBY, Lee
Study in design B&H 6

HOVHANESS, Alan
Alleluia and fugue BB(R) 10
Armenian rhapsody No. 1 PIC(R) 4
Armenian rhapsody No. 2 BB(R) 4
Armenian rhapsody No. 3 4
CFP(R)
Celestial fantasy BB(R) 7
In memory of an artist (suite, 7
Op. 163) CFP(R)
Psalm and fugue, Op. 40a 6
CFP(R)
Symphony No. 16, Op. 202 16
CFP(R)

HOWARD, John Tasker
Mosses from an old manse 5.5
EM

HUSTED, Benjamin
Fugue for strings EV 6

IVES, Charles
Hymn (largo cantabile) PIC 4

JAMES, Philip
Suite No. 1 BB 16
Preamble. Musette.
Interlude. Fugue.

JONES, Charles
Introduction and rondo CFP 12

KAY, Ulysses
Six dances MCA 12
Suite for strings CFP(R) 14

KOCH, John
Elegy VAL 2

LA MONTAINE, John
Colloquy for strings PJS(R) 13
Recitative, aria and finale 12
PJS(R)

LANE, Richard
Passacaglia CF 6

LEE, Dai-Keong
Introduction and allegro MCA 7.5

LEES, Benjamin
Interlude for strings B&H 11

LUENING, Otto
Suite B&H 10
Overture. Song. Dance.

McBRIDE, Robert
Pumpkin-eater's little fugue 3
AMP

McKAY, George F.
From outdoor life GAL 6
Canyon vista.
On the road.
Halyard and capstan (sea- 4
shanty suite) S-B
Haul on the bowline. Shallo
Brown. Poor old man.
Missouri harmony EV 7
By morning light. To worlds
on high. O joyful sound.

	Duration (min)		Duration (min)
Port Royal 1861 (folk song suite) S-B Hold your light on Canaan shore. Go down in lonesome valley. Heaven shall be my home.	8	Study in sonority AMP(R) 10 vln (or any multiple thereof)	9
Symphonetta in D GAL	3.5	ROGERS, Bernard Allegory TP	6
		Soliloquy CF	7
MENNINI, Louis Arioso CF	6.5	RUGGLES, Carl Portals AME(R)	6
MOORE, Douglas Cotillion suite CF Grand march. Polka. Waltz. Galop. Cake walk. Quickstep.	15	SCHRAMM, Harold Invocation MCA	5
		SCHUMAN, William Symphony for strings (Symphony No. 5) GS(R)	17
NIBLOCK, James Trigon B&H	7	SHAPERO, Harold Serenade in D-major SMPC(R)	28
NIXON, Roger Air for strings MIL	5	SHULMAN, Alan The Benjamin Franklin quartet WEIN(R)	7
OVERTON, Hall Symphony for strings CFP(R)	21	STARER, Robert Elegy MCA	4
PERSICHETTI, Vincent Introit for strings EV	3	STEVENS, Halsey Overture HME	5.5
Symphony for strings, Op. 61 EV(R)	22	STILL, William Grant Danzas de Panama SMPC Tamborito. Mejorana y Socavon. Punto. Cumbia y congo.	6
PHILLIPS, Burrill Concert piece CF	9		
PORTER, Quincy Music for strings MER Ukrainian suite CF	8 13	STOUT, Alan Ricercare and aria CFP(R)	4.5
POZDRO, John Rondo gioioso S-B	5	THOMSON, Virgil Cantabile for strings MER	4.5
PREVIN, Andre Portrait for strings MCA	6	TRIMBLE, Lester Notturno CFP(R)	7
RAPHLING, Sam Suite MER(R)	13	VAN VACTOR, David Introduction and presto AME(R)	7
RICHTER, Marga Lament BB	11	VERRALL, John Divertimento for strings GAL	11
RIEGGER, Wallingford Canon and fugue, Op. 33 FLAM(R)	8		
Romanza, Op. 56a AMP	5		

	Duration (min)

	Duration (min)

VINCENT, John
The Benjamin Franklin suite 7
MIL

WALDROP, Gid
Pressures B&H 7

WASHBURN, Robert
Suite for strings OX 5
(See also "String Quartet")

WEBER, Ben
Serenade B&H 14

WEIGEL, Eugene
Sonata VAL 8

WHEAR, Paul W.
Olympiad: Concertino EV 9

WHITE, Paul
Sinfonietta EV(R) 18

WILLIAMS, John T.
Essay MCA(R) 9.5

WILSON, Don
Dedication GAL 5.5

YARDUMIAN, Richard
Cantus animae et cordis EV(R) 15

SMALL OR CHAMBER ORCHESTRA

		Duration* (min)
ARGENTO, Dominick		
Overture to The Boor B&H	fl, ob, 2 cl, bsn, 2 hn, trp, timp, pno, str	5
Royal invitation or homage to the Queen of Tonga B&H(R)	fl, 2 ob, 2 bsn, 2 hn, str	23
BABBITT, Milton		
Composition for twelve instruments (1948; rev. 1954) AMP	fl, ob, cl, bsn, hn, trp, hp, cel, vln, vla, vlc, c-b	7
BARATI, George		
Chamber concerto CFP(R) (See also "String Orchestra")	fl, ob, cl, bsn, str	23
BAZELON, Irwin		
Suite WEIN Prelude. Serenade. Scherzo and trio. Rondo. Fugato. Finale.	fl, ob (E-hn), cl, bsn, hn, trp, timp, str	17
BEREZOWSKY, Nicolai		
Introduction and allegro MER	fl, ob, cl, bsn, hn, str	9
BERGER, Arthur		
Serenade concertante CFP(R)	vln, fl, ob, cl, bsn solos; 2 hn, trp, str	9
BERRY, Wallace		
Five pieces for small orchestra CF(R) Evocation. Variation. Fantasy. Chorale. Fugue.	fl, ob, cl, bsn, hn, trp, trb, timp, hp, str	18
BROWN, Earle		
Available forms I AMP(R)	fl, ob, 2 cl, b-cl, bsn, hn, trp, trb, hp, pno, str, perc I, perc II	10-20

*Approximate

		Duration (min)
CHOU, Wen-Chung		
Landscapes CFP(R)	2 fl (picc), 2 ob (E-hn), 2 hn,	7.5
Under the cliff in the bay.	2 trp, timp, perc, hp, str	
Sorrow of parting.		
One streak of dying light.		
COPLAND, Aaron		
Dance panels (ballet in 7 sections)	2 fl, ob, 2 cl, bsn, 2 hn,	26
B&H(R)	2 trp, trb, perc, str	
(See also "Piano, Two Hands")		
Down a country lane B&H	2 fl, ob, 2 cl, bsn, 2 hn,	3
	trp, trb, str	
From "Billy the Kid" (arr. composer)		5
B&H		
Prairie night.	fl, ob, cl, bsn, vln, vla, vlc, c-b	
Celebration dance.	picc, ob, cl, bsn, vln, c-b	
Music for the movies (1942) B&H(R)	fl, ob, cl, bsn, hn, 2 trp,	16
New England countryside.	trb, perc, hp, pno, str	
Barley wagons. Sunday traffic.		
Story of Grovers Corners.		
Threshing machines.		
Music for radio (1937) (Saga of the	2 fl, 2 ob, 2 cl, bsn, 3 sax,	12
prairie) B&H(R)	2 hn, 3 trp, 2 trb, 2 tba,	
	timp, perc, hp, pno, cel, str	
Music for the theater (1925) B&H(R)	fl, ob, cl, bsn, 2 trp, trb,	22
Prologue. Dance. Interlude.	perc, pno, str	
Burlesca. Epilogue.		
Quiet city B&H	E-hn, trp, str	9
Waltz from "Billy the Kid" B&H	fl, ob, 2 cl, bsn, hn, 2 trp,	4
	trb, hp, 2 vln, vla, vlc, c-b	
COWELL, Henry		
Old American country set AMP	2 fl, 2 ob, 2 cl, bsn, 2 hn,	15
Blarneying lilt. Meeting house.	2 trp, trb, tba, perc, str	
Camallye. Charivari. Corn-		
huskin' hornpipe.		
Persian set CFP(R)	fl, cl, tar or man, vln I,	15
	vln II, c-b, pno	
Polyphonica AMP(R)	fl, ob, cl, bsn, hn, trp, trb,	4
	str	
Saturday night at the fire house AMP	fl, 2 ob, 2 cl, 2 bsn, 2 hn,	4
	2 trp, perc, pno, str	
CRESTON, Paul		
Two choric dances, Op. 17a GS(R)	fl, ob, cl, bsn, trp, timp,	24
	perc, pno, str	
ETLER, Alvin		
Elegy (1959) AMP	fl, ob, 2 cl, 2 bsn, 2 hn, str	4.5
FELDMAN, Morton		
Atlantis CFP(R)	(graph)	8
FINNEY, Ross Lee		
Three pieces CFP(R)	fl, ob, cl, bsn, trp, timp,	10
	2 pno, cel, str, tape recorder	
FRACKENPOHL, Arthur		
Little suite EV	fl, ob, 2 cl, bsn, 2 sax, 2 hn,	4

Duration
(min)

March.   Minuet.   Jig.   2 trp, 2 trb, tba, perc, str

GABURO, Kenneth
Elegy TP(R)   2 fl, 2 ob, 2 cl, 2 trp, 3 trb, str 13

GIANNINI, Vittorio
Frescobaldiana (from 3 org pieces by   fl, ob, E-hn, 2 cl, bsn, c-bsn, 15
   Frescobaldi) COL(R)   4 hn, C-trp, 2 trb, b-& c-b
   Toccata. Aria. Fuga.   trb, timp, str

HAIEFF, Alexei
Divertimento B&H(R)   fl (picc), ob (E-hn), cl, 2 trp,   12
   Prelude. Aria. Scherzo.   2 trb, str
   Lullaby. Finale.

HARRIS, Roy
Evening piece MIL(R)   fl, ob, 2 cl (b-cl), hn, trp,   6
                                           trb, solo vln, str
Radio piece CF   2 fl, 2 ob, 2 cl, 2 bsn, hn,   8
                                           trp, trb, timp, perc, pno, str

HARRISON, Lou
Alleluia NME   2 fl (picc), ob, cl, bsn (c-bsn),   7
                                           2 hn, hp, str
Seven pastorales PIC   2 fl, ob, bsn, hp, str   17

HARTLEY, Walter
Partita for chamber orchestra GAL(R) fl, ob, cl, bsn, 2 hn, trp, str 16

HELM, Everett
Sinfonia da camera AMP(R)   ob, cl, bsn, hn, hpcd (or pno),   18
                                           str

HOVHANESS, Alan
Anahid (fantasy), Op. 57 CFP(R)   fl, E-hn, trp, timp, perc, str   14
Circe (ballet), Op. 204 CFP(R)   15
   (See also "Full Symphony")
Janabar PIC(R)   trp, pno, str   35
Khrimian Hairig, Op. 49 CFP(R)   trp, str   9
Kohar, Op. 66 CFP(R)   fl, E-hn, timp, str   8
Saint Vartan symphony, Op. 180   E-flat sax, a-sax, hn, 4 trp,   36
   PIC(R)   trb, perc, pno, str
Symphony No. 6, Op. 173 ("Celestial   fl, ob, cl, bsn, hn, trp,   14
   gate") CFP(R)   timp, chimes, hp, str
Symphony No. 8, Op. 179 ("Arjuna")   fl, E-hn, cl, bsn, hn, timp,   25
   CFP(R)   pno, str
Symphony No. 13 (in one mov), Op.   fl, E-hn, cl, bsn, hn, perc,   18
   190 CFP(R)   hp, str
Zartik parkim (awake, my glory),   fl, cl, 2 hn, trp, timp, cmb,   15
   Op. 77 PIC(R)   tam-tam, pno, str
   Zankag. Tampoug. Srynk.

IVES, Charles
The gong on the hook and ladder, or,   fl, cl, bsn, 2 trp, trb, sn-dr,   2
   Fireman's parade on Main Street   tri, timp, gong (ad lib), pno,
   PIC   str
The rainbow (after a poem by   fl, E-hn (or bsn), pno, str   2
   William Wordsworth) PIC

Duration
(min)

A set of pieces NME(R)   7
  In the cage.   ob (or fl) ad lib, E-hn, timp,
                                  pno, str
  In the inn.   cl, bsn (or E-flat B-sax),
                                  timp, pno, str
  In the night.   E-hn (or A-cl), bells, pno,
                                  hp (or pno II), str
Symphony No. 3 ("The camp meeting")   fl, ob, cl, bsn, 2 hn, trb,   17
  AMP(R)   bells, str
  Old folks gatherin'.   Children's
  day.   Communion.
Tone roads, No. 1 PIC   fl, cl, bsn, str   8
Tone roads, No. 3 PIC   fl, cl, trp, trb, chimes, pno, str 9
The unanswered question PIC   2 fl, ob (or fl III), cl (or fl   8
                                  IV), trp (or E-hn, cl or ob), str

KELLEY, Robert
A miniature symphony No. 1, Op. 14   fl, ob, cl, bsn, 2 hn, trp,   10
  GAL(R)   trb, timp, str

KENNAN, Kent
Promenade CF(R)   fl, ob, 2 cl, 2 hn, 2 trp (or   4
                                  cor), trb, tba, perc, hp (or
                                  pno)

KORN, Peter Jona
Variations on a tune from The   fl, ob, 2 cl, bsn, 2 hn, trp,   27
  Beggar's Opera B&H   trb, hp, cel, perc, str

KUBIK, Gail
Folk song suite SMPC(R)   fl, ob, 2 cl, bsn, 2 hn, 2 trp, 10
  Whoopee-ti-yi-yo.   Two hymn tunes   trb, timp, pno, str
  of Billings (When Jesus wept;
  Chester).   Camptown races.
Music for dancing SMPC   fl, ob, 2 cl, bsn, 2 hn, 2 trp,   9
                                  trb, tba, timp, pno, str

KUPFERMAN, Meyer
Little symphony WEIN(R)   fl (picc), 2 ob, 2 bsn, 2 hn, str 19

KURKA, Robert
Serenade, Op. 25 WEIN(R)   2 fl, 2 ob, 2 cl, 2 bsn, 2 hn,   21
                                  2 trp, timp, str

LA MONTAINE, John
Interlude from "The Songs of Songs"   picc, ob, 2 fl, cl, bsn, E-hn,   6
  PJS(R)   hp, pno, str
A summer's day GS   fl, ob, cl, hn, trp, hp, str   5

LEWIS, Peter
Evolution TP   fl, ob, cl, bsn, 2 hn, trp, trb, 9
                                  tba, perc, str

LUENING, Otto
Prelude to a hymn tune by William   fl, ob, cl, bsn, hn, pno, str   10
  Billings CFP

MAGANINI, Quinto
Sylvan symphony EM   fl, ob, cl, bsn, 2 hn, str   17
  Crags.   Daybreak.   Frogs.

Duration
(min)

McPHEE, Colin
Concerto for wind orchestra CFP(R)   4 picc, 3 fl, 3 cl, 3 c-bsn,   15
4 hn, 3 trp, 3 trb, tba,
perc, hp, pno, c-b

MOEVS, Robert
Musica da camera EBM(R)   2 fl, 3 cl, 2 bsn, hn, vln,   12.5
vla, vlc, hp, perc

MOORE, Douglas
Farm journal CF   2 fl (picc), 2 ob, 2 cl, 2 bsn,   15
Up early. Sunday clothes.   2 hn, trp, timp, perc, str
Lamplight. Harvest song.

MORAN, Robert
Interiors CFP   (graph)   9-10
(See also "Full Symphony" and
"Percussion")

PHILLIPS, Burrill
Scena HAR   fl, ob, 2 cl, bsn, 2 hn,   7
2 trp, trb, timp, str

PISTON, Walter
Divertimento AMP   fl, ob, cl, bsn, 2 vln, vla,   11
vlc, c-b
Sinfonietta B&H(R)   2 fl, 2 ob, 2 cl, 2 bsn,   17
2 hn, str

PRESSER, William
Arctic night EV   fl, ob, 2 cl, 2 hn, 2 trp,   5
3 trb, tba, timp, str

RAPHLING, Sam
Rhapsody COL(R)   ob, trp, str   10

REYNOLDS, Roger
Wedge CFP(R)   2 fl (picc), 2 trp, 2 trb, tba,   7.5
(See also "Percussion")   perc, c-b, vib, pno

RIEGGER, Wallingford
Dichotomy, Op. 12 AMP(R)   fl, ob, cl, bsn, hn, 2 trp,   12
perc, pno, str
Scherzo PIC(R)   fl, ob, cl, bsn, hn, trp,   7
timp, str

ROGERS, Bernard
Elegy to memory of Franklin D.   fl, 2 hn, timp, str   8
Roosevelt EV(R)
Fantasia TP   hn, timp, str   9
Leaves from the tale of Pinocchio   Narr; fl (picc), ob, cl, bsn (c-   22
SMPC(R)   bsn), hn, trp, trb, timp, perc,
He is born...and rejoices. The   glock, xyl, hp, pno, str (also
talking cricket. Parade of the   performable with Narr & pno)
actors. At the marionette theater.
The cat and the fox. The fairy with
azure hair. The field of wonders.
The serpent and the smoking tail.
Flight with a pigeon. He rescues
his father. A real boy!
The silver world SMPC   fl (picc), ob, str   10

		Duration (min)
RUGGLES, Carl		
Men and mountains AME(R)	fl, 2 ob (E-hn), cl, bsn, 2 hn, 2 trp, trb, pno, perc, str	15
SANDERS, Robert		
Little symphony No. 3 GAL(R)	fl, ob, cl, bsn, 2 hn, trp, timp, str	13
SCHULLER, Gunther		
Contours AMP	fl (picc), ob, cl, b-cl, bsn, hn, trp, trb, perc, hp, str	23
Entrada. Interlude. Capriccio. Interlude. Partita. Interlude. Lamento. Interlude.		
Little fantasy SHAW(R)	picc, fl, ob, cl, bsn, 2 hn, C-trp, trb, perc, str	4
SCHWARTZ, Elliott		
Texture AB	fl, ob, cl, bsn, trp, trb, hn, str (for solo or in choirs)	7.5
SHIFRIN, Seymour		
Kammer-sinfonie CFP(R)	fl, 2 cl (b-cl), 2 hn, 2 trb, str	20
SOLLBERGER, Harvey		
Chamber variations for 12 players MM(R)	fl, a-fl (picc), ob, cl (b-cl), bsn, 2 perc, vln, vla, vlc, c-b, pno	17
STARER, Robert		
Concerto a tre MCA(R)	cl, trp, trb, str	18
STILL, William Grant		
Darker America CF(R)	2 fl, 2 ob, 2 cl, 2 bsn, hn, trp, trb, perc, pno, str	9
SWANSON, Howard		
Night music WEIN(R)	fl, ob, cl, bsn, hn, str	9
THOMSON, Virgil		
Suite from The River SMPC(R)	fl, 2 ob, cl, bsn, 2 hn, 2 trp, 2 trb, perc, str	25
The old South. Industrial expansion. Soil erosion and floods. Finale.		
WARD, Robert		
Night music GAL(R)	fl, ob, cl, bsn, 2 trp, hn, hp, str	6
Symphony No. 3 GAL(R)	2 (picc), 2 (E-hn), 2 (b-cl), 2 ob, 2 trp, hn, pno, str	21
Fantasia. Arioso. Rondo.		
WEBER, Ben		
Dolmen, an elegy for winds and strings, Op. 58 EBM(R)	fl, ob, cl, bsn, hn, trp, trb, str, pno	9
WILDER, Alec		
Slow dance BI	fl, ob, 3 cl, b-cl, bsn, pno, perc, str	7
Theme and variations BI	fl, ob, 3 cl, b-cl, bsn, pno, str	7
WUORINEN, Charles		
Evolutio transcripta MM	2 ob, 2 hn, bsn, str	7

STRING OR CHAMBER ORCHESTRA WITH SOLO INSTRUMENT OR VOICE

	Solo	Duration* (min)
AMRAM, David		
The American bell CFP(R)	Narr; cham; text: Archibald MacLeish	45
Shakespearean concerto CFP(R)	ob, 2 hn; str	22
BARBER, Samuel		
Capricorn concerto, Op. 21 GS	fl, ob, trp; str	14
Four songs for voice and orchestra GS(R)	med-high voice	8
I hear an army	fl, ob, cl, 2 bsn, 3 trp, 2 hn, 2 trb, hp, str; text: James Joyce	
Monks and raisins	2 ob, 3 cl, 2 bsn, 2 trp, hn, str; text: Jose Garcia Villa	
Nocturne	fl, ob, 2 cl, bsn, 2 trp, timp, hp, str; text: Frederick Prokosch	
Sure on this shining night	ob, cl, bsn, 2 trp, timp, hp, str; text: James Agee	
A hand of bridge, Op. 35 GS(R)	S, m-S, T, B voices; perc, pno, str; text: Stephen Spender	9
Knoxville: summer of 1915, Op. 24 GS(R)	S voice; fl, ob, cl, bsn, 2 hn, trp, tri, hp, str; text: James Agee	16
BARLOW, Wayne		
Lyrical piece CF(R)	cl; str	4.5
Winter's passed CF	ob; str	5
BAVICCHI, John		
Concerto OX	cl; str	20
BERNSTEIN, Leonard		
Serenade GS(R)	vln; str, hp, perc	32
Phaedrus. Pausanias. Aristophanes. Erixymathus. Agathon. Socrates. Alcibiades.		
BINGHAM, Seth		
Connecticut suite, Op. 56 HWG(R)	org; str (optional trp, trb)	14
Town meeting. Picnic. Autumn haze. Old Yale.		
BUCCI, Mark		
Concerto for a singing instrument FM(R) (For contents, see "Solo Vocal")	high voice (vocalise); hp, pno (cel), str	16.5
CANNING, Thomas		
Fantasy on a hymn by Justin Morgan CF	str qrt solo; str qrt II and str orch	10
CARTER, Elliott		
Double concerto AMP(R)	hpcd & pno; with 2 cham orch:	23

*Approximate

	Solo	Duration (min)
	I: fl, hn, trp, trb, perc, vla, c-b II: ob, cl, bsn, 2 hn, perc, vln, vlc	
CLOKEY, Joseph W.		
Partita in G-minor HWG(R)	org; str	8
COPLAND, Aaron		
Concerto (1948) B&H(R)	cl; str, hp, pno	17.5
(Also used for score of "The pied piper (1951), " a ballet; see "String Orchestra")		
Old American songs B&H(R)	Bar; fl(& picc), ob, 2 cl, bsn,	25
(For contents, see "Solo Vocal")	2 hn, trp, trb, hp; str; text: trad	
Quiet city (1940) B&H	trp, E-hn(or ob); str	9
COWELL, Henry		
Air and scherzo AMP	a-sax; cham	8
Fiddler's jig AMP	vln; str	3
Variations on thirds CFP(R)	2 solo vla; cham	11.5
CRESTON, Paul		
Partita MCA	vln, fl(or 2 vln); str	16
Preamble. Sarabande. Burlesk. Air. Tarantella.		
CURTIS, Edgar		
Concerto CFP(R)	org; str	21
DELLO JOIO, Norman		
Lamentation of Saul CF(R)	Bar; full or cham; text: from play, David, by D.H. Lawrence	20
DIAMOND, David		
Elegies SMPC(R)	fl and E hn; str	18
In memory of Edward Estlin Cummings. In memory of William Faulkner.		
DI DOMENICO, Robert		
Concerto MJQ(R)	vln; cham	18
DONOVAN, Richard		
Ricercare B&H	ob; str	6
DRUCKMAN, Jacob		
Dark upon the harp TP	T; cham; text: Biblical	17.5
EPSTEIN, David		
Four songs (a cycle) MER(R)	S, solo hn; str	10
(For contents, see "Solo Vocal Music")		
ETLER, Alvin		
Concerto (1967) AB	brass quintet (2 trp, hn, trb, b-trb); str, perc	18
Concerto for clarinet (1962) AMP(R)	cl; 3 trp, 2 trb, 2 c-b, perc	19

	Solo	Duration (min)
EVETT, Robert		
Concerto CFP(R)	hpcd; trp, timp, perc, cel, str	20
FINE, Irving		
Notturno B&H	hp; str	15
FLAGELLO, Nicolas		
The land GEN(R)	B-Bar; cham;	24
(For contents, see "Solo Vocal Music")	text: Alfred Lord Tennyson	
L'Infinito GEN(R)	med voice; cham;	4.5
	text: Giacomo Leopardi	
FOOTE, Arthur		
A night piece S-B	fl; str	4.5
FOSS, Lukas		
Song of anguish CF(R)	Bar; cham; text: Biblical	19
Time cycle CF(R)	S; cham	22
(For contents, see "Solo Vocal Music")		
FULEIHAN, Anis		
Concerto SMPC(R)	pno; str	20
Rhapsody CF	vlc; str	18
GAUL, Harvey		
Thanksgiving JF	org; str, timp	8
GILLIS, Don		
Four scenes from yesterday B&H		16
Courthouse square	ob; timp, perc, cel(or pno), hp, str	
North Harris	fl; perc, cel, hp, str	
Retrospection MIL(R)	vln; str, cel, pno, hp, perc	5.5
GIUFFRE, James		
Mobiles MJQ(R)	cl; str	21
Piece for clarinet and string orchestra MJQ(R)	cl; str	18
Threshold MJQ(R)	vib, pno, c-b, dr; cham	10
GOEB, Roger		
Fantasy AMP	ob; str	6
GOODMAN, Joseph		
Concertante for woodwind quintet AB(R)	fl, ob, cl, bsn, hn; cham	22
GOULD, Morton		
Dialogues CHAP	pno; str	22
Recitative and chorale. Embellishments and rondo. Dirge and meditation. Variations and coda. (See also "Piano, Four-Hands")		
GRIFFES, Charles		
Poem GS	fl; 2 hn, timp, str	9

	Solo	Duration (min)
HAIEFF, Alexei Eclogue: "La nouvelle Héloise" CHAP	hp; str	7
HANSON, Howard Concerto No. 3, Op. 22 (1941) CF(R) Serenade, Op. 35 (1945) CF	org; hp, str fl; hp, str	15 6
HARRISON, Lou Concerto CFP(R) (See also "Percussion")	vln; perc orch	15
HELM, Everett Concerto for 5 solo instruments AMP(R)	vln, fl, ob, bsn, trp; perc, str	14
HOIBY, Lee Pastorale dances, Op. 4 GS(R)	fl; cham	7
HOSMER, James Rhapsody MM(R)	fl; str	5
HOVHANESS, Alan Artik, Op. 78 CFP(R) Alleluia. Ballata. Laude. Canzona (To a mountain range). Processional. Canon. Aria. Intonazione.	hn; str	15
Avak, the healer, Op. 65 PIC(R)	S voice, C-trp; str; text: Alan Hovhaness	20
Concerto No. 2 CFP(R) Pastoral. Aria. Allegro. Aria. Presto. Recitative and lullaby. Hymn.	vln; str	20
Concerto No. 3, "Diran" KING Canzona. Aria.	bar hn; str	10
Concerto, Op. 114 CFP(R)	harmonica; str	10
Elibris (Dawn god of Urardu), Op. 50 PIC(R)	fl; str	7
The holy city CFP(R)	susp chime or bell in A, trp, str	8
Lousadzak (Coming of light), Op. 48 PIC(R)	pno; str	15
Overture, Op. 76, No. 1 CFP(R)	trb; str	5
Prayer of St. Gregory PIC	trp; str	4
Processional and fugue, Op. 76, No. 5 CFP(R)	trp(or cl); str	5
Talin, Op. 93 CFP(R) Chant. Estampie. Canzona.	vla; str	14
Tsaikerk (Evening song), Op. 53 PIC(R)	vln; fl, timp, str	10
JACOBI, Frederick Concertino EV(R)	pno; str	17
JOHNSON, Hunter For an unknown soldier VAL	fl; str	8

	Solo	Duration (min)
JOHNSON, J.J.		
Rondeau MJQ(R)	vib, pno, c-b, dr; cham	18
KENNAN, Kent		
Night soliloquy CF	fl; pno, str	4
KIRCHNER, Leon		
Concerto AMP(R)	soli: vln, vlc; fl, ob, cl, bsn, c-bsn, hn, 2 trp, 2 trb, timp, 3 perc	19
Toccata AMP(R)	solo winds: ob, cl, bsn, trp, hn, trb; perc, str	14
KOHS, Ellis		
Chamber concerto MER(R)	vla; str nonnette	17
Legend AMP	ob; str	6
Passacaglia HWG(R)	org; str	12
KORN, Peter Jona		
Concertino B&H	hn; str	14
KOUTZEN, Boris		
Concert piece MER(R)	vlc; str	10
Concertino GEN(R)	pno; str	15
KUBIK, Gail		
Gerald McBoing Boing (A children's tale) SMPC (also performable with Narr, pno, solo perc)	Narr; cham	9
KURKA, Robert		
Ballad WEIN(R)	hn; str	8
LEES, Benjamin		
Declamations WEIN(R)	pno; str	9.5
LEWIS, John		
The Queen's fancy MJQ(R) (See also "Jazz Combos")	vib, pno, c-b, dr; cham	8
LoPRESTI, Ronald		
Nocturne CF	vla; str	6.5
LUENING, Otto		
Concertino CFP(R)	fl; str	20
MAYER, William		
Concert piece B&H	trp; str	9
MORAVIANS, Music of the		
Ten sacred songs CFP (For contents, see "Vocal Music")	S; str, org(or pno); texts: Biblical	15
NEMIROFF, Isaac		
Concerto MM(R)	ob; str	15

	Solo	Duration (min)
PERRY, Julia		
Stabat Mater SMPC	A; str orch (or str qrt); text: liturgical	17
PERSICHETTI, Vincent		
The hollow men EV	trp; str	7.5
PHILLIPS, Burrill		
Concert piece CF (See also "Band")	bsn; str	6
PHILLIPS, Peter		
Concerto grosso MJQ(R)	vib, pno, c-b, dr; cham	24
PINKHAM, Daniel		
Sonata No. 1 ECS	org; str	6
Sonata No. 2 ECS	org; str	10
Three lyric scenes BOS (For contents, see "Solo Vocal Music")	med voice; str; text: W. H. Auden	10
PISTON, Walter		
Capriccio AMP(R)	hp; str	8
Concertino AMP	pno; 2 fl, 2 ob, 2 cl, 2 bsn, 2 hn, str	14
Fantasy (1953) AMP	E-hn; hp, str	10
Prelude and allegro AMP(R)	org; str	12
PORTER, Quincy		
Fantasy on a pastoral theme (1946)CF	org; str	10
Three Elizabethan songs YUP(R) (For contents, see "Solo Vocal Music")	med voice; fl, ob, bsn, 2 vln, vla, vlc, c-b	14
PRESSER, William		
Rondo TP	trb; str	5
RAPHLING, Sam		
Concerto BI(R)	trp; str	7
Rhapsody (or "Sonata") COL(R)	hn; ob, str	7
Warble for lilac-time EM	fl; str	10
RICHTER, Marga		
Aria and toccata MIL(R)	vla; str	9
ROGERS, Bernard		
Allegory TP(R)	2 fl, mar; str	10
Fantasia TP(R)	hn; timp, str	9
The musicians of Bremen TP	Narr; cham; text: from Grimm's fairy tales	22
The silver world SMPC The silver world. Hobby horse. Marche Chinoise. Princess. Tug of war.	fl, ob; str	10.5
Soliloquy CF	fl; str	6
Soliloquy (No. 2) EV(R)	bsn; str	5

	Solo	Duration (min)
SCHULLER, Gunther		
Journey into jazz AMP(R)	Narr, jazz ensemble (2 sax, trp, c-b, dr); fl, ob, cl, bsn, hn, trp, hp, perc, str; text: Nat Hentoff	15
SCHUMAN, William		
Concerto GS	pno; cham	20
SIEGMEISTER, Elie		
Concerto MCA(R)	fl; cham	21
SOWERBY, Leo		
"Classic" concerto HWG(R)	org; str	16
Medieval poem CF	org, solo woman's or boy's voice (vocalise); fl, 2 ob, 3 cl, bsn, 2 hn, trp, timp, perc, str	16
STARER, Robert		
Concerto MCA(R)	vla; str, perc	24
Invocation MIL(R)	trp; str	8
SWIFT, Richard		
Concerto UCP(R)	pno; cham	15
SYDEMAN, William		
Concerto da camera No. III AMP(R)	vln; cham	14
Lament of Elektra ECS	S; cham; text adapted by W. Sydeman from the Greek drama	8
THOMSON, Virgil		
Concerto COL	fl; hp, str, perc	15
The feast of love GS	Bar; cham; text: See "Solo Vocal Music"	12
TOWNSEND, Douglas		
Chamber concerto No. 2, Op. 6 MER(R)	trb or bar; str	10
TRIMBLE, Lester		
Concerto CFP(R)	fl, ob, cl, bsn; str	18
VALENTINE, Robert		
Concerto in D-major CHAP	fl or ob; str, continuo	12
WAGNER, Joseph		
Rhapsody (two themes with variations) B&H	cl; str, pno	9.5
WARD-STEINMAN, David		
Concerto grosso MJQ(R)	a-sax, b-sax, trp, trb; cham	17
WILDER, Alec		
Air for flute BI	fl; str, perc	6
Air for oboe BI	ob; str, perc	6
Concerto AMP	ob; str, perc	24

FULL SYMPHONY ORCHESTRA
for classical orchestra (winds in pairs) or larger

	Duration* (min)		Duration (min)

ADLER, Samuel
Summer stock (overture) 5
(1955) AMP

ANTHEIL, George
Capitol of the world GS(R) 14
The tailor shop. Medita-
tion. Knife dance and
Farruga.
McKonkey's ferry WEIN(R) 7.5
Over the plains WEIN(R) 7.5
Symphony No. 5 ("Joyous") 22
MCA(R)
Symphony No. 6 WEIN(R) 24

ARGENTO, Dominick
Variations for orchestra 28
B&H(R)
Nocturne. Barcarolle.
Burlesca. Serenade.
Toccata. Recitative and
aria with S solo.

BACON, Ernst
From these states (Gathered 15
along unpaved roads) AMP
Laying the rails (a sledge-
hammer song). Source of
the Tennessee. The sunless
pines. The Saluda barn
dance. The cliff dwellers.
Wizard oil. Storm over
Huron. Lullaby to a sick
child. Polly's murder.
Hickory Gap. The timber-
line express.

BARATI, George
The dragon and the phoenix 14
CFP(R)
Polarization CFP(R) 16

BARBER, Samuel
Die Natali, Op. 37 (chorale 16
preludes for Christmas) GS
Essay No. 1, Op. 12 GS 7.5
Essay No. 2, Op. 17 GS(R) 9.5
Intermezzo (from Act IV from 4
Vanessa) GS
Medea's meditation and dance 13
of vengeance, Op. 23A GS(R)

Medea (suite), Op. 23 GS 22
Parados. Choros (Medea &
Jason). The young princess.
Choros. Medea. Kantikos
Agonais. Exodos.
Music for a scene from 8
Shelley, Op. 7 GS(R)
Night flight, Op. 19a (rev. 7.5
version of 2nd mov from
Second Symphony) GS
Overture to School for scandal, 7.5
Op. 5 GS
Souvenirs, Op. 28 (ballet suite) 19
GS(R)
Waltz. Schottische. Pas de
deux. Two-step. Hesitation-
tango. Galop.
Symphony No. 1, Op. 9 GS(R) 18.5

BASSETT, Leslie
Variations for orchestra CFP(R) 22.5

BAZELON, Irwin
Concert overture WEIN(R) 10
Short symphony (testament to 14
a big city) B&H(R)
(See also "Percussion")

BENNETT, Robert Russell
Suite of old American dances 16
CHAP(R)
Serenade. Spiritual.
Celebration.

BERGER, Arthur
Ideas of order CFP(R) 12

BERGSMA, William
Carol on twelfth night GAL(R) 8
Chameleon variations GAL(R) 12
Gold and Señor Commandante 11
(suite for orchestra from
the ballet) GAL
Siesta. Furious dance.
Sinister dance. Tender dance.
Music on a quiet theme B&H(R) 8
Paul Bunyon suite CF 12
Dance of the blue ox. Country
dance. Night.
Serenade, to await the moon 13
GAL(R)

*Approximate

Duration (min)

BERNSTEIN, Leonard
On the waterfront (symphonic   23
  suite) (1955) GS(R)
Overture to Candide GS   4.5
Symphonic dances from West   10
  Side Story GS(R)

BILIK, Jerry H.
American Civil War fantasy   8
  SMPC
  (See also "Band")

BLACKWOOD, Easley
Symphony No. 1 EV(R)   30
Symphony No. 2 GS(R)   24

BRITAIN, Radie
Heroic poem AME(R)   13

BROWN, Earle
Available forms II AMP(R)   10-20
  NOTE: for 98 players re-
  quiring 2 conductors)
  (See also "Piano, Four
  Hands")
Folio and 4 systems AMP(R)   varies
  piano (s) and/or instruments

CACAVAS, John
Overture concertante BI   4
Western scenario CF   8

CADMAN, Charles Wakefield
Dark dancers of the Mardi Gras 10
  (With pno obbligato)EM

CAGE, John
The seasons (ballet in one act) 15
  (1947) CFP(R)

CARPENTER, John Alden
Sea drift (symphonic poem) GS(R) 15

CARTER, Elliott
Holiday overture (1944-61)   10
  AMP(R)
Suite from the ballet Minotaur 25
  AMP(R)
  Overture.
  Scene I: Pasiphae's apart-
    ments in the royal palace
    (Pasiphae; Entrance of the
    bulls; Bull's dance with
    Pasiphae).
  Scene II: Before the labyrinth
    (Ariadne and Theseus; The

Duration (min)

  labyrinth; Theseus' farewell on entering the labyrinth; Theseus fights and
  kills the minotaur; Ariadne
  rewinds her thread; Theseus
  and the Greeks emerge from
  the labyrinth; Theseus and
  the Greeks prepare to leave
  Crete).
Symphony No. 1 AMP(R)   25
Variations (1954-55) AMP(R)   24

CAZDEN, Norman
Six definitions, Op. 25 AMP(R) 8.5
Stony Hollow JS   7
  (See also "Piano, Four Hands")

CHADWICK, George W.
Jubilee and noël (from   14
  Symphonic sketches) GS
Rip Van Winkle (overture) CF   10
Symphonic sketches GS(R)   31
  Jubilee. Noël. Hobgoblin.
  A vagrom ballad.

CHOU, Wen-Chung
All in the spring wind CFP(R)   8
And the fallen petals CFP(R)   10

COKER, Wilson
Lyric statement TP(R)   8

COPLAND, Aaron
Appalachian spring (ballet suite) 23
  (1944) B&H(R)
Billy the kid (ballet suite)   22
  (1938) B&H(R)
  The open prairie. Street in
  a frontier town. Card game
  at night (prairie night). Gun
  battle. Celebration (dance
  after Billy's capture). Billy's
  death. The open prairie again.
Connotations B&H(R)   19
Dance symphony (1925) B&H(R)   17
Danzon Cubano (1942) B&H   6
Down a country lane B&H   3
Fanfare for the common man   2
  (1942) B&H
Inscape B&H(R)   12
John Henry (1940, rev. 1952)   4
  B&H
Letter from home (1944, rev.   7
  1962) B&H
Lincoln portrait (1942) (with 14
  Narr) B&H(R)

	Duration (min)
Music for a great city B&H(R)	24
The skyline. Night thoughts. Subway jam. Toward the bridge.	
Orchestral variations (1957) B&H(R)	14
Our town (suite) B&H(R)	9
An outdoor overture (1938) B&H	9.5
Preamble for a solemn occasion (1949) (Narr--optional. Text based on part of the Preamble to the United Nations Charter) B&H(R)	6
The red pony (1948) (suite) B&H(R)	23
Morning on the ranch. The gift. Dream march and circus music. Walk to the bunkhouse. Grandfather's story. Happy ending.	
Rodeo (dance episodes from ballet) (1942) B&H	18
Buckaroo holiday. Corral nocturne. Saturday night waltz. Hoe-down.	
El salón México (1936) B&H(R)	11.5
Short symphony (Symphony No. 2) (1933) B&H(R) (For cham ver, see "Strings with Voice and/or Winds Percussion")	15
Statements (1934) B&H(R)	18.5
Militant. Cryptic. Dogmatic. Subjective. Jingo. Prophetic.	
Symphonic ode (1929, rev. 1955) B&H(R)	19
Symphony No. 1 (1928) (orch version of Symphony for Organ (1924)) B&H(R)	25
Prelude. Scherzo. Finale.	
Symphony No. 3 (1946) B&H(R)	40
Symphony No. 3 (rev., 1966) B&H(R)	40
Tender land (suite) (1954) B&H(R)	19
Introduction and love music. Party scene. Finale: The promise of living.	
Variations on a Shaker tune B&H	3
Waltz from Billy the kid (1938) B&H(R)	4

COWELL, Henry

Ancient desert drone AMP(R)	5
Hymn and fuguing tune No. 3 AMP	7
Hymn and fuguing tune No. 16 CFP(R)	6

	Duration (min)
Overture SMPC(R)	10
Symphonic set, Op. 17 B&H(R)	12
Symphony No. 4, "Short symphony" AMP(R)	19
Hymn. Ballad. Dance. Fuguing tune.	
Symphony No. 11, "Seven rituals of music" (1953) AMP(R)	22
Symphony No. 12 AMP(R)	15
Symphony No. 13 (Madras) CFP(R)	20
Symphony No. 15 (Thesis) AMP(R)	22
Synchrony CFP(R)	15
Twilight CFP(R)	8

CRESTON, Paul

Corinthians: XIII, Op. 82 MIL(R)	14
Dance overture, Op. 62 SHAW	12
Spanish bolero. English country-dance. French loure. American square-dance.	
Invocation and dance, Op. 58 GS(R)	12
Janus, Op. 77 COL(R)	12
Lydian ode, Op. 67 COL(R)	12
Pre-classic suite, Op. 71 COL(R)	10
Courante. Pavane. Galliard.	
Symphony No. 1, Op. 20 GS(R)	20
Symphony No. 2, Op. 35 GS(R)	24
Introduction and song. Interlude and dance.	
Symphony No. 3, Op. 48 ("3 mysteries") SHAW(R)	27
The Nativity. The Crucifixion. The Resurrection.	
Two choric dances, Op. 17B GS(R) (12 min each)	24
Walt Whitman, Op. 53 COL(R)	12

DAHL, Ingolf

Aria sinfonica AB(R)	17
Quodlibet on American folk tunes CFP(R)	5.5
"The fancy blue devil's break-down, " featuring tunes such as: Boston fancy; Deep blue sea; The devil's dream; Old fiddler's breakdown; California Joe; Old Zip Coon.	
(See also "Piano, Eight Hands")	

	Duration (min)

DAWSON, William
Negro folk symphony SHAW — 20

DELLO JOIO, Norman
Epigraph CF(R) — 7
New York profiles CF(R) — 20
Prelude--"The Cloisters."
Caprice--"The park."
Chorale fantasy--"The tomb."
Festal dance--"Little Italy."
Serenade CF(R) — 16
Three songs of Chopin EBM(R) — 6
The lovers. The ring.
The wish.
The triumph of St. Joan CF(R) — 27
The maid. The warrior.
The saint.
Variations, chaconne, and finale — 21
CF(R)

DIAMOND, David
Music for Romeo and Juliet — 18
B&H(R)
Psalm SMPC — 7
Symphony No. 4 (1945) GS(R) — 16
Symphony No. 6 W-7 — 25
Symphony No. 7 SMPC(R) — 16
Symphony No. 8 SMPC(R) — 28
Timon of Athens (A symphonic — 8.5
portrait after Shakespeare)
MCA(R)
The world of Paul Klee SMPC(R) — 12
The dance of the grieving child.
The black prince. Pastorale.
The twittering machine.

DIEMER, Emma Lou
Symphonie antique MIL — 10

DONATO, Anthony
Two orchestral pieces EV — 14
The plains. Prairie schooner.

DUKELSKY, Vladimir (DUKE, Vernon)
Ode to the milky way COL(R) — 6
Symphony No. 3 in E-major — 25
COL(R)

ELKUS, Albert I.
Impressions from a Greek — 17
tragedy KAL

ELWELL, Herbert
The happy hypocrite (ballet — 15
suite) CF
Introduction and allegro AME(R) — 11.5

	Duration (min)

ENGEL, Lehman
The creation (with Narr) AMP — 30
Jackson (overture) CFP(R) — 12

EPSTEIN, David
Sonority--variations for — 15
orchestra MCA(R)

ERICKSON, Frank
Air for orchestra BI — 4

ETLER, Alvin
Convivialities (1968) AB(R) — 11
Dramatic overture (1956) AMP — 9
Triptych (1961) AMP(R) — 16

FELDMAN, Morton
Intersection CFP(R) (graph) — varies
Marginal intersection CFP(R) — varies
(graph)
...out of "last pieces" — varies
CFP(R) (graph)
Structures CFP(R) — 12

FETLER, Paul
Contrasts AME(R) — 22

FINE, Irving
Diversions MIL — 8
Symphony (1962) MIL(R) — 24

FINNEY, Ross Lee
Hymn, fuguing and holiday — 10
CF(R)
Symphony No. 1 (communiqué — 22
1943) CFP(R)
Introduction. Dramatic
statement. Elegy.
Scherzo. Interlude.
Symphony No. 2 CFP(R) — 21
Symphony No. 3 CFP(R) — 22
Variations CFP(R) — 12

FLANAGAN, William
Concert ode PIC(R) — 10
Divertimento MIL(R) — 15

FLETCHER, Grant
An American overture MIL(R) — 5.5

FOSS, Lukas
Ode (1944, revised 1958) CF — 10

FRACKENPOHL, Arthur
Little suite EV — 4
March. Minuet. Jig.

	Duration (min)
Short overture B&H	3.5
Song for orchestra EV	4
FULEIHAN, Anis	
Accent on percussion SMPC	4
Accent on precision SMPC	4
Mediterranean suite GS	14
Shepherds. Peasants. Priests and priestesses. Musicians. Dancers.	
GEORGE, Earl	
Thanksgiving overture B&H(R)	5
GERSCHEFSKI, Edwin	
Classic symphony, Op. 4 BEL	20
GERSHWIN, George	
An American in Paris W-7	16
Cuban overture W-7	10
GIANNINI, Vittorio	
Divertimento COL(R)	14
Divertimento No. 2 COL(R)	18
Symphony No. 1 (in 1 movement) COL(R)	20
Symphony No. 2 CHAP	22
Symphony No. 4 COL(R)	20
GILLIS, Don	
The January February march B&H	4
Portrait of a frontier town B&H(R)	18
Chamber of Commerce. Where the West begins. Ranch house party. Prairie sunset. Main Street. Saturday night.	
Short overture to an unwritten opera B&H(R)	4
Symphony No. 5 1/2 B&H(R)	13.5
Perpetual motion. Spiritual. Scherzofrenia. Conclusion.	
GIUFFRE, James	
Hex MJQ(R)	4.5
GOLD, Ernest	
Allegorical overture AMP(R)	6
GOLDMAN, Richard Franko	
The Lee rig TP	4
GORDAN, Phillip	
Little Baroque suite CF	8

	Duration (min)
GOTTSCHALK, Louis Moreau	
Andante (from A night in the tropics) EM	6
GOULD, Morton	
American salute (based on "When Johnny comes marching home") MIL	5
American symphonette No. 2 MIL(R)	9
Moderately fast. Pavane. Racy.	
Americana (mood sketches) CF	8
Corn cob (barn dance). Indian nocturne. Hillbilly. Night song.	
Columbia (broadsides for orchestra on Columbian themes) CHAP	13
Hail Columbia. Columbia the gem of the ocean.	
Cowboy rhapsody MIL(R)	12.5
Declaration suite CHAP(R)	20
Liberty bell. Midnight ride. Concord bridge. Summer '76. Celebration.	
Fall River legend (ballet suite) CHAP(R)	24
Prologue. Elegy. Church social. Serenade. Hymnal variations. Cotillion. Epilogue.	
Festive music CHAP	11
Jekyll and Hyde variations CHAP(R)	22
Latin-American symphonette MIL(R)	18
Rhumba. Tango. Guaracha. Conga.	
Spirituals MIL(R)	17.5
Proclamation. Sermon. A little bit of sin. Protest. Jubilee.	
Symphonette No. 2 MIL(R)	9
Venice (audiograph) for double orchestra and two brass choirs (2 trp, 2 trb each) CHAP(R)	26
Vivaldi gallery for divided orchestra and string quartet CHAP(R)	25
GREEN, Ray	
Symphony No. 2 AME(R)	28

	Duration (min)
GRIFFES, Charles T.	
The pleasure dome of Kubla Khan GS(R)	15
The white peacock (from Roman sketches) GS	6
GROFE, Ferde	
Grand Canyon suite ROB	32
Sunrise. The painted desert. On the trail. Sunset. Cloudburst.	
Hudson River suite ROB(R)	26
The river. Hendrik Hudson. Rip van Winkle. Albany night boat. New York.	
Mississippi suite LF	16
Father of the waters. Huckleberry Finn. Old Creole days. Mardi Gras.	
On the trail (from Grand Canyon suite) ROB	7
GRUENBERG, Louis	
The creation, Op. 23 TP	15
GUTCHE, Gene	
Bongo divertimento GAL(R)	5
Genghis Kahn, Op. 37 GAL(R)	8
Note: no strings used other than double basses	
Holofernes overture, Op. 27, No. 1 GAL(R)	9
Raquel, Op. 38 GAL(R)	8
HADLEY, Henry	
Enchanted castle CF	8
Herod overture CF	7.5
HAIEFF, Alexei	
Symphony No. 2 CHAP(R)	21
Symphony No. 3 CHAP(R)	21
HANSON, Howard	
Elegy in memory of Serge Koussevitsky CF(R)	12
For the first time CF(R)	16
Lux aeterna (with vla obbligato) (from Symphony No. 4) CF	15
Merry Mount (suite) W-7	16
Symphony No. 1, "The Nordic" (1923), Op. 21 CF	28
Symphony No. 2, "The Romantic" (1930), Op. 30 CF	25
Symphony No. 3 (1937) CF	35
Symphony No. 4, "The Requiem" (1943), Op. 34 CF	22

	Duration (min)
Kyrie. Requiescat. Dies irae. Lux aeterna.	
Symphony No. 5, "Sinfonia Sacra" (1955) CF	13
HARRIS, Roy	
Elegy AMP	6
Horn of plenty AMP(R)	10
Kentucky spring CF(R)	10
Melody CF	10
Ode to consonance AMP	10
Ode to friendship MIL	5
Radio piece CF	8
Symphony No. 3 (in one mov) GS(R)	18
Symphony No. 7 AMP(R)	19
Symphony No. 9 AMP(R)	22
"When Johnny comes marching home" (overture)GS(R)	8
HARRISON, Lou	
Simfony in free style CFP(R)	5
HEIDEN, Bernhard	
Euphorion AMP(R)	12
HELM, Everett	
Cambridge suite CFP(R)	16
Three Gospel hymns AMP(R)	15
HERDER, Ronald	
Movements for orchestra AMP(R)	11.5
HERRMANN, Bernard	
For the fallen (a berceuse) BB(R)	7.5
HILL, Edward Burlingham	
Lilacs B&H(R)	19
HOVHANESS, Alan	
Circe (Symphony No. 18), Op. 204a CFP(R)	15
(See also "Small or Chamber Orchestra")	
Concerto No. 1, Op. 88, "Arevakal" AMP(R)	15
Allegretto. Canzona. Estampie. Allegro vivace. Hymn. Ballata.	
Concerto No. 7, Op. 116 AMP(R)	20
Concerto No. 8, Op. 117 CFP(R)	20

Duration
(min)

Duration
(min)

Floating world (ballad for   12
orchestra), Op. 209 CFP(R)
Fra Angelico CFP(R)   16.5
Macedonian mountain dance   3
CFP(R)
Meditation on Orpheus, Op.   13
155 CFP(R)
Monadnock, Fantasy, Op. 2   5
CFP(R)
Mountain of prophecy AMP(R)   10
Mysterious mountain AMP(R)   17
Prelude and quadruple fugue   7
AMP
Symphony No. 1, Op. 17,   21
"Exile" CFP(R)
Symphony No. 3, Op. 148   22
CFP(R)
Symphony No. 5, Op. 170   10
CFP(R)
Symphony No. 11, Op. 186   27
CFP(R)
Symphony No. 13, Op. 190   18
CFP(R)
Symphony No. 15, Op. 199   20
("Silver pilgrimage") CFP(R)
Mt. Ravana. Marava
princess. River of medita-
tion. Heroic gates of peace.
Symphony No. 19 (Vishnu)   30
CFP(R)
Variations and fugue, Op. 18   13
CFP(R)
Vision from high rock, Op.   11
123 CFP(R)

HOWE, Mary
Rock GAL(R)   11
Stars and sand GAL(R)   6

HUGGLER, John
Elegy, Op. 2 CFP(R)   6

INGALLS, Albert M.
Song of peace NAK   4.5

IVES, Charles
Robert Browning overture PIC(R) 24
Symphony No. 2 PIC(R)   35
Symphony No. 4 AMP(R)   26
NOTE: a large work for a
greatly expanded orchestra
Three places in New England   25
MER(R)
The St. Gaudens in Boston
Common. Putman's camp
in Redding, Connecticut.

From the Housatonic at
Stockbridge.
Variations on "America"   8
(orchestrated by William
Schuman from Ives' orig-
inal work for organ) TP

JACOBI, Frederick
Music hall (an overture) MCA(R) 6

JOHNSON, Hunter
Suite from Letter to the   23
World (1950) GAL(R)
(a synthesis of dance, music
and poetry, describing the
legend of Emily Dickinson.
Originally written for and
performed by Martha
Graham in 1940)
I. Because I see New
Englandly: Introduction;
Life is a spell; I open
every door.
II. Ancestress: I'm sorry for
the dead today; It's coming,
the postponeless creature;
Looking at death is dying;
Gay, ghastly holiday.
III. The little tippler: In the
name of the bee, and of
the butterfly, and of the
breeze, amen; Saints with
vanished slate and pencil
solve our April day; Party
scene: Let us play yester-
day.
IV. Leaf at love turned back:
There came a day at sum-
mer's full; I thought that
such were for the saints;
Soul, wilt thou toss again?
V. Coda: This is my letter
to the world.
NOTE: In addition to the
above, 3 shorter suites
may be drawn from the
complete suite, as follows:
Short suite No. 1 (from   11
Letter to the World) GAL(R)
I. Because I see New
Englandly.
II. Ancestress.
Short suite No. 2 (from   14
Letter to the World) GAL(R)
I. Ancestress.
II. The little tippler.

Duration (min)

	Duration (min)
Short suite No. 3 (from Letter to the World) GAL(R)	12
I. The little tippler.	
II. Leaf at love turned back.	
III. Coda: This is my letter to the world.	
The little tippler (three dances from Letter to the World) GAL(R)	6
JOHNSTON, Jack	
Bunker Hill fantasy EV	4.5
JONES, Charles	
Little symphony for the New Year TP(R)	4
KAY, Hersey	
Cakewalk (ballet suite after Gottschalk) B&H(R)	23.5
Grand walkaround. Three variations. Freebee. Magic act.	
Western symphony B&H(R)	25
KAY, Ulysses	
Fantasy variations MCA(R)	15
"Markings" (symphonic essay-- a tribute to Dag Hammarskjold) MCA(R)	18
Of new horizons (overture) CFP(R)	8
Serenade AMP(R)	18
Suite AMP(R)	18
Fanfare. Three-four.	
Scherzo. Olden tune.	
Finale.	
Umbrian scene MCA(R)	15
KELLEY, Robert	
Symphony No. 2 GAL	28
Intense and energetic (seed-time); Calm (summer); Festive (harvest); Dirge (winter).	
KENNEDY, John Brodbin	
Symphonic fantasy B&H(R)	14
KERR, Harrison	
Symphony No. 1 B&H(R)	16
KIRCHNER, Leon	
Sinfonia in two parts MER(R)	19

	Duration (min)
KIRK, Theron	
Intrada CF(R)	4.5
KOHN, Karl	
Interludes CF(R)	12
KORN, Peter Jona	
In medias res B&H(R)	3.5
KOUTZEN, Boris	
Valley Forge AME(R)	12
KUBIK, Gail	
Bachata (Cuban dance) SMPC(R)	5
A mirror for the sky (overture) COL(R)	8
Senario for orchestra COL(R)	25
Symphony in E-flat major SMPC(R)	38
Symphony No. 2 in F-major COL(R)	35
Symphony No. 3 COL(R)	22
Thunderbolt overture CHAP	7
KUPFERMAN, Meyer	
Devil dance WEIN	8
KURKA, Robert	
Serenade WEIN(R)	21
LA MONTAINE, John	
Birds of paradise CF(R)	6
Canons for orchestra PJS(R)	10
Canticle for orchestra PJS(R)	6
Jubilant overture PJS(R)	6
Overture: "From sea to shining sea" PJS(R)	8
LAYTON, Billy Jim	
Divertimento, Op. 6 GS(R)	6
LAZAROF, Henri	
Structures sonores AMP(R)	28.5
Introduction. Polyphonie I. Etude I. Polyphonie II. Etude II. Polyphonie III.	
LEE, Dai-Keong	
Introduction and allegro MCA	7.5
LEES, Benjamin	
Concerto for orchestra B&H(R)	22
Divertimento burlesca B&H(R)	22
Profiles WEIN(R)	7
Prologue, capriccio and epilogue B&H(R)	11

	Duration (min)		Duration (min)
Symphony No. 2 B&H(R)	20	MAYER, William	
		Overture for an American	10
LEVY, Marvin David		B&H	
Kyros (dance poem) B&H	20		
		McBRIDE, Robert	
LEWIS, John		Mexican rhapsody CF	8
Original sin (a ballet) MJQ(R)	24	Pumpkin eater's little fugue	4
		AMP	
LICHTER, Charles			
Vermont summer GAL	9	McDONALD, Harl	
		The legend of the Arkansas	6
LOEFFLER, Charles Martin		traveler EV(R)	
A Pagan poem, Op. 14 GS(R)	22	Three poems EV(R)	12
LO PRESTI, Ronald		McKAY, George F.	
The masks CF(R)	5	Sinfonia No. 1 (A short	7
		symphony) W-7	
LUENING, Otto		Prelude. Dance. Finale.	
Prelude to a hymn tune by	5	Symphonette in D-major	11
William Billings CFP(R)		GAL(R)	
Two symphonic interludes	8.5	Symphonie miniature S-B	10
CFP(R)		March to tomorrow. A	
		prairie poem. Rondino	
MacDOWELL, Edward		on a jovial theme.	
Suite No. 1, Op. 42 KAL	32		
In a haunted forest. Summer		McKAY, Neil	
idyll. In October. The		Symphony No. 1 KAL	22
shepherdess' song. Forest			
spirits.		McPHEE, Colin	
Suite No. 2, Op. 48, "Indian"	30	Symphony No. 3 CFP(R)	20
AMP			
Legend. Love song. In		MECHEM, Kirke	
war time. Dirge. Village		Symphony No. 1 ECS(R)	18
festival.		Symphony No. 2, Op. 29	18
		ECS(R)	
MAGANINI, Quinto			
Americanese EM	11	MENNIN, Peter	
Old Connecticut tune.		Canto CF(R)	8
A village festival. A chant		Concertato, "Moby Dick"	10
for Washington's funeral.		CF(R)	
		Folk overture HAR	8
MARTINO, Donald		Symphony No. 3 HAR	20
Contemplations ECS(R)	10	Symphony No. 5 CF(R)	21
		Symphony No. 6 CF(R)	25
MARTIRANO, Salvatore		Symphony No. 7 CF(R)	25
Contrasto AMP	9		
		MIDDLETON, Jean B.	
MASON, Daniel Gregory		Symphony in C-major (1942;	16
Chanticleer (festival overture),	8	revised 1962) B&H(R)	
Op. 27 AME(R)			
A Lincoln symphony AME(R)	34	MITCHELL, Lyndol	
The candidate from Spring-		"Shivaree" from Kentucky	4
field. "Massa Linkum."		Mountain Portraits CF(R)	
Old Abe's yarns. 1865.			

Duration (min)

MOORE, Douglas
Down East suite CF(R)   10
(See also "Violin")
In memoriam EV   7
Pageant of P.T. Barnum   14
(suite) CF
Boyhood at Bethel. Joice
Heth. General and Mrs.
Tom Thumb. Jenny Lind.
Circus parade.
Symphony No. 2 in A-major   22
GS(R)

MORAN, Robert
Interiors CFP (graph)   9-10
(See also "Small or Chamber
Orchestra" and "Percussion")

MORRIS, Harold
Prospice symphony EM   33

MUCZYNSKI, Robert
Dovetail overture GS   4.5

NELSON, Ron
Jubilee B&H   7
Sarabande (for Katharine in   6
April) B&H
Savannah River holiday CF(R)   9

OVERTON, Hall
Sonorities for orchestra MJQ(R)   7
Symphony No. 2 CFP(R)   14

PERLE, George
Three movements for orchestra   16
TP(R)
Prelude. Contrasts. Ostinato.

PERSICHETTI, Vincent
Dance overture EV   8
Serenade No. 5 EV(R)   11
Prelude. Poem. Interlude.
Capriccio. Dialogue. Burla.
Symphony No. 4, Op. 51 EV   24

PHILLIPS, Burrill
McGuffey's readers (suite with   16.5
Narr) CF(R)
The one horse shay. John
Alden and Priscilla. The
midnight ride of Paul Revere.

PINKHAM, Daniel
Catacoustical measures CFP(R)   4.5

Duration (min)

Signs of the Zodiac CFP(R)   21
Sp (opt) text: from
"Symnetrics" by David
McCord
Aries: Ram; Taurus: Bull;
Gemini: Twins; Cancer:
Crab; Leo: Lion; Virgo:
Virgin; Libra: Balance;
Scorpio: Scorpion; Sagit-
tarius: Archer; Capricornus:
Goat; Aquarius: Water bearer;
Pisces: Fishes.
Symphony No. 1 CFP(R)   16
Symphony No. 2 CFP(R)   16

PISTON, Walter
Concerto for orchestra (1933)   14
AMP(R)
Lincoln Center festival over-   12
ture AMP(R)
Pine tree fantasy AMP(R)   10
Prelude and fugue AMP(R)   13
Second suite for orchestra   24
AMP(R)
Prelude. Sarabande. Inter-
mezzo. Passacaglia and fugue.
Serenata (1956) AMP(R)   15
Suite for orchestra AMP(R)   15
Suite from the ballet, The   17
incredible flutist AMP(R)
Introduction. Dance of the
vendors. Entrance of the
customers. Tango of the
merchant's daughters.
Entry of the circus. Circus
march. Solo of the flutist.
Minuet. Spanish waltz.
Eight o'clock. Siciliano.
Polka finale.
Symphony No. 1 GS(R)   27
Symphony No. 2 AMP(R)   26
Symphony No. 3 B&H(R)   30
Symphony No. 4 (1950) AMP(R)   23
Symphony No. 5 (1954) AMP(R)   22
Symphony No. 6 (1955) AMP(R)   25
Symphony No. 7 (1960) AMP(R)   19
Symphony No. 8 AMP(R)   20
Three New England sketches   17
(1959) AMP(R)
Seaside. Summer evening.
Mountains.
Toccata B&H(R)   9
Variations on a theme by   11
E.B. Hill (1936) AMP

Duration
(min)

PORTER, Quincy
Symphony No. 2 CFP(R)   25

POWELL, John
Natchez on the hill (three   4
    Virginian country dances)
    GS(R)

POWELL, Mel
Stanzas GS(R)   7

PREVIN, André
Overture to a comedy MCA(R)   9

READ, Gardner
First overture HE(R)   8
Night flight, Op. 44 CFP(R)   7

REYNOLDS, Roger
Graffiti CFP(R)   9

RIEGGER, Wallingford
The cry, Op. 22 PIC(R)   6
Dance rhythms, Op. 58 AMP   8
Evocation, Op. 17a PIC(R)   4
Music for orchestra, Op. 50   7
    AMP
New dance, Op. 18b AMP(R)   5
    (See also "Band")
Suite for younger orchestra,   7
    Op. 56 AMP
Symphony No. 3, Op. 42   23
    (rev. version) AMP(R)
Symphony No. 4, Op. 63 AMP(R) 24

ROBERTSON, Leroy
Passacaglia GAL(R)   12
Punch and Judy overture GAL   11

ROCHBERG, George
Night music TP(R)   12
Serenata d'estate MCA(R)   5
Symphony No. 1 TP(R)   25
Symphony No. 2 TP(R)   26
Time-span (II) MCA(R)   10
Zodiac TP(R)   14
    (orchestral version of "12
    bagatelles for piano")

ROGERS, Bernard
Apparitions (scenes from The   15
    Temptation of St. Anthony)
    MCA(R)
    (See also "Band")
Characters from Hans Christian 11
    Anderson EV(R)

Duration
(min)

The shirt collar. The rose
tree. The snow queen.
The emperor's new clothes.
Five fairy tales KAL   12
Tinder-box soldier. Song
of Rapunzel. Story of a
darning needle. Dance of
the twelve princesses.
Ride of Koschei, the
Deathless.
Three Japanese dances TP(R)   12
Dance with pennons.
Mourning dance (with m-S
solo; text: John Masefield).
Dance with swords.

ROREM, Ned
Design B&H(R)   17.5
Eagles B&H(R)   8.5
Ideas for easy orchestra B&H   11
Lions (a dream (1963) B&H(R)   13.5
    (See also "Percussion")
Symphony No. 3 B&H(R)   23.5

ROYCE, Edward
Far ocean (symphonic poem) CF   7

RUGGLES, Carl
Organum AME(R)   8

SANDERS, Robert
Little symphony No. 2 COL(R)   15
Little symphony No. 3 GAL(R)   14
Saturday night CF   9

SCHICKELE, Peter
Celebration with bells EV   4
The civilian barber (overture)   6
    EV

SCHULLER, Gunther
American triptych AMP(R)   14
Composition in three parts   15
    AMP(R)
Spectra AMP   23

SCHUMAN, William
American festival overture   9
    GS(R)
Circus overture (sideshow)   7
    GS(R)
Credendum TP(R)   18
    Declaration. Chorale. Finale.
Judith (choreographic poem)   24
    GS(R)

Duration (min)

New England triptych (3 pieces   13
  after William Billings) TP(R)
  Be glad then, America.
  When Jesus wept. Chester.
  Newsreel, in five shots GS(R)   8
  Horse race. Fashion show.
  Tribal dance. Monkeys at
  the zoo. Parade.
The orchestra song TP(R)   3.5
Prayer in time of war GS(R)   15
Symphony No. 3 GS(R)   29
  Passacaglia and fugue.
  Chorale and toccata.
Symphony No. 4 GS(R)   25
Symphony No. 6 GS(R)   27
Symphony No. 7 TP(R)   26
Symphony No. 8 TP(R)   27
Undertow (choreographic epi-   25
  sodes) GS(R)
Variations on "America" (1963)   8
  (based on a piece for organ
  by Charles Ives) TP

SESSIONS, Roger
The black maskers (suite)   23
  (1928) EBM(R)
  Dance. Scene.
  Dirge. Finale.
Divertimento (1959) EBM(R)   20
Symphony No. 1 EBM(R)   22
Symphony No. 2 GS(R)   30
Symphony No. 3 EBM(R)   32
Symphony No. 4 EBM(R)   24

SHAPERO, Harold
Symphony for classical orches-   40
  tra SMPC(R)

SHEPHERD, Arthur
Horizons (4 Western pieces)   30
  AME(R)
  Westward. The lone prairie.
  The old Chisholm Trail.
  Canyons.
Overture to a drama AME(R)   12

SHIFRIN, Seymour
Three pieces for orchestra   17
  CFP(R)

SHULMAN, Alan
A Laurentian overture CHAP(R)   9
Waltzes for orchestra CHAP(R)   8.5

SIEGMEISTER, Elie
Divertimento SHAW(R)   16

Duration (min)

From my window CHAP(R)   9
  Housewives' chatter. Moon
  on the pavement. Kids
  playing tag. Sunday after-
  noon. Distant parade.
  Jitterbug.
Sunday in Brooklyn EBM(R)   15
  Prospect Park. Sunday
  driver. Family at home.
  Children's story. Coney
  Island.
Symphony No. 2 MCA(R)   27
Symphony No. 3 MCA(R)   18
Wilderness road MCA(R)   6

SMITH, Hale
Contours for orchestra CFP(R)   9

SMITH, Russell
Can-can and waltz CFP(R)   8
Tetrameron CFP(R)   12

SOWERBY, Leo
Concert overture MER   9
Medieval poem CF   16
Prairie (a symphonic poem)CF   17
Set of four ironics CF(R)   18

STARER, Robert
Dalton set (suite) MCA   10
  Prelude. Serenade.
  Waltz. March.
Mutabili MCA(R)   11
Prelude and rondo giocoso   10
  MCA(R)
Samson Agonistes MCA(R)   13
Symphony No. 2 in one move-   12
  ment MCA(R)

STEVENS, Halsey
Symphonic dances CFP(R)   15

STILL, William Grant
Afro-American symphony JF(R)   28
  Longing. Sorrow.
  Humor. Aspiration.
Bells MCA(R)   7
  Phantom chapel.
  Fairy knoll.
Darker America CF   9
From the Black Belt CF   8
In memoriam MCA(R)   6
Orchestral suite from "Sahdji" 20.5
  CF(R)
Poem MCA(R)   15
Wood notes SMPC(R)   27

Duration
(min)

Singing river. Autumn night.
Moon dusk. Whippoor will's
shoes.

STILLMAN-KELLEY, Edgar
Alladin suite AME(R)   28
Symphony in B-flat major, "New   40
England" EM(R)
Symphony in four movements,   30
"Gulliver--his voyage to
Lilliput" EM(R)

SWANSON, Howard
Short symphony WEIN(R)   12

SYDEMAN, William
Orchestral abstractions CFP(R)   15
Study for orchestra No. III   15
AMP(R)

TALMA, Louise
Toccata CF(R)   12

TAYLOR, Deems
Through the looking glass (5   28
pictures from Lewis Carroll)
JF
Dedication. The garden of
live flowers. Jabberwocky.
Looking glass insects. The
white knight.

THOMPSON, Randall
Symphony No. 1 ECS   24
Symphony No. 2 ECS(R)   28

THOMSON, Virgil
Acadian songs and dances   15
(from The Louisiana story)GS
Sadness. Papa's tune. A
narrative. The alligator and
the 'coon. Super-sadness.
Walking song. The squeeze
box.
Eleven chorale preludes B&H(R) 18
Fugue and chorale on Yankee   4
Doodle (from the film: "Tues-
day in November") GS
Fugues and cantilenas B&H(R)   18
Louisiana story (suite) GS(R)   17
Pastorale. Chorale.
Passacaglia. Fugue.
The plow that broke the plains   15
(suite) MER
Prelude. Pastorale. Cattle.
Blues Drought. Devastation.

Duration
(min)

Sea piece with birds GS(R)   5
A solemn music and a joyful   12
fugue GS(R)
The Seine at night GS(R)   8
Symphony on a hymn tune   21
SMPC(R)
Symphony No. 2 MCA   15
Wheatfield at noon GS(R)   6

TRIMBLE, Lester
Five episodes MCA   11
Second symphony MCA(R)   27
Sonic landscape MCA(R)   10
Symphony in 2 movements   15
CFP(R)

TURNER, Charles
Encounter GS(R)   8

VAN VACTOR, David
Overture to a comedy, No. 2   16
AME(R)

VINCENT, John
Rondo rhapsody MIL(R)   8
Suite from ballet Three Jacks   15
MIL(R)
Fanfare and Jack-be-Nimble.
Jack Spratt. The house that
Jack built.
Symphonic poem after Des-   18.5
cartes MIL(R)
Introduction. Cogito, ergo
sum. Intuitions. Vortex.
Meditations. Folium (passa-
caglia). Exaltation. Con-
templation. Finale.
Symphony in D-major MIL(R)   18

WAGENAAR, Bernard
Divertimento CF   12
Cortège. Paspy.
Pastorale. Rondo.

WAGNER, Joseph
Northland evocation SMPC(R)   13

WARD, Robert
Adagio and allegro PIC(R)   12
Concert music GAL(R)   8
Divertimento for orchestra   14
GAL(R)
Fanfare. Intermezzo. Finale.
Euphony GAL(R)   10
Jubilation (overture) GAL(R)   8
Prairie overture GAL   7

	Duration (min)
Symphony No. 1 GAL(R)	15
Symphony No. 2 GAL(R)	24
Symphony No. 4 GAL(R)	26

WASHBURN, Robert
St. Lawrence overture B&H(R)   6
Three pieces for orchestra OX(R) 5

WATSON, Walter
A folk fantasia SHAW   5

WEBER, Ben
Prelude and passacaglia AMP(R) 11

WEISGALL, Hugo
Overture in F TP(R)   9.5

WHEAR, Paul
Catskill legend EV   6

WHITE, Paul
Five miniatures EV   15
1. By the lake. 2. Caravan
song. 3. Waltz for Teenie's

	Duration (min)
doll. 4. Hippo dance.	
5. Mosquito dance.	

WILDER, Alec
Carl Sandburg suite (based on   16
tunes from The American
songbag) AMP
Hey, Betty Martin. Lo que
digo. Way up on Clinch
Mountain

WILLIAMS, John T.
Symphony No. 1 MCA(R)   24

YARDUMIAN, Richard
Armenian suite EV(R)   17
Introduction. Song. Lullaby.
Dance No. 1. Interlude.
Dance No. 2. Interlude.
Cantus animae et cordis EV(R)   15
Chorale prelude (on plainsong: 9
"Veni, sancte spiritus") EV(R)
Symphony No. 1 EV(R)   23

FULL SYMPHONY ORCHESTRA WITH SOLO INSTRUMENT OR VOICE

	Solo	Duration* (min)
AUSTIN, Larry		
Improvisations for orchestra and jazz soloists MJQ(R)	trp, a-sax, cl, t-sax, b-sax, c-b, dr	15
BARATI, George		
Concerto CFP(R)	vlc	27
BARBER, Samuel		
Andromache's farewell, Op. 39 GS(R)	S voice; text: from The Trojan Women by Euripides; trans: John Patrick Creagh	12
Concerto, Op. 14 GS(R)	vln	22
Concerto, Op. 22 GS(R)	vlc	26
Concerto, Op. 38 GS(R)	pno	26
Toccata festiva, Op. 36 GS(R)	org	14
Two scenes from Antony and Cleopatra GS(R)	S voice; Shakespeare; adapted by Franco Zeffirelli	15.5
1. Give me some music.		
2. Death of Cleopatra.		
BECKER, J. J.		
Concerto TP(R)	hn	15

*Approximate

	Solo	Duration (min)
BEREZOWSKY, Nicolai		
Concerto EV(R)	hp	14
Concerto B&H(R)	vln	20
BERNSTEIN, Leonard		
Symphony No. 2: Age of anxiety GS(R)	pno	30
Part 1: Prologue. The seven ages.		
The seven stages.		
Part 2: The dirge. The masque.		
The epilogue.		
Jeremiah symphony W-7	m-S; text: Biblical	23
Prophecy. Profanation.		
Lamentation.		
BINGHAM, Seth		
Concerto in G-minor HWG(R)	org	19
BUCCI, Marc		
Concerto FM(R)	fl	15
BURLEIGH, Cecil		
Concerto No. 2 CF(R)	vln	25
Concerto No. 3 CF(R)	vln	25
CACAVAS, John		
The day the orchestra played B&H	Narr; text: Charles O. Wood	18
CAGE, John		
Concert (1957-58) CFP	pno	19.5
CARPENTER, John Alden		
Concertino GS	pno	26
Concerto GS(R)	vln	23
CARTER, Elliott		
Concerto AMP(R)	pno	26
COOLEY, Carlton		
Concertino HE	vla	20
Introduction. Aria. Finale.		
COPLAND, Aaron		
"Jazz" concerto (1926) B&H(R)	pno	16
Lincoln portrait B&H(R)	Narr; text: from Lincoln's	14
(See also "Band")	writings	
Symphony B&H(R)	org	25
CORIGLIANO, John		
The Cloisters GS(R)	med voice;	7.5
(For contents, see "Solo Vocal Music")	text: William Hoffman	
COWELL, Henry		
Concerto CFP(R)	perc	19
(See also "Percussion")		
Toccanta B&H(R)	S; vocalise	9
(See also "Solo Vocal Music" and		

	Solo	Duration (min)
"Strings with Voice and/or Winds, Percussion")		
CRESTON, Paul		
Concerto, Op. 21 GS(R)	mar	15
Concerto GS(R)	sax	16
Concerto, Op. 65 COL(R)	vln	20
Concerto, Op. 75 COL(R)	acdn	20
Concerto, Op. 78 COL(R)	vln	20
Dance variations, Op. 30 GS(R)	Col	6
Fantasy, Op. 42 GS(R)	trb	10
DELLO JOIO, Norman		
Antiphonal fantasy EBM(R)	org	15
Concertante CF(R)	cl	17
Fantasy and variations CF(R)	pno	22
Lamentation of Saul CF(R)	Bar; text: adapted from the play, "David," by D.H. Lawrence	5
Ricercari CF(R)	pno	20
DIAMOND, David		
Concerto SMPC(R)	pno	21
Concerto SMPC(R)	vlc	20
DUKELSKY, Vladimir (DUKE, Vernon)		
Concerto CF(R)	vlc	28
Concerto CF(R)	vln	26
EATON, John		
Holy sonnets of John Donne SHAW (For contents, see "Solo Vocal Music")	S	7
ELLSTEIN, Abraham		
"Negev" concerto MIL(R)	pno	18
ELMORE, Robert		
Concerto GAL(R)	org	27
EVETT, Robert		
Concerto CFP(R)	hpcd	20
FARBERMAN, Harold		
Concerto COL(R) (See also "Percussion")	timp	14
FINNEY, Ross Lee		
Concerto CFP(R)	vln	35
Concerto CFP(R) (See also "Percussion")	perc	15
FLAGELLO, Nicolas		
Capriccio GEN(R)	vlc	16
Concerto Antoniano GEN(R)	fl	26
Contemplatzioni di Michelangelo GEN(R) (For contents, see "Solo Vocal Music")	high voice; text: Michelangelo	20.5

	Solo	Duration (min)
An island in the moon GEN(R) (For contents, see "Solo Vocal Music")	high voice; text: William Blake	16
FLOYD, Carlisle		
The mystery (5 songs of motherhood) B&H (For contents, see "Solo Vocal Music")	S; text: Gabriela Mistral; trans: Anita K. Fleet	15
Pilgrimage B&H(R) (For contents, see "Solo Vocal Music")	Bar; text: Biblical	20
FOSS, Lukas		
Concerto SMPC(R)	ob	14.5
Concerto No. 2 (1949) CF(R)	pno	34
Song of anguish CF(R)	Bar; text: Biblical	20
Song of songs GS (For contents, see "Solo Vocal Music")	high voice; text: Biblical	27
Time cycle CF(R) (For contents, see "Solo Vocal Music")	S	22
FREED, Isadore		
Rhapsody CF(R)	vla	9
GABURO, Kenneth		
Ideas and transformation No. 1 TP(R)	vln	9
GERSHWIN, George		
Concerto in F-major W-7	pno	30
Rhapsody in blue W-7	pno	16
Second rhapsody W-7	pno	12.5
GIANNINI, Vittorio		
Concerto W-7	trp	16
Psalm 130 COL(R)	c-b or vlc	12
GILLIS, Don		
Three short pieces MIL(R)	fl	7
GIUFFRE, James		
Concerto COL(R)	vla	16
GOTTSCHALK, Louis Moreau		
Grand tarantelle, Op. 67 B&H	pno	7
GOULD, Morton		
Dance variations CHAP(R) Chaconne. Arabesques. Pas de deux ("Tango"). Tarantella.	2 pno	22
Interplay MIL(R) With vigor and drive. Gavotte. Blues. Very fast.	pno	14.5
GRIFFES, Charles		
Five poems from the ancient Far East GS(R) (For contents, see "Solo Vocal Music")	med voice	13

	Solo	Duration (min)
Lament of Ian the Proud GS(R)	med or high voice; text: Fiona MacLeod	4
Rose of the night GS(R)	high voice; text: Fiona MacLeod	4
Thy dark eyes to mine GS(R)	high voice; text: Fiona MacLeod	4
HAIEFF, Alexei		
Concerto B&H(R)	pno	24.5
HANSON, Howard		
Concerto, Op. 36 (1948) CF(R)	pno	20.5
Four Psalms CF(R)	T; text: Biblical	17.5
1. God is our refuge and strength (Psalm 46)		
2. O Lord, rebuke me Thine anger (Psalm 6)		
3. O clap your hands (Psalm 47)		
4. O Lord, our God, how excellent Thy name (Psalm 8)		
HARRIS, Roy		
Give me the splendid silent sun AMP	Bar; text: Walt Whitman	15
HOIBY, Lee		
Pastoral dances GS(R)	fl	7
The tides of sleep B&H(R)	low voice; text: Thomas Wolfe	17
HOVHANESS, Alan		
Concerto, Op. 174 CFP(R)	acdn	11
Fantasy on Japanese wood prints, Op. 211 CFP(R) (See also "Percussion")	xy	12
HUGGLER, John		
Divertimento CFP(R)	vla	11
Sculptures CFP(R)	S; text: Robinson Jeffers	14
JACOBI, Frederick		
Concerto TP(R)	vlc	20
Concerto MCA(R)	vln	24
Night piece and dance B&H(R)	fl	8
JOHNSON, J. J.		
Senario MJQ(R)	trb	13
KANITZ, Ernest		
Concerto TP(R)	bsn	14
KIRCHNER, Leon		
Concerto No. 2 AMP(R)	pno	30
KOHN, Karl		
Episodes CF(R)	pno	12
KUBIK, Gail		
Concerto in D CHAP(R)	vln	23

	Solo	Duration (min)
Symphony concertante COL(R)	trp, vla, pno	24
KURKA, Robert		
Concerto WEIN(R)	mar	20
LA MONTAINE, John		
Birds of paradise, Op. 34 CF(R)	pno	13
Concerto, Op. 9 GAL(R)	pno	25
Fragments from "The Song of Songs" PJS(R)	S; text: Biblical	30
(For contents, see "Solo Vocal Music")		
Songs of the rose of Sharon BB(R)	S; text: Biblical	15
(For contents, see "Solo Vocal Music")		
LANE, Richard		
Four songs CF(R)	m-S	16
(For contents, see "Solo Vocal Music")		
LEES, Benjamin		
Concerto No. 1 B&H(R)	pno	24
Concerto No. 2 B&H(R)	pno	24
Concerto B&H(R)	vln	21
Songs of the night B&H(R)	S	10
(For contents, see "Solo Vocal Music")		
LEVY, Marvin David		
One person B&H(R)	A; text: Elinor Wylie	19
LEWIS, John		
Jazz ostinato MJQ(R)	vib, pno, c-b, dr	6
The spiritual MJQ(R)	vib, pno, c-b	6
LOEFFLER, Charles Martin		
Five Irish fantasies GS(R)	high voice;	15
The hosting of sidhe. The host of	text: William Butler Yeats	
the air. The fiddler of Dooney.		
Ballad for the fox hunt. Caitilin		
ni Vallachain.		
LUENING, Otto		
Fantasia CFP(R)	str qrt	12
MACDOWELL, Edward		
Concerto No. 1 in A-minor, Op. 15 GS	pno	26
Concerto No. 2 in D-minor, Op. 23 GS	pno	26
MAGANINI, Quinto		
Tualumne (a Californian rhapsody) EM	trp obb	14
MARTINO, Donald		
Concerto ECS(R)	pno	18
MAYER, William		
Octagon MCA(R)	pno	26

	Solo	Duration (min)
McDONALD, Harl		
Suite "from childhood" EV(R)	hp	24
McPHEE, Colin		
Tabuh-Tabuhan AMP(R)	2 pno	17
Ostinatos. Nocturne. Finale.		
(See also "Percussion")		
MOORE, Douglas		
Down East suite CF(R)	vln	15
NORTH, Alex		
Revue MIL(R)	cl	15.5
PANETTI, Joan		
Concerto AB(R)	pno	15
PARRIS, Robert		
Concerto CFP(R)	timp: 5 kettledrums	15
PERSICHETTI, Vincent		
Concertino EV(R)	pno	9
Concerto, Op. 90 EV(R)	pno	27
PHILLIPS, Donald		
Concerto in jazz MIL(R)	pno	8.5
PILHOFER, Phil		
Three pieces for jazz quartet and	gtr, pno, c-b, dr	14
orchestra MJQ(R)		
PINKHAM, Daniel		
Now the trumpet summons us again	S; text: from the Inaugural	4
CFP(R)	Address by John F. Kennedy	
PISTON, Walter		
Concerto (1957) AMP(R)	vla	19
Concerto B&H(R)	vln	23
Variations AMP(R)	vlc	16
PORTER, Quincy		
Three Elizabethan songs YUP(R)	med voice;	7
(For contents, see "Solo Vocal Music")	text: anon and Shakespeare	
POWELL, John		
Rhapsodie négre GS	pno	14
RAMSIER, Paul		
Divertimento concertante on a theme	c-b or vlc	9.5
of Couperin GS(R)		
(For contents, see "Cello" or		
"Double Bass")		
RAPHLING, Sam		
Concerto No. 1 MIL(R)	pno	10
Concerto No. 3 MER(R)	pno	21

	Solo	Duration (min)
Minstrel rhapsody MIL(R)	pno	4.5
REED, Alfred		
Rhapsody B&H(R)	vla	12
REIF, Paul		
Birches B&H(R)	S or T; text: Robert Frost	12.5
RIEGGER, Wallingford		
The dying of the light, Op. 59 AMP	med-high voice; text: Dylan Thomas	4
ROBERTSON, Leroy		
Concerto GAL(R)	vln	27
ROGERS, Bernard		
Portrait TP(R)	vln	24
ROREM, Ned		
Six songs CFP(R) (For contents, see "Solo Vocal Music")	high voice	7
SCHULLER, Gunther		
Concertino for jazz quartet and orchestra MJQ(R)	vib, pno, c-b, dr	19
Concerto AMP(R)	pno	20
Contrasts AMP(R)	woodwind quintet	15
Recitative and rondo AMP(R)	vln	11
Threnos AMP(R)	ob	15
Variants (a ballet) MJQ(R)	vib, pno, c-b, dr	18
SCHUMAN, William		
Concerto (1950; rev. 1956; final rev. 1959) TP(R)	vln	26
Song of Orpheus TP(R)	vlc	20
SESSIONS, Roger		
Concerto EBM(R)	pno	18
Concerto EBM(R)	vln	35
Idyll of Theocritus EBM(R)	S; text: Virgil	42
Psalm 140 EBM(R)	S; text: Biblical	8
SHULMAN, Alan		
Concerto CHAP(R)	vlc	23.5
Theme and variations CHAP(R)	vla	13.5
SIEGMEISTER, Elie		
Concerto SF(R)	cl	14
Concerto MCA(R)	fl	21
SMITH, William O.		
Interplay MJQ(R)	vib, pno, c-b, dr	14
Variants for jazz soloists and orchestra MJQ(R)	cl, c-b, dr	18
SOWERBY, Leo		
Concert piece HWG(R)	org	20

	Solo	Duration (min)
Concerto HWG(R)	vla	25
STARER, Robert		
Concerto No. 2 MCA(R)	pno	16
(See also "Band")		
STILL, William Grant		
Dismal swamp NME(R)	pno	12
Suite MCA(R)	vln	15
THOMSON, Virgil		
Concerto COL(R)	vlc	22
Five songs from William Blake COL(R)	med voice	16
(For contents, see "Solo Vocal Music")		
TUTHILL, Burnet		
Concerto EV(R)	cl	12
VINCENT, John		
Miracle of the cherry tree MIL(R)	A; text: trad	5
WAGNER, Joseph		
Introduction and rondo CHAP(R)	trp	8
WARD, Robert		
Sacred songs for pantheists GAL(R)	S	15
(For contents, see "Solo Vocal Music")		
WEISGALL, Hugo		
A garden eastward TP(R)	high voice; text: Moses Ibn Ezra; Eng. ver: Milton Feist	16.5
WIENER, Ivan		
Fantasie concertante AB(R)	c-b	6
WUORINEN, Charles		
Concerto MM(R)	pno	20
YON, Pietro		
Concerto Gregoriano JF(R)	org	20

7. OPERA

Composer, Title and Publisher	Author of Text or Libretto	Type	Acts	Voices	Duration* (min)
ADLER, Samuel					
Outcasts of Poker Flat TP(R)	Judah Stamfer (based on short story by Bret Hart)	comedy	1	S, m-S, T, Bar, B, Ch	45
ARGENTO, Dominick					
The boor B&H(R)	John Olon-Scrymgeour (based on play by Anton Chekov)	opera buffa	1	S, T, B-Bar	55
The masque of angels B&H(R)	John Olon-Scrymgeour	drama	1	S, m-S, 4 T, B, B-Bar	75
ASCHAFFENBURG, Walter					
Bartleby TP(R)	Jay Leyda (based on the story by Herman Melville)	drama	pro-logue, 2	S, contralto, 2 T, Bar, B-Bar, 2 B, Ch	83
BARAB, Seymour					
Chanticleer B&H(R)	M. C. Richards (based on Chaucer's "Nun's Priest's Tale")	comedy	1	S, m-S, T, Bar	40
A game of chance B&H(R)	Evelyn Draper	comedy	1	2 S, m-S, B-Bar	40
Little Red Riding Hood B&H(R)	Seymour Barab	comedy	1	S, m-S, Bar	50
BARBER, Samuel					
Antony and Cleopatra GS(R)	Shakespeare, adapted by Franco Zeffirelli	drama	3	2 S, m-S, A, 9 T, 5 Bar, 12 B, Ch	180
A hand of bridge, Op. 35 GS(R)	Gian Carlo Menotti	comedy	1	S, A, T, Bar	9
Vanessa, Op. 32 GS(R)	Gian Carlo Menotti	drama	4	S, m-S, A, T, Bar, 2 B, Ch	120
BEESON, Jack					
Hello out there MIL(R)	Jack Beeson (based on play by William Saroyan)	drama	1	m-S, T, Bar, 2 Sp	35
Lizzie Borden (a family portrait) B&H(R)	Kenward Elmslie (based on senario by Richard Plant)	drama	3	2 S, m-S, T, Bar, B-Bar, Ch	120

*Approximate

Composer, Title and Publisher	Author of Text or Libretto	Type	Acts	Voices	Dura- tion (min)
BERNSTEIN, Leonard					
Candide GS	Lillian Hellman (based on play by Voltaire)	comedy	2, 7sc	Col, S, m-S, 2 T, 2 Bar, B, Ch	120
Trouble in Tahiti GS(R)	Leonard Bernstein	satire	1	S, m-S, T, Bar, B-Bar	45
BEREZOWSKY, Nicolai					
Babar the elephant CF(R)	based on Babar stories of Jean de Brunhoff; lyrics by Judith Randal; libretto by Dorothy Heyward	comedy	1	3 S, 2 m-S, 5 Bar (1 Narr), B-Bar	50
BLITZSTEIN, Marc					
Regina CHAP(R)	Marc Blitzstein (based on play, The Little Foxes, by Lillian Hellman)	drama	3	3 S, m-S, 2 T, 4 Bar, B, 2 Sp	120
BUCCI, Mark					
Sweet Betsy from Pike FM	Mark Bucci	comedy	1	S, m-S; or T, B-Bar	25
Tale for a deaf ear FM	Mark Bucci	drama	1	3 S (or S, 2 m-S), T, Bar	46
CALDWELL, Mary E.					
A gift of song (a family Christmas opera) B&H(R)	Mary E. Caldwell	comedy	3sc	3 S, m-S, T, 2 Bar, Sp	65
COPLAND, Aaron					
The second hurricane (1937) B&H(R)	Edwin Denby	drama	2	7 children's voices, 3 Sp, Ch	92
The tender land (1954) B&H(R)	Horace Everett	folk	2	2 S, m-S, A, 2 T, 2 Bar, B, Sp, Ch	100
DELLO JOIO, Norman					
The ruby COL(R)	William Mass (based on "A night at the inn" by Lord Dunsany)	melo- drama	1	S, 2 T, Bar, B, 3 Sp	55
DOUGHERTY, Celius					
Many moons GS(R)	James Thurber	comedy	3 sc	S, m-S, T, Bar	40
FLOYD, Carlisle					
Markheim B&H(R)	Robert Louis Stevenson	drama	1	2 T, B-Bar	70
Slow dusk B&H(R)	Carlisle Floyd	drama	1	S, m-S, T, B	38
The sojourner and Mollie Sinclair B&H(R)	Carlisle Floyd	comedy- drama	1	S, m-S, T, 2 Bar, Ch	70
Susannah B&H(R)	Carlisle Floyd	drama	2	3 S, 2 m-S, 4 T, 2 Bar,	105

Composer, Title and Publisher	Author of Text or Libretto	Type	Acts	Voices	Duration (min)
Wuthering heights B&H(R)	Carlisle Floyd (based on novel by Emily Brontë)	drama	3	B-Bar, Ch 2 S, m-S, 4 T, Bar, B, Ch	130
FOSS, Lukas					
Introductions and good-byes CF(R)	Gian Carlo Menotti	comedy	1	S, A, T, B	9
The jumping frog of Calaveras County CF(R)	Jean Karsavina (based on short story by Mark Twain)	comedy	2	m-S, 2 T, 2 Bar, B, Ch	45
GERSHWIN, George					
Porgy and Bess CHAP(R)	Du Bose Hey-ward	drama	3	3 S, A, 3 m-S, 6 T, B-Bar, 5 B, Ch	150
GIANNINI, Vittorio					
Beauty and the beast COL(R)	Robert A. Simon	fantasy	2 sc	S, 2 m-S, A, 2 T, Bar, Ch	60
Taming of the shrew COL(R)	Vittorio Giannini & D. Fee (based on Shakespeare's play)	comedy	3, 4 sc	2 S, 5 T, 3 Bar, 4 B	150
GREENBERG, Noah (Ed.)					
The play of Daniel (a 13th century musical drama) OX	based on trans-cription from Brit-ish Museum Eger-ton 2615 by Rev. Rembert Weakland; narration by W.H. Auden	drama	1	2 S, 5 T, 5 Bar, 2 B, Narr, Ch	60
The play of Herod (a 12th century musical drama) OX	trans: William L. Smoldon	drama	1	2 S, m-S, 5 T, 4 Bar, 3 B, Ch	60
HARRISON, Lou					
Rapunzel PIC(R)	William Morris	drama	1 sc	S	40
HAUFRECHT, Herbert					
Boney Quillen BB(R)	adapted by com-poser from three folk tales	comedy	1	2 S, 2 A, T, 3 Bar, Ch	30
HERRMANN, Bernard					
Wuthering Heights HWG(R)	adapted from novel by Emily Brontë by Lucille Fletcher	drama	4	S, 2 m-S, T, 2 Bar, Sp, Ch	120
HOIBY, Lee					
Natalia Petrovna B&H(R)	William Ball (based on Turge-nev's A Month in the Country	drama	2	Col, 3 S, m-S, 3 T, Bar, B	120
The scarf GS(R)	Harry Duncan (based on story by Anton Chekov)	drama	1	S, T, Bar	45

Composer, Title and Publisher	Author of Text or Libretto	Type	Acts	Voices	Duration (min)
HOLLINGSWORTH, Stanley					
The mother COL(R)	S. Hollingsworth & John Sandel (based on story by Hans Christian Anderson)	drama	1	Col, S, 2 m-S, T, B-Bar	45
HOVHANESS, Alan					
The burning house, Op. 185 CFP	Alan Hovhaness	drama	1	2 Bar, Ch (8 Bar)	26
Pilate, Op. 196 CFP(R) (See also "Percussion")	Alan Hovhaness	drama	1	A, 2 B, Ch (TTBB)	30
Spirit of the avalanche, Op. 197 CFP(R)	Alan Hovhaness	drama	1	Col, 2 Bar, Ch (Bar)	35
Wind drum, Op. 183 CFP(R) 1. Overture. 2. Stone, water. 3. Dance of ocean mist. 4. Island of mist. 5. Dance of waving branches. 6. Snow mountain. 7. Dance of new leaves. 8. Three hills. 9. Dance of singing trees. 10. Moan. 11. Dance of black-haired mountain storm. 12. Time, turn back. 13. The flute of Azura. 14. Sun, melt. 15. Dance of spring winds. 16. Trees singing. 17. Dance of steep hills. 18. Approach, O spirit. 19. Dance of ocean slumber. 20. One, compassionate-ever. 21. Lullaby of ocean night. (See also "Percussion")	Alan Hovhaness	dance/ drama	1	A or B, Ch (with dancer, solo or group)	26
JOHNSON, Lochrem					
A letter to Emily MER(R)	L. Johnson	drama	1	S, m-S, Bar, B	40
KOUTZEN, Boris					
You never know GEN(R)	Boris Koutzen	comedy	1	S, T, Bar	50
KREUTZ, Arthur					
Sourwood mountain COL(R)	Zoe Lunde Schiller	folk	1	2 S, 3 Bar (or T, Bar, B), 3 Sp	45
The university greys COL(R)	Zoe Lunde Schiller (based on historical account by Maud M. Brown)	drama	2	2 S, m-S, 2 Bar	120

Composer, Title and Publisher	Author of Text or Libretto	Type	Acts	Voices	Dura-tion (min)
KUBIK, Gail					
Boston baked beans CHAP(R)	Gail Kubik	fable	1	S, B	20
KUPFERMAN, Meyer					
Draagenfut girl GEN(R)	M. Kupferman	comedy	2	3 S, 2 m-S, 2 T, Bar, B, SSA Ch	120
In a garden TP(R)	Gertrude Stein	fantasy	1	S, T, Bar	15
KURKA, Robert					
The good soldier Schweik WEIN(R)	Lewis Allan (based on a novel by Jaruslav Hasek)	drama	2	2 S, A, 2 T, 2 Bar	120
LA MONTAINE, John					
Novellis, novellis GS(R)	John La Montaine, adapted from two English medieval plays	pageant opera	5 sc	boy S, 2 S, A, 2 T, Bar, B-Bar, Sp	60
The shepherdes playe, Op. 38 PJS(R)	adapted by composer from 4 medieval Corpus Christi plays: Coventry: (text of Robert Croo, 1534); Chester: (texts of George Bellin, 1592 & 1600 & Jas. Miller, 1607; Wakefield: ed. of George England, 1836; York: ed. of Lucy Toulmin Smith, 1885	pageant opera	1	Narr and double Ch	40
LEVY, Marvin David					
Escorial B&H(R)	Michel de Ghelde-rode; English version by Lionel Abel	drama	1	T, Bar, B, silent role	40
Mourning becomes Electra B&H(R)	Eugene O'Neill	drama	3	3 S, T (or high Bar), 2 Bar, B-Bar, B	180
MAYER, William					
One Christmas long ago GAL(R)	William Mayer (based on story by Raymond Mac-Donald Alden)	fantasy	5 sc	2 boy S, S, m-S, 2 Bar, B-Bar, mime	60
MOORE, Douglas					
The ballad of Baby Doe CHAP(R)	John Latouche	drama	8 sc	2 S, 4 m-S, A, 2 T, Bar, B-Bar, B, Ch	120
The devil and Daniel Webster B&H(R)	Stephen Vincent Benét	folk	1	m-S, 3 T, 3 Bar, 2 B, 3 Sp, Ch	60
The emperor's new clothes CF(R)	Raymond Abrash-kin (based on a	fantasy	1, 4 sc	3 T, Bar, 4 Sp, Ch	14

Composer, Title and Publisher	Author of Text or Libretto	Type	Acts	Voices	Duration (min)
	fairy tale by Hans Christian Anderson)				
Gallantry GS(R)	Arnold Sundgaard	soap opera satire	1	S, m-S, T, Bar, 3 dancers	35
The headless horseman ECS(R)	Stephen Vincent Benét	comedy	1	2 S, m-S, 2 T, B, Ch	50
The wings of the dove GS(R)	Ethan Ayer (based on novel by Henry James)	drama	6 sc	2 S, m-S, A, 2 T, 4 Bar	120
MOSS, Lawrence The brute TP(R)	Eric Bentley (based on a play by Anton Chekhov)	comedy	1	S, T, Bar	30
OWEN, Richard A fisherman called Peter GEN(R)	Biblical	drama	5 sc	S, m-S, 2 T, 3 Bar, Narr, Ch	45
PASATIERI, Thomas Opera Triptych					
1. The Women TP(R)	Thomas Pasatieri	drama	1	S, m-S, Bar	13
2. La Divina TP(R)	Thomas Pasatieri	opera buffa	1	Col, contralto, T, Bar	25
3. Padrevia TP(R)	Thomas Pasatieri	drama	1	S, T, B-Bar, Narr	52
ROREM, Ned Miss Julie B&H(R)	adapted by Kenward Elmslie from the play by August Strindberg	drama	2	3 S, m-S, 2 T, B-Bar	120
SCHULLER, Gunther The visitation AMP(R)	G. Schuller after a motive by Franz Kafka	drama	3	2 S, 2 m-S, 6 T, 4 Bar, B-Bar, 3 B, Ch	150
SCHUMAN, William The mighty Casey GS(R)	Jeremy Gury	comedy	1	S, T, 3 Bar	75
SESSIONS, Roger Montezuma EBM(R)	G. Antonio Borgese	drama	3	9 S, m-S, 9 T, 8 Bar, 3 B, Ch	150
SIEGMEISTER, Elie Darling Corie CHAP(R)	Lewis Allan	folk	1	S, m-S, T, 2 Bar, B	45
The mermaid in lock No. 7 CFP(R)	Edward Mabley	comedy	3 sc	S, A, Bar, B-Bar, Ch of dancers	45
Miranda and the dark young man SHAW	Edward Eager	satire	1	S, m-S, Bar, B-Bar	60
SIMEONE, Harry The emperor's new	Jay Johnson	fable	2	2 S, A, T,	60

Composer, Title and Publisher	Author of Text or Libretto	Type	Acts	Voices	Duration (min)
clothes SHAW(R)				2 Bar, B, Ch	
SMITH, Russell					
The unicorn in the garden GS(R)	Joseph Longstreth (based on a fable by James Thurber)	comedy	1	Col, m-S, 2 Bar	25
TAYLOR, Deems					
The king's henchman JF(R)	Edna St. Vincent Millay	drama	3	S, m-S, 3 T, 2 Bar, 2 B, Ch	140
Peter Ibbetson JF(R)	Constance Collier & Deems Taylor (based on novel by George du Maurier)	drama	3, 9 sc	5 S, 3 m-S, A, 4 T, 6 Bar, 2 B, Ch	140
Ramuntcho JF(R)	Deems Taylor	drama	3	2 S, m-S, A, 4 T, 4 Bar, 2 B, Ch	140
THOMPSON, Randall					
The nativity according to St. Luke ECS	Biblical	drama	7 sc	S, m-S, A, T, 3 Bar, B, Ch	100
Solomon and Balkis ECS	R. Thompson (based on a short story by Rudyard Kipling)	comedy	1	2 S, m-S, T, Bar, Ch	40
THOMSON, Virgil					
Four saints in three acts MER(R)	Gertrude Stein	drama	3	3 S, 3 A, 4 T, 2 Bar, B, Ch	120
The mother of us all MER(R)	Gertrude Stein	drama	2, 8 sc	5 S, 3 m-S, 3 A, 4 T, 5 Bar, 3 B-Bar, 2 B, Ch	120
WARD, Robert					
The crucible GAL(R)	Bernard Stambler (based on play by Arthur Miller)	drama	4	4 S, 2 m-S, 2 A, 4 T, 2 Bar, 2 B	120
Pantaloon (He who gets slapped) GAL(R)	Bernard Stambler (based on play by Andreyev)	drama	3	2 S, 2 T, 2 Bar	150
WEISGALL, Hugo					
Purgatory TP(R)	William Butler Yeats	drama	1	T, Bar	35
Six characters in search of an author TP(R)	Denis Johnston (based on a play by Luigi Pirandello)	drama	3	Col, 2 S, 2 m-S, 2 A, 2 T, 3 Bar, 2 B, Ch	120
The stronger TP(R)	Richard Hart (based on a play by August Strindberg)	drama	1	Col, B, Mu	25
The tenor TP(R)	Karl Shapiro & Ernst Lert	tragi-comedy	1	2 S, 2 T, Bar, B	75
WILDER, Alec					
The lowland sea GS(R)	Arnold Sundgaard	folk	1	S, T, Bar, B, Ch	55
Sunday excursion GS(R)	Arnold Sundgaard	comedy	1	S, A, T, Bar, B	25

8. BAND
(Including Wind Symphony)

ADLER, Samuel
Diptych CFP(R) — 15
Southwestern sketches OX — 15

AITKEN, Hugh
Suite in six EV — 9
  Overture. Dance. Chorale.
  Interlude. March. Finale.

AMRAM, David
Concerto for horn and wind — 15
  symphony CFP(R)
King Lear variations for wind — 15
  symphony CFP(R)

BARBER, Samuel
Commando march GS — 4

BASSETT, Leslie
Designs, images and textures — 11
  CFP
  Oil painting. Water color.
  Pen and ink drawing.
  Mobile. Bronze sculpture.

BECK, John Ness
Reflection EV — 4

BENNETT, Robert Russell
Concerto grosso CFP(R) — 16
Kentucky (from life) CFP(R) — 17
Ohio River suite CFP(R) — 20
  1. The Allegheny 1859 (Pre-
     lude; andante--"prayer
     meeting song;" allegro--
     "Saturday night jig")
  2. The Monongahela 1909
     (Prelude; allegretto--
     "banjos across the river;"
     moderato--"the ballad of
     the mines")
  3. The Ohio 1959 (Prelude;
     tranquillo--"counterpoint
     of two rivers;" allegro
     con ritmo--"this is it")

*Approximate

Suite of old American dances — 16
  CHAP
  Cakewalk. Schottisch.
  Western one-step. Wall-
  flower waltz. Rag.
Symphonic songs for band — 12.5
  CHAP
  Serenade. Spiritual.
  Celebration.
Three humoresques CFP(R) — 9
West Virginia epic CFP(R) — 10

BENSON, Warren
The leaves are falling EBM — 11.5
Polyphonies for percussion — 5.5
  MCA(R)
  (See also "Percussion")
Remembrance SHAW — 14
The solitary dancer for wind — 7
  ensemble MCA
Symphony for drums and wind — 21
  orchestra CFP(R)
  Invocation. Contemplation.
  Declaration.
  (See also "Percussion")
Transylvania fanfare SHAW — 7

BERGSMA, William
March with trumpets GAL — 6

BERNSTEIN, Elmer
Pennsylvania overture CFP — 8

BERNSTEIN, Leonard
Danzon (from "Fancy Free") — 3
  (arr. John Krance) W-7

BEVERSDORF, Thomas
Symphony for winds and per- — 14
  cussion SMC
  (See also "Percussion")

BILIK, Jerry H.
American Civil War fantasy — 8
  SMPC
  (See also "Full Symphony
  Orchestra")

311

	Duration (min)
BRIGHT, Houston	
Concerto grosso No. 1 SHAW	3.5
Marche de concert S-B	3
Passacaglia SHAW	5
Prelude and fugue in F-minor SHAW	4
BROWN, Rayner	
Concerto for organ and band WIM	16
BROWNE, Philip	
Sonoro and brioso S-B	7
CACAVAS, John	
La bella Roma FM	3
March of the golden brass CHAP	3
Overture in miniature EV	3
Rhapsody for band CF	3
Symphonic prelude CF	4
Western senario CF	6
CARTER, Charles	
Proclamation MIL	6
State fair suite GS	6
Off to the fair. Merry-go-round. Farmer Jones. The race.	
Symphonic overture CF	4.5
CARPENTER, John Alden	
Song of freedom (optional unison chorus) GS	3
CAZDEN, Norman	
On the death of a Spanish child MER	5
CHANCE, John Barnes	
Incantation and dance B&H	5
Introduction and capriccio for piano and 24 winds B&H (R)	8
Variations on a Korean folk song B&H	4
CHOU, Wen-Chung	
Metaphors (four seasons) for wind symphony CFP(R)	17
Spring. Summer. Autumn. Winter.	
Riding the wind (for wind symphony) CFP(R)	7
COKER, Wilson	
Concerto for tenor-bass trombone & symphonic band TP	10

	Duration (min)
With bugle, fife and drum (overture) TP	6.5
COPLAND, Aaron	
Emblems B&H	14
Lincoln portrait B&H(R) Narr (See also "Full Symphony Orchestra with Solo")	14
An outdoor overture B&H	9.5
Variations on a Shaker melody ("simple gifts") B&H	6
COWELL, Henry	
Animal magic MCA	6
Celtic set GS	12
Reel. Caoine. Hornpipe.	
A curse and a blessing PIC	7
Hymn and fuguing tune No. 1 MCA	3
Little concerto for piano and band AMP	12
Shipshape overture GS	8
CRESTON, Paul	
Celebration overture, Op. 61 SHAW	8
Concerto for alto saxophone and band GS(R)	16
Legend MCA	6.5
Prelude and dance, Op. 76 COL	7
Zanoni, Op. 40 GS	7
DAHL, Ingolf	
Sinfonietta for band AB	17
deGASTYNE, Serge	
Prelude to a play EV	6
DELLO JOIO, Norman	
From every horizon: a tone poem to New York EBM	7.5
Scenes from "The Louvre" EBM	10
The portals. Children's gallery. The kings of France. Nativity paintings. Finale.	
Variants on a medieval tune EBM	12
DILL, William	
Modeerf (chant spiritualistic) EV	3
DONATO, Anthony	
Cowboy reverie B&H	6
The hidden fortress B&H	8

	Duration (min)		Duration (min)
EFFINGER, Cecil		GIANNINI, Vittorio	
Silver plume, Op. 66 EV	4	Dedication overture COL	7.5
		Fantasia COL	5
ERICKSON, Frank		Praeludium and allegro COL	7
Alla marcia BI	7	Symphony No. 3 COL	15
Arietta and rondo BI	3.5	Variations and fugue COL	15
Ceremonial BI	4		
Chanson and bourree BI	3.5	GILLIS, Don	
Concertino for trumpet and band	12	Celebration scene from	4
CF		"Twinkle toes ballet" MIL	
Double concerto BI(R) trp, trb	12	Cyclometric overture NAK	8
Fantasy for band BI	4	Dialogue MIL(R) solo trb	7.5
Feria BI	4	Instant music FM	varies
First symphony BI(R)	8	The January February March	4
Neo-classic suite BI	6.5	B&H	
Sinfonia. Intermezzo-		The land of wheat NAK	23
passacaglia. Bourree-finale.		1st mov: The land and the	
Rondo giocoso BI	7.5	people; 2nd mov: The	
Saturnalia GS	7	planting; 3rd mov: The	
Second symphony BI	12	fields in summer; 4th	
Intrada. Intermezzo. Finale.		mov: The lazy days; 5th	
Summer holiday BI	4	mov: Thrashing bee and	
Tamerlane BI	4.5	Saturday spree; 6th mov:	
Toccata BI	3.5	Harvest celebration.	
		Men of music (overture) VB	8.5
FARRELL, Kenneth L.		Two exotic dances from	7
Two impressions VB	4	"Twinkle toes ballet" MIL	
FRACKENPOHL, Arthur		GOLDMAN, Edwin Franko	
Academic processional march	5	Scherzo SHAW	4
SHAW		(Also published with solo trp)	
Allegro giocoso SHAW	3		
Cantilena for band EBM	3.5	GORDON, Philip	
Chorale episode EV	4	American frontier EV	3
Prelude and march SHAW	5	Colonial diary EV	5
Rondo marziale SHAW	4	New England chronicle BI	3.5
Seaway valley EV	3.5	Olympia S-B	3.5
		Prairie saga TP	6
FULEIHAN, Anis		Robert Burns overture CF	3.5
Accent on percussion SMPC	4		
(See also "Percussion")		GOULD, Morton	
		American symphonette No. 2,	3
GEORGE, Thom Ritter		1st movement MIL	
Hymn and toccata SHAW	12	Ballad CHAP	6
Proclamations B&H	7	Battle hymn (based on "Battle	4
		hymn of the republic") CHAP	
GERSCHEFSKI, Edwin		Folk suite overture MIL	3
Streamline, Op. 17 WIT	3	Jericho (a rhapsody) MIL	12
		Pavanne (from American sym-	3
GERSHWIN, George		phonette No. 2) MIL	
An American in Paris (arr.	6	Prisms CHAP	25
John Krance) W-7		Revolutionary prelude and	8
Rhapsody in blue (arr. Ferde	16	prologue CHAP	
Grofe) W-7		Saint Lawrence suite CHAP	9.5
Second prelude (arr. John	4	Dedication. Quickstep.	
Krance) W-7		Chansonnette. Commemoration	

	Duration (min)

march.
Santa Fe saga CHAP   9
Symphony for band CHAP   16

GREEN, Ray
Folksong fantasys (with solo   25
   trp) AME
John Henry (choral prelude)
Wayfarin' stranger (ballad)
De Lawd knows (spiritual-
   scherzo)
Cod liver ile (fugue-finale)
Kentucky mountain running set   6
   GS

GROFE, Ferde
Death Valley suite ROB   16
Funeral mountains. '49er
   emigrant train. Desert
   water hole. Sand storm.
On the trail (from Grand Canyon   7
   suite) ROB

GROSS, Charles
An American folk suite EBM   8
Songs of the sea EBM   8
A-rovin'. Shenandoah.
   Hulla baloo belay.

GRUNDMAN, Clare
American folk rhapsody B&H   10
My little Mohee. Shantyman's
   life. Sourwood Mountain.
   Sweet Betsy from Pike.
Burlesque B&H   4
Holiday B&H   5
Interval town B&H   7
2nd St. and 7th Ave.; 4th St.
   and 5th Ave.; 3rd St. and
   6th Ave.; Octave Circle.
Little English suite B&H   7
   1. The leather bottle.
   2. Roving. 3. We met.
   4. The Vicar of Bray.
Little suite for band B&H   8
   Prelude. Ballad. Festival.
A medieval story B&H   3.5
Music for a carnival B&H   5
Western dance B&H   4.5

HADDAD, Don
Grand processional SHAW   5

HADLEY, Henry
Concert overture GS   6
Prelude (from Suite ancienne) CF   4

	Duration (min)

Youth triumphant (overture)   6
   CF

HANSON, Howard
Centennial march CF   5.5
Chorale and alleluia CF   6

HARRIS, Roy
Cimarron (symphonic overture)   6
   MIL

HARTLEY, Gerald
A fuguing tune SHAW   3

HARTLEY, Walter
Concerto for saxophone and   11.5
   band TP
Sinfonietta No. 4 MCA   11

HARVEY, Russell
Band sonata NAK   9

HAUFRECHT, Herbert
Parade to the bull ring (1943)   3
   MCA
Symphony for brass and timpani   9
   B&H
   Dona nobis. Elegy. Jubilation.
   (See also "Percussion")
Walkin' the road (1944) MCA   3

HAZELMAN, Herbert
Gallic gallop (freely adapted   6
   from Auber's Crown
   Diamonds) B&H
A short ballet for awkward   12
   dancers SHAW

HEISINGER, Brent
Essay for band SHAW   4.5
Fantasia for band CF   5

HOLMAN, Willis
Festival prologue for wind   8
   symphony CFP(R)

HOVHANESS, Alan
Return and rebuild the deso-   11
   late places (for wind
   symphony) CFP(R) solo trp
Symphony No. 4 (for wind   18
   symphony), Op. 165 CFP(R)
Symphony No. 7, "Nanga   14
   Parvat" (for wind symphony),
   Op. 178 CFP(R)

	Duration (min)		Duration (min)

Symphony No. 14, "Ararat" for 14
  wind symphony CFP(R)

IVES, Charles
  The son of a gambolier (arr. 3.5
    Jonathan Elkus) PIC

JENKINS, Joseph Willcox
  American overture TP 6
  Three images for band EV 8

JOHNSTON, Donald O.
  Essay for trumpet and band 5
    W-7
  Prelude S-B 7

KAY, Ulysses
  Short suite AMP 7
  Solemn prelude AMP 5
  Trigon (for wind symphony) 12
    CFP(R)

KECHLEY, Gerald R.
  Suite for concert band AMP 11

KENNAN, Kent
  Night soliloquy CF   solo fl 4

KEPNER, Fred
  Cuban fantasy S-B 10
  Native dance.   The sea.
  Havana terrace.

KERN, Jerome
  Songs CHAP 7.5
  Who.   They didn't believe me.
  I've told every little star.
  The touch of your hand.   She
  didn't say yes.   Yesterdays.
  Look for the silver lining.

KIRK, Theron
  Aylesford variations S-B 5
  Smokey Mountain suite S-B 7

KLEIN, John
  Festival dance SMPC 4

KOHS, Ellis
  Life with Uncle (Sam) suite 14
    AMP
  Reveille.   Goldbrick.   First
  sergeant and little Joe.
  Tactical march.   Mail call.
  First morning of a furlough.

KORTE, Karl
  Prairie song EV   solo trp 4.5

KUBIK, Gail
  Stewball (variations on Ameri- 16
    can folk tune, "Stewball")
    SMPC

LaGASSEY, Homer
  Sea portrait NAK 8
  Sequoia NAK 6

LANG, Philip J.
  Period piece (gavotte) GS 4
  Trumpet and drum MIL(R) 5
    solo trp
    (See also "Percussion")

LATHAM, William
  Court festival S-B 4
    Intrada.   Pavan.   Galliard.
    "The horses" branle.
  Honors day S-B 3
  Il pasticcio (overture) S-B 4
  Passacaglia and fugue SHAW 7
  Plymouth S-B 3
  Proud heritage S-B 3
  Quiet time S-B (for cham band) 3
  Serenade for band SHAW 5
  Suite for trumpet and band 6
    TP
  Three by four S-B 3
  Three choral preludes S-B 5.5
    Break forth, O beauteous
    heavenly light.   O sacred
    head now wounded.   Now
    thank we all our God.

LEWIS, John (arr. Peter Phillips)
  Django SF 5
  Perceptions I SF 36
  The queen's fancy SF 5
  Three jazz moods (based on 11
    "Three little feelings") SF

LIVINGSTON, David
  Mirage BI 5
  Pastoral for winds BI 5.5
  Prelude and fugue BI 6.5

LLOYD, Norman
  A Walt Whitman overture MER 6

LOMBARDO, Robert
  In my craft or sullen art CPE 8
  Narr; text: Dylan Thomas

	Duration (min)
LoPRESTI, Ronald	
Elegy for a young American TP	5.5
Pageant overture TP	6
MacDOWELL, Edward	
Sea pieces (arr.) (For contents, see "Piano Solo") SHAW	8
MAGANINI, Quinto	
Review of the Allied-African command EM	4
MAILMAN, Martin	
Concertino for trumpet and band MIL(R)	10
Geometrics in sound MIL	10
Liturgical music for band MIL	10
Introit. Kyrie.	
Gloria. Alleluia.	
MALTBY, Richard	
Threnody (tribute to memory of John F. Kennedy) W-7 Narr	7.5
Trumpet nocturne MIL	3.5
MAXWELL, Everett	
Jubilant brass (march) SMC	3
Wall of brass (march) SMC	3
McBETH, W. Francis	
Battaglia SMC	5
Cantique and faranade SMC	5
Two symphonic fanfares SMC	5
McBRIDE, Robert	
Country music fantasy for wind symphony CFP(R)	5
Fugato (on a well-known theme) CF	4
Hill-country symphony (for wind symphony) CFP(R)	10.5
Lonely landscape MCA	6
Sunday in Mexico (for wind symphony) CFP(R)	15
Technicolor AMP	5
McCAULEY, William A.	
Metropolis (concert suite) OX	6.5
1. City Hall ceremony.	
2. Lonesome newcomer.	
3. Rush hour.	
McKAY, George Frederick	
Burlesque march AMP	4
Forty-niners (American rhapsody) TP	7

	Duration (min)
Railroaders (5 pieces for band) TP	8.5
Steel drivin' man. Midnight special. Comin' round the mountain. Lonesome whistle. Brave engineer.	
Three street corner sketches GS	8
A window shopper. Whistling newsboy. Daydream.	
Western youth (march giocoso) TP	2.5
McLEAN, Barton	
Rondo SHAW	4
McPHEE, Colin	
Concerto for wind symphony CFP	12
MEACHAM, F.W.	
American patrol CF	3
MENNIN, Peter	
Canzona (1951) CF	7
MILLER, Frederick	
Procession and interlude S-B	3
MITCHELL, Lyndol	
River suite SHAW	15
When Johnny comes marching home CFP(R) SATB with wind symphony and dr; text: trad (See also "Mixed Chorus" and "Percussion")	9
MOORE, Douglas	
The people's choice GAL	7
Three contemporaries (suite) CF	6
Careful Etta. Grievin' Annie. Fiddlin' Joe.	
MORRISSEY, John J.	
Bayou beguine MCA	5
Concertino EBM	7
Maestoso. Pavane. Finale.	
Dance fantasy for band EBM	5.5
Display piece for band EBM	5.5
Divertissement EBM	6.5
Prelude. Interlude. Waltz. March.	
Gala for band CF	3.5
Ghost town GS	4

	Duration (min)		Duration (min)
Medieval fresco EBM	6	Masquerade for band EV	12
Music for a ceremony CF	5	Pageant CF	7
Viva Mexico!: A symphonic		Psalm EV	8
suite EBM		Serenade for band EV	6
NOTE: The following move-		Pastoral. Humoreske.	
ments are published as		Nocturne. Intermezzo.	
separate scores.		Capriccio.	
1st mov: Processional	3.5	Symphony, Op. 69 EV	16
2nd mov: Fiesta of the Charros	2.5		
3rd mov: The bells of San	3.5	PHILLIPS, Burrill	
Miguel		Concert piece CF solo bsn	6
4th mov: Pueblo de Los	4.5	(See also "String or Cham-	
Angeles		ber Orchestra with Solo")	
5th mov: Parade	3		
		PHILLIPS, Peter	
MUTCHLER, Ralph		Continuum for band BI	5.5
Concerto grosso for jazz combo	8		
and symphonic band KSM		PISTON, Walter	
		Tunbridge fair B&H	5
NELSON, Oliver			
Concerto CFP(R) soli: xy, mar,	9	POLIFRONE, Jon	
vib; wind symphony		Partita for band, Op. 20 CF	12
(See also "Percussion")		Prelude. Siciliana. Gigue.	
NELSON, Ron		PORTER, Quincy	
Mayflower overture B&H	7	Concerto for wind symphony	8
		CFP(R)	
NIBLOCK, James			
La folia variations MIL	6	POTTENGER, Harold	
Soliloquy and dance S-B	5	Suite S-B	12
NIXON, Roger		QUINN, J. Mark	
Elegy and fanfare march CF	9	Chorale of the winds NAK	9
Fiesta del Pacifico B&H	8	Portrait of the land NAK	3.5
Nocturne GAL	8		
Reflections TP	8	READ, Gardner	
		Two moods GS	4.5
O'NEILL, John			
An April overture BI	5	REED, Alfred	
		Ceremony of flourishes BI	9.5
O'REILLY, John		A festival prelude EBM	5
Concerto for trumpet and	7.5	Passacaglia FM	6
winds SHAW		Rahoon (after James Joyce):	8.5
		a rhapsody EBM solo cl	
PERLE, George		Song of Threnos BI	8.5
Solemn procession TP	3.5	A symphonic prelude (based on	6
		"Black is the color of my	
PERSICHETTI, Vincent		true love's hair") EBM	
Bagatelles EV	5		
Chorale prelude: So pure the	4	REED, H. Owen	
star EV		La fiesta Mexicana MIL	20
Chorale prelude: turn not thy	5	Prelude and Aztec dance.	
face EV		Mass. Festival.	
Divertimento TP	11	Missouri shindig MIL	6
Prologue. Song. Dance.		Renascence MIL	9.5
Burlesque. Soliloquy. March.		Spiritual AMP	6.5

	Duration (min)		Duration (min)
REX, Harley		RUSSELL, Armand	
Camminando MIL	3.5	Theme and fantasia EBM	9
RIEGGER, Wallingford		SCHINSTINE, William	
Dance rhythms, Op. 58a AMP	8	Tympendium (suite) KSM	8
New dance, Op.18 AMP	5	Tympolero KSM solo trp	8
(See also "Full Symphony Orchestra")			
		SCHMIDT, William	
Passacaglia and fugue TP	8	Chorale, march and fugato	5
Processional, Op. 36 MCA	7	WIM	
ROCHBERG, George		SCHULLER, Gunther	
Apocalyptica TP(R)	20	Meditation AMP	6.5
RODGERS, Richard		SCHUMAN, William	
Cinderella (overture for concert band) WMC	6	The band song TP	3.5
		Chester (overture) TP	6
Victory at sea (arr. Robert Russel Bennett) CHAP	46	George Washington bridge GS	7
		News reel in five shots GS	8
The song of the high seas. The Pacific boils over. Guadalcanal march. D-day. Hard work and horse play. Theme of the fast carriers. Beneath the Southern Cross. Mare Nostrum. Victory at sea.		Horse-race. Fashion show. Tribal dance. Monkeys at the zoo. Parade.	
		When Jesus wept (from New England Triptych) TP	3
RODGERS, Richard and Lorenz Hart		SCHWARTZ, Elliott	
Songs CHAP	9	Memorial 1963 GEN (with org)	5
Johnny one-note. I could write a book. This can't be love. There's a small hotel. Falling in love with you. I didn't know what time it was. Where or when.			
		SEIBERT, Bob	
		Medusa's head (concert march) KSM	5
		SESSIONS, Roger	
		Finale from "Black Maskers Suite" EBM	4.5
ROGERS, Bernard			
Apparitions (scenes from The Temptation of St. Anthony) MCA(R)	15	SHIFRIN, Seymour	
		Concerto CFP(R) soli: trp, perc; wind symphony	18
(See also "Full Symphony Orchestra")		(See also "Percussion")	
Three Japanese dances TP	11		
Dance with pennons. Mourning dance. Dance with swords.		SIEGMEISTER, Elie	
		American folk music GS	11
Tribal drums (from Africa, a symphony in 2 movements)TP	7	A-roving. Roll, Jordan, roll. Johnny has gone for a soldier. Buffalo gals. Bury me not on the lone prairie. Go down Moses. Li'l David. The Erie Canal. Every night when the sun goes in. Peter Gray. The streets of Laredo. Skip to my Lou. Sweet Betsy from Pike. Going down the road. Poor wayfar-	
ROREM, Ned			
Sinfonia for 15 wind instruments CFP(R)	9		

Duration (min)

ing stranger.
Deep sea chanty CF   1.5
Five American folk songs CF   10
Sourwood mountain. Doney
gal. The monkey's wedding.
Black is the color of my
true love's hair. M'sieu
Bainjo.
Hootenanny (suite No. 2) CF   8.5
Part I: Old Joe Clarke
   (square dance)
Part II: Buckeye Jim
   (lullaby)
   Motherless child
   (spiritual)
   Get along little dogies
   (cowboy song)
Part III: Bound for the prom-
   ised land (pioneer song)
Pastoral MCA   5
Prairie legend AMP   7
Summer day EBM   4
Wilderness road MCA   6

SMITH, Hale
Expansions EBM   7
Somersault FM   7
Take a chance (an aleatoric epi-   varies
   sode for band) FM

SOMERS, Harry
Symphony for woodwinds, brass   18
   and percussion CFP(R)
   (See also "Percussion")

SOUSA, John Philip
King cotton B&H   3
Stars and stripes forever B&H   3
Thunderer MIL   3

STARER, Robert
Concerto No. 2 MCA(R) solo pno   16
   (See also "Full Symphony
   with Solo")
Dirge MCA   4
Fanfare, pastorale and serenade   3
   EBM

STILL, William Grant
Folk suite BI   8
From the Delta MCA   8
To you America SMPC   11

SUMERLIN, Macon
Fanfare, andante and fugue   6
   WIM

Duration (min)

TANNER, Paul
Aria for trombone and band   5
   WIM
Concerto for 2 trombones   7.5
   and band WIM

THOMSON, Virgil
At the beach CF solo trp   5
A solemn music GS   5

TUTHILL, Burnet
Concerto for double bass and   12
   wind orchestra CF(R)
   solo c-b
Prelude and rondo S-B   5
Rondo concertante S-B   4
   (with 2 solo cl)

VAN VACTOR, David
Passacaglia, chorale and   12
   scamper S-B

VELKE, Fritz
Concertino SHAW   10
Fanfare and rondo SHAW   4.5
Foray at Fairfax SHAW   7
Quartal piece SHAW   5

VERRALL, John
Holiday moods (suite) (1946)   6
   BOS
Saturday in the woods.
   Sunday mood. Summer
   evening shadows. Morn-
   ing on the river.
A northern overture (1946) BOS 4

WAGNER, Joseph
Eulogy MCA   4

WALKER, Richard
A lyrical overture JS   5

WARD, Robert
American youth concerto TP   4.5
Clarinet escapades TP   6
Fantasia for brass choir and   13
   timpani GAL
Jubilation (overture) GAL   8
Night fantasy GAL   4
Prairie (overture) GAL   7

WASHBURN, Robert
Burlesk B&H   5
March and chorale SHAW   4
Ode for band SHAW   6

	Duration (min)		Duration (min)
Overture, "Elkhart 1960" SHAW	4	Puppet overture SHAW	5
Partita B&H	6		
Symphony for band OX	15		

WEED, Maurice
Introduction and scherzo NAK   8

WHEAR, Paul W.
Antietam EV   8
Nocturne EV   5

WHITE, Donald H.
Dichotomy SHAW   8
Miniature set SHAW   11.5
   Prelude. Monologue. Inter-
   lude. Dialogue. Postlude.
Recitative, air and dance COL   8

WILLIAMS, Clifton
Arioso S-B   2
Dedicatory overture EBM   8
Dramatic essay S-B (with   5
   solo trp)
Fanfare and allegro S-B   5
Festival S-B   6.5
Pastorale S-B   3.5
The ramparts EBM   6
Regal procession S-B   3.5
Solemn fugue S-B   3
Symphonic suite S-B   7
   Intrada. Chorale. March.
   Antique dance. Jubilee.

WORK, Julian
Autumn walk SHAW   5
Driftwood patterns SHAW   6
Portraits from the Bible SHAW   15
   Moses. Ruth. Shadrach,
   Meshach and Abednego.
Processional hymn SHAW   6
Stand the storm SHAW   10

YODER, Paul
Hurricane! NAK   5
Relax! (a rumba) NAK   3.5

ZANINELLI, Luigi
Festa SHAW   4.5
Hymn and variations SHAW   5
Margaret suite SHAW   6
   The city by night.
   The city by day.
   A little girl filled with
   sadness. A little girl
   filled with joy.

KEY TO PUBLISHERS

AB — Alexander Broude, Inc.
120 West 57th Street
New York, N. Y. 10019

ABE — Aldo Bruzzichelli Editions
c/o Alexander Broude, Inc.
120 West 57th Street
New York, N. Y. 10019

ABP — Abington Press
201 8th Avenue South
Nashville, Tennessee 37202

AM — Anfor Music Publishers
17 West 60th Street
New York, N. Y. 10023

AME — American Music Edition
263 East 7th Street
New York, N. Y. 10009

AMP — Associated Music Publishers, Inc.
609 Fifth Avenue
New York, N. Y. 10017
Agents overseas:
Albania, Austria, Bulgaria,
Czechoslovakia, Greece,
Hungary, Poland, Rumania,
Yugoslavia:...Doblinger,
Vienna, Austria
Australia;...Allan & Co. Ltd.,
Melbourne
Belgium, Netherlands,
Switzerland, West Germany:
...B. Schott's Soehne,
Mainz, Germany
Denmark, Finland, Norway,
Sweden:...Wilhelm Hansen,
Copenhagen, Denmark
France:...Editions Max
Eschig, Paris
Italy:...G. Ricordi, Milan
Spain:...Union Musical
Española, Madrid
United Kingdom & Irish
Free State:...Schott & Co.
Ltd., London

AP — Apogee Press, Inc.
c/o World Library Publications, Inc.

2145 Central Parkway
Cincinnati, Ohio 45214

AUG — Augsburg Publishing House
426 South Fifth Street
Minneapolis, Minnesota 55415

BB — Broude Brothers Limited
Music Publishers
56 West 45th Street
New York, N. Y. 10036

BCM — Bowdoin College Music Press
New Brunswick, Maine

BCS — Bennington College Series
c/o Alexander Broude, Inc.
120 West 57th Street
New York, N. Y. 10019

BEL — Belwin, Inc.
Rockville Center, N. Y. 11571

B&H — Boosey & Hawkes
30 West 57th Street
New York, N. Y. 10019
(for rental); for sales, address:
Oceanside, New York, N. Y.
11572
Agents overseas:
Australia:...Boosey &
Hawkes (Australia) Pty.
Ltd., Sydney
Austria:...Theater-Verlag
Eirich, Vienna
Belgium & France:...
Boosey & Hawkes, S. A.,
Paris
Canada:...Boosey & Hawkes
(Canada) Ltd., Toronto
Denmark:...Wilhelm Hansen, Copenhagen
England:...Boosey & Hawkes
Music Publishers Ltd.,
London
Germany & Switzerland:...
Boosey & Hawkes GmbH,
Bonn
Hungary:...Kultura,
Budapest

Italy:...Carisch S. p. a.,
Milan
Netherlands:...Albersen &
Co., The Hague
Norway:...Norsk Musik-
forlag a/s, Oslo
South Africa:...Boosey &
Hawkes (S. Africa) Pty.
Ltd., Johannesburg
South America:...Barry &
Cia, Buenos Aires,
Argentina
Spain:...Robert Achard,
Madrid
Sweden:...Carl Gehrmans
Musikforlag, Stockholm

BI   Bourne Co. (formerly Bourne, Inc.)
136 West 52nd Street
New York, N.Y. 10019

BOS   The Boston Music Company
116 Boylston Street
Boston, Mass. 02116

CF   Carl Fischer, Inc.
56-62 Cooper Square
New York, N.Y. 10003

CFP   C.F. Peters Corporation
373 Park Avenue South
New York, N.Y. 10016
Agents overseas:
Austria & Germany:...C.F.
Peters, Frankfurt/Main
Belgium:...Schott Freres,
Brussels
Norway:...Harold Lyche &
Co., Oslo
Switzerland:...Edition Eulen-
burg, Zurich
All other countries:...
Hinrichsen Edition Ltd.,
London
with following exception:
Countries of Western Hemis-
phere, Japan and The Phil-
ippines, which should order
C.F. Peters publications
from the office in New
York, N.Y.

CHAP Chappell & Co., Inc.
609 Fifth Avenue
New York, N.Y. 10017
Agents overseas:
Australia:...Chappel & Co.
Ltd., Sydney

England:...Chappell & Co.
Ltd., London
France:...S.A.F. Chappell,
Paris

CMP   Continuo Music Press, Inc.
c/o Alexander Broude, Inc.
120 West 57th Street
New York, N.Y. 10019

COL   Franco Colombo, Inc.
16 West 61st Street
New York, N.Y. 10023
Agents overseas:
Australia:...G. Ricordi &
Co., Sydney
Argentina:...Ricordi
Americana S.A.,
Buenos Aires
Brazil:...Ricordi Bra-
sileira S.A., São Paulo
Canada:...Leeds Music
Ltd., Toronto
England:...G. Ricordi &
Co. (London) Ltd.,
London
France:...Edition Salabert,
Paris
Germany:...G. Ricordi &
Co., Frankfurt/Main
Italy:...G. Ricordi & Co.,
Milan
Mexico:...G. Ricordi &
Co., Mexico City, D.F.
Switzerland:...Symphonia
Verlag, Basel

COR   Cor Music Publications
67 Bell Place
Massapequa, N.Y.

CPE   Composer/Performer Edition
330 University Avenue
Davis, California 05616

CPH   Concordia Publishing House
358 South Jefferson Avenue
St. Louis, Missouri 63118

CPI   The Composers Press, Inc.
c/o Robert B. Brown Music Co.
1709 No. Kenmore Avenue
Hollywood, California 90027

EBM   Edward B. Marks Music Corp.
136 West 52nd Street
New York, N.Y. 10019
Agent overseas:

England:...Schott & Co. Ltd., London

ECS   E.C. Schirmer Music Company
600 Washington Street
Boston, Mass. 02111

EM   Edition Musicus
333 West 52nd Street
New York, N.Y. 10019

EV   Elkan-Vogel Co.
1712-14-16 Sansom Street
Philadelphia, Pa. 19103
Sole agents in U.S.A.
Durand Edition
Henry Lemoine & Co.,
Jean Jobert
Editions Philippo
Organ catalogues: Edition
Heuwekemeijer, La
Schola Cantorum & Pro-
cure Generale, Ars Nova

FAM   Fine Arts Music Press
Tulsa, Oklahoma

FLAM   Harold Flammer, Inc.
251 West 19th Street
New York, N.Y. 10011

FM   Frank Music Corp.
119 West 57th Street
New York, N.Y. 10019
Agents overseas:
Brazil:...Fermata Do Brazil
LTDA, São Paulo
Canada:...Frank Music Co.
(Canada) Ltd., Toronto
England:...Frank Music
Company Ltd., London
Italy:...Edizioni Frank
Music S.r.l., Milan
Re: Mexico:...Ariston Music
Inc., New York, N.Y.

GAL   Galaxy Music Corporation
2121 Broadway
New York, N.Y. 10023
Agents overseas:
England:...Galliard Ltd.,
London
Germany:...Heinrichshofen's
verlag, Wilhelmshaven

GEN   General Music Publishing Co., Inc.
53 East 54th Street
New York, N.Y. 10022

GS   G. Schirmer, Inc.
609 Fifth Avenue
New York, N.Y. 10017
Agents overseas:
Australia:...Allan & Co.
Ltd., Melbourne (for
orch & opera rental
materials)
Austria:...Universal Edi-
tion, Vienna (for orch
& opera rental materials)
Denmark, Norway, Sweden:
...Wilhelm Hansen,
Copenhagen
England:...Chappell & Co.
Ltd., London (materials
for sale)
France also for Belgium,
Czechoslovakia, Greece,
Hungary, Israel, Poland,
Portugal, Spain, & Yugo-
slavia:...Edition Salabert,
Paris (for orch & opera
rentals)
Germany:...Anton Benjamin,
Hamburg (for orch rent-
als); August Seith, Mu-
nich (materials for sale)
Italy:...G. Ricordi & Co.,
Milan
Netherlands:...Albersen &
Co., The Hague (for
orch rentals)

HAR   Hargail Music Press
157 West 57th Street
New York, N.Y. 10019

HE   Henri Elkan Music Publisher
1316 Walnut Street
Philadelphia, Pa. 19107
Agent overseas:
Belgium:...metropolis
Frankrijklei 24,
Antwerpen 1

HME   Helios Music Edition
c/o Mark Foster Music Co.
Box 783
Marquette, Michigan 49855

HWG   The H.W. Gray Company, Inc.
159 East 48th Street
New York, N.Y. 10017
Agent overseas:
England:...Novello & Co.,
Ltd., London

JC   Joshua Corporation
c/o General Music Publishing
Co, Inc.
53 East 54th Street
New York, N.Y. 10022

JF   J. Fischer & Bro.
Harristown Road
Glen Rock, New Jersey 07452

JS   Spratt Music Publishers (formerly
Jack Spratt Music Company)
17 West 60th Street
New York, N.Y. 10023

KAL   Edwin F. Kalmus
1345 New York Avenue
Huntington Station, L.I., N.Y.
11748

KING   Robert King Music Company
North Easton, Mass. 02356

KSM   KSM Publishing Co.
507 North Willomet
Dallas, Texas 75208

LF   Leo Feist
c/o The Big 3 Music Corporation
1540 Broadway
New York, N.Y. 10019

L-G   Lawson-Gould Music Publishers,
Inc.
609 Fifth Avenue
New York, N.Y. 10017

MA   Musical Americana
5458 Montgomery Avenue
Philadelphia, Pa. 19131

MCA   Music Corporation of America
543 West 43rd Street
New York, N.Y. 10036

MER   Mercury Music Corporation
c/o Theodore Presser Company
Presser Place
Bryn Mawr, Pa. 19010

MIL   Mills Music, Inc.
1790 Broadway
New York, N.Y. 10019
    Agents overseas:
        Central & South America:...
        Editora Musical Mills Ltda,
        São Paulo, Brazil;
        Mills Music de Mexico,

Mexico City, D.F.
England:...Mills Music
Ltd., London
France:...Mills France,
Paris
Germany:...Mills Musik-
verlag GmbH, Berlin-
Halensee
Netherlands:...Mills-
Holland N.V., Amster-
dam
Spain & Portugal:...Edi-
torial Mills Music
Española, Madrid

MJQ   MJQ Music, Inc.
200 West 57th Street
New York, N.Y. 10019

MM   McGinnis & Marx
201 West 86th Street, Apt. 706
New York, N.Y. 10024

MMC   Miller Music Corporation
c/o The Big 3 Music Corporation
1540 Broadway
New York, N.Y. 10019

MP   Music for Percussion, Inc.
17 West 60th Street
New York, N.Y. 10023

MPC   Mark Press Company
c/o Mark Foster Music Co.
Box 783
Marquette, Michigan

M&R   McLaughlin & Reilly Co.
45 Franklin Street
Boston 19, Mass.

NAK   Neil A. Kjos Music Co. Publishers
525 Busse Highway
Park Ridge, Illinois 60068

NME   New Music Edition
c/o Theodore Presser Company
Presser Place
Bryn Mawr, Pa. 19010

OX   Oxford University Press
200 Madison Avenue
New York, N.Y. 10016

PAU   Pan American Union
c/o Southern Music Publishing
Co.
1619 Broadway

New York, N.Y. 10019

PIC   Peer International Corporation
c/o Southern Music Publishing Co.
1619 Broadway
New York, N.Y. 10019

PJS   Paul J. Sifler
3947 Fredonia Drive
Hollywood 28, California

RBB   Robert B. Brown Music Co.
1709 No. Kenmore Avenue
Hollywood, California 90027

RDR   R.D. Row Music Company
353 Newbury Street
Boston 15, Mass.

ROB   Robbins Music Corporation
c/o The Big 3 Music Corporation
1540 Broadway
New York, N.Y. 10019

S-B   Summy-Birchard Company
1834 Ridge Avenue
Evanston, Illinois 60204

SE   Spire Editions
c/o World Library Publications,
Inc.
2145 Central Parkway
Cincinnati, Ohio 45214

SF   Sam Fox Publishing Co., Inc.
1841 Broadway
New York, N.Y. 10023

SHAW   Shawnee Press, Inc.
Delaware Water Gap, Pa. 18327

SMC   Southern Music Company
1100 Broadway--P.O. Box 329
San Antonio, Texas

SMPC   Southern Music Publishing Co., Inc.
1619 Broadway
New York, N.Y. 10019
Agents overseas:
Australia:...Southern Music
Publishing Company (Aus-
tralasia) Pty. Ltd., Sydney
Canada:...Southern Music
Publishing Company (Can-
ada) Ltd., Montreal
Central & South America:...
Ricordi Americana, S.A.
Buenos Aires, Argentina

European countries:...
Peer Musikverlag
GmbH, Hamburg,
Germany
Japan:...Southern Music
Publishing Company
(Japan) Ltd., Tokyo
Mexico:...Promotoro His-
pana Americana de
Musica, Mexico City,
D.F.
New Zealand:...Southern
Music Publishing Com-
pany (New Zealand) Pty.
Ltd., Auckland C. 1

TEN   Tenuto Publications
c/o Theodore Presser Company
Presser Place
Bryn Mawr, Pa. 19010

TP   Theodore Presser Company
Presser Place
Bryn Mawr, Pa. 19010
Agents overseas:
Austria:...Universal Edi-
tion, Vienna; Haydn
Mozart Presse, Vienna;
Philharmonia Pocket
Scores, Vienna
England:...Universal Edi-
tion, London
France:...Editions Musi-
cales Transatlantiques,
Paris; Heugel & Cie,
Paris
Germany:...Impero Verlag,
Wilhelmshaven
Switzerland:...Universal
Edition, Zurich

TPI   Twayne Publishers, Inc.
31 Union Square
New York, N.Y. 10003
(NOTE: The songs by Paul
Nordoff [see "Solo Vocal
Music"] to texts of Robert
Burns are published in the
book, Songs and Poems of
Robert Burns, by Twayne
Publishers, Inc.)

TRAN   Transcontinental Music Publications
1674 Broadway
New York, N.Y. 10019

UCP	University of California Press Berkeley, California 94720
UWP	University of Washington Press c/o Galaxy Music Corporation 2121 Broadway New York, N. Y. 10023
VAL	The New Valley Music Press Sage Hall, Smith College Northampton, Mass. 01060
VB	Volkwein Bros., Inc. 117 Sandusky Street Pittsburgh, Pa. 15212
WEIN	Weintraub Music Company 33 West 60th Street New York, N. Y. 10023
WIM	Western International Music, Inc. 2859 Holt Avenue Los Angeles, California 90034
WIT	M. Witmark and Sons 488 Madison Avenue New York, N. Y. 10022
WLP	World Library Publications, Inc. 2145 Central Parkway Cincinnati, Ohio 45214
WMC	Williamson Music Co. 609 Fifth Avenue New York, N. Y. 10017
W-7	Warner Bros.--Seven Arts Music 488 Madison Avenue New York, N. Y. 10022
WWN	W. W. Norton Co. 55 Fifth Avenue New York, N. Y. 10003
YUP	Yale University Press 92A Yale Station New Haven, Connecticut 06520

Biblical (cont.) 72, 73, 74, 75, 76,
77, 79, 80, 81, 82, 83, 84, 85, 86,
87, 88, 89, 90, 91, 93, 94, 95, 96,
98, 99, 100, 101, 102, 104, 105,
106, 108, 109, 110, 111, 112, 113,
114, 115, 116, 117, 118, 119, 120,
122, 124, 125, 127, 128, 129, 131,
132, 133, 135, 136, 137, 138, 139,
140, 143, 144, 146, 147, 148, 149,
150, 151, 152, 153, 154, 155, 156,
157, 158, 160, 161, 162, 163, 164,
165, 166, 167, 168, 169, 170, 171,
172, 229, 230, 231, 240, 257, 262,
275, 277, 279, 296, 298, 299, 300,
302, 309, 310
Bickel, Mary 34
Bierce, Ambrose 255
Billings, William 11, 56
Binyon, Laurence 50
Bishop, Elizabeth 43
Bixby, James T. 30, 32
Black, James Alexander 127
Blake, William 10, 14, 15, 16, 17,
19, 20, 23, 25, 26, 32, 35, 36, 38,
41, 42, 47, 48, 53, 60, 61, 62, 65,
67, 68, 75, 94, 98, 103, 115, 118,
119, 126, 129, 130, 132, 135, 139,
146, 147, 150, 151, 230, 298, 303
Blitzstein, Marc 305
Blow, John 112
Bogardus, Edgar 45
Boggs, Tom 134
Boleyn, Anne 21
Bonar, Horatius 90
Bonner, Samuel 117, 171
Borgers, Edward 110, 169
Borgese, G. Antonia 309
Borland, Hal 79
Bossidy, J.C. 95
Bottomley, Gordon 127
Bowles, Paul 13
Bowles, Jane 13
Bowring, John 29, 30, 81, 160
Bradford, William 116
Bradley, Marcia 48
Brant, Henry 103
Bridges, Robert 58, 59, 70, 150
Bright, Houston 60, 121, 154
British Museum Egenton 2615
Brontë, Emily 10, 20, 59, 121, 134,
306
Brooke, Rupert 26, 30
Brooks, Jonathan 118
Brooks, Phillips 83
Brown, Beatrice C. 122
Brown, Maud Morrow 307
Brown, Myra Lockwood 77
Brown, Simon 70

Browning, Elizabeth Barrett 17
Browning, Pack 53, 153
Browning, Robert 17, 30, 42, 43,
79
Brubeck, Dave and Iola 61, 154
Bruce, Richard 111, 170
Bryant, William Cullen 59, 105, 123
Bryner, Witter 96
Bucci, Mark 305
Buchanan, Robert 102, 167
Bullet, Gerald 111
Bunyan, John 18
Burgess, George 81
Burlin, Natalie Curtis 97
Burns, Robert 10, 25, 33, 38, 41,
85, 91
Burr, Amelia J. 75
Burroughs, John 53
Buson, Taniquchi 40, 131
Butler, H. Montagu 70
Buxton, John 104
Byers, Irene 41
Byles, Dr. 56
Bynner, Witter 38, 128
Byron, Lord 30, 31, 126, 131, 134
Byrom, John 104

Cage, John 14
Caldwell, Mary E. 305
Callaway, Dorothy 10
Campbell, Charles Atwood 87, 162
Campion, Thomas 47, 97, 111,
114, 115, 151, 165, 231
Camus 73
Canby, Edward T. 61
Cancioneros, the (15th cent.) 22
Cander, Alan 112
Cane, Melville 72
Carew, Thomas 130
Carpenter, John Alden 61, 62, 121,
141, 154
Carpenter, William Boyd 58
Carr, Albert Lee 62
Carr, Benjamin 14
Carroll, Lewis 46, 60, 72, 89,
126, 136, 144, 154, 294
Carryl, G.W. 69, 109
Carus, Paul 119
Chang, Chang Wen- 26
Chapin, Katherine G. 81
Chapman, Henry G. 128
Charles I 13
Chatterton, Thomas 10, 27
Chaucer, Geoffrey 48, 52, 72, 122,
150, 158, 242, 304
Chauvenet, W.M. 15
Chekov, Anton 304, 306, 309
Cherbury, Lord Herbert of 73

337

340

O'Reilly, John 317
Overton, Hall (1920 -) 183, 221, 268, 291
Owen, Harold 210, 211, 236
Owen, Richard 38, 309

Palmer, Robert (1915 -) 98, 183, 189, 201, 221, 223, 229
Panetti, Joan 38, 183, 301
Papale, Henry 98
Parchman, Gen 262
Parker, Alice 148, 165, 262
Parker, Horatio (1863-1919) 98, 165, 193
Parris, Herman (1903 -) 211, 238, 244, 248
Parris, Robert (1924 -) 203, 248, 262, 301
Pasatieri, Thomas 309
Paschke, Richard 262
Payson, Albert 262
Peloquin, C. Alexander 98, 165
Peninger, David 98
Perle, George (1915 -) 99, 183, 199, 201, 203, 204, 207, 211, 212, 217, 221, 291, 317
Perry, Julia (1927 -) 38, 205, 229, 280
Persichetti, Vincent (1915 -) 38, 39, 99, 133, 134, 148, 149, 166, 183, 189, 194, 199, 201, 203, 207, 213, 216, 218, 221, 223, 229, 234, 238, 241, 268, 280, 291, 301, 317
Peter, Johann F. 224
Peter, Simon (1743-1819) 99
Peters, Mitchell 262
Peterson, Wayne 99
Pfautsch, Lloyd (1921 -) 39, 99, 100, 134, 149, 166, 194
Phillips, Burrill (1907 -) 100, 134, 149, 166, 183, 189, 207, 212, 217, 244, 246, 268, 273, 280, 291, 317
Phillips, Donald 189, 301
Phillips, Peter 204, 280, 317
Piket, Frederick 134
Pilhofer, Phil 301
Pinkham, Daniel (1923 -) 39, 40, 100, 101, 102, 134, 135, 149, 166, 167, 184, 194, 199, 207, 209, 211, 221, 224, 229, 241, 244, 262, 280, 291, 301
Piston, Walter (1894 -) 102, 149, 167, 184, 194, 199, 201, 207, 209, 217, 218, 222, 224, 229, 234, 239, 248, 273, 280, 291, 301, 317
Planchart, A.E. 262
Polifrone, Jon 194, 317
Polin, Claire 207

Porter, Quincy (1897-1966) 40, 184, 194, 199, 201, 203, 214, 217, 218, 222, 229, 239, 268, 280, 292, 301, 317
Pottenger, Harold 317
Powell, John (1882-1963) 40, 102, 199, 292, 301
Powell, Laurence 234
Powell, Mel (1923 -) 40, 135, 184, 222, 229, 239, 292
Powell, Morgan (1938 -) 251
Pozdro, John (1923 -) 102, 268
Presser, William 40, 194, 207, 209, 211, 212, 214, 216, 229, 234, 236, 239, 242, 244, 246, 248, 273, 280
Price, Paul 262
Preston, John E. 102, 167
Previn, Andre 184, 268, 292
Purvis, Richard (1915 -) 102, 103, 135, 167, 194

Quinn, J. Mark (1936 -) 317

Ramey, Phillip 262
Ramsier, Paul 203, 204, 301
Rancy, James 224
Raphling, Sam (1910 -) 40, 41, 103, 184, 189, 199, 207, 209, 211, 212, 214, 215, 234, 244, 246, 268, 273, 280, 301, 302
Raymond, Lewis 244
Read, Daniel (1757-1836) 103, 194
Read, Gardner (1913 -) 41, 103, 136, 184, 194, 200, 202, 207, 214, 215, 239, 248, 292, 317
Reck, David 41, 216, 230
Reed, Alfred 103, 168, 211, 239, 302, 317
Reed, H. Owen (1910 -) 204, 211, 242, 248, 317
Reichenbach, Herman 103, 104, 136, 149
Reif, Paul 41, 184, 239, 302
Reinagle, Alexander (1756-1809) 41, 194
Reuning, Sanford H. 184, 262
Revicki, Roberto 136
Rex, Harley 318
Reynolds, Roger (1934 -) 104, 168, 184, 207, 222, 230, 236, 239, 262, 273, 292
Reynolds, Verne (1926 -) 207, 244, 245, 248
Rhodes, Phillip 136, 204
Richards, Howard 104
Richter, Marga (1926 -) 104, 202, 268, 280
Riegger, Wallingford (1885-1961) 104,

Smith, Kent 195
Smith, Leland 185
Smith, Melville (1898 -) 45
Smith, Russell (1927 -) 109, 110, 137, 138, 169, 195, 293, 310
Smith, Warren 264
Smith, William O. 231, 234, 302
Sokoloff, Noel (1923 -) 200
Sollberger, Harvey 202, 208, 231, 234, 236, 274
Somers, Harry 264, 319
Songer, Lewis 264
Sousa, John Philip (1854-1932) 319
Sowerby, Leo (1895-1968) 110, 138, 169, 185, 195, 200, 202, 209, 213, 216, 222, 231, 239, 242, 281, 293, 302, 303
Spaulding, Albert 185
Spies, Claudio 110, 138, 150, 185
Starer, Robert Lee (1924 -) 45, 110, 111, 150, 169, 170, 185, 190, 200, 205, 208, 209, 211, 213, 217, 222, 231, 234, 244, 245, 264, 268, 274, 281, 293, 303, 319
Stearns, Peter Pindar (1931 -) 185
Stein, Leon 236
Stern, Robert 234, 264
Sterne, Colin (1921 -) 45
Stevens, Bernard 245
Stevens, Halsey (1908 -) 111, 138, 150, 170, 185, 186, 195, 200, 202, 204, 205, 208, 211, 212, 213, 214, 215, 216, 217, 219, 231, 234, 236, 268, 293
Stewart, Kensey D. 111
Still, William Grant (1895 -) 45, 111, 170, 186, 195, 200, 209, 212, 222, 234, 268, 274, 293, 294, 303, 319
Stillman-Kelley, Edgar 294
Stoessel, Albert (1894-1943) 219
Stone, Don 195, 236
Stout, Alan (1932 -) 111, 170, 195, 204, 212, 268
Straight, Willard 186
Strang, Gerald 264
Strilko, Anthony (1931 -) 45, 46, 112, 195
Subotnick, Morton 186, 231, 242
Suderburg, Robert 112
Sumerlin, Macon 319
Summerlin, Edward 112, 170
Summers, Stanley 237
Swan, Frederick L. 195
Swanson, Howard (1909 -) 46, 150, 186, 200, 204, 245, 274, 294
Swift, Richard 281
Sydeman, William (1928 -) 46, 112, 138, 170, 186, 204, 209, 211, 217,

231, 234, 239, 264, 281, 294

Talma, Louise (1906 -) 186, 190, 294
Tanner, Paul 215, 244, 319
Tanner, Peter 112
Taylor, Clifford 46
Taylor, Corin H. 248
Taylor, Deems (1885-1966) 112, 186, 222, 294, 310
Tepper, Albert 235
Terry, Frances (1884 -) 200
Thomas, Alan 138
Thome, Joel 264
Thompson, Randall (1899 -) 47, 113, 114, 138, 139, 150, 151, 170, 171, 219, 222, 231, 294, 310
Thomson, Virgil (1896 -) 47, 48, 114, 115, 139, 151, 171, 186, 187, 190, 195, 200, 208, 213, 222, 231, 240, 248, 264, 268, 274, 281, 294, 303, 310, 319
Thomson, William 115
Tirro, Frank (1935 -) 115, 171
Townsend, Douglas (1921 -) 190, 208, 215, 217, 231, 235, 237, 281
Travis, Roy 187
Trimble, Lester (1923 -) 48, 115, 139, 187, 202, 223, 231, 242, 268, 281, 294
Trowbridge, Luther (1892 -) 209, 211, 213
Trubitt, Allen R. 115
Tubb, Monte 115
Tull, Fisher 249, 264
Turner, Charles (1921 -) 48, 200, 294
Turner, Godfrey (1913 -) 249
Tuthill, Burnet (1888 -) 204, 208, 209, 211, 212, 213, 215, 235, 237, 303, 319
Tuthill, George 264
Tweedy, Donald (1890 -) 204

Ulrich, E.J. 208, 214, 264

Valentine, Robert 281
Van Vactor, David (1906 -) 115, 231, 268, 294, 319
Van de Vate, Nancy 202
Vardi, Emmanuel (1915 -) 200, 202
Velke, Fritz (1930 -) 319
Verrall, John (1908 -) 115, 139, 171, 187, 202, 219, 223, 239, 246, 268, 319
Vincent, John (1902 -) 48, 116, 151, 223, 224, 269, 294, 303

347